CISSP®
Official (ISC)²®
Practice Tests

CISSP®
Official (ISC)²®
Practice Tests

David Seidl

Mike Chapple

SYBEX®
A Wiley Brand

Executive Editor: Jim Minatel
Development Editor: Kim Wimpsett
Technical Editors: Jeff Parker and Addam Schroll
Production Editor: Christine O'Connor
Copy Editors: Judy Flynn and Elizabeth Welch
Editorial Manager: Mary Beth Wakefield
Production Manager: Kathleen Wisor
Book Designers: Bill Gibson and Judy Fung
Proofreader: Nancy Carrasco
Indexer: Ted Laux
Project Coordinator, Cover: Brent Savage
Cover Designer: Wiley
Cover Image: Getty Images Inc./Jeremy Woodhouse

Copyright © 2016 by John Wiley & Sons, Inc., Indianapolis, Indiana

Published simultaneously in Canada

ISBN: 978-1-119-25228-3
ISBN: 978-1-119-28804-6 (ebk.)
ISBN: 978-1-119-25229-0 (ebk.)

Manufactured in the United States of America

Library of Congress Control Number: 2016941726

10 9 8 7 6

For Renee, the most patient and caring person I know. Thank you for being the heart of our family.
—MJC

This book is for Lauren, who supports me through each writing endeavor, and for the wonderful teachers and professors who shared both their knowledge and their lifelong love of learning with me.
—DAS

Acknowledgments

The authors would like to thank the many people who made this book possible. Jim Minatel at Wiley Publishing helped us extend the Sybex CISSP franchise to include this new title and gain important support from the International Information Systems Security Consortium (ISC)². Carole Jelen, our agent, worked on a myriad of logistic details and handled the business side of the book with her usual grace and commitment to excellence. Addam Schroll, our technical editor, pointed out many opportunities to improve our work and deliver a high-quality final product. Jeff Parker's technical proofing ensured a polished product. Kim Wimpsett served as developmental editor and managed the project smoothly. Many other people we'll never meet worked behind the scenes to make this book a success.

About the Authors

Mike Chapple, Ph.D., CISSP is an author of the best-selling *CISSP (ISC)² Certified Information Systems Security Professional Official Study Guide,* Sybex, 2015, now in its seventh edition. He is an information security professional with two decades of experience in higher education, the private sector, and government.

Mike currently serves as Senior Director for IT Service Delivery at the University of Notre Dame. In this role, he oversees the information security, data governance, IT architecture, project management, strategic planning, and product management functions for Notre Dame. Mike also serves as a concurrent assistant professor in the university's Computing and Digital Technologies department, where he teaches undergraduate courses on information security.

Before returning to Notre Dame, Mike served as Executive Vice President and Chief Information Officer of the Brand Institute, a Miami-based marketing consultancy. Mike also spent four years in the information security research group at the National Security Agency and served as an active duty intelligence officer in the U.S. Air Force.

He is a technical editor for *Information Security Magazine* and has written 20 books, including *Cyberwarfare: Information Operations in a Connected World* (Jones & Bartlett, 2015), *the CompTIA Security+ Training Kit* (Microsoft Press, 2013), and the *CISSP Study Guide* (Sybex, 7th edition, 2015).

Mike earned both his BS and Ph.D. degrees from Notre Dame in computer science & engineering. He also holds an MS in computer science from the University of Idaho and an MBA from Auburn University.

David Seidl CISSP is the Senior Director for Campus Technology Services at the University of Notre Dame. As the Senior Director for CTS, David is responsible for central platform and operating system support, database administration and services, identity and access management, application services, and email and digital signage. Prior to his current role, he was Notre Dame's Director of Information Security.

David teaches a popular course on networking and security for Notre Dame's Mendoza College of Business. In addition to his professional and teaching roles, he has co-authored the *CompTIA Security+ Training Kit* (Microsoft Press, 2013) and *Cyberwarfare: Information Operations in a Connected World* (Jones & Bartlett, 2015), and served as the technical editor for the 6th (Sybex, 2012) and 7th (Sybex, 2015) editions of the *CISSP Study Guide*. David holds a bachelor's degree in communication technology and a master's degree in information security from Eastern Michigan University, as well as CISSP, GPEN, and GCIH certifications.

Contents

Introduction

CISSP Official (ISC)² Practice Tests is a companion volume to the CISSP (ISC)² Certified Information Systems Security Professional Official Study Guide. If you're looking to test your knowledge before you take the CISSP exam, this book will help you by providing a combination of 1,300 questions that cover the CISSP Common Body of Knowledge and easy-to-understand explanations of both right and wrong answers.

If you're just starting to prepare for the CISSP exam, we highly recommend that you use the CISSP (ISC)² Certified Information Systems Security Professional Official Study Guide, 7th Edition Stewart/Chapple/Gibson, Sybex, 2015, to help you learn about each of the domains covered by the CISSP exam. Once you're ready to test your knowledge, use this book to help find places where you may need to study more, or to practice for the exam itself.

Since this is a companion to the CISSP Study Guide, this book is designed to be similar to taking the CISSP exam. It contains multipart scenarios as well as standard multiple-choice questions similar to those you may encounter in the certification exam itself. The book itself is broken up into 10 chapters: 8 domain-centric chapters with 100 questions about each domain, and 2 chapters that contain 250-question practice tests to simulate taking the exam itself.

CISSP Certification

The CISSP certification is offered by the International Information System Security Certification Consortium, or (ISC)², a global nonprofit. The mission of (ISC)² is to support and provide members and constituents with credentials, resources, and leadership to address cyber, information, software, and infrastructure security to deliver value to society. They achieve this mission by delivering the world's leading information security certification program. The CISSP is the flagship credential in this series and is accompanied by several other (ISC)² programs:

- Systems Security Certified Practitioner (SSCP)
- Certified Authorization Professional (CAP)
- Certified Secure Software Lifecycle Professional (CSSLP)
- Certified Cyber Forensic Professional (CCFP)
- HealthCare Information Security Privacy Practitioner (HCISPP)
- Certified Cloud Security Professional (CCSP)

There are also three advanced CISSP certifications for those who wish to move on from the base credential to demonstrate advanced expertise in a domain of information security:

- Information Systems Security Architecture Professional (CISSP-ISSAP)
- Information Systems Security Engineering Professional (CISSP-ISSEP)
- Information Systems Security Management Professional (CISSP-ISSMP)

The CISSP certification covers eight domains of information security knowledge. These domains are meant to serve as the broad knowledge foundation required to succeed in the information security profession. They include:

- Security and Risk Management
- Asset Security
- Security Engineering
- Communication and Network Security
- Identity and Access Management
- Security Assessment and Testing
- Security Operations
- Software Development Security

The CISSP domains are periodically updated by (ISC)². The last revision in April 2015 changed from 10 domains to the 8 listed here, and included a major realignment of topics and ideas. At the same time, a number of new areas were added or expanded to reflect changes in common information security topics.

Complete details on the CISSP Common Body of Knowledge (CBK) are contained in the Candidate Information Bulletin (CIB). The CIB, which includes a full outline of exam topics, can be found on the ISC² website at www.isc2.org.

Taking the CISSP Exam

The CISSP exam is a 6-hour exam that consists of 250 questions covering the eight domains. Passing requires achieving a score of at least 700 out of 1,000 points. It's important to understand that this is a scaled score, meaning that not every question is worth the same number of points. Questions of differing difficulty may factor into your score more or less heavily. That said, as you work through these practice exams, you might want to use 70 percent as a yardstick to help you get a sense of whether you're ready to sit for the actual exam. When you're ready, you can schedule an exam via links provided on the (ISC)² website—tests are offered in locations throughout the world.

Questions on the CISSP exam are provided in both multiple-choice form and what (ISC)² calls "advanced innovative" questions, which are drag and drop and hotspot questions, both of which are offered in computer-based testing environments. Innovative questions are scored the same as traditional multiple-choice questions and have only one right answer.

Computer-Based Testing Environment

Almost all CISSP exams are now administered in a computer-based testing (CBT) format. You'll register for the exam through the Pearson Vue website and may take the exam in the language of your choice. It is offered in English, French, German, Portuguese, Spanish, Japanese, Simplified Chinese, Korean, and a format for the visually impaired.

You'll take the exam in a computer-based testing center located near your home or office. The centers administer many different exams, so you may find yourself sitting in the same room as a student taking a school entrance examination and a healthcare professional earning a medical certification. If you'd like to become more familiar with the testing environment, the Pearson Vue website offers a virtual tour of a testing center:

`https://home.pearsonvue.com/test-taker/Pearson-Professional-Center-Tour.aspx`

When you sit down to take the exam, you'll be seated at a computer that has the exam software already loaded and running. It's a pretty straightforward interface that allows you to navigate through the exam. You can download a practice exam and tutorial from Pearson at:

`http://www.vue.com/athena/athena.asp`

Exam Retake Policy

If you don't pass the CISSP exam, you shouldn't panic. Many individuals don't reach the bar on their first attempt but gain valuable experience that helps them succeed the second time around. When you retake the exam, you'll have the benefit of familiarity with the CBT environment and CISSP exam format. You'll also have time to study up on the areas where you felt less confident.

After your first exam attempt, you must wait 30 days before retaking the computer-based exam. If you're not successful on that attempt, you must then wait 90 days before your third attempt and 180 days before your fourth attempt. You may not take the exam more than three times in a single calendar year.

Work Experience Requirement

Candidates who wish to earn the CISSP credential must not only pass the exam but also demonstrate that they have at least five years of work experience in the information security field. Your work experience must cover activities in at least two of the eight domains of the CISSP program and must be paid, full-time employment. Volunteer experiences or part-time duties are not acceptable to meet the CISSP experience requirement.

You may be eligible to waive one of the five years of the work experience requirement based on your educational achievements. If you hold a bachelor's degree or four-year equivalent, you may be eligible for a degree waiver that covers one of those years. Similarly, if you hold one of the information security certifications on the current (ISC)² credential waiver list (`https://www.isc2.org/credential_waiver/default.aspx`), you may also waive a year of the experience requirement. You may not combine these two programs. Holders of both a certification and an undergraduate degree must still demonstrate at least four years of experience.

If you haven't yet completed your work experience requirement, you may still attempt the CISSP exam. Individuals who pass the exam are designated Associates of (ISC)^2 and have six years to complete the work experience requirement.

Recertification Requirements

Once you've earned your CISSP credential, you'll need to maintain your certification by paying maintenance fees and participating in continuing professional education (CPE). As long as you maintain your certification in good standing, you will not need to retake the CISSP exam.

Currently, the annual maintenance fees for the CISSP credential are $85 per year. Individuals who hold one of the advanced CISSP concentrations will need to pay an additional $35 annually for each concentration they hold.

The CISSP CPE requirement mandates earning at least 40 CPE credits each year toward the 120-credit three-year requirement. (ISC)^2 provides an online portal where certificants may submit CPE completion for review and approval. The portal also tracks annual maintenance fee payments and progress toward recertification.

Using This Book to Practice

This book is composed of 10 chapters. Each of the first eight chapters covers a domain, with a variety of questions that can help you test your knowledge of real-world, scenario, and best practices–based security knowledge. The final two chapters are complete practice exams that can serve as timed practice tests to help determine if you're ready for the CISSP exam.

We recommend taking the first practice exam to help identify where you may need to spend more study time, and then using the domain-specific chapters to test your domain knowledge where it is weak. Once you're ready, take the second practice exam to make sure you've covered all of the material and are ready to attempt the CISSP exam.

Chapter

1

Security and Risk Management (Domain 1)

1. What is the final step of a quantitative risk analysis?

   A. Determine asset value.

   B. Assess the annualized rate of occurrence.

   C. Derive the annualized loss expectancy.

   D. Conduct a cost/benefit analysis.

2. An evil twin attack that broadcasts a legitimate SSID for an unauthorized network is an example of what category of threat?

   A. Spoofing

   B. Information disclosure

   C. Repudiation

   D. Tampering

3. Under the Digital Millennium Copyright Act (DMCA), what type of offenses do not require prompt action by an Internet service provider after it receives a notification of infringement claim from a copyright holder?

   A. Storage of information by a customer on a provider's server

   B. Caching of information by the provider

   C. Transmission of information over the provider's network by a customer

   D. Caching of information in a provider search engine

4. FlyAway Travel has offices in both the European Union and the United States and transfers personal information between those offices regularly. Which of the seven requirements for processing personal information states that organizations must inform individuals about how the information they collect is used?

   A. Notice

   B. Choice

   C. Onward Transfer

   D. Enforcement

5. Which one of the following is not one of the three common threat modeling techniques?

   A. Focused on assets

   B. Focused on attackers

   C. Focused on software

   D. Focused on social engineering

6. Which one of the following elements of information is not considered personally identifiable information that would trigger most US state data breach laws?

   A. Student identification number

   B. Social Security number

    C. Driver's license number

    D. Credit card number

7. In 1991, the federal sentencing guidelines formalized a rule that requires senior executives to take personal responsibility for information security matters. What is the name of this rule?

    A. Due diligence rule

    B. Personal liability rule

    C. Prudent man rule

    D. Due process rule

8. Which one of the following provides an authentication mechanism that would be appropriate for pairing with a password to achieve multifactor authentication?

    A. Username

    B. PIN

    C. Security question

    D. Fingerprint scan

9. What United States government agency is responsible for administering the terms of safe harbor agreements between the European Union and the United States under the EU Data Protection Directive?

    A. Department of Defense

    B. Department of the Treasury

    C. State Department

    D. Department of Commerce

10. Yolanda is the chief privacy officer for a financial institution and is researching privacy issues related to customer checking accounts. Which one of the following laws is most likely to apply to this situation?

    A. GLBA

    B. SOX

    C. HIPAA

    D. FERPA

11. Tim's organization recently received a contract to conduct sponsored research as a government contractor. What law now likely applies to the information systems involved in this contract?

    A. FISMA

    B. PCI DSS

    C. HIPAA

    D. GISRA

12. Chris is advising travelers from his organization who will be visiting many different countries overseas. He is concerned about compliance with export control laws. Which of the following technologies is most likely to trigger these regulations?

A. Memory chips

B. Office productivity applications

C. Hard drives

D. Encryption software

13. Bobbi is investigating a security incident and discovers that an attacker began with a normal user account but managed to exploit a system vulnerability to provide that account with administrative rights. What type of attack took place under the STRIDE model?

A. Spoofing

B. Repudiation

C. Tampering

D. Elevation of privilege

14. You are completing your business continuity planning effort and have decided that you wish to accept one of the risks. What should you do next?

A. Implement new security controls to reduce the risk level.

B. Design a disaster recovery plan.

C. Repeat the business impact assessment.

D. Document your decision-making process.

15. Which one of the following control categories does not accurately describe a fence around a facility?

A. Physical

B. Detective

C. Deterrent

D. Preventive

16. Tony is developing a business continuity plan and is having difficulty prioritizing resources because of the difficulty of combining information about tangible and intangible assets. What would be the most effective risk assessment approach for him to use?

A. Quantitative risk assessment

B. Qualitative risk assessment

C. Neither quantitative nor qualitative risk assessment

D. Combination of quantitative and qualitative risk assessment

17. What law provides intellectual property protection to the holders of trade secrets?

A. Copyright Law

B. Lanham Act

C. Glass-Steagall Act

D. Economic Espionage Act

18. Which one of the following principles imposes a standard of care upon an individual that is broad and equivalent to what one would expect from a reasonable person under the circumstances?

A. Due diligence

B. Separation of duties

C. Due care

D. Least privilege

19. Darcy is designing a fault tolerant system and wants to implement RAID-5 for her system. What is the minimum number of physical hard disks she can use to build this system?

A. One

B. Two

C. Three

D. Five

20. Which one of the following is an example of an administrative control?

A. Intrusion detection system

B. Security awareness training

C. Firewalls

D. Security guards

21. Keenan Systems recently developed a new manufacturing process for microprocessors. The company wants to license the technology to other companies for use but wishes to prevent unauthorized use of the technology. What type of intellectual property protection is best suited for this situation?

A. Patent

B. Trade secret

C. Copyright

D. Trademark

22. Which one of the following actions might be taken as part of a business continuity plan?

A. Restoring from backup tapes

B. Implementing RAID

C. Relocating to a cold site

D. Restarting business operations

23. When developing a business impact analysis, the team should first create a list of assets. What should happen next?

   A. Identify vulnerabilities in each asset.

   B. Determine the risks facing the asset.

   C. Develop a value for each asset.

   D. Identify threats facing each asset.

24. Mike recently implemented an intrusion prevention system designed to block common network attacks from affecting his organization. What type of risk management strategy is Mike pursuing?

   A. Risk acceptance

   B. Risk avoidance

   C. Risk mitigation

   D. Risk transference

25. Which one of the following is an example of physical infrastructure hardening?

   A. Antivirus software

   B. Hardware-based network firewall

   C. Two-factor authentication

   D. Fire suppression system

26. Which one of the following is normally used as an authorization tool?

   A. ACL

   B. Token

   C. Username

   D. Password

27. The International Information Systems Security Certification Consortium uses the logo below to represent itself online and in a variety of forums. What type of intellectual property protection may it use to protect its rights in this logo?

   A. Copyright

   B. Patent

   C. Trade secret

   D. Trademark

28. Mary is helping a computer user who sees the following message appear on his computer screen. What type of attack has occurred?

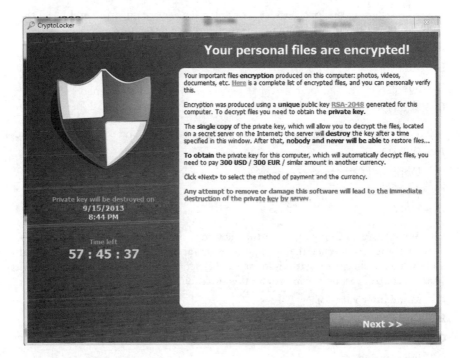

A. Availability

B. Confidentiality

C. Disclosure

D. Distributed

29. Which one of the following organizations would not be automatically subject to the terms of HIPAA if they engage in electronic transactions?

A. Healthcare provider

B. Health and fitness application developer

C. Health information clearinghouse

D. Health insurance plan

30. John's network begins to experience symptoms of slowness. Upon investigation, he realizes that the network is being bombarded with ICMP ECHO REPLY packets and believes that his organization is the victim of a Smurf attack. What principle of information security is being violated?

A. Availability

B. Integrity

    C. Confidentiality

    D. Denial

31. Renee is designing the long-term security plan for her organization and has a three- to five-year planning horizon. What type of plan is she developing?

    A. Operational

    B. Tactical

    C. Summary

    D. Strategic

32. What government agency is responsible for the evaluation and registration of trademarks?

    A. USPTO

    B. Library of Congress

    C. TVA

    D. NIST

33. The Acme Widgets Company is putting new controls in place for its accounting department. Management is concerned that a rogue accountant may be able to create a new false vendor and then issue checks to that vendor as payment for services that were never rendered. What security control can best help prevent this situation?

    A. Mandatory vacation

    B. Separation of duties

    C. Defense in depth

    D. Job rotation

34. Which one of the following categories of organizations is most likely to be covered by the provisions of FISMA?

    A. Banks

    B. Defense contractors

    C. School districts

    D. Hospitals

35. Robert is responsible for securing systems used to process credit card information. What standard should guide his actions?

    A. HIPAA

    B. PCI DSS

    C. SOX

    D. GLBA

36. Which one of the following individuals is normally responsible for fulfilling the operational data protection responsibilities delegated by senior management, such as validating data integrity, testing backups, and managing security policies?

A. Data custodian

B. Data owner

C. User

D. Auditor

37. Alan works for an e-commerce company that recently had some content stolen by another website and republished without permission. What type of intellectual property protection would best preserve Alan's company's rights?

A. Trade secret

B. Copyright

C. Trademark

D. Patent

38. Florian receives a flyer from a federal agency announcing that a new administrative law will affect his business operations. Where should he go to find the text of the law?

A. United States Code

B. Supreme Court rulings

C. Code of Federal Regulations

D. Compendium of Laws

39. Tom is installing a next-generation firewall (NGFW) in his data center that is designed to block many types of application attacks. When viewed from a risk management perspective, what metric is Tom attempting to lower?

A. Impact

B. RPO

C. MTO

D. Likelihood

40. Which one of the following individuals would be the most effective organizational owner for an information security program?

A. CISSP-certified analyst

B. Chief information officer

C. Manager of network security

D. President and CEO

41. What important function do senior managers normally fill on a business continuity planning team?

A. Arbitrating disputes about criticality

B. Evaluating the legal environment

C. Training staff

D. Designing failure controls

42. You are the CISO for a major hospital system and are preparing to sign a contract with a Software-as-a-Service (SaaS) email vendor and want to ensure that its business continuity planning measures are reasonable. What type of audit might you request to meet this goal?

    A. SOC-1

    B. FISMA

    C. PCI DSS

    D. SOC-2

43. Gary is analyzing a security incident and, during his investigation, encounters a user who denies having performed an action that Gary believes he did perform. What type of threat has taken place under the STRIDE model?

    A. Repudiation

    B. Information disclosure

    C. Tampering

    D. Elevation of privilege

44. Beth is the security administrator for a public school district. She is implementing a new student information system and is testing the code to ensure that students are not able to alter their own grades. What principle of information security is Beth enforcing?

    A. Integrity

    B. Availability

    C. Confidentiality

    D. Denial

45. Which one of the following issues is not normally addressed in a service-level agreement (SLA)?

    A. Confidentiality of customer information

    B. Failover time

    C. Uptime

    D. Maximum consecutive downtime

46. Joan is seeking to protect a piece of computer software that she developed under intellectual property law. Which one of the following avenues of protection would not apply to a piece of software?

    A. Trademark

    B. Copyright

    C. Patent

    D. Trade secret

Questions 47–49 refer to the following scenario.

Juniper Content is a web content development company with 40 employees located in two offices: one in New York and a smaller office in the San Francisco Bay Area. Each office has a local area network protected by a perimeter firewall. The LAN contains modern switch equipment connected to both wired and wireless networks.

Each office has its own file server, and the IT team runs software every hour to synchronize files between the two servers, distributing content between the offices. These servers are primarily used to store images and other files related to web content developed by the company. The team also uses a SaaS-based email and document collaboration solution for much of their work.

You are the newly appointed IT manager for Juniper Content and you are working to augment existing security controls to improve the organization's security.

47. Users in the two offices would like to access each other's file servers over the Internet. What control would provide confidentiality for those communications?

    A. Digital signatures

    B. Virtual private network

    C. Virtual LAN

    D. Digital content management

48. You are also concerned about the availability of data stored on each office's server. You would like to add technology that would enable continued access to files located on the server even if a hard drive in a server fails. What integrity control allows you to add robustness without adding additional servers?

    A. Server clustering

    B. Load balancing

    C. RAID

    D. Scheduled backups

49. Finally, there are historical records stored on the server that are extremely important to the business and should never be modified. You would like to add an integrity control that allows you to verify on a periodic basis that the files were not modified. What control can you add?

    A. Hashing

    B. ACLs

    C. Read-only attributes

    D. Firewalls

50. What law serves as the basis for privacy rights in the United States?

    A. Privacy Act of 1974

    B. Fourth Amendment

    C. First Amendment

    D. Electronic Communications Privacy Act of 1986

51. Which one of the following is not normally included in business continuity plan documentation?

A. Statement of accounts

B. Statement of importance

C. Statement of priorities

D. Statement of organizational responsibility

52. An accounting employee at Doolitte Industries was recently arrested for participation in an embezzlement scheme. The employee transferred money to a personal account and then shifted funds around between other accounts every day to disguise the fraud for months. Which one of the following controls might have best allowed the earlier detection of this fraud?

A. Separation of duties

B. Least privilege

C. Defense in depth

D. Mandatory vacation

53. Which one of the following is not normally considered a business continuity task?

A. Business impact assessment

B. Emergency response guidelines

C. Electronic vaulting

D. Vital records program

54. Which information security goal is impacted when an organization experiences a DoS or DDoS attack?

A. Confidentiality

B. Integrity

C. Availability

D. Denial

55. Yolanda is writing a document that will provide configuration information regarding the minimum level of security that every system in the organization must meet. What type of document is she preparing?

A. Policy

B. Baseline

C. Guideline

D. Procedure

56. Who should receive initial business continuity plan training in an organization?

A. Senior executives

B. Those with specific business continuity roles

C. Everyone in the organization

D. First responders

57. James is conducting a risk assessment for his organization and is attempting to assign an asset value to the servers in his data center. The organization's primary concern is ensuring that it has sufficient funds available to rebuild the data center in the event it is damaged or destroyed. Which one of the following asset valuation methods would be most appropriate in this situation?

   A. Purchase cost

   B. Depreciated cost

   C. Replacement cost

   D. Opportunity cost

58. The Computer Security Act of 1987 gave a federal agency responsibility for developing computer security standards and guidelines for federal computer systems. What agency did the act give this responsibility to?

   A. National Security Agency

   B. Federal Communications Commission

   C. Department of Defense

   D. National Institute of Standards and Technology

59. Which one of the following is not a requirement for an invention to be patentable?

   A. It must be new.

   B. It must be invented by an American citizen.

   C. It must be nonobvious.

   D. It must be useful.

60. Frank discovers a keylogger hidden on the laptop of his company's chief executive officer. What information security principle is the keylogger most likely designed to disrupt?

   A. Confidentiality

   B. Integrity

   C. Availability

   D. Denial

61. What is the formula used to determine risk?

   A. Risk = Threat * Vulnerability

   B. Risk = Threat / Vulnerability

   C. Risk = Asset * Threat

   D. Risk = Asset / Threat

62. The graphic below shows the NIST risk management framework with step 4 missing. What is the missing step?

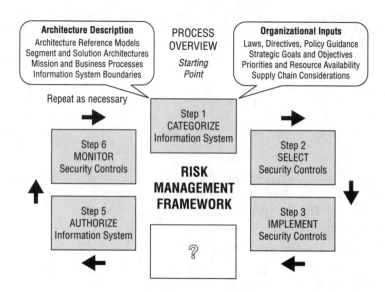

A. Assess security controls

B. Determine control gaps

C. Remediate control gaps

D. Evaluate user activity

63. HAL Systems recently decided to stop offering public NTP services because of a fear that its NTP servers would be used in amplification DDoS attacks. What type of risk management strategy did HAL pursue with respect to its NTP services?

A. Risk mitigation

B. Risk acceptance

C. Risk transference

D. Risk avoidance

64. Susan is working with the management team in her company to classify data in an attempt to apply extra security controls that will limit the likelihood of a data breach. What principle of information security is Susan trying to enforce?

A. Availability

B. Denial

C. Confidentiality

D. Integrity

65. Which one of the following components should be included in an organization's emergency response guidelines?

    A. List of individuals who should be notified of an emergency incident

    B. Long-term business continuity protocols

    C. Activation procedures for the organization's cold sites

    D. Contact information for ordering equipment

66. Who is the ideal person to approve an organization's business continuity plan?

    A. Chief information officer

    B. Chief executive officer

    C. Chief information security officer

    D. Chief operating officer

67. Which one of the following actions is not normally part of the project scope and planning phase of business continuity planning?

    A. Structured analysis of the organization

    B. Review of the legal and regulatory landscape

    C. Creation of a BCP team

    D. Documentation of the plan

68. Gary is implementing a new RAID-based disk system designed to keep a server up and running even in the event of a single disk failure. What principle of information security is Gary seeking to enforce?

    A. Denial

    B. Confidentiality

    C. Integrity

    D. Availability

69. Becka recently signed a contract with an alternate data processing facility that will provide her company with space in the event of a disaster. The facility includes HVAC, power, and communications circuits but no hardware. What type of facility is Becka using?

    A. Cold site

    B. Warm site

    C. Hot site

    D. Mobile site

70. What is the threshold for malicious damage to a federal computer system that triggers the Computer Fraud and Abuse Act?

    A. $500

    B. $2,500

    C. $5,000

    D. $10,000

71. Ben is seeking a control objective framework that is widely accepted around the world and focuses specifically on information security controls. Which one of the following frameworks would best meet his needs?

    A. ITIL

    B. ISO 27002

    C. CMM

    D. PMBOK Guide

72. Which one of the following laws requires that communications service providers cooperate with law enforcement requests?

    A. ECPA

    B. CALEA

    C. Privacy Act

    D. HITECH Act

73. Every year, Gary receives privacy notices in the mail from financial institutions where he has accounts. What law requires the institutions to send Gary these notices?

    A. FERPA

    B. GLBA

    C. HIPAA

    D. HITECH

74. Which one of the following agreements typically requires that a vendor not disclose confidential information learned during the scope of an engagement?

    A. NCA

    B. SLA

    C. NDA

    D. RTO

75. Which one of the following is not an example of a technical control?

    A. Router ACL

    B. Firewall rule

    C. Encryption

    D. Data classification

76. Which one of the following stakeholders is not typically included on a business continuity planning team?

    A. Core business function leaders

    B. Information technology staff

    C. CEO

    D. Support departments

77. Ben is designing a messaging system for a bank and would like to include a feature that allows the recipient of a message to prove to a third party that the message did indeed come from the purported originator. What goal is Ben trying to achieve?

  A. Authentication

  B. Authorization

  C. Integrity

  D. Nonrepudiation

78. What principle of information security states that an organization should implement overlapping security controls whenever possible?

  A. Least privilege

  B. Separation of duties

  C. Defense in depth

  D. Security through obscurity

79. Which one of the following is not a goal of a formal change management program?

  A. Implement change in an orderly fashion.

  B. Test changes prior to implementation.

  C. Provide rollback plans for changes.

  D. Inform stakeholders of changes after they occur.

80. Ben is responsible for the security of payment card information stored in a database. Policy directs that he remove the information from the database, but he cannot do this for operational reasons. He obtained an exception to policy and is seeking an appropriate compensating control to mitigate the risk. What would be his best option?

  A. Purchasing insurance

  B. Encrypting the database contents

  C. Removing the data

  D. Objecting to the exception

81. The Domer Industries risk assessment team recently conducted a qualitative risk assessment and developed a matrix similar to the one shown below. Which quadrant contains the risks that require the most immediate attention?

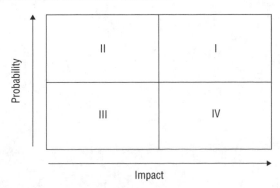

    A. I

    B. II

    C. III

    D. IV

82. Tom is planning to terminate an employee this afternoon for fraud and expects that the meeting will be somewhat hostile. He is coordinating the meeting with Human Resources and wants to protect the company against damage. Which one of the following steps is most important to coordinate in time with the termination meeting?

    A. Informing other employees of the termination

    B. Retrieval of photo ID

    C. Calculation of final paycheck

    D. Revocation of electronic access rights

83. Rolando is a risk manager with a large-scale enterprise. The firm recently evaluated the risk of California mudslides on its operations in the region and determined that the cost of responding outweighed the benefits of any controls it could implement. The company chose to take no action at this time. What risk management strategy did Rolando's organization pursue?

    A. Risk avoidance

    B. Risk mitigation

    C. Risk transference

    D. Risk acceptance

84. Helen is the owner of a website that provides information for middle and high school students preparing for exams. She is concerned that the activities of her site may fall under the jurisdiction of the Children's Online Privacy Protection Act (COPPA). What is the cutoff age below which parents must give consent in advance of the collection of personal information from their children under COPPA?

    A. 13

    B. 15

    C. 17

    D. 18

85. Tom is considering locating a business in the downtown area of Miami, Florida. He consults the FEMA flood plain map for the region, shown below, and determines that the area he is considering lies within a 100-year flood plain.

What is the ARO of a flood in this area?

    A. 100

    B. 1

    C. 0.1

    D. 0.01

86. You discover that a user on your network has been using the Wireshark tool, as shown in the following screen shot. Further investigation revealed that he was using it for illicit purposes. What pillar of information security has most likely been violated?

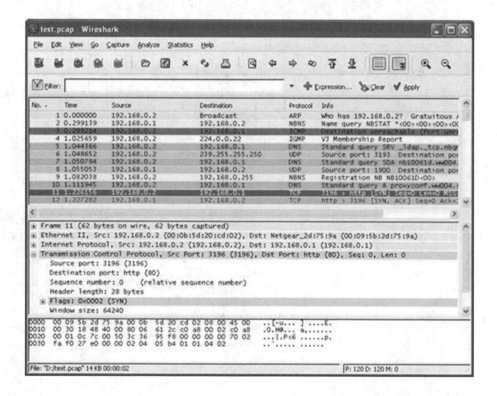

A. Integrity

B. Denial

C. Availability

D. Confidentiality

87. Alan is performing threat modeling and decides that it would be useful to decompose the system into the key elements shown in the following illustration. What tool is he using?

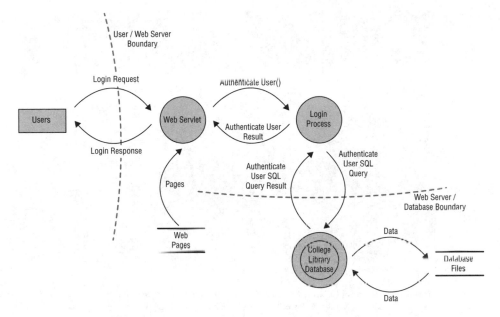

Image reprinted from *CISSP (ISC)² Certified Information Systems Security Professional Official Study Guide, 7th Edition* © John Wiley & Sons 2015, reprinted with permission.

A. Vulnerability assessment

B. Fuzzing

C. Reduction analsis

D. Data modeling

88. What law governs the handling of information related to the financial statements of publicly traded companies?

A. GLBA

B. PCI DSS

C. HIPAA

D. SOX

89. Craig is selecting the site for a new data center and must choose a location somewhere within the United States. He obtained the earthquake risk map below from the United States Geological Survey. Which of the following would be the safest location to build his facility if he were primarily concerned with earthquake risk?

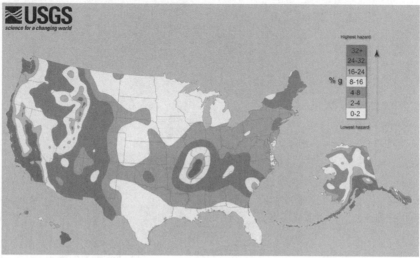

(Source: US Geological Survey)

Image reprinted from CISSP (ISC)[2] Certified Information Systems Security Professional Official Study Guide, 7th Edition © John Wiley & Sons 2015, reprinted with permission.

    A. New York

    B. North Carolina

    C. Indiana

    D. Florida

90. Which one of the following tools is most often used for identification purposes and is not suitable for use as an authenticator?

    A. Password

    B. Retinal scan

    C. Username

    D. Token

91. Which type of business impact assessment tool is most appropriate when attempting to evaluate the impact of a failure on customer confidence?

    A. Quantitative

    B. Qualitative

    C. Annualized loss expectancy

    D. Reduction

92. Which one of the following is the first step in developing an organization's vital records program?

    A. Identifying vital records

    B. Locating vital records

C. Archiving vital records

D. Preserving vital records

93. Which one of the following security programs is designed to provide employees with the knowledge they need to perform their specific work tasks?

A. Awareness

B. Training

C. Education

D. Indoctrination

94. Which one of the following security programs is designed to establish a minimum standard common denominator of security understanding?

A. Training

B. Education

C. Indoctrination

D. Awareness

95. Ryan is a security risk analyst for an insurance company. He is currently examining a scenario in which a hacker might use a SQL injection attack to deface a web server due to a missing patch in the company's web application. In this scenario, what is the threat?

A. Unpatched web application

B. Web defacement

C. Hacker

D. Operating system

Questions 96–98 refer to the following scenario.

Henry is the risk manager for Atwood Landing, a resort community in the Midwestern United States. The resort's main data center is located in northern Indiana in an area that is prone to tornados. Henry recently undertook a replacement cost analysis and determined that rebuilding and reconfiguring the data center would cost $10 million.

Henry consulted with tornado experts, data center specialists, and structural engineers. Together, they determined that a typical tornado would cause approximately $5 million of damage to the facility. The meteorologists determined that Atwood's facility lies in an area where they are likely to experience a tornado once every 200 years.

96. Based upon the information in this scenario, what is the exposure factor for the effect of a tornado on Atwood Landing's data center?

A. 10%

B. 25%

C. 50%

D. 75%

97. Based upon the information in this scenario, what is the annualized rate of occurrence for a tornado at Atwood Landing's data center?

   A. 0.0025

   B. 0.005

   C. 0.01

   D. 0.015

98. Based upon the information in this scenario, what is the annualized loss expectancy for a tornado at Atwood Landing's data center?

   A. $25,000

   B. $50,000

   C. $250,000

   D. $500,000

99. John is analyzing an attack against his company in which the attacker found comments embedded in HTML code that provided the clues needed to exploit a software vulnerability. Using the STRIDE model, what type of attack did he uncover?

   A. Spoofing

   B. Repudiation

   C. Information disclosure

   D. Elevation of privilege

100. Which one of the following is an administrative control that can protect the confidentiality of information?

   A. Encryption

   B. Non-disclosure agreement

   C. Firewall

   D. Fault tolerance

Chapter 2

Asset Security (Domain 2)

1. Angela is an information security architect at a bank and has been assigned to ensure that transactions are secure as they traverse the network. She recommends that all transactions use TLS. What threat is she most likely attempting to stop, and what method is she using to protect against it?

   A. Man-in-the-middle, VPN

   B. Packet injection, encryption

   C. Sniffing, encryption

   D. Sniffing, TEMPEST

2. COBIT, Control Objectives for Information and Related Technology, is a framework for IT management and governance. Which data management role is most likely to select and apply COBIT to balance the need for security controls against business requirements?

   A. Business owners

   B. Data processors

   C. Data owners

   D. Data stewards

3. What term is used to describe a starting point for a minimum security standard?

   A. Outline

   B. Baseline

   C. Policy

   D. Configuration guide

4. When media is labeled based on the classification of the data it contains, what rule is typically applied regarding labels?

   A. The data is labeled based on its integrity requirements.

   B. The media is labeled based on the highest classification level of the data it contains.

   C. The media is labeled with all levels of classification of the data it contains.

   D. The media is labeled with the lowest level of classification of the data it contains.

5. The need to protect sensitive data drives what administrative process?

   A. Information classification

   B. Remanence

   C. Transmitting data

   D. Clearing

6. How can a data retention policy help to reduce liabilities?

   A. By ensuring that unneeded data isn't retained

   B. By ensuring that incriminating data is destroyed

   C. By ensuring that data is securely wiped so it cannot be restored for legal discovery

   D. By reducing the cost of data storage required by law

7. Staff in an IT department who are delegated responsibility for day-to-day tasks hold what data role?

  A. Business owner

  B. User

  C. Data processor

  D. Custodian

8. Susan works for an American company that conducts business with customers in the European Union. What is she likely to have to do if she is responsible for handling PII from those customers?

  A. Encrypt the data at all times.

  B. Label and classify the data according to HIPAA.

  C. Conduct yearly assessments to the EU DPD baseline.

  D. Comply with the US-EU Safe Harbor requirements.

9. Ben has been tasked with identifying security controls for systems covered by his organization's information classification system. Why might Ben choose to use a security baseline?

  A. It applies in all circumstances, allowing consistent security controls.

  B. They are approved by industry standards bodies, preventing liability.

  C. They provide a good starting point that can be tailored to organizational needs.

  D. They ensure that systems are always in a secure state.

10. What term is used to describe overwriting media to allow for its reuse in an environment operating at the same sensitivity level?

  A. Clearing

  B. Erasing

  C. Purging

  D. Sanitization

11. Which of the following classification levels is the US government's classification label for data that could cause damage but wouldn't cause serious or grave damage?

  A. Top Secret

  B. Secret

  C. Confidential

  D. Classified

12. What issue is common to spare sectors and bad sectors on hard drives as well as overprovisioned space on modern SSDs?

  A. They can be used to hide data.

  B. They can only be degaussed.

    C. They are not addressable, resulting in data remanence.

    D. They may not be cleared, resulting in data remanence.

13. What term describes data that remains after attempts have been made to remove the data?

    A. Residual bytes

    B. Data remanence

    C. Slack space

    D. Zero fill

For questions 14, 15, and 16, please refer to the following scenario:

Your organization regularly handles three types of data: information that it shares with customers, information that it uses internally to conduct business, and trade secret information that offers the organization significant competitive advantages. Information shared with customers is used and stored on web servers, while both the internal business data and the trade secret information are stored on internal file servers and employee workstations.

14. What civilian data classifications best fit this data?

    A. Unclassified, confidential, top secret

    B. Public, sensitive, private

    C. Public, sensitive, proprietary

    D. Public, confidential, private

15. What technique could you use to mark your trade secret information in case it was released or stolen and you need to identify it?

    A. Classification

    B. Symmetric encryption

    C. Watermarks

    D. Metadata

16. What type of encryption should you use on the file servers for the proprietary data, and how might you secure the data when it is in motion?

    A. TLS at rest and AES in motion

    B. AES at rest and TLS in motion

    C. VPN at rest and TLS in motion

    D. DES at rest and AES in motion

17. What does labeling data allow a DLP system to do?

    A. The DLP system can detect labels and apply appropriate protections.

    B. The DLP system can adjust labels based on changes in the classification scheme.

    C. The DLP system can notify the firewall that traffic should be allowed through.

    D. The DLP system can delete unlabeled data.

18. Why is it cost effective to purchase high-quality media to contain sensitive data?

    A. Expensive media is less likely to fail.

    B. The value of the data often far exceeds the cost of the media.

    C. Expensive media is easier to encrypt.

    D. More expensive media typically improves data integrity.

19. Chris is responsible for workstations throughout his company and knows that some of the company's workstations are used to handle proprietary information. Which option best describes what should happen at the end of their lifecycle for workstations he is responsible for?

    A. Erasing

    B. Clearing

    C. Sanitization

    D. Destruction

20. Which is the proper order from least to most sensitive for US government classifications?

    A. Confidential, Secret, Top Secret

    B. Confidential, Classified, Secret

    C. Top Secret, Secret, Classified, Public, Classified, Top Secret

    D. Public, Unclassified, Classified, Top Secret

21. What scenario describes data at rest?

    A. Data in an IPsec tunnel

    B. Data in an e-commerce transaction

    C. Data stored on a hard drive

    D. Data stored in RAM

22. If you are selecting a security standard for a Windows 10 system that processes credit cards, what security standard is your best choice?

    A. Microsoft's Windows 10 security baseline

    B. The CIS Windows 10 baseline

    C. PCI DSS

    D. The NSA Windows 10 baseline

Use the following scenario for questions 23, 24, and 25.

The Center for Internet Security (CIS) works with subject matter experts from a variety of industries to create lists of security controls for operating systems, mobile devices, server software, and network devices. Your organization has decided to use the CIS benchmarks for your systems. Answer the following questions based on this decision.

23. The CIS benchmarks are an example of what practice?

   A. Conducting a risk assessment

   B. Implementing data labeling

   C. Proper system ownership

   D. Using security baselines

24. Adjusting the CIS benchmarks to your organization's mission and your specific IT systems would involve what two processes?

   A. Scoping and selection

   B. Scoping and tailoring

   C. Baselining and tailoring

   D. Tailoring and selection

25. How should you determine what controls from the baseline a given system or software package should receive?

   A. Consult the custodians of the data.

   B. Select based on the data classification of the data it stores or handles.

   C. Apply the same controls to all systems.

   D. Consult the business owner of the process the system or data supports.

26. What problem with FTP and Telnet makes using SFTP and SSH better alternatives?

   A. FTP and Telnet aren't installed on many systems.

   B. FTP and Telnet do not encrypt data.

   C. FTP and Telnet have known bugs and are no longer maintained.

   D. FTP and Telnet are difficult to use, making SFTP and SSH the preferred solution.

27. The government defense contractor that Saria works for has recently shut down a major research project and is planning on reusing the hundreds of thousands of dollars of systems and data storage tapes used for the project for other purposes. When Saria reviews the company's internal processes, she finds that she can't reuse the tapes and that the manual says they should be destroyed. Why isn't Saria allowed to degauss and then reuse the tapes to save her employer money?

   A. Data permanence may be an issue.

   B. Data remanence is a concern.

   C. The tapes may suffer from bitrot.

   D. Data from tapes can't be erased by degaussing.

28. Information maintained about an individual that can be used to distinguish or trace their identity is known as what type of information?

   A. Personally identifiable information (PII)

   B. Personal health information (PHI)

   C. Social Security number (SSN)

   D. Secure identity information (SII)

29. What is the primary information security risk to data at rest?

   A. Improper classification

   B. Data breach

   C. Decryption

   D. Loss of data integrity

30. Full disk encryption like Microsoft's BitLocker is used to protect data in what state?

   A. Data in transit

   B. Data at rest

   C. Unlabeled data

   D. Labeled data

31. Sue's employer has asked her to use an IPsec VPN to connect to its network. When Sue connects, what does the IPsec VPN allow her to do?

   A. Send decrypted data over a public network and act like she is on her employer's internal network.

   B. Create a private encrypted network carried via a public network and act like she is on her employer's internal network.

   C. Create a virtual private network using TLS while on her employer's internal network.

   D. Create a tunneled network that connects her employer's network to her internal home network.

32. What is the primary purpose of data classification?

   A. It quantifies the cost of a data breach.

   B. It prioritizes IT expenditures.

   C. It allows compliance with breach notification laws.

   D. It identifies the value of the data to the organization.

33. Fred's organization allows downgrading of systems for reuse after projects have been finished and the systems have been purged. What concern should Fred raise about the reuse of the systems from his Top Secret classified project for a future project classified as Secret?

    A. The Top Secret data may be commingled with the Secret data, resulting in a need to relabel the system.

    B. The cost of the sanitization process may exceed the cost of new equipment.

    C. The data may be exposed as part of the sanitization process.

    D. The organization's DLP system may flag the new system due to the difference in data labels.

34. Which of the following concerns should not be part of the decision when classifying data?

    A. The cost to classify the data

    B. The sensitivity of the data

    C. The amount of harm that exposure of the data could cause

    D. The value of the data to the organization

35. Which of the following is the least effective method of removing data from media?

    A. Degaussing

    B. Purging

    C. Erasing

    D. Clearing

36. Safe Harbor is part of a US program to meet what European Union law?

    A. The EU CyberSafe Act

    B. The Network and Information Security (NIS) directives

    C. The General Data Protection Regulation (GDPR)

    D. The EU Data Protection Directive

Use the following scenario to answer questions 37, 38, and 39.

The healthcare company that Lauren works for handles HIPAA data as well as internal business data, protected health information, and day-to-day business communications. Its internal policy uses the following requirements for securing HIPAA data at rest and in transit.

Classification	Handling Requirements
Confidential (HIPAA)	Encrypt at rest and in transit.
	Full disk encryption required for all workstations.
	Files can only be sent in encrypted form, and passwords must be transferred under separate cover.
	Printed documents must be labeled with "HIPAA handling required."
Private (PHI)	Encrypt at rest and in transit.
	PHI must be stored on secure servers, and copies should not be kept on local workstations.
	Printed documents must be labeled with "Private."

Classification	Handling Requirements
Sensitive (business confidential)	Encryption is recommended but not required.
Public	Information can be sent unencrypted.

Using the table, answer the following questions.

37. What type of encryption would be appropriate for HIPAA documents in transit?

  A. AES256

  B. DES

  C. TLS

  D. SSL

38. Lauren's employer asks Lauren to classify patient X-ray data that has an internal patient identifier associated with it but does not have any way to directly identify a patient. The company's data owner believes that exposure of the data could cause damage (but not exceptional damage) to the organization. How should Lauren classify the data?

  A. Public

  B. Sensitive

  C. Private

  D. Confidential

39. What technology could Lauren's employer implement to help prevent confidential data from being emailed out of the organization?

  A. DLP

  B. IDS

  C. A firewall

  D. UDP

40. A US government database contains Secret, Confidential, and Top Secret data. How should it be classified?

  A. Top Secret

  B. Confidential

  C. Secret

  D. Mixed classification

41. What tool is used to prevent employees who leave from sharing proprietary information with their new employers?

  A. Encryption

  B. NDA

    C. Classification

    D. Purging

42. What encryption algorithm is used by both BitLocker and Microsoft's Encrypting File System?

    A. Blowfish

    B. Serpent

    C. AES

    D. 3DES

43. Chris is responsible for his organization's security standards and has guided the selection and implementation of a security baseline for Windows PCs in his organization. How can Chris most effectively make sure that the workstations he is responsible for are being checked for compliance and that settings are being applied as necessary?

    A. Assign users to spot-check baseline compliance.

    B. Use Microsoft Group Policy.

    C. Create startup scripts to apply policy at system start.

    D. Periodically review the baselines with the data owner and system owners.

44. What term is used to describe a set of common security configurations, often provided by a third party?

    A. Security policy

    B. Baseline

    C. DSS

    D. SP 800

45. What type of policy describes how long data is retained and maintained before destruction?

    A. Classification

    B. Audit

    C. Record retention

    D. Availability

46. Which attack helped drive vendors to move away from SSL toward TLS-only by default?

    A. POODLE

    B. Stuxnet

    C. BEAST

    D. CRIME

47. What security measure can provide an additional security control in the event that backup tapes are stolen or lost?

    A. Keep multiple copies of the tapes.

    B. Replace tape media with hard drives.

   C. Use appropriate security labels.

   D. Use AES256 encryption.

48. Joe works at a major pharmaceutical research and development company and has been tasked with writing his organization's data retention policy. As part of its legal requirements, the organization must comply with the US Food and Drug Administration's Code of Federal Regulations Title 21. To do so, it is required to retain records with electronic signatures. Why would a signature be part of a retention requirement?

   A. It ensures that someone has reviewed the data.

   B. It provides confidentiality.

   C. It ensures that the data has not been changed.

   D. It validates who approved the data.

49. What protocol is preferred over Telnet for remote server administration via the command line?

   A. SCP

   B. SFTP

   C. WDS

   D. SSH

50. What method uses a strong magnetic field to erase media?

   A. Magwipe

   B. Degaussing

   C. Sanitization

   D. Purging

51. What primary issue does personnel retention deal with?

   A. Employees quitting

   B. Employees not moving on to new positions

   C. Knowledge gained after employment

   D. Knowledge gained during employment

52. Alex works for a government agency that is required to meet US federal government requirements for data security. To meet these requirements, Alex has been tasked with making sure data is identifiable by its classification level. What should Alex do to the data?

   A. Classify the data.

   B. Encrypt the data.

   C. Label the data.

   D. Apply DRM to the data.

53. Ben is following the NIST Special Publication 800-88 guidelines for sanitization and disposition as shown in the following diagram. He is handling information that his

organization classified as sensitive, which is a moderate security categorization in the NIST model. If the media is going to be sold as surplus, what process does Ben need to follow?

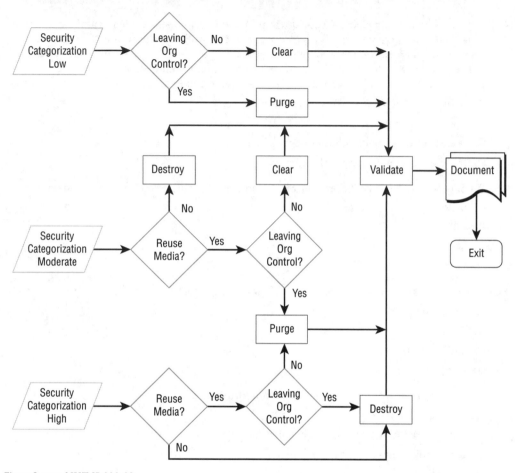

Figure Source: NIST SP 800-88

   A. Destroy, validate, document

   B. Clear, purge, document

   C. Purge, document, validate

   D. Purge, validate, document

54. What methods are often used to protect data in transit?

   A. Telnet, ISDN, UDP

   B. Encrypted storage media

   C. AES, Serpent, IDEA

   D. TLS, VPN, IPsec

55. Which data role is described as the person who has ultimate organizational responsibility for data?

   A. System owners

   B. Business owners

   C. Data owners

   D. Mission owners

56. What US government agency oversees compliance with the Safe Harbor framework for organizations wishing to use the personal data of EU citizens?

   A. The FAA

   B. The FDA

   C. The DoD

   D. The Department of Commerce

For questions 57, 58, and 59, use the following scenario.

Chris has recently been hired into a new organization. The organization that Chris belongs to uses the following classification process:

   1. Criteria are set for classifying data.

   2. Data owners are established for each type of data.

   3. Data is classified.

   4. Required controls are selected for each classification.

   5. Baseline security standards are selected for the organization.

   6. Controls are scoped and tailored.

   7. Controls are applied and enforced.

   8. Access is granted and managed.

Use the classification process to answer the following questions.

57. If Chris is one of the data owners for the organization, what steps in this process is he most likely responsible for?

   A. He is responsible for steps 3, 4, and 5.

   B. He is responsible for steps 1, 2, and 3.

   C. He is responsible for steps 5, 6, and 7.

   D. All of the steps are his direct responsibility.

58. Chris manages a team of system administrators. What data role are they fulfilling if they conduct steps 6, 7, and 8 of the classification process?

   A. They are system owners and administrators.

   B. They are administrators and custodians.

   C. They are data owners and administrators.

   D. They are custodians and users.

59. If Chris's company operates in the European Union and has been contracted to handle the data for a third party, what role is his company operating in when it uses this process to classify and handle data?

   A. Business owners

   B. Mission owners

   C. Data processors

   D. Data administrators

60. Which of the following is not a part of the European Union's Data Protection principles?

   A. Notice

   B. Reason

   C. Security

   D. Access

61. Ben's company, which is based in the EU, hires a third-party organization that processes data for it. Who has responsibility to protect the privacy of the data and ensure that it isn't used for anything other than its intended purpose?

   A. Ben's company is responsible.

   B. The third-party data processor is responsible.

   C. The data controller is responsible.

   D. Both organizations bear equal responsibility.

62. Major Hunter, a member of the US armed forces, has been entrusted with information that, if exposed, could cause serious damage to national security. Under US government classification standards, how should this data be classified?

   A. Unclassified

   B. Top Secret

   C. Confidential

   D. Secret

63. When a computer is removed from service and disposed of, the process that ensures that all storage media has been removed or destroyed is known as what?

   A. Sanitization

   B. Purging

   C. Destruction

   D. Declassification

64. Linux systems that use bcrypt are using a tool based on what DES alternative encryption scheme?

   A. 3DES

   B. AES

   C. Diffie-Hellman

   D. Blowfish

65. Susan works in an organization that labels all removable media with the classification level of the data it contains, including public data. Why would Susan's employer label all media instead of labeling only the media that contains data that could cause harm if it was exposed?

   A. It is cheaper to order all prelabeled media.

   B. It prevents sensitive media from not being marked by mistake.

   C. It prevents reuse of public media for sensitive data.

   D. Labeling all media is required by HIPAA.

66. Data stored in RAM is best characterized as what type of data?

   A. Data at rest

   B. Data in use

   C. Data in transit

   D. Data at large

67. What issue is the validation portion of the NIST SP 800-88 sample certificate of sanitization intended to help prevent?

   A. Destruction

   B. Reuse

   C. Data remanence

   D. Attribution

68. Why is declassification rarely chosen as an option for media reuse?

   A. Purging is sufficient for sensitive data.

   B. Sanitization is the preferred method of data removal.

   C. It is more expensive than new media and may still fail.

   D. Clearing is required first.

69. NIST SP 800-60 provides a process shown in the following diagram to assess information systems. What process does this diagram show?

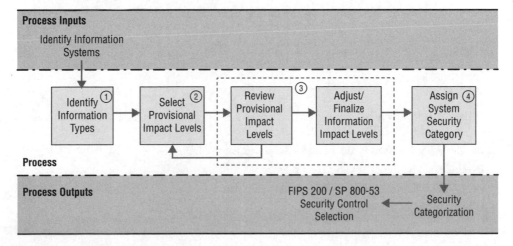

Figure Source: NIST SP 800-60

A. Selecting a standard and implementing it

B. Categorizing and selecting controls

C. Baselining and selecting controls

D. Categorizing and sanitizing

The following image shows a typical workstation and server and their connections to each other and the Internet. Use the image to answer questions 70, 71, and 72.

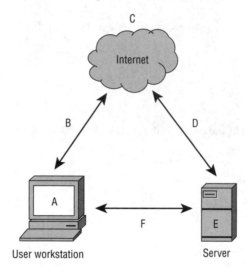

70. Which letters should be associated with data at rest?

A. A, B, and C

B. C and E

C. A and E

D. B, D, and F

71. What would be the best way to secure data at points B, D, and F?

A. AES256

B. SSL

C. TLS

D. 3DES

72. What is the best way to secure files that are sent from workstation A via the Internet service (C) to remote server E?

A. Use AES at rest at point A, and TLS in transit via B and D.

B. Encrypt the data files and send them.

C. Use 3DES and TLS to provide double security.

D. Use full disk encryption at A and E, and use SSL at B and D.

73. Incineration, crushing, shredding, and disintegration all describe what stage in the life cycle of media?

   A. Sanitization

   B. Degaussing

   C. Purging

   D. Destruction

74. The European Union (EU) Data Protection Directive's seven principles do not include which of the following key elements?

   A. The need to inform subjects when their data is being collected

   B. The need to set a limit on how long data is retained

   C. The need to keep the data secure

   D. The need to allow data subjects to be able to access and correct their data

75. Why might an organization use unique screen backgrounds or designs on workstations that deal with data of different classification levels?

   A. To indicate the software version in use

   B. To promote a corporate message

   C. To promote availability

   D. To indicate the classification level of the data or system

76. Charles has been asked to downgrade the media used for storage of private data for his organization. What process should Charles follow?

   A. Degauss the drives, and then relabel them with a lower classification level.

   B. Pulverize the drives, and then reclassify them based on the data they contain.

   C. Follow the organization's purging process, and then downgrade and replace labels.

   D. Relabel the media, and then follow the organization's purging process to ensure that the media matches the label.

77. Which of the following tasks are not performed by a system owner per NIST SP 800-18?

   A. Develops a system security plan

   B. Establishes rules for appropriate use and protection of data

   C. Identifies and implements security controls

   D. Ensures that system users receive appropriate security training

78. Susan needs to provide a set of minimum security requirements for email. What steps should she recommend for her organization to ensure that the email remains secure?

   A. All email should be encrypted.

   B. All email should be encrypted and labeled.

   C. Sensitive email should be encrypted and labeled.

   D. Only highly sensitive email should be encrypted.

79. What term describes the process of reviewing baseline security controls and selecting only the controls that are appropriate for the IT system you are trying to protect?

   A. Standard creation

   B. CIS benchmarking

   C. Baselining

   D. Scoping

80. What data role does a system that is used to process data have?

   A. Mission owner

   B. Data owner

   C. Data processor

   D. Custodian

81. Which of the following will be superceded in 2018 by the European Union's General Data Protection Regulation (GDPR)

   A. The EU Data Protection Directive

   B. NIST SP 800-12

   C. The EU Personal Data Protection Regulation

   D. COBIT

82. What type of health information is the Health Insurance Portability and Accountability Act required to protect?

   A. PII

   B. PHI

   C. SHI

   D. HPHI

83. What encryption algorithm would provide strong protection for data stored on a USB thumb drive?

   A. TLS

   B. SHA1

   C. AES

   D. DES

84. Lauren's multinational company wants to ensure compliance with the EU Data Protection Directive. If she allows data to be used against the requirements of the notice principle and against what users selected in the choice principle, what principle has her organization violated?

   A. Onward transfer

   B. Data integrity

   C. Enforcement

   D. Access

85. What is the best method to sanitize a solid-state drive (SSD)?

- **A.** Clearing
- **B.** Zero fill
- **C.** Disintegration
- **D.** Degaussing

For questions 86, 87, and 88, use the following scenario.

As shown in the following security life cycle diagram (loosely based on the NIST reference architecture), NIST uses a five-step process for risk management. Using your knowledge of data roles and practices, answer the following questions based on the NIST framework process.

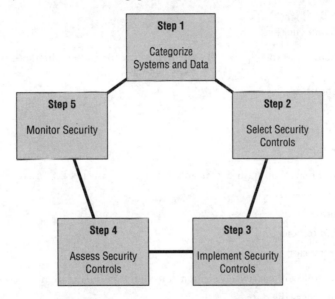

86. What data role will own responsibility for step 1, the categorization of information systems, to whom will they delegate step 2, and what data role will be responsible for step 3?

- **A.** Data owners, system owners, custodians
- **B.** Data processors, custodians, users
- **C.** Business owners, administrators, custodians
- **D.** System owners, business owners, administrators

87. If the systems that are being assessed all handle credit card information (and no other sensitive data), at what step would the PCI DSS first play an important role?

- **A.** Step 1
- **B.** Step 2
- **C.** Step 3
- **D.** Step 4

88. What data security role is primarily responsible for step 5?

    A. Data owners

    B. Data processors

    C. Custodians

    D. Users

89. Susan's organization performs a zero fill on hard drives before they are sent to a third-party organization to be shredded. What issue is her organization attempting to avoid?

    A. Data remanence while at the third-party site

    B. Mishandling of drives by the third party

    C. Classification mistakes

    D. Data permanence

90. Embedded data used to help identify the owner of a file is an example of what type of label?

    A. Copyright notice

    B. DLP

    C. Digital watermark

    D. Steganography

91. Retaining and maintaining information for as long as it is needed is known as what?

    A. Data storage policy

    B. Data storage

    C. Asset maintenance

    D. Record retention

92. Which of the following activities is not a consideration during data classification?

    A. Who can access the data

    B. What the impact would be if the data was lost or breached

    C. How much the data cost to create

    D. What protection regulations may be required for the data

93. What type of encryption is typically used for data at rest?

    A. Asymmetric encryption

    B. Symmetric encryption

    C. DES

    D. OTP

94. Which data role is tasked with granting appropriate access to staff members?

    A. Data processors

    B. Business owners

    C. Custodians

    D. Administrators

95. Which California law requires conspicuously posted privacy policies on commercial websites that collect the personal information of California residents?

    A. The Personal Information Protection and Electronic Documents Act

    B. The California Online Privacy Protection Act

    C. California Online Web Privacy Act

    D. California Civil Code 1798.82

96. Fred is preparing to send backup tapes off site to a secure third-party storage facility. What steps should Fred take before sending the tapes to that facility?

    A. Ensure that the tapes are handled the same way the original media would be handled based on their classification.

    B. Increase the classification level of the tapes because they are leaving the possession of the company.

    C. Purge the tapes to ensure that classified data is not lost.

    D. Encrypt the tapes in case they are lost in transit.

97. Which of the following does not describe data in motion?

    A. Data on a backup tape that is being shipped to a storage facility

    B. Data in a TCP packet

    C. Data in an e-commerce transaction

    D. Data in files being copied between locations

98. A new law is passed that would result in significant financial harm to your company if the data that it covers was stolen or inadvertently released. What should your organization do about this?

    A. Select a new security baseline.

    B. Relabel the data.

    C. Encrypt all of the data at rest and in transit.

    D. Review its data classifications and classify the data appropriately.

99. Ed has been asked to send data that his organization classifies as confidential and proprietary via email. What encryption technology would be appropriate to ensure that the contents of the files attached to the email remain confidential as they traverse the Internet?

    A. SSL

    B. TLS

    C. PGP

    D. VPN

100. Which mapping correctly matches data classifications between nongovernment and government classification schemes?

A. Top Secret - Confidential/Proprietary

Secret – Private

Confidential – Sensitive

B. Secret - Business confidential

Classifed - Proprietary

Confidential - Business Internal

C. Top Secret - Business sensitive

Secret - Business internal

Confidential - Business proprietary

D. Secret - Proprietary

Classified - Private

Unclassified - Public

Chapter

3

Security Engineering (Domain 3)

1. Matthew is the security administrator for a consulting firm and must enforce access controls that restrict users' access based upon their previous activity. For example, once a consultant accesses data belonging to Acme Cola, a consulting client, they may no longer access data belonging to any of Acme's competitors. What security model best fits Matthew's needs?

   A. Clark-Wilson

   B. Biba

   C. Bell-LaPadula

   D. Brewer-Nash

2. Referring to the figure shown below, what is the earliest stage of a fire where it is possible to use detection technology to identify it?

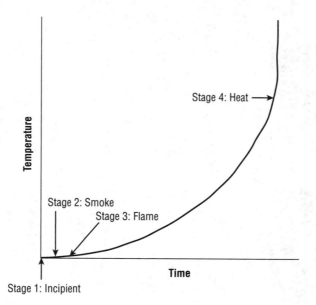

Image reprinted from *CISSP (ISC)² Certified Information Systems Security Professional Official Study Guide, 7th Edition* © John Wiley & Sons 2015, reprinted with permission.

   A. Incipient

   B. Smoke

   C. Flame

   D. Heat

3. Ralph is designing a physical security infrastructure for a new computing facility that will remain largely unstaffed. He plans to implement motion detectors in the facility but would also like to include a secondary verification control for physical presence. Which one of the following would best meet his needs?

    A. CCTV

    B. IPS

    C. Turnstiles

    D. Faraday cages

4. Harry would like to retrieve a lost encryption key from a database that uses m of n control with m = 4 and n = 8. What is the minimum number of escrow agents required to retrieve the key?

    A. 2

    B. 4

    C. 8

    D. 12

5. Fran's company is considering purchasing a web-based email service from a vendor and eliminating its own email server environment as a cost-saving measure. What type of cloud computing environment is Fran's company considering?

    A. SaaS

    B. IaaS

    C. CaaS

    D. PaaS

6. Bob is a security administrator with the federal government and wishes to choose a digital signature approach that is an approved part of the federal Digital Signature Standard under FIPS 186-4. Which one of the following encryption algorithms is not an acceptable choice for use in digital signatures?

    A. DSA

    B. HAVAL

    C. RSA

    D. ECDSA

7. Harry would like to access a document owned by Sally and stored on a file server. Applying the subject/object model to this scenario, who or what is the subject of the resource request?

    A. Harry

    B. Sally

    C. Server

    D. Document

8. Michael is responsible for forensic investigations and is investigating a medium severity security incident that involved the defacement of a corporate website. The web server in question ran on a virtualization platform, and the marketing team would like to get the website up and running as quickly as possible. What would be the most reasonable next step for Michael to take?

    A. Keep the website offline until the investigation is complete.

    B. Take the virtualization platform offline as evidence.

    C. Take a snapshot of the compromised system and use that for the investigation.

    D. Ignore the incident and focus on quickly restoring the website.

9. Helen is a software engineer and is developing code that she would like to restrict to running within an isolated sandbox for security purposes. What software development technique is Helen using?

    A. Bounds

    B. Input validation

    C. Confinement

    D. TCB

10. What concept describes the degree of confidence that an organization has that its controls satisfy security requirements?

    A. Trust

    B. Credentialing

    C. Verification

    D. Assurance

11. What type of security vulnerability are developers most likely to introduce into code when they seek to facilitate their own access, for testing purposes, to software they developed?

    A. Maintenance hook

    B. Cross-site scripting

    C. SQL injection

    D. Buffer overflow

12. In the figure shown below, Sally is blocked from reading the file due to the Biba integrity model. Sally has a Secret security clearance and the file has a Confidential classification. What principle of the Biba model is being enforced?

    A. Simple Security Property

    B. Simple Integrity Property

    C. *-Security Property

    D. *-Integrity Property

13. Tom is responsible for maintaining the security of systems used to control industrial processes located within a power plant. What term is used to describe these systems?

    A. POWER

    B. SCADA

    C. HAVAL

    D. COBOL

14. Sonia recently removed an encrypted hard drive from a laptop and moved it to a new device because of a hardware failure. She is having difficulty accessing encrypted content on the drive despite the fact that she knows the user's password. What hardware security feature is likely causing this problem?

    A. TCB

    B. TPM

    C. NIACAP

    D. RSA

15. Marcy would like to continue using some old DES encryption equipment to avoid throwing it away. She understands that running DES multiple times improves the security of the algorithm. What is the minimum number of times she must run DES on the same data to achieve security that is cryptographically strong by modern standards?

    A. 2

    B. 3

    C. 4

    D. 12

Questions 16–19 refer to the following scenario.

Alice and Bob would like to use an asymmetric cryptosystem to communicate with each other. They are located in different parts of the country but have exchanged encryption keys by using digital certificates signed by a mutually trusted certificate authority.

16. If Alice wishes to send Bob an encrypted message, what key does she use to encrypt the message?

    A. Alice's public key

    B. Alice's private key

    C. Bob's public key

    D. Bob's private key

17. When Bob receives the encrypted message from Alice, what key does he use to decrypt the message?

    A. Alice's public key

    B. Alice's private key

    C. Bob's public key

    D. Bob's private key

18. Which one of the following keys would Bob not possess in this scenario?

    A. Alice's public key

    B. Alice's private key

    C. Bob's public key

    D. Bob's private key

19. Alice would also like to digitally sign the message that she sends to Bob. What key should she use to create the digital signature?

    A. Alice's public key

    B. Alice's private key

    C. Bob's public key

    D. Bob's private key

20. What name is given to the random value added to a password in an attempt to defeat rainbow table attacks?

    A. Hash

    B. Salt

    C. Extender

    D. Rebar

21. Which one of the following is not an attribute of a hashing algorithm?

    A. They require a cryptographic key.

    B. They are irreversible.

    C. It is very difficult to find two messages with the same hash value.

    D. They take variable-length input.

22. What type of fire suppression system fills with water when the initial stages of a fire are detected and then requires a sprinkler head heat activation before dispensing water?

    A. Wet pipe

    B. Dry pipe

    C. Deluge

    D. Preaction

23. Susan would like to configure IPsec in a manner that provides confidentiality for the content of packets. What component of IPsec provides this capability?

    A. AH

    B. ESP

    C. IKE

    D. ISAKMP

24. Which one of the following cryptographic goals protects against the risks posed when a device is lost or stolen?

   A. Nonrepudiation

   B. Authentication

   C. Integrity

   D. Confidentiality

25. What logical operation is described by the truth table below?

Input 1	Input 2	Output
0	0	0
0	1	1
1	0	1
1	1	0

   A. OR

   B. AND

   C. XOR

   D. NOR

26. How many bits of keying material does the Data Encryption Standard use for encrypting information?

   A. 56 bits

   B. 64 bits

   C. 128 bits

   D. 256 bits

27. In the figure shown below, Harry's request to write to the data file is blocked. Harry has a Secret security clearance and the data file has a Confidential classification. What principle of the Bell-LaPadula model blocked this request?

   A. Simple Security Property

   B. Simple Integrity Property

   C. *-Security Property

   D. Discretionary Security Property

28. Florian and Tobias would like to begin communicating using a symmetric cryptosystem but they have no prearranged secret and are not able to meet in person to exchange keys. What algorithm can they use to securely exchange the secret key?

    A. IDEA

    B. Diffie-Hellman

    C. RSA

    D. MD5

29. Under the Common Criteria, what element describes the security requirements for a product?

    A. TCSEC

    B. ITSEC

    C. PP

    D. ST

30. Which one of the following is not one of the basic requirements for a cryptographic hash function?

    A. The function must work on fixed-length input.

    B. The function must be relatively easy to compute for any input.

    C. The function must be one way.

    D. The function must be collision free.

31. How many possible keys exist for a cipher that uses a key containing 5 bits?

    A. 10

    B. 16

    C. 32

    D. 64

32. What cryptographic principle stands behind the idea that cryptographic algorithms should be open to public inspection?

    A. Security through obscurity

    B. Kerchoff principle

    C. Defense in depth

    D. Heisenburg principle

33. Referring to the figure shown below, what is the name of the security control indicated by the arrow?

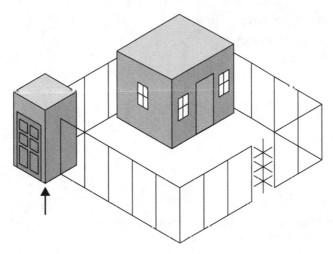

Image reprinted from *CISSP (ISC)² Certified Information Systems Security Professional Official Study Guide, 7th Edition* © John Wiley & Sons 2015, reprinted with permission.

    A. Mantrap

    B. Turnstile

    C. Intrusion prevention system

    D. Portal

34. Which one of the following does not describe a standard physical security requirement for wiring closets?

    A. Place only in areas monitored by security guards.

    B. Do not store flammable items in the closet.

    C. Use sensors on doors to log entries.

    D. Perform regular inspections of the closet.

35. In the figure shown below, Sally is blocked from writing to the data file by the Biba integrity model. Sally has a Secret security clearance and the file is classified Top Secret. What principle is preventing her from writing to the file?

A. Simple Security Property

B. Simple Integrity Property

C. *-Security Property

D. *-Integrity Property

36. Which one of the following security controls is least often required in Bring Your Own Device (BYOD) environments?

A. Remote wiping

B. Passcodes

C. Application control

D. Device encryption

37. What is the minimum number of independent parties necessary to implement the Fair Cryptosystems approach to key escrow?

A. 1

B. 2

C. 3

D. 4

38. In what state does a processor's scheduler place a process when it is prepared to execute but the CPU is not currently available?

A. Ready

B. Running

C. Waiting

D. Stopped

39. Alan is reviewing a system that has been assigned the EAL1 evaluation assurance level under the Common Criteria. What is the degree of assurance that he may have about the system?

A. It has been functionally tested.

B. It has been structurally tested.

C. It has been formally verified, designed, and tested.

D. It has been methodically designed, tested, and reviewed.

40. Which one of the following components is used to assign classifications to objects in a mandatory access control system?

A. Security label

B. Security token

C. Security descriptor

D. Security capability

41. What type of software program exposes the code to anyone who wishes to inspect it?

   A. Closed source

   B. Open-source

   C. Fixed source

   D. Unrestricted source

42. Adam recently configured permissions on an NTFS filesystem to describe the access that different users may have to a file by listing each user individually. What did Adam create?

   A. An access control list

   B. An access control entry

   C. Role-based access control

   D. Mandatory access control

43. Betty is concerned about the use of buffer overflow attacks against a custom application developed for use in her organization. What security control would provide the strongest defense against these attacks?

   A. Firewall

   B. Intrusion detection system

   C. Parameter checking

   D. Vulnerability scanning

44. Which one of the following terms is not used to describe a privileged mode of system operation?

   A. User mode

   B. Kernel mode

   C. Supervisory mode

   D. System mode

45. James is working with a Department of Defense system that is authorized to simultaneously handle information classified at the Secret and Top Secret levels. What type of system is he using?

   A. Single state

   B. Unclassified

   C. Compartmented

   D. Multistate

46. Kyle is being granted access to a military computer system that uses System High mode. What is not true about Kyle's security clearance requirements?

   A. Kyle must have a clearance for the highest level of classification processed by the system, regardless of his access.

   B. Kyle must have access approval for all information processed by the system.

   C. Kyle must have a valid need to know for all information processed by the system.

   D. Kyle must have a valid security clearance.

47. Gary intercepts a communication between two individuals and suspects that they are exchanging secret messages. The content of the communication appears to be the image shown below. What type of technique may the individuals use to hide messages inside this image?

   A. Visual cryptography

   B. Steganography

   C. Cryptographic hashing

   D. Transport layer security

48. Which one of the following terms accurately describes the Caesar cipher?

   A. Transposition cipher

   B. Block cipher

   C. Shift cipher

   D. Strong cipher

49. In the ring protection model shown below, what ring contains the operating system's kernel?

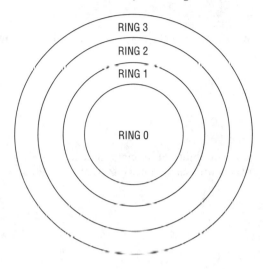

- **A.** Ring 0
- **B.** Ring 1
- **C.** Ring 2
- **D.** Ring 3

50. In an Infrastructure as a Service (IaaS) environment where a vendor supplies a customer with access to storage services, who is normally responsible for removing sensitive data from drives that are taken out of service?

- **A.** Customer's security team
- **B.** Customer's storage team
- **C.** Customer's vendor management team
- **D.** Vendor

51. Which one of the following is an example of a code, not a cipher?

- **A.** Data Encryption Standard
- **B.** "One if by land; two if by sea"
- **C.** Shifting letters by three
- **D.** Word scramble

52. Which one of the following systems assurance processes provides an independent third-party evaluation of a system's controls that may be trusted by many different organizations?

- **A.** Certification
- **B.** Definition

   C. Verification

   D. Accreditation

53. Process _____ ensures that any behavior will affect only the memory and resources associated with a process.

   A. Restriction

   B. Isolation

   C. Limitation

   D. Parameters

54. Harold is assessing the susceptibility of his environment to hardware failures and would like to identify the expected lifetime of a piece of hardware. What measure should he use for this?

   A. MTTR

   B. MTTF

   C. RTO

   D. MTO

55. What type of fire extinguisher is useful only against common combustibles?

   A. Class A

   B. Class B

   C. Class C

   D. Class D

56. Gary is concerned about applying consistent security settings to the many mobile devices used throughout his organization. What technology would best assist with this challenge?

   A. MDM

   B. IPS

   C. IDS

   D. SIEM

57. Alice sent a message to Bob. Bob would like to demonstrate to Charlie that the message he received definitely came from Alice. What goal of cryptography is Bob attempting to achieve?

   A. Authentication

   B. Confidentiality

   C. Nonrepudiation

   D. Integrity

58. Rhonda is considering the use of new identification cards for physical access control in her organization. She comes across a military system that uses the card shown below. What type of card is this?

A. Smart card

B. Proximity card

C. Magnetic stripe card

D. Phase three card

59. Gordon is concerned about the possibility that hackers may be able to use the Van Eck radiation phenomenon to remotely read the contents of computer monitors in his facility. What technology would protect against this type of attack?

A. TCSEC

B. SCSI

C. GHOST

D. TEMPEST

60. In the diagram shown below of security boundaries within a computer system, what component's name has been replaced with XXX?

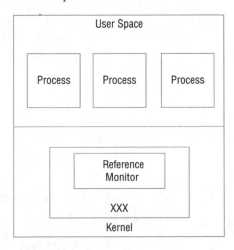

    A. Kernel

    B. TCB

    C. Security perimeter

    D. User execution

61. Sherry conducted an inventory of the cryptographic technologies in use within her organization and found the following algorithms and protocols in use. Which one of these technologies should she replace because it is no longer considered secure?

    A. MD5

    B. 3DES

    C. PGP

    D. WPA2

62. What action can you take to prevent accidental data disclosure due to wear leveling on an SSD device before reusing the drive?

    A. Reformatting

    B. Disk encryption

    C. Degaussing

    D. Physical destruction

63. Tom is a cryptanalyst and is working on breaking a cryptographic algorithm's secret key. He has a copy of an intercepted message that is encrypted and he also has a copy of the decrypted version of that message. He wants to use both the encrypted message and its decrypted plaintext to retrieve the secret key for use in decrypting other messages. What type of attack is Tom engaging in?

    A. Chosen ciphertext

    B. Chosen plaintext

    C. Known plaintext

    D. Brute force

64. A hacker recently violated the integrity of data in James's company by modifying a file using a precise timing attack. The attacker waited until James verified the integrity of a file's contents using a hash value and then modified the file between the time that James verified the integrity and read the contents of the file. What type of attack took place?

    A. Social engineering

    B. TOCTOU

    C. Data diddling

    D. Parameter checking

65. What standard governs the creation and validation of digital certificates for use in a public key infrastructure?

    A. X.509

    B. TLS

    C. SSL

    D. 802.1x

66. What is the minimum fence height that makes a fence difficult to climb easily, deterring most intruders?

    A. 3 feet

    B. 4 feet

    C. 5 feet

    D. 6 feet

67. Johnson Widgets strictly limits access to total sales volume information, classifying it as a competitive secret. However, shipping clerks have unrestricted access to order records to facilitate transaction completion. A shipping clerk recently pulled all of the individual sales records for a quarter and totaled them up to determine the total sales volume. What type of attack occurred?

    A. Social engineering

    B. Inference

    C. Aggregation

    D. Data diddling

68. What physical security control broadcasts false emanations constantly to mask the presence of true electromagnetic emanations from computing equipment?

    A. Faraday cage

    B. Copper-infused windows

    C. Shielded cabling

    D. White noise

69. In a Software as a Service cloud computing environment, who is normally responsible for ensuring that appropriate firewall controls are in place to protect the application?

    A. Customer's security team

    B. Vendor

    C. Customer's networking team

    D. Customer's infrastructure management team

70. Alice has read permissions on an object and she would like Bob to have those same rights. Which one of the rules in the Take-Grant protection model would allow her to complete this operation?

    A. Create rule

    B. Remove rule

    C. Grant rule

    D. Take rule

71. In what type of attack does the attacker replace the legitimate BIOS on a computer with a malicious alternative that allows them to take control of the system?

A. Phlashing

B. Phreaking

C. Phishing

D. Phogging

72. Which one of the following computing models allows the execution of multiple concurrent tasks within a single process?

A. Multitasking

B. Multiprocessing

C. Multiprogramming

D. Multithreading

73. Alan intercepts an encrypted message and wants to determine what type of algorithm was used to create the message. He first performs a frequency analysis and notes that the frequency of letters in the message closely matches the distribution of letters in the English language. What type of cipher was most likely used to create this message?

A. Substitution cipher

B. AES

C. Transposition cipher

D. 3DES

74. The Double DES (2DES) encryption algorithm was never used as a viable alternative to the original DES algorithm. What attack is 2DES vulnerable to that does not exist for the DES or 3DES approach?

A. Chosen ciphertext

B. Brute force

C. Man in the middle

D. Meet in the middle

75. Grace would like to implement application control technology in her organization. Users often need to install new applications for research and testing purposes, and she does not want to interfere with that process. At the same time, she would like to block the use of known malicious software. What type of application control would be appropriate in this situation?

A. Blacklisting

B. Greylisting

C. Whitelisting

D. Bluelisting

76. Warren is designing a physical intrusion detection system for his data center and wants to include technology that issues an alert if the communications lines for the alarm system are unexpectedly cut. What technology would meet this requirement?

   A. Heartbeat sensor

   B. Emanation security

   C. Motion detector

   D. Faraday cage

77. John and Gary are negotiating a business transaction and John must demonstrate to Gary that he has access to a system. He engages in an electronic version of the "magic door" scenario shown below. What technique is John using?

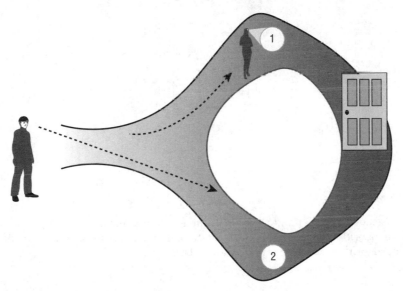

Image reprinted from *CISSP (ISC)² Certified Information Systems Security Professional Official Study Guide, 7th Edition* © John Wiley & Sons 2015, reprinted with permission.

   A. Split-knowledge proof

   B. Zero-knowledge proof

   C. Logical proof

   D. Mathematical proof

78. Raj is selecting an encryption algorithm for use in his organization and would like to be able to vary the strength of the encryption with the sensitivity of the information. Which one of the following algorithms allows the use of different key strengths?

   A. Blowfish

   B. DES

    C. Skipjack

    D. IDEA

79. Referring to the fire triangle shown below, which one of the following suppression materials attacks a fire by removing the fuel source?

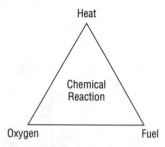

Image reprinted from *CISSP (ISC)²
Certified Information Systems Security
Professional Official Study Guide, 7th
Edition* © John Wiley & Sons 2015,
reprinted with permission.

    A. Water

    B. Soda acid

    C. Carbon dioxide

    D. Halon

80. Howard is choosing a cryptographic algorithm for his organization and he would like to choose an algorithm that supports the creation of digital signatures. Which one of the following algorithms would meet his requirement?

    A. RSA

    B. DES

    C. AES

    D. Blowfish

81. Laura is responsible for securing her company's web-based applications and wishes to conduct an educational program for developers on common web application security vulnerabilities. Where can she turn for a concise listing of the most common web application issues?

    A. CVE

    B. NSA

    C. OWASP

    D. CSA

82. The Bell-LaPadula and Biba models implement state machines in a fashion that uses what specific state machine model?

   A. Information flow

   B. Noninterference

   C. Cascading

   D. Feedback

83. The _____ of a process consist(s) of the limits set on the memory addresses and resources that the process may access.

   A. Perimeter

   B. Confinement limits

   C. Metes

   D. Bounds

84. What type of motion detector senses changes in the electromagnetic fields in monitored areas?

   A. Infrared

   B. Wave pattern

   C. Capacitance

   D. Photoelectric

85. Which one of the following fire suppression systems uses a suppressant that is no longer manufactured due to environmental concerns?

   A. FM-200

   B. Argon

   C. Inergen

   D. Halon

86. Which one of the following statements is correct about the Biba model of access control?

   A. It addresses confidentiality and integrity.

   B. It addresses integrity and availability.

   C. It prevents covert channel attacks.

   D. It focuses on protecting objects from integrity threats.

87. In Transport Layer Security, what type of key is used to encrypt the actual content of communications between a web server and a client?

   A. Ephemeral session key

   B. Client's public key

   C. Server's public key

   D. Server's private key

88. Beth would like to include technology in a secure area of her data center to protect against unwanted electromagnetic emanations. What technology would assist her with this goal?

    A. Heartbeat sensor

    B. Faraday cage

    C. Piggybacking

    D. WPA2

89. In a virtualized computing environment, what component is responsible for enforcing separation between guest machines?

    A. Guest operating system

    B. Hypervisor

    C. Kernel

    D. Protection manager

90. Rick is an application developer who works primarily in Python. He recently decided to evaluate a new service where he provides his Python code to a vendor who then executes it on their server environment. What type of cloud computing environment is this service?

    A. SaaS

    B. PaaS

    C. IaaS

    D. CaaS

91. A software company developed two systems that share information. System A provides information to the input of System B, which then reciprocates by providing information back to System A as input. What type of composition theory best describes this practice?

    A. Cascading

    B. Feedback

    C. Hookup

    D. Elementary

92. Tommy is planning to implement a power conditioning UPS for a rack of servers in his data center. Which one of the following conditions will the UPS be unable to protect against if it persists for an extended period of time?

    A. Fault

    B. Blackout

    C. Sag

    D. Noise

93. Which one of the following humidity values is within the acceptable range for a data center operation?

    A. 0%

    B. 10%

    C. 25%

    D. 40%

94. Chris is designing a cryptographic system for use within his company. The company has 1,000 employees, and they plan to use an asymmetric encryption system. How many total keys will they need?

   A. 500

   B. 1,000

   C. 2,000

   D. 4,950

95. What term is used to describe the formal declaration by a designated approving authority (DAA) that an IT system is approved to operate in a specific environment?

   A. Certification

   B. Accreditation

   C. Evaluation

   D. Approval

96. Object-oriented programming languages use a black box approach to development, where users of an object do not necessarily need to know the object's implementation details. What term is used to describe this concept?

   A. Layering

   B. Abstraction

   C. Data hiding

   D. Process isolation

97. Todd wants to add a certificate to a certificate revocation list. What element of the certificate goes on the list?

   A. Serial number

   B. Public key

   C. Digital signature

   D. Private key

98. Alison is examining a digital certificate presented to her by her bank's website. Which one of the following requirements is not necessary for her to trust the digital certificate?

   A. She knows that the server belongs to the bank.

   B. She trusts the certificate authority.

   C. She verifies that the certificate is not listed on a CRL.

   D. She verifies the digital signature on the certificate.

99. Which one of the following is an example of a covert timing channel when used to exfiltrate information from an organization?

   A. Sending an electronic mail message

   B. Posting a file on a peer-to-peer file sharing service

    C. Typing with the rhythm of Morse code

    D. Writing data to a shared memory space

100. Which one of the following would be a reasonable application for the use of self-signed digital certificates?

    A. E-commerce website

    B. Banking application

    C. Internal scheduling application

    D. Customer portal

Chapter

4

Communication and Network Security (Domain 4)

1. What important factor listed below differentiates Frame Relay from X.25?

   A. Frame Relay supports multiple PVCs over a single WAN carrier connection.

   B. Frame Relay is a cell-switching technology instead of a packet-switching technology like X.25.

   C. Frame Relay does not provide a Committed Information Rate (CIR).

   D. Frame Relay only requires a DTE on the provider side.

2. During a security assessment of a wireless network, Jim discovers that LEAP is in use on a network using WPA. What recommendation should Jim make?

   A. Continue to use LEAP. It provides better security than TKIP for WPA networks.

   B. Use an alternate protocol like PEAP or EAP-TLS and implement WPA2 if supported.

   C. Continue to use LEAP to avoid authentication issues, but move to WPA2.

   D. Use an alternate protocol like PEAP or EAP-TLS, and implement Wired Equivalent Privacy to avoid wireless security issues.

3. Ben has connected his laptop to his tablet PC using an 802.11g connection. What wireless network mode has he used to connect these devices?

   A. Infrastructure mode

   B. Wired extension mode

   C. Ad hoc mode

   D. Stand-alone mode

4. Lauren's and Nick's PCs simultaneously send traffic by transmitting at the same time. What network term describes the range of systems on a network that could be affected by this same issue?

   A. The subnet

   B. The supernet

   C. A collision domain

   D. A broadcast domain

5. Sarah is manually reviewing a packet capture of TCP traffic and finds that a system is setting the RST flag in the TCP packets it sends repeatedly during a short period of time. What does this flag mean in the TCP packet header?

   A. RST flags mean "Rest." The server needs traffic to briefly pause.

   B. RST flags mean "Relay-set." The packets will be forwarded to the address set in the packet.

   C. RST flags mean "Resume Standard." Communications will resume in their normal format.

   D. RST means "Reset." The TCP session will be disconnected.

6. Gary is deploying a wireless network and wants to deploy the fastest possible wireless technology. Of the 802.11 standards listed below, which is the fastest 2.4 GHz option he has?

    A. 802.11a

    B. 802.11g

    C. 802.11n

    D. 802.11ac

7. What common applications are associated with each of the following TCP ports: 23, 25, 143, and 515?

    A. Telnet, SFTP, NetBIOS, and LPD

    B. SSH, SMTP, POP3, and ICMP

    C. Telnet, SMTP, IMAP, and LPD

    D. Telnet, SMTP, POP3, and X Windows

8. Chris is configuring an IDS to monitor for unencrypted FTP traffic. What ports should Chris use in his configuration?

    A. TCP 20 and 21

    B. TCP 21 only

    C. UDP port 69

    D. TCP port 21 and UDP port 21

9. FHSS, DSSS, and OFDM all use what wireless communication method that occurs over multiple frequencies simultaneously?

    A. Wi-Fi

    B. Spread Spectrum

    C. Multiplexing

    D. Orthogonal modulation

10. Which authentication protocol commonly used for PPP links encrypts both the username and password and uses a challenge/response dialog that cannot be replayed and periodically reauthenticates remote systems throughout its use in a session?

    A. PAP

    B. CHAP

    C. EAP

    D. LEAP

11. Which of the following options is not a common best practice for securing a wireless network?

    A. Turn on WPA2.

    B. Enable MAC filtering if used for a relatively small group of clients.

    C. Enable SSID broadcast.

    D. Separate the access point from the wired network using a firewall, thus treating it as external access.

12. What network topology is shown in the image below?

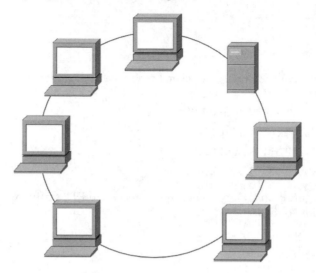

 A. A ring

 B. A bus

 C. A star

 D. A mesh

Chris is designing layered network security for his organization. Using the diagram below, answer questions 13 through 15.

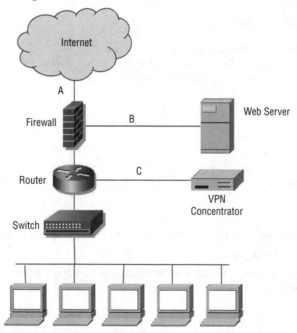

13. What type of firewall design is shown in the diagram?

   A. A single-tier firewall

   B. A two-tier firewall

   C. A three-tier firewall

   D. A four-tier firewall

14. If the VPN grants remote users the same access to network and system resources as local workstations have, what security issue should Chris raise?

   A. VPN users will not be able to access the web server.

   B. There is no additional security issue; the VPN concentrator's logical network location matches the logical network location of the workstations.

   C. VPN bypasses the firewall, creating additional risks.

   D. VPN users should only connect from managed PCs.

15. If Chris wants to stop cross-site scripting attacks against the web server, what is the best device for this purpose, and where should he put it?

   A. A firewall, location A

   B. An IDS, location A

   C. An IPS, location B

   D. A WAF, location C

16. Susan is deploying a routing protocol that maintains a list of destination networks with metrics that include the distance in hops to them and the direction traffic should be sent to them. What type of protocol is she using?

   A. A link-state protocol

   B. A link-distance protocol

   C. A destination metric protocol

   D. A distance-vector protocol

17. Ben has configured his network to not broadcast a SSID. Why might Ben disable SSID broadcast, and how could his SSID be discovered?

   A. Disabling SSID broadcast prevents attackers from discovering the encryption key. The SSID can be recovered from decrypted packets.

   B. Disabling SSID broadcast hides networks from unauthorized personnel. The SSID can be discovered using a wireless sniffer.

   C. Disabling SSID broadcast prevents issues with beacon frames. The SSID can be recovered by reconstructing the BSSID.

   D. Disabling SSID broadcast helps avoid SSID conflicts. The SSID can be discovered by attempting to connect to the network.

18. What network tool can be used to protect the identity of clients while providing Internet access by accepting client requests, altering the source addresses of the requests, mapping requests to clients, and sending the modified requests out to their destination?

    A. A gateway

    B. A proxy

    C. A router

    D. A firewall

19. During troubleshooting, Chris uses the `nslookup` command to check the IP address of a host he is attempting to connect to. The IP he sees in the response is not the IP that should resolve when the lookup is done. What type of attack has likely been conducted?

    A. DNS spoofing

    B. DNS poisoning

    C. ARP spoofing

    D. A Cain attack

20. A remote access tool that copies what is displayed on a desktop PC to a remote computer is an example of what type of technology?

    A. Remote node operation

    B. Screen scraping

    C. Remote control

    D. RDP

21. Which email security solution provides two major usage modes: (1) signed messages that provide integrity, sender authentication, and nonrepudiation; and (2) an enveloped message mode that provides integrity, sender authentication, and confidentiality?

    A. S/MIME

    B. MOSS

    C. PEM

    D. DKIM

22. During a security assessment, Jim discovers that the organization he is working with uses a multilayer protocol to handle SCADA systems and recently connected the SCADA network to the rest of the organization's production network. What concern should he raise about serial data transfers carried via TCP/IP?

    A. SCADA devices that are now connected to the network can now be attacked over the network.

    B. Serial data over TCP/IP cannot be encrypted.

    C. Serial data cannot be carried in TCP packets.

    D. TCP/IP's throughput can allow for easy denial of service attacks against serial devices.

23. What type of key does WEP use to encrypt wireless communications?

    A. An asymmetric key

    B. Unique key sets for each host

    C. A predefined shared static key

    D. Unique asymmetric keys for each host

24. An attack that causes a service to fail by exhausting all of a system's resources is what type of attack?

    A. A worm

    B. A denial of service attack

    C. A virus

    D. A Smurf attack

25. What speed and frequency range is used by 802.11n?

    A. 54 Mbps, 5 GHz

    B. 200+ Mbps, 5GHz

    C. 200+ Mbps, 2.4 and 5 GHz

    D. 1 Gbps, 5 GHz

26. The Address Resolution Protocol (ARP) and the Reverse Address Resolution Protocol (RARP) operate at what layer of the OSI model?

    A. Layer 1

    B. Layer 2

    C. Layer 3

    D. Layer 4

27. Which of the following is a converged protocol that allows storage mounts over TCP, and which is frequently used as a lower-cost alternative to Fibre Channel?

    A. MPLS

    B. SDN

    C. VoIP

    D. iSCSI

28. Chris is building an Ethernet network and knows that he needs to span a distance of over 150 meters with his 1000Base-T network. What network technology should he use to help with this?

    A. Install a repeater or a concentrator before 100 meters.

    B. Use Category 7 cable, which has better shielding for higher speeds.

    C. Install a gateway to handle the distance.

    D. Use STP cable to handle the longer distance at high speeds.

Lauren's organization has used a popular instant messaging service for a number of years. Recently, concerns have been raised about the use of instant messaging. Using the diagram below, answer questions 29 through 31 about instant messaging.

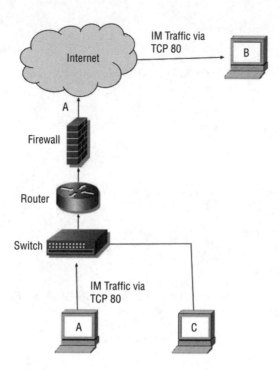

29. What protocol is the instant messaging traffic most likely to use based on the diagram?

    A. AOL

    B. HTTP

    C. SMTP

    D. HTTPS

30. What security concern does sending internal communications from A to B cause?

    A. The firewall does not protect system B.

    B. System C can see the broadcast traffic from system A to B.

    C. It is traveling via an unencrypted protocol.

    D. IM does not provide nonrepudiation.

31. How could Lauren's company best address a desire for secure instant messaging for users of internal systems A and C?

    A. Use a 3rd party instant messaging service.

    B. Implement and use a locally hosted IM service.

    C. Use HTTPS.

    D. Discontinue use of IM and instead use email, which is more secure.

32. Which of the following drawbacks is a concern when multilayer protocols are allowed?

    A. A range of protocols may be used at higher layers.

    B. Covert channels are allowed.

    C. Filters cannot be bypassed.

    D. Encryption can't be incorporated at multiple layers.

33. What network topology is shown in the image below?

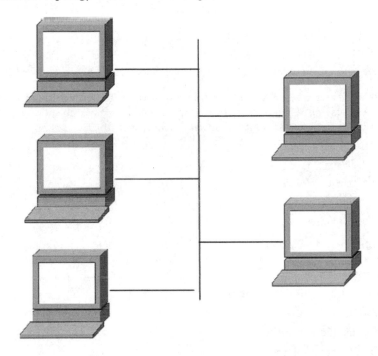

    A. A ring

    B. A star

    C. A bus

    D. A mesh

34. Chris uses a cellular hot spot (modem) to provide Internet access when he is traveling. If he leaves the hot spot connected to his PC while his PC is on his organization's corporate network, what security issue might he cause?

    A. Traffic may not be routed properly, exposing sensitive data.

    B. His system may act as a bridge from the Internet to the local network.

    C. His system may be a portal for a reflected DDoS attack.

    D. Security administrators may not be able to determine his IP address if a security issue occurs.

35. In her role as an information security professional, Susan has been asked to identify areas where her organization's wireless network may be accessible even though it isn't intended to be. What should Susan do to determine where her organization's wireless network is accessible?

    A. A site survey

    B. Warwalking

    C. Wardriving

    D. A design map

36. The DARPA TCP/IP model's Application layer matches up to what three OSI model layers?

    A. Application, Presentation, and Transport

    B. Presentation, Session, and Transport

    C. Application, Presentation, and Session

    D. There is not a direct match. The TCP model was created before the OSI model.

37. One of Susan's attacks during a penetration test involves inserting false ARP data into a system's ARP cache. When the system attempts to send traffic to the address it believes belongs to a legitimate system, it will instead send that traffic to a system she controls. What is this attack called?

    A. RARP Flooding

    B. ARP cache poisoning

    C. A denial of ARP attack

    D. ARP buffer blasting

38. Sue modifies her MAC address to one that is allowed on a network that uses MAC filtering to provide security. What is the technique Sue used, and what non-security issue could her actions cause?

    A. Broadcast domain exploit, address conflict

    B. Spoofing, token loss

    C. Spoofing, address conflict

    D. Sham EUI creation, token loss

39. Jim's audit of a large organization's traditional PBX showed that Direct Inward System Access (DISA) was being abused by third parties. What issue is most likely to lead to this problem?

    A. The PBX was not fully patched.

    B. The dial-in modem lines use unpublished numbers.

    C. DISA is set up to only allow local calls.

    D. One or more users' access codes have been compromised.

40. SMTP, HTTP, and SNMP all occur at what layer of the OSI model?

    A. Layer 4

    B. Layer 5

    C. Layer 6

    D. Layer 7

41. Lauren uses the ping utility to check whether a remote system is up as part of a penetration testing exercise. If she wants to filter ping out by protocol, what protocol should she filter out from her packet sniffer's logs?

A. UDP

B. TCP

C. IP

D. ICMP

42. Lauren wants to provide port-based authentication on her network to ensure that clients must authenticate before using the network. What technology is an appropriate solution for this requirement?

A. 802.11a

B. 802.3

C. 802.15.1

D. 802.1x

43. Ben has deployed a 1000Base-T 1 gigabit network and needs to run a cable to another building. If Ben is running his link directly from a switch to another switch in that building, what is the maximum distance Ben can cover according to the 1000Base-T specification?

A. 2 kilometers

B. 500 meters

C. 185 meters

D. 100 meters

44. Jim's remote site has only ISDN as an option for connectivity. What type of ISDN should he look for to get the maximum speed possible?

A. BRI

B. BPRI

C. PRI

D. D channel

45. SPIT attacks target what technology?

A. Virtualization platforms

B. Web services

C. VoIP systems

D. Secure Process Internal Transfers

46. What does a bluesnarfing attack target?

A. Data on IBM systems

B. An outbound phone call via Bluetooth

C. 802.11b networks

D. Data from a Bluetooth-enabled device

47. Which of the following options includes standards or protocols that exist in layer 6 of the OSI model?

A. NFS, SQL, and RPC

B. TCP, UDP, and TLS

C. JPEG, ASCII, and MIDI

D. HTTP, FTP, SMTP

48. What network topology is shown below?

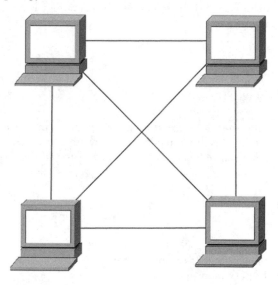

A. A ring

B. A bus

C. A star

D. A mesh

49. There are four common VPN protocols. Which group of four below contains all of the common VPN protocols?

A. PPTP, LTP, L2TP, IPsec

B. PPP, L2TP, IPsec, VNC

C. PPTP, L2F, L2TP, IPsec

D. PPTP, L2TP, IPsec, SPAP

50. What network technology is best described as a token-passing network that uses a pair of rings with traffic flowing in opposite directions?

A. A ring topology

B. Token Ring

C. FDDI

D. SONET

51. Which OSI layer includes electrical specifications, protocols, and interface standards?

    A. The Transport layer

    B. The Device layer

    C. The Physical layer

    D. The Data Link layer

52. Ben is designing a Wi-Fi network and has been asked to choose the most secure option for the network. Which wireless security standard should he choose?

    A. WPA2

    B. WPA

    C. WEP

    D. AES

53. If your organization needs to allow attachments in email to support critical business processes, what are the two best options for helping to avoid security problems caused by attachments?

    A. Train your users and use anti-malware tools.

    B. Encrypt your email and use anti-malware tools.

    C. Train your users and require S/MIME for all email.

    D. Use S/MIME by default and remove all ZIP (.zip) file attachments.

54. Segmentation, sequencing, and error checking all occur at what layer of the OSI model that is associated with SSL, TLS, and UDP?

    A. The Transport layer

    B. The Network layer

    C. The Session layer

    D. The Presentation layer

55. The Windows ipconfig command displays the following information:

    BC-5F-F4-7B-4B-7D

    What term describes this, and what information can be gathered from it?

    A. The IP address, the network location of the system

    B. The MAC address, the network interface card's manufacturer

    C. The MAC address, the media type in use

    D. The IPv6 client ID, the network interface card's manufacturer

56. Chris has been asked to choose between implementing PEAP and LEAP for wireless authentication. What should he choose, and why?

    A. LEAP, because it fixes problems with TKIP, resulting in stronger security

    B. PEAP, because it implements CCMP for security

    C. LEAP, because it implements EAP-TLS for end-to-end session encryption

    D. PEAP, because it can provide a TLS tunnel that encapsulates EAP methods, protecting the entire session

57. Ben is troubleshooting a network and discovers that the NAT router he is connected to has the 192.168.x.x subnet as its internal network and that its external IP is 192.168.1.40. What problem is he encountering?

    A. 192.168.x.x is a non-routable network and will not be carried to the Internet.

    B. 192.168.1.40 is not a valid address because it is reserved by RFC 1918.

    C. Double NATing is not possible using the same IP range.

    D. The upstream system is unable to de-encapsulate his packets and he needs to use PAT instead.

58. What is the default subnet mask for a Class B network?

    A. 255.0.0.0

    B. 255.255.0.0

    C. 255.254.0.0

    D. 255.255.255.0

59. Jim's organization uses a traditional PBX for voice communication. What is the most common security issue that its internal communications are likely to face, and what should he recommend to prevent it?

    A. Eavesdropping, encryption

    B. Man-in-the-middle attacks, end-to-end encryption

    C. Eavesdropping, physical security

    D. Wardialing, deploy an IPS

60. What common security issue is often overlooked with cordless phones?

    A. Their signal is rarely encrypted and thus can be easily monitored.

    B. They use unlicensed frequencies.

    C. They can allow attackers access to wireless networks.

    D. They are rarely patched and are vulnerable to malware.

61. Lauren's organization has deployed VoIP phones on the same switches that the desktop PCs are on. What security issue could this create, and what solution would help?

    A. VLAN hopping, use physically separate switches.

    B. VLAN hopping, use encryption.

    C. Caller ID spoofing, MAC filtering

    D. Denial of service attacks, use a firewall between networks.

62. Which type of firewall can be described as "a device that filters traffic based on its source, destination and the port it is sent from or is going to"?

    A. A static packet filtering firewall

    B. An Application layer gateway firewall

    C. A dynamic packet filtering firewall

    D. A stateful inspection firewall

63. A phreaking tool used to manipulate line voltages to steal long-distance service is known as what type of box?

    A. A black box

    B. A red box

    C. A blue box

    D. A white box

64. Data streams occur at what three layers of the OSI model?

    A. Application, Presentation, and Session

    B. Presentation, Session, and Transport

    C. Physical, Data Link, and Network

    D. Data Link, Network, and Transport

65. Chris needs to design a firewall architecture that can support a DMZ, a database, and a private internal network in a secure manner that separates each function. What type of design should he use, and how many firewalls does he need?

    A. A four-tier firewall design with two firewalls

    B. A two-tier firewall design with three firewalls

    C. A three-tier firewall design with at least one firewall

    D. A single-tier firewall design with three firewalls

66. Lauren's networking team has been asked to identify a technology that will allow them to dynamically change the organization's network by treating the network like code. What type of architecture should she recommend?

    A. A network that follows the 5-4-3 rule

    B. A converged network

    C. A software-defined network

    D. A hypervisor-based network

67. Jim's organization uses fax machines to receive sensitive data. Since the fax machine is located in a public area, what actions should Jim take to deal with issues related to faxes his organization receives?

    A. Encrypt the faxes and purge local memory.

    B. Disable automatic printing and purge local memory.

    C. Encrypt faxes and disable automatic printing.

    D. Use link encryption and enable automatic printing.

68. Cable modems, ISDN, and DSL are all examples of what type of technology?

   A. Baseband

   B. Broadband

   C. Digital

   D. Broadcast

69. What type of firewall design is shown in the image below?

   A. Single tier

   B. Two tier

   C. Three tier

   D. Next generation

70. During a review of her organization's network, Angela discovered that it was suffering from broadcast storms and that contractors, guests, and organizational administrative staff were on the same network segment. What design change should Angela recommend?

   A. Require encryption for all users.

   B. Install a firewall at the network border.

   C. Enable spanning tree loop detection.

   D. Segment the network based on functional requirements.

71. ICMP, RIP, and network address translation all occur at what layer of the OSI model?

   A. Layer 1

   B. Layer 2

   C. Layer 3

   D. Layer 4

Use the following scenario to help guide your answers in the following three questions.

Ben is an information security professional at an organization that is replacing its physical servers with virtual machines. As the organization builds its virtual environment, it is decreasing the number of physical servers it uses while purchasing more powerful servers to act as the virtualization platforms.

72. The IDS Ben is responsible for is used to monitor communications in the data center using a mirrored port on the data center switch. What traffic will Ben see once the majority of servers in the data center have been virtualized?

    A. The same traffic he currently sees

    B. All inter-VM traffic

    C. Only traffic sent outside of the VM environment

    D. All inter-hypervisor traffic

73. The VM administrators recommend enabling cut and paste between virtual machines. What security concern should Ben raise about this practice?

    A. It can cause a denial of service condition.

    B. It can serve as a covert channel.

    C. It can allow viruses to spread.

    D. It can bypass authentication controls.

74. Ben is concerned about exploits that allow VM escape. What option should Ben suggest to help limit the impact of VM escape exploits?

    A. Separate virtual machines onto separate physical hardware based on task or data types.

    B. Use VM escape detection tools on the underlying hypervisor.

    C. Restore machines to their original snapshots on a regular basis.

    D. Use a utility like Tripwire to look for changes in the virtual machines.

75. WPA2's Counter Mode Ciper Block Chaining Message Authentication Mode Protocol (CCMP) is based on which common encryption scheme?

    A. DES

    B. 3DES

    C. AES

    D. TLS

76. When a host on an Ethernet network detects a collision and transmits a jam signal, what happens next?

    A. The host that transmitted the jam signal is allowed to retransmit while all other hosts pause until that transmission is received successfully.

    B. All hosts stop transmitting and each host waits a random period of time before attempting to transmit again.

    C. All hosts stop transmitting and each host waits a period of time based on how recently it successfully transmitted.

    D. Hosts wait for the token to be passed and then resume transmitting data as they pass the token.

77. IPX, AppleTalk, and NetBEUI are all examples of what?

    A. Routing protocols

    B. UDP protocols

    C. Non-IP protocols

    D. TCP protocols

78. What is the speed of a T3 line?

   A. 128 kbps

   B. 1.544 Mbps

   C. 44.736 Mbps

   D. 155 Mbps

79. What type of firewall design does the image below show?

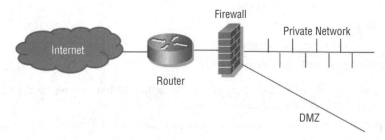

   A. A single-tier firewall

   B. A two-tier firewall

   C. A three-tier firewall

   D. A fully protected DMZ firewall

80. What challenge is most common for endpoint security system deployments?

   A. Compromises

   B. The volume of data

   C. Monitoring encrypted traffic on the network

   D. Handling non-TCP protocols

81. What type of address is 127.0.0.1?

   A. A public IP address

   B. An RFC 1918 address

   C. An APIPA address

   D. A loopback address

82. Susan is writing a best practices statement for her organizational users who need to use Bluetooth. She knows that there are many potential security issues with Bluetooth and wants to provide the best advice she can. Which of the following sets of guidance should Susan include?

   A. Use Bluetooth's built-in strong encryption, change the default PIN on your device, turn off discovery mode, and turn off Bluetooth when it's not in active use.

   B. Use Bluetooth only for those activities that are not confidential, change the default PIN on your device, turn off discovery mode, and turn off Bluetooth when it's not in active use.

    C. Use Bluetooth's built-in strong encryption, use extended (8 digit or longer) Bluetooth PINs, turn off discovery mode, and turn off Bluetooth when it's not in active use.

    D. Use Bluetooth only for those activities that are not confidential, use extended (8 digit or longer) Bluetooth PINs, turn off discovery mode, and turn off Bluetooth when it's not in active use.

83. What type of firewall is known as a second-generation firewall?

    A. Static packet filtering firewalls

    B. Application-level gateway firewalls

    C. Stateful inspection firewalls

    D. Unified Threat Management

84. Steve has been tasked with implementing a network storage protocol over an IP network. What storage-centric converged protocol is he likely to use in his implementation?

    A. MPLS

    B. FCoE

    C. SDN

    D. VoIP

85. What type of network device modulates between an analog carrier signal and digital information for computer communications?

    A. A bridge

    B. A router

    C. A brouter

    D. A modem

86. Which list presents the layers of the OSI model in the correct order?

    A. Presentation, Application, Session, Transport, Network, Data Link, Physical

    B. Application, Presentation, Session, Network, Transport, Data Link, Physical

    C. Presentation, Application, Session, Transport, Data Link, Network, Physical

    D. Application, Presentation, Session, Transport, Network, Data Link, Physical

87. A denial of service (DoS) attack that sends fragmented TCP packets is known as what kind of attack?

    A. Christmas tree

    B. Teardrop

    C. Stack killer

    D. Frag grenade

88. Modern dial-up connections use what dial-up protocol?

    A. SLIP

    B. SLAP

    C. PPTP

    D. PPP

89. One of the findings that Jim made when performing a security audit was the use of non-IP protocols in a private network. What issue should Jim point out that may result from the use of these non-IP protocols?

    A. They are outdated and cannot be used on modern PCs.

    B. They may not be able to be filtered by firewall devices.

    C. They may allow Christmas tree attacks.

    D. IPX extends on the IP protocol and may not be supported by all TCP stacks.

90. Angela needs to choose between EAP, PEAP, and LEAP for secure authentication. Which authentication protocol should she choose and why?

    A. EAP, because it provides strong encryption by default

    B. LEAP, because it provides frequent re-authentication and changing of WEP keys

    C. PEAP, because it provides encryption and doesn't suffer from the same vulnerabilities that LEAP does

    D. None of these options can provide secure authentication, and an alternate solution should be chosen.

91. Lauren has been asked to replace her organization's PPTP implementation with an L2TP implementation for security reasons. What is the primary security reason that L2TP would replace PPTP?

    A. L2TP can use IPsec.

    B. L2TP creates a point-to-point tunnel, avoiding multipoint issues.

    C. PPTP doesn't support EAP.

    D. PPTP doesn't properly encapsulate PPP packets.

92. Jim is building a research computing system that benefits from being part of a full mesh topology between systems. In a five-node full mesh topology design, how many connections will an individual node have?

    A. Two

    B. Three

    C. Four

    D. Five

93. What topology correctly describes Ethernet?

    A. A ring

    B. A star

    C. A mesh

    D. A bus

94. What type of attack is most likely to occur after a successful ARP spoofing attempt?

    A. A DoS attack

    B. A Trojan

    C. A replay attack

    D. A man-in-the-middle attack

95. What speed is Category 3 UTP cable rated for?

    A. 5 Mbps

    B. 10 Mbps

    C. 100 Mbps

    D. 1000 Mbps

96. What issue occurs when data transmitted over one set of wires is picked up by another set of wires?

    A. Magnetic interference

    B. Crosstalk

    C. Transmission absorption

    D. Amplitude modulation

97. What two key issues with the implementation of RC4 make Wired Equivalent Privacy (WEP) even weaker than it might otherwise be?

    A. Its use of a static common key and client-set encryption algorithms

    B. Its use of a static common key and a limited number of initialization vectors

    C. Its use of weak asymmetric keys and a limited number of initialization vectors

    D. Its use of a weak asymmetric key and client-set encryption algorithms

98. Chris is setting up a hotel network, and needs to ensure that systems in each room or suite can connect to each other, but systems in other suites or rooms cannot. At the same time, he needs to ensure that all systems in the hotel can reach the Internet. What solution should he recommend as the most effective business solution?

    A. Per-room VPNs

    B. VLANs

    C. Port security

    D. Firewalls

99. During a forensic investigation, Charles is able to determine the Media Access Control address of a system that was connected to a compromised network. Charles knows that MAC addresses are tied back to a manufacturer or vendor and are part of the fingerprint of the system. To which OSI layer does a MAC address belong?

    A. The Application layer

    B. The Session layer

    C. The Physical layer

    D. The Data Link layer

100. Ben knows that his organization wants to be able to validate the identity of other organizations based on their domain name when receiving and sending email. What tool should Ben recommend?

    A. PEM

    B. S/MIME

    C. DKIM

    D. MOSS

Chapter 5

Identity and Access Management (Domain 5)

1. Which of the following is best described as an access control model that focuses on subjects and identifies the objects that each subject can access?

   A. An access control list

   B. An implicit denial list

   C. A capability table

   D. A rights management matrix

2. Jim's organization-wide implementation of IDaaS offers broad support for cloud-based applications. The existing infrastructure for Jim's company does not have in-house identity management staff, and does not use centralized identity services but uses Active Directory for AAA services. Which of the following choices is the best option to recommend to handle the company's onsite identity needs?

   A. Integrate onsite systems using OAuth.

   B. Use an on-premise third-party identity service.

   C. Integrate onsite systems using SAML.

   D. Design an in-house solution to handle the organization's unique needs.

3. Which of the following is not a weakness in Kerberos?

   A. The KDC is a single point of failure.

   B. Compromise of the KDC would allow attackers to impersonate any user.

   C. Authentication information is not encrypted.

   D. It is susceptible to password guessing.

4. Voice pattern recognition is what type of authentication factor?

   A. Type 1

   B. Type 2

   C. Type 3

   D. Type 4

5. If Susan's organization requires her to log in with her username, a PIN, a password, and a retina scan, how many distinct types of factor has she used?

   A. One

   B. Two

   C. Three

   D. Four

6. Which of the following items are not commonly associated with restricted interfaces?

   A. Shells

   B. Keyboards

   C. Menus

   D. Database views

7. During a log review, Saria discovers a series of logs that show login failures as shown here:

Jan 31 11:39:12 ip-10-0-0-2 sshd[29092]: Invalid user admin from remotehost passwd=orange

Jan 31 11:39:20 ip-10-0-0-2 sshd[29098]: Invalid user admin from remotehost passwd=Orang3

Jan 31 11:39:23 ip-10-0-0-2 sshd[29100]: Invalid user admin from remotehost passwd=Orange93

Jan 31 11:39:31 ip-10-0-0-2 sshd[29106]: Invalid user admin from remotehost passwd=Orangutan1

Jan 31 20:40:53 ip-10-0-0-254 sshd[30520]: Invalid user admin from remotehost passwd=Orangemonkey

What type of attack has Saria discovered?

A. A brute force attack

B. A man-in-the-middle attack

C. A dictionary attack

D. A rainbow table attack

8. What type of attack can be prevented by using a trusted path?

A. Dictionary attacks

B. Brute force attacks

C. Man-in-the-middle attacks

D. Login spoofing

9. What major issue often results from decentralized access control?

A. Access outages may occur.

B. Control is not consistent.

C. Control is too granular.

D. Training costs are high.

10. Callback to a home phone number is an example of what type of factor?

A. Type 1

B. Somewhere you are

C. Type 3

D. Geographic

11. Kathleen needs to set up an Active Directory trust to allow authentication with an existing Kerberos K5 domain. What type of trust does she need to create?

A. A shortcut trust

B. A forest trust

    C. An external trust

    D. A realm trust

12. Which of the following AAA protocols is the most commonly used?

    A. TACACS

    B. TACACS+

    C. XTACACS

    D. Super TACACS

13. Which of the following is not a single sign-on implementation?

    A. Kerberos

    B. ADFS

    C. CAS

    D. RADIUS

14. As seen in the following image, a user on a Windows system is not able to use the "Send Message" functionality. What access control model best describes this type of limitation?

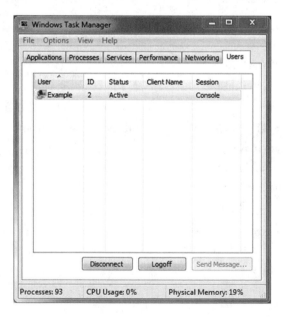

    A. Least privilege

    B. Need to know

    C. Constrained interface

    D. Separation of duties

15. What type of access controls allow the owner of a file to grant other users access to it using an access control list?

  A. Role based

  B. Non-discretionary

  C. Rule based

  D. Discretionary

16. Alex's job requires him to see personal health information (PHI) to ensure proper treatment of patients. His access to their medical records does not provide access to patient addresses or billing information. What access control concept best describes this control?

  A. Separation of duties

  B. Constrained interfaces

  C. Context-dependent control

  D. Need to know

Using your knowledge of the Kerberos logon process and the following diagram, answer questions 17, 18, and 19.

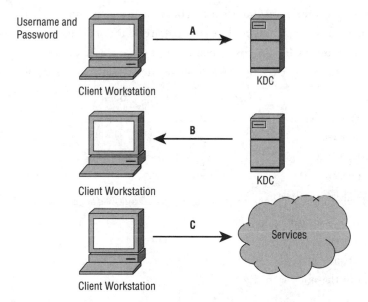

17. At point A in the diagram, the client sends the username and password to the KDC. How is the username and password protected?

  A. 3DES encryption

  B. TLS encryption

  C. SSL encryption

  D. AES encryption

18. At point B in the diagram, what two important elements does the KDC send to the client after verifying that the username is valid?

   A. An encrypted TGT and a public key

   B. An access ticket and a public key

   C. An encrypted, time-stamped TGT and a symmetric key encrypted with a hash of the user's password

   D. An encrypted, time-stamped TGT and an access token

19. What tasks must the client perform before it can use the TGT?

   A. It must generate a hash of the TGT and decrypt the symmetric key.

   B. It must accept the TGT and decrypt the symmetric key.

   C. It must decrypt the TGT and the symmetric key.

   D. It must send a valid response using the symmetric key to the KDC and must install the TGT.

20. Jacob is planning his organization's biometric authentication system and is considering retina scans. What concern may be raised about retina scans by others in his organization?

   A. Retina scans can reveal information about medical conditions.

   B. Retina scans are painful because they require a puff of air in the user's eye.

   C. Retina scanners are the most expensive type of biometric device.

   D. Retina scanners have a high false positive rate and will cause support issues.

21. Mandatory access control is based on what type of model?

   A. Discretionary

   B. Group based

   C. Lattice based

   D. Rule based

22. Which of the following is not a type of attack used against access controls?

   A. Dictionary attack

   B. Brute force attack

   C. Teardrop

   D. Man-in-the-middle attack

23. What is the best way to provide accountability for the use of identities?

   A. Logging

   B. Authorization

   C. Digital signatures

   D. Type 1 authentication

24. Jim has worked in human relations, payroll, and customer service roles in his company over the past few years. What type of process should his company perform to ensure that he has appropriate rights?

   A. Re-provisioning

   B. Account review

   C. Privilege creep

   D. Account revocation

25. Biba is what type of access control model?

   A. MAC

   B. DAC

   C. Role BAC

   D. ABAC

26. Which of the following is a client/server protocol designed to allow network access servers to authenticate remote users by sending access request messages to a central server?

   A. Kerberos

   B. EAP

   C. RADIUS

   D. OAuth

27. What type of access control is being used in the following permission listing:

Storage Device X

User1: Can read, write, list

User2: Can read, list

User3: Can read, write, list, delete

User4: Can list

   A. Resource-based access controls

   B. Role-based access controls

   C. Mandatory access controls

   D. Rule-based access controls

28. Angela uses a sniffer to monitor traffic from a RADIUS server configured with default settings. What protocol should she monitor and what traffic will she be able to read?

   A. UDP, none. All RADIUS traffic is encrypted.

   B. TCP, all traffic but the passwords, which are encrypted

   C. UDP, all traffic but the passwords, which are encrypted

   D. TCP, none. All RADIUS traffic is encrypted.

29. Which of the following is not part of a Kerberos authentication system?

   A. KDC

   B. TGT

   C. AS

   D. TS

30. When an application or system allows a logged-in user to perform specific actions, it is an example of what?

   A. Roles

   B. Group management

   C. Logins

   D. Authorization

31. Alex has been employed by his company for over a decade and has held a number of positions in the company. During an audit, it is discovered that he has access to shared folders and applications due to his former roles. What issue has Alex's company encountered?

   A. Excessive provisioning

   B. Unauthorized access

   C. Privilege creep

   D. Account review

32. Which of the following is not a common threat to access control mechanisms?

   A. Fake login pages

   B. Phishing

   C. Dictionary attacks

   D. Man-in-the-middle attacks

33. What term properly describes what occurs when two or more processes require access to the same resource and must complete their tasks in the proper order for normal function?

   A. Collisions

   B. Race conditions

   C. Determinism

   D. Out-of-order execution

34. What type of access control scheme is shown in the following table?

Highly Sensitive	Red	Blue	Green
Confidential	Purple	Orange	Yellow
Internal Use	Black	Gray	White
Public	Clear	Clear	Clear

    A. RBAC

    B. DAC

    C. MAC

    D. TBAC

35. Which of the following is not a valid LDAP DN (distinguished name)?

    A. cn=ben+ou=sales

    B. ou=example

    C. cn=ben,ou=example;

    D. ou=example,dc=example,dc=com+dc=org

36. When a subject claims an identity, what process is occurring?

    A. Login

    B. Identification

    C. Authorization

    D. Token presentation

37. Dogs, guards, and fences are all common examples of what type of control?

    A. Detective

    B. Recovery

    C. Administrative

    D. Physical

38. Susan's organization is updating its password policy and wants to use the strongest possible passwords. What password requirement will have the highest impact in preventing brute force attacks?

    A. Change maximum age from 1 year to 180 days.

    B. Increase the minimum password length from 8 characters to 16 characters.

    C. Increase the password complexity so that at least three character classes (such as uppercase, lowercase, numbers, and symbols) are required.

    D. Retain a password history of at least four passwords to prevent reuse.

39. What is the stored sample of a biometric factor called?

    A. A reference template

    B. A token store

    C. A biometric password

    D. An enrollment artifact

40. When might an organization using biometrics choose to allow a higher FRR instead of a higher FAR?

    A. When security is more important than usability

    B. When false rejection is not a concern due to data quality

   C. When the CER of the system is not known

   D. When the CER of the system is very high

41. Susan is working to improve the strength of her organization's passwords by changing the password policy. The password system that she is using allows upper- and lower-case letters as well as numbers but no other characters. How much additional complexity does adding a single character to the minimum length of passwords for her organization create?

   A. 26 times more complex

   B. 62 times more complex

   C. 36 times more complex

   D. 2^62 times more complex

42. Which pair of the following factors are key for user acceptance of biometric identification systems?

   A. The FAR

   B. The throughput rate and the time required to enroll

   C. The CER and the ERR

   D. How often users must reenroll and the reference profile requirements

Alex is in charge of SAML integration with a major third-party partner that provides a variety of business productivity services for his organization. Using the following diagram and your knowledge of SAML integrations and security architecture design, answer questions 43, 44, and 45.

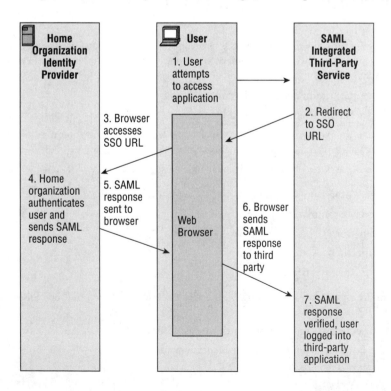

43. Alex is concerned about eavesdropping on the SAML traffic and also wants to ensure that forged assertions will not be successful. What should he do to prevent these potential attacks?

    A. Use SAML's secure mode to provide secure authentication.

    B. Implement TLS using a strong cipher suite, which will protect against both types of attacks.

    C. Implement TLS using a strong cipher suite and use digital signatures.

    D. Implement TLS using a strong cipher suite and message hashing.

44. If Alex's organization is one that is primarily made up of offsite, traveling users, what availability risk does integration of critical business applications to onsite authentication create and how could he solve it?

    A. Third-party integration may not be trustworthy; use SSL and digital signatures.

    B. If the home organization is offline, traveling users won't be able to access third-party applications; implement a hybrid cloud/local authentication system.

    C. Local users may not be properly redirected to the third-party services; implement a local gateway.

    D. Browsers may not properly redirect; use host files to ensure that issues with redirects are resolved.

45. What solution can best help address concerns about third parties that control SSO directs as shown in step 2 in the diagram?

    A. An awareness campaign about trusted third parties

    B. TLS

    C. Handling redirects at the local site

    D. Implementing an IPS to capture SSO redirect attacks

46. Susan has been asked to recommend whether her organization should use a mandatory access control scheme or a discretionary access control scheme. If flexibility and scalability is an important requirement for implementing access controls, which scheme should she recommend and why?

    A. MAC, because it provides greater scalability and flexibility because you can simply add more labels as needed

    B. DAC, because allowing individual administrators to make choices about the objects they control provides scalability and flexibility

    C. MAC, because compartmentalization is well suited to flexibility and adding compartments will allow it to scale well

    D. DAC, because a central decision process allows quick responses and will provide scalability by reducing the number of decisions required and flexibility by moving those decisions to a central authority

47. Which of the following tools is not typically used to verify that a provisioning process was followed in a way that ensures that the organization's security policy is being followed?

    A. Log review

    B. Manual review of permissions

    C. Signature-based detection

    D. Review the audit trail

48. Lauren needs to send information about services she is provisioning to a third-party organization. What standards-based markup language should she choose to build the interface?

    A. SAML

    B. SOAP

    C. SPML

    D. XACML

49. During a penetration test, Chris recovers a file containing hashed passwords for the system he is attempting to access. What type of attack is most likely to succeed against the hashed passwords?

    A. A brute force attack

    B. A pass-the-hash attack

    C. A rainbow table attack

    D. A salt recovery attack

50. Google's identity integration with a variety of organizations and applications across domains is an example of which of the following?

    A. PKI

    B. Federation

    C. Single sign-on

    D. Provisioning

51. Lauren starts at her new job and finds that she has access to a variety of systems that she does not need access to to accomplish her job. What problem has she encountered?

    A. Privilege creep

    B. Rights collision

    C. Least privilege

    D. Excessive privileges

52. When Chris verifies an individual's identity and adds a unique identifier like a user ID to an identity system, what process has occurred?

    A. Identity proofing

    B. Registration

    C. Directory management

    D. Session management

53. Jim configures his LDAP client to connect to an LDAP directory server. According to the configuration guide, his client should connect to the server on port 636. What does this indicate to Jim about the configuration of the LDAP server?

    A. It requires connections over SSL/TLS.

    B. It supports only unencrypted connections.

    C. It provides global catalog services.

    D. It does not provide global catalog services.

54. The X.500 standards cover what type of important identity systems?

    A. Kerberos

    B. Provisioning services

    C. Biometric authentication systems

    D. Directory services

55. Microsoft's Active Directory Domain Services is based on which of the following technologies?

    A. RADIUS

    B. LDAP

    C. SSO

    D. PKI

56. Lauren is responsible for building a banking website. She needs proof of the identity of the users who register for the site. How should she validate user identities?

    A. Require users to create unique questions that only they will know.

    B. Require new users to bring their driver's license or passport in person to the bank.

    C. Use information that both the bank and the user have such as questions pulled from their credit report.

    D. Call the user on their registered phone number to verify that they are who they claim to be.

57. By default, in what format does OpenLDAP store the value of the userPassword attribute?

    A. In the clear

    B. Salted and hashed

    C. MD5 hashed

    D. Encrypted using AES256 encryption

58. A new customer at a bank that uses fingerprint scanners to authenticate its users is surprised when he scans his fingerprint and is logged in to another customer's account. What type of biometric factor error occurred?

    A. A registration error

    B. A Type 1 error

    C. A Type 2 error

    D. A time of use, method of use error

59. What type of access control is typically used by firewalls?

    A. Discretionary access controls

    B. Rule-based access controls

    C. Task-based access control

    D. Mandatory access controls

60. When you input a user ID and password, you are performing what important identity and access management activity?

    A. Authorization

    B. Validation

    C. Authentication

    D. Login

61. Kathleen works for a data center hosting facility that provides physical data center space for individuals and organizations. Until recently, each client was given a magnetic-strip-based keycard to access the section of the facility where their servers are located, and they were also given a key to access the cage or rack where their servers reside. In the past month, a number of servers have been stolen, but the logs for the passcards show only valid IDs. What is Kathleen's best option to make sure that the users of the passcards are who they are supposed to be?

    A. Add a reader that requires a PIN for passcard users.

    B. Add a camera system to the facility to observe who is accessing servers.

    C. Add a biometric factor.

    D. Replace the magnetic stripe keycards with smart cards.

62. Which of the following is a ticket-based authentication protocol designed to provide secure communication?

    A. RADIUS

    B. OAuth

    C. SAML

    D. Kerberos

63. What type of access control is composed of policies and procedures that support regulations, requirements, and the organization's own policies?

    A. Corrective

    B. Logical

    C. Compensating

    D. Administrative

64. In a Kerberos environment, when a user needs to access a network resource, what is sent to the TGS?

    A. A TGT

    B. An AS

    C. The SS

    D. A session key

65. Which objects and subjects have a label in a MAC model?

    A. Objects and subjects that are classified as Confidential, Secret, or Top Secret have a label.

    B. All objects have a label, and all subjects have a compartment.

    C. All objects and subjects have a label.

    D. All subjects have a label and all objects have a compartment.

Chris is the identity architect for a growing e-commerce website that wants to leverage social identity. To do this, he and his team intend to allow users to use their existing Google accounts as their primary accounts when using the e-commerce site. This means that when a new user initially connects to the e-commerce platform, they are given the choice between using their Google+ account using OAuth 2.0, or creating a new account on the platform using their own email address and a password of their choice.

Using this information and the following diagram of an example authentication flow, answer questions 66, 67, and 68.

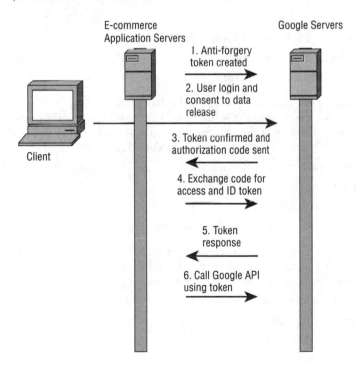

66. When the e-commerce application creates an account for a Google+ user, where should that user's password be stored?

    A. The password is stored in the e-commerce application's database.

    B. The password is stored in memory on the e-commerce application's server.

    C. The password is stored in Google's account management system.

    D. The password is never stored; instead, a salted hash is stored in Google's account management system.

67. Which system or systems is/are responsible for user authentication for Google+ users?

    A. The e-commerce application

    B. Both the e-commerce application and Google servers

    C. Google servers

    D. The diagram does not provide enough information to determine this.

68. What type of attack is the creation and exchange of state tokens intended to prevent?

    A. XSS

    B. CSRF

    C. SQL injection

    D. XACML

69. Questions like "What is your pet's name?" are examples of what type of identity proofing?

    A. Knowledge-based authentication

    B. Dynamic knowledge-based authentication

    C. Out-of-band identity proofing

    D. A Type 3 authentication factor

70. Lauren builds a table that includes assigned privileges, objects, and subjects to manage access control for the systems she is responsible for. Each time a subject attempts to access an object, the systems check the table to ensure that the subject has the appropriate rights to the objects. What type of access control system is Lauren using?

    A. A capability table

    B. An access control list

    C. An access control matrix

    D. A subject/object rights management system

71. During a review of support incidents, Ben's organization discovered that password changes accounted for more than a quarter of its help desk's cases. Which of the following options would be most likely to decrease that number significantly?

    A. Two-factor authentication

    B. Biometric authentication

    C. Self-service password reset

    D. Passphrases

72. Brian's large organization has used RADIUS for AAA services for its network devices for years and has recently become aware of security issues with the unencrypted information transferred during authentication. How should Brian implement encryption for RADIUS?

   A. Use the built-in encryption in RADIUS.

   B. Implement RADIUS over its native UDP using TLS for protection.

   C. Implement RADIUS over TCP using TLS for protection.

   D. Use an AES256 pre-shared cipher between devices.

73. Jim wants to allow cloud-based applications to act on his behalf to access information from other sites. Which of the following tools can allow that?

   A. Kerberos

   B. OAuth

   C. OpenID

   D. LDAP

74. Ben's organization has had an issue with unauthorized access to applications and workstations during the lunch hour when employees aren't at their desk. What are the best type of session management solutions for Ben to recommend to help prevent this type of access?

   A. Use session IDs for all access and verify system IP addresses of all workstations.

   B. Set session time-outs for applications and use password protected screensavers with inactivity time-outs on workstations.

   C. Use session IDs for all applications, and use password protected screensavers with inactivity time-outs on workstations.

   D. Set session time-outs for applications and verify system IP addresses of all workstations.

75. Lauren is an information security analyst tasked with deploying technical access controls for her organization. Which of the following is not a logical or technical access control?

   A. Passwords

   B. Firewalls

   C. RAID arrays

   D. Routers

76. The financial services company that Susan works for provides a web portal for its users. When users need to verify their identity, the company uses information from third-party sources to ask questions based on their past credit reports, such as, "Which of the following streets did you live on in 2007?" What process is Susan's organization using?

   A. Identity proofing

   B. Password verification

   C. Authenticating with Type 2 authentication factor

   D. Out-of-band identity proofing

77. The US government CAC is an example of what form of Type 2 authentication factor?

   A. A token

   B. A biometric identifier

   C. A smart card

   D. A PIV

78. What authentication technology can be paired with OAuth to perform identity verification and obtain user profile information using a RESTful API?

A. SAML

B. Shibboleth

C. OpenID Connect

D. Higgins

79. Jim has Secret clearance and is accessing files that use a mandatory access control scheme to apply the Top Secret, Secret, Confidential, and Unclassified label scheme. If his rights include the ability to access all data of his clearance level or lower, what classification levels of data can he access?

A. Top Secret and Secret

B. Secret, Confidential, and Unclassified

C. Secret data only

D. Secret and Unclassified

80. The security administrators at the company that Susan works for have configured the workstation she uses to allow her to log in only during her work hours. What type of access control best describes this limitation?

A. Constrained interface

B. Context-dependent control

C. Content-dependent control

D. Least privilege

81. When Lauren uses a fingerprint scanner to access her bank account, what type of authentication factor is she using?

A. Type 1

B. Type 2

C. Type 3

D. Type 4

82. Which of the following is not an access control layer?

A. Physical

B. Policy

C. Administrative

D. Technical

83. Ben uses a software based token which changes its code every minute. What type of token is he using?

A. Asynchronous

B. Smart card

C. Synchronous

D. Static

84. What type of token-based authentication system uses a challenge/response process in which the challenge has to be entered on the token?

    A. Asynchronous

    B. Smart card

    C. Synchronous

    D. RFID

Ben's organization is adopting biometric authentication for its high-security building's access control system. Using the following chart, answer questions 85, 86, and 87 about the organization's adoption of the technology.

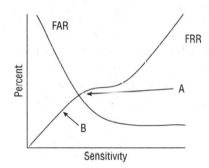

85. Ben's company is considering configuring its systems to work at the level shown by point A on the diagram. To what level is it setting the sensitivity?

    A. The FRR crossover

    B. The FAR point

    C. The CER

    D. The CFR

86. At point B, what problem is likely to occur?

    A. False acceptance will be very high.

    B. False rejection will be very high.

    C. False rejection will be very low.

    D. False acceptance will be very low.

87. What should Ben do if the FAR and FRR shown in this diagram does not provide an acceptable performance level for his organization's needs?

    A. Adjust the sensitivity of the biometric devices.

    B. Assess other biometric systems to compare them.

    C. Move the CER.

    D. Adjust the FRR settings in software.

88. What LDAP authentication mode can provide secure authentication?

    A. Anonymous

    B. SASL

    C. Simple

    D. S-LDAP

89. Which of the following Type 3 authenticators is appropriate to use by itself rather than in combination with other biometric factors?

    A. Voice pattern recognition

    B. Hand geometry

    C. Palm scans

    D. Heart/pulse patterns

90. What danger is created by allowing the OpenID relying party to control the connection to the OpenID provider?

    A. It may cause incorrect selection of the proper OpenID provider.

    B. It creates the possibility of a phishing attack by sending data to a fake OpenID provider.

    C. The relying party may be able to steal the client's username and password.

    D. The relying party may not send a signed assertion.

91. Jim is implementing a cloud identity solution for his organization. What type of technology is he putting in place?

    A. Identity as a Service

    B. Employee ID as a Service

    C. Cloud-based RADIUS

    D. OAuth

92. RAID-5 is an example of what type of control?

    A. Administrative

    B. Recovery

    C. Compensation

    D. Logical

93. When Alex sets the permissions shown in the following image as one of many users on a Linux server, what type of access control model is he leveraging?

```
$ chmod 731 alex.txt
$ ls -la
total 12
drwxr-xr-x 2 alex root 4096 Feb 27 19:26 .
drwxr-xr-x 3 root root 4096 Feb 27 19:25 ..
-rwx-wx--x 1 alex alex   15 Feb 27 19:26 alex.txt
$ █
```

    A. Role-based access control

    B. Rule-based access control

    C. Mandatory access control

    D. Discretionary access control

94. What open protocol was designed to replace RADIUS—including support for additional commands and protocols, replacing UDP traffic with TCP, and providing for extensible commands—but does not preserve backward compatibility with RADIUS?

    A. TACACS

    B. RADIUS-NG

    C. Kerberos

    D. Diameter

95. LDAP distinguished names (DNs) are made up of comma-separated components called relative distinguished names (RDNs) that have an attribute name and a value. DNs become less specific as they progress from left to right. Which of the following LDAP DN best fits this rule?

    A. uid=ben,ou=sales,dc=example,dc=com

    B. uid=ben,dc=com,dc=example

    C. dc=com,dc=example,ou=sales,uid=ben

    D. ou=sales,dc=com,dc=example

96. Susan is troubleshooting Kerberos authentication problems with symptoms including TGTs that are not accepted as valid and an inability to receive new tickets. If the system she is troubleshooting is properly configured for Kerberos authentication, her username and password are correct, and her network connection is functioning, what is the most likely issue?

    A. The Kerberos server is offline.

    B. There is a protocol mismatch.

    C. The client's TGTs have been marked as compromised and de-authorized.

    D. The Kerberos server and the local client's time clocks are not synchronized.

97. Kerberos, KryptoKnight, and SESAME are all examples of what type of system?

    A. SSO

    B. PKI

    C. CMS

    D. Directory

98. Which of the following types of access controls do not describe a lock?

    A. Physical

    B. Directive

    C. Preventative

    D. Deterrent

99. What authentication protocol does Windows use by default for Active Directory systems?

    A. RADIUS

    B. Kerberos

    C. OAuth

    D. TACACS+

100. Alex configures his LDAP server to provide services on 636 and 3269. What type of LDAP services has he configured based on LDAP's default ports?

    A. Unsecure LDAP and unsecure global directory

    B. Unsecure LDAP and secure global directory

    C. Secure LDAP and secure global directory

    D. Secure LDAP and unsecure global directory

Chapter
6

Security Assessment and Testing (Domain 6)

1. During a port scan, Susan discovers a system running services on TCP and UDP 137-139 and TCP 445, as well as TCP 1433. What type of system is she likely to find if she connects to the machine?

   A. A Linux email server

   B. A Windows SQL server

   C. A Linux file server

   D. A Windows workstation

2. Which of the following is a method used to design new software tests and to ensure the quality of tests?

   A. Code auditing

   B. Static code analysis

   C. Regression testing

   D. Mutation testing

3. During a port scan, Lauren found TCP port 443 open on a system. Which tool is best suited to scanning the service that is most likely running on that port?

   A. zzuf

   B. Nikto

   C. Metasploit

   D. sqlmap

4. What message logging standard is commonly used by network devices, Linux and Unix systems, and many other enterprise devices?

   A. Syslog

   B. Netlog

   C. Eventlog

   D. Remote Log Protocol (RLP)

5. Alex wants to use an automated tool to fill web application forms to test for format string vulnerabilities. What type of tool should he use?

   A. A black box

   B. A brute-force tool

   C. A fuzzer

   D. A static analysis tool

6. Susan needs to scan a system for vulnerabilities, and she wants to use an open source tool to test the system remotely. Which of the following tools will meet her requirements and allow vulnerability scanning?

   A. Nmap

   B. OpenVAS

   C. MBSA

   D. Nessus

7. NIST Special Publication 800-53A describes four major types of assessment objects that can be used to identify items being assessed. If the assessment covers IPS devices, which of the types of assessment objects is being assessed?

A. A specification

B. A mechanism

C. An activity

D. An individual

8. Jim has been contracted to perform a penetration test of a bank's primary branch. In order to make the test as real as possible, he has not been given any information about the bank other than its name and address. What type of penetration test has Jim agreed to perform?

A. A crystal box penetration test

B. A gray box penetration test

C. A black box penetration test

D. A white box penetration test

9. As part of a penetration test, Alex needs to determine if there are web servers that could suffer from the 2014 Heartbleed bug. What type of tool could he use, and what should he check to verify that the tool can identify the problem?

A. A vulnerability scanner, to see whether the scanner has a signature or test for the Heartbleed CVE number

B. A port scanner, to see whether the scanner properly identifies SSL connections

C. A vulnerability scanner, to see whether the vulnerability scanner detects problems with the Apache web server

D. A port scanner, to see whether the port scanner supports TLS connections

10. In a response to a Request for Proposal, Susan receives a SAS-70 Type 1 report. If she wants a report that includes operating effectiveness detail, what should Susan ask for as followup and why?

A. An SAS-70 Type II, because Type I only covers a single point in time

B. An SOC Type 1, because Type II does not cover operating effectiveness

C. An SOC Type 2, because Type I does not cover operating effectiveness

D. An SAC-70 Type 3, because Types 1 and 2 are outdated and no longer accepted

11. During a wireless network penetration test, Susan runs aircrack-ng against the network using a password file. What might cause her to fail in her password-cracking efforts?

A. Use of WPA2 encryption

B. Running WPA2 in Enterprise mode

C. Use of WEP encryption

D. Running WPA2 in PSK mode

12. Which type of SOC report is best suited to provide assurance to users about an organization's security, availability, and the integrity of their service operations?

   A. An SOC 1 Type 2 report

   B. An SOC 2 report

   C. An SOC 3 report

   D. An SOC 1 Type 1 report

13. What type of testing is used to ensure that separately developed software modules properly exchange data?

   A. Fuzzing

   B. Dynamic testing

   C. Interface testing

   D. API checksums

14. Which of the following is not a potential problem with active wireless scanning?

   A. Accidently scanning apparent rogue devices that actually belong to guests

   B. Causing alarms on the organization's wireless IPS

   C. Scanning devices that belong to nearby organizations

   D. Misidentifying rogue devices

15. Ben uses a fuzzing tool that develops data models and creates fuzzed data based on information about how the application uses data to test the application. What type of fuzzing is Ben doing?

   A. Mutation

   B. Parametric

   C. Generational

   D. Derivative

16. Saria wants to log and review traffic information between parts of her network. What type of network logging should she enable on her routers to allow her to perform this analysis?

   A. Audit logging

   B. Flow logging

   C. Trace logging

   D. Route logging

17. Jim has been contracted to conduct a gray box penetration test, and his clients have provided him with the following information about their networks so that he can scan them.

   Data center: 10.10.10.0/24

   Sales: 10.10.11.0/24

   Billing: 10.10.12.0/24

   Wireless: 192.168.0.0/16

What problem will Jim encounter if he is contracted to conduct a scan from offsite?

   A. The IP ranges are too large to scan efficiently.

   B. The IP addresses provided cannot be scanned.

   C. The IP ranges overlap and will cause scanning issues.

   D. The IP addresses provided are RFC 1918 addresses.

18. Karen's organization has been performing system backups for years but has not used the backups frequently. During a recent system outage, when administrators tried to restore from backups they found that the backups had errors and could not be restored. Which of the following options should Karen avoid when selecting ways to ensure that her organization's backups will work next time?

   A. Log review

   B. MTD verification

   C. Hashing

   D. Periodic testing

Questions 19, 20, and 21 refer to the following scenario.

The company that Jennifer works for has implemented a central logging infrastructure, as shown in the following image. Use this diagram and your knowledge of logging systems to answer the following questions.

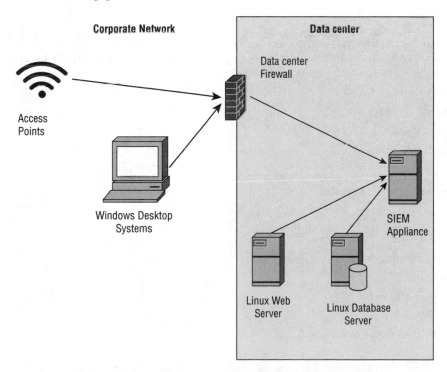

19. Jennifer needs to ensure that all Windows systems provide identical logging information to the SIEM. How can she best ensure that all Windows desktops have the same log settings?

    A. Perform periodic configuration audits.

    B. Use Group Policy.

    C. Use Local Policy.

    D. Deploy a Windows syslog client.

20. During normal operations, Jennifer's team uses the SIEM appliance to monitor for exceptions received via syslog. What system shown does not natively have support for syslog events?

    A. Enterprise wireless access points

    B. Windows desktop systems

    C. Linux web servers

    D. Enterprise firewall devices

21. What technology should an organization use for each of the devices shown in the diagram to ensure that logs can be time sequenced across the entire infrastructure?

    A. Syslog

    B. NTP

    C. Logsync

    D. SNAP

22. During a penetration test, Danielle needs to identify systems, but she hasn't gained sufficient access on the system she is using to generate raw packets. What type of scan should she run to verify the most open services?

    A. A TCP connect scan

    B. A TCP SYN scan

    C. A UDP scan

    D. An ICMP scan

23. During a port scan using nmap, Joseph discovers that a system shows two ports open that cause him immediate worry:

    21/open

    23/open

What services are likely running on those ports?

    A. SSH and FTP

    B. FTP and Telnet

    C. SMTP and Telnet

    D. POP3 and SMTP

24. Saria's team is working to persuade their management that their network has extensive vulnerabilities that attackers could exploit. If she wants to conduct a realistic attack as part of a penetration test, what type of penetration test should she conduct?

    A. Crystal box

    B. Gray box

    C. White box

    D. Black box

25. What method is commonly used to assess how well software testing covered the potential uses of a an application?

    A. A test coverage analysis

    B. A source code review

    C. A fuzz analysis

    D. A code review report

26. Testing that is focused on functions that a system should not allow are an example of what type of testing?

    A. Use case testing

    B. Manual testing

    C. Misuse case testing

    D. Dynamic testing

27. What type of monitoring uses simulated traffic to a website to monitor performance?

    A. Log analysis

    B. Synthetic monitoring

    C. Passive monitoring

    D. Simulated transaction analysis

28. Which of the following vulnerabilities is unlikely to be found by a web vulnerability scanner?

    A. Path disclosure

    B. Local file inclusion

    C. Race condition

    D. Buffer overflow

29. Jim uses a tool that scans a system for available services, then connects to them to collect banner information to determine what version of the service is running. It then provides a report detailing what it gathers, basing results on service fingerprinting, banner information, and similar details it gathers combined with CVE information. What type of tool is Jim using?

    A. A port scanner

    B. A service validator

    C. A vulnerability scanner

    D. A patch management tool

30. Emily builds a script that sends data to a web application that she is testing. Each time the script runs, it sends a series of transactions with data that fits the expected requirements of the web application to verify that it responds to typical customer behavior. What type of transactions is she using, and what type of test is this?

A. Synthetic, passive monitoring

B. Synthetic, use case testing

C. Actual, dynamic monitoring

D. Actual, fuzzing

31. What passive monitoring technique records all user interaction with an application or website to ensure quality and performance?

A. Client/server testing

B. Real user monitoring

C. Synthetic user monitoring

D. Passive user recording

32. Earlier this year, the information security team at Jim's employer identified a vulnerability in the web server that Jim is responsible for maintaining. He immediately applied the patch and is sure that it installed properly, but the vulnerability scanner has continued to incorrectly flag the system as vulnerable due to the version number it is finding even though Jim is sure the patch is installed. Which of the following options is Jim's best choice to deal with the issue?

A. Uninstall and reinstall the patch.

B. Ask the information security team to flag the system as patched and not vulnerable.

C. Update the version information in the web server's configuration.

D. Review the vulnerability report and use alternate remediation options.

33. Angela wants to test a web browser's handling of unexpected data using an automated tool. What tool should she choose?

A. Nmap

B. zzuf

C. Nessus

D. Nikto

34. STRIDE, which stands for Spoofing, Tampering, Repudiation, Information Disclosure, Denial of Service, Elevation of Privilege, is useful in what part of application threat modeling?

A. Vulnerability assessment

B. Misuse case testing

C. Threat categorization

D. Penetration test planning

35. Why should passive scanning be conducted in addition to implementing wireless security technologies like wireless intrusion detection systems?

   A. It can help identify rogue devices.

   B. It can test the security of the wireless network via scripted attacks.

   C. Their short dwell time on each wireless channel can allow them to capture more packets.

   D. They can help test wireless IDS or IPS systems.

36. During a penetration test, Lauren is asked to test the organization's Bluetooth security. Which of the following is not a concern she should explain to her employers?

   A. Bluetooth scanning can be time consuming.

   B. Many devices that may be scanned are likely to be personal devices.

   C. Bluetooth passive scans may require multiple visits at different times to identify all targets.

   D. Bluetooth active scans can't evaluate the security mode of Bluetooth devices.

37. What term describes software testing that is intended to uncover new bugs introduced by patches or configuration changes?

   A. Nonregression testing

   B. Evolution testing

   C. Smoke testing

   D. Regression testing

38. Which of the tools cannot identify a target's operating system for a penetration tester?

   A. Nmap

   B. Nessus

   C. Nikto

   D. sqlmap

39. Susan needs to predict high-risk areas for her organization and wants to use metrics to assess risk trends as they occur. What should she do to handle this?

   A. Perform yearly risk assessments.

   B. Hire a penetration testing company to regularly test organizational security.

   C. Identify and track key risk indicators.

   D. Monitor logs and events using a SIEM device.

40. What major difference separates synthetic and passive monitoring?

   A. Synthetic monitoring only works after problems have occurred.

   B. Passive monitoring cannot detect functionality issues.

   C. Passive monitoring only works after problems have occurred.

   D. Synthetic monitoring cannot detect functionality issues.

41. Chris uses the standard penetration testing methodology shown here. Use this methodology and your knowledge of penetration testing to answer the following questions about tool usage during a penetration test.

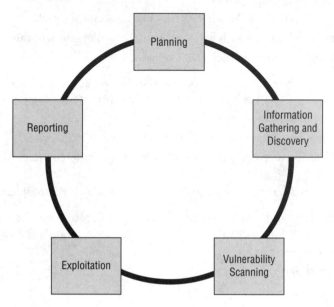

What task is the most important during Phase 1, Planning?

    A. Building a test lab

    B. Getting authorization

    C. Gathering appropriate tools

    D. Determining if the test is white, black, or gray box

42. Which of the following tools is most likely to be used during discovery?

    A. Nessus

    B. john

    C. Nmap

    D. Nikto

43. Which of these concerns is the most important to address during planning to ensure the reporting phase does not cause problems?

    A. Which CVE format to use

    B. How the vulnerability data will be stored and sent

    C. Which targets are off limits

    D. How long the report should be

44. What four types of coverage criteria are commonly used when validating the work of a code testing suite?

   A. Input, statement, branch, and condition coverage

   B. Function, statement, branch, and condition coverage

   C. API, branch, bounds, and condition coverage

   D. Bounds, branch, loop, and condition coverage

45. As part of his role as a security manager, Jacob provides the following chart to his organization's management team. What type of measurement is he providing for them?

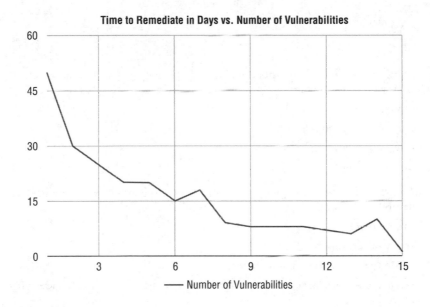

Time to Remediate in Days vs. Number of Vulnerabilities

   A. A coverage rate measure

   B. A key performance indicator

   C. A time to live metric

   D. A business criticality indicator

46. What does using unique user IDs for all users provide when reviewing logs?

   A. Confidentiality

   B. Integrity

   C. Availability

   D. Accountability

47. Which of the following is not an interface that is typically tested during the software testing process?

   A. APIs

   B. Network interfaces

   C. UIs

   D. Physical interfaces

48. What protocol is used to handle vulnerability management data?

   A. VML

   B. SVML

   C. SCAP

   D. VSCAP

49. Misconfiguration, logical and functional flaws, and poor programming practices are all causes of what type of issue?

   A. Fuzzing

   B. Security vulnerabilities

   C. Buffer overflows

   D. Race conditions

50. Which of the following strategies should not be used to handle a vulnerability identified by a vulnerability scanner?

   A. Install a patch.

   B. Use a workaround fix.

   C. Update the banner or version number.

   D. Use an application layer firewall or IPS to prevent attacks against the identified vulnerability.

51. During a penetration test Saria calls her target's help desk claiming to be the senior assistant to an officer of the company. She requests that the help desk reset the officer's password because of an issue with his laptop while traveling and persuades them to do so. What type of attack has she successfully completed?

   A. Zero knowledge

   B. Help desk spoofing

   C. Social engineering

   D. Black box

52. In this image, what issue may occur due to the log handling settings?

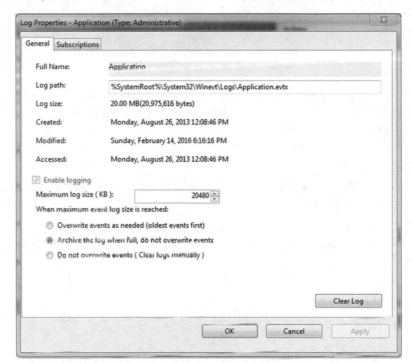

A. Log data may be lost when the log is archived.

B. Log data may be overwritten.

C. Log data may not include needed information.

D. Log data may fill the system disk.

53. Which of the following is not a hazard associated with penetration testing?

A. Application crashes

B. Denial of service

C. Exploitation of vulnerabilities

D. Data corruption

54. Which NIST special publication covers the assessment of security and privacy controls?

A. 800-12

B. 800-53A

C. 800-34

D. 800-86

55. What type of port scanning is known as "half open" scanning?

A. TCP Connect

B. TCP ACK

C. TCP SYN

D. Xmas

56. Lauren is performing a review of a third-party service organization and wants to determine if the organization's policies and procedures are effectively enforced over a period of time. What type of industry standard assessment report should she request?

A. SSAE 16 SOC 1 Type I

B. SAS 70 Type I

C. SSAE 16 SOC 1 Type II

D. SAS 70 Type II

57. Jim is working with a penetration testing contractor who proposes using Metasploit as part of her penetration testing effort. What should Jim expect to occur when Metasploit is used?

A. Systems will be scanned for vulnerabilities.

B. Systems will have known vulnerabilities exploited.

C. Services will be probed for buffer overflow and other unknown flaws.

D. Systems will be tested for zero-day exploits.

58. During a third-party audit, Jim's company receives a finding that states, "The administrator should review backup success and failure logs on a daily basis, and take action in a timely manner to resolve reported exceptions." What is the biggest issue that is likely to result if Jim's IT staff need to restore from a backup?

A. They will not know if the backups succeeded or failed.

B. The backups may not be properly logged.

C. The backups may not be usable.

D. The backup logs may not be properly reviewed.

59. Jim is helping his organization decide on audit standards for use throughout their international organization. Which of the following is not an IT standard that Jim's organization is likely to use as part of its audits?

A. COBIT

B. SSAE-16

C. ITIL

D. ISO27002

60. Which of the following best describes a typical process for building and implementing an Information Security Continuous Monitoring program as described by NIST Special Publication 800-137?

   A. Define, establish, implement, analyze and report, respond, review, and update

   B. Design, build, operate, analyze, respond, review, revise

   C. Prepare, detect and analyze, contain, respond, recover, report

   D. Define, design, build, monitor, analyze, react, revise

61. Lauren's team conducts regression testing on each patch that they release. What key performance measure should they maintain to measure the effectiveness of their testing?

   A. Time to remediate vulnerabilities

   B. A measure of the rate of defect recurrence

   C. A weighted risk trend

   D. A measure of the specific coverage of their testing

62. Which of the following types of code review is not typically performed by a human?

   A. Software inspections

   B. Code review

   C. Static program analysis

   D. Software walkthroughs

Susan is the lead of a Quality Assurance team at her company. They have been tasked with the testing for a major release of their company's core software product. Use your knowledge of code review and testing to answer the following three questions.

63. Susan's team of software testers are required to test every code path, including those that will only be used when an error condition occurs. What type of testing environment does her team need to ensure complete code coverage?

   A. White box

   B. Gray box

   C. Black box

   D. Dynamic

64. As part of the continued testing of their new application, Susan's quality assurance team has designed a set of test cases for a series of black box tests. These functional tests are then run, and a report is prepared explaining what has occurred. What type of report is typically generated during this testing to indicate test metrics?

   A. A test coverage report

   B. A penetration test report

   C. A code coverage report

   D. A line coverage report

65. As part of their code coverage testing, Susan's team runs the analysis in a nonproduction environment using logging and tracing tools. Which of the following types of code issues is most likely to be missed during testing due to this change in the operating environment?

    A. Improper bounds checking

    B. Input validation

    C. A race condition

    D. Pointer manipulation

66. What step should occur after a vulnerability scan finds a critical vulnerability on a system?

    A. Patching

    B. Reporting

    C. Remediation

    D. Validation

67. Kathleen is reviewing the code for an application. She first plans the review, conducts an overview session with the reviewers and assigns roles, and then works with the reviewers to review materials and prepare for their roles. Next, she intends to review the code, rework it, and ensure that all defects found have been corrected.

What type of review is Kathleen conducting?

    A. A dynamic test

    B. Fagan inspection

    C. Fuzzing

    D. A Roth-Parker review

68. Danielle wants to compare vulnerabilities she has discovered in her data center based on how exploitable they are, if exploit code exists, as well as how hard they are to remediate. What scoring system should she use to compare vulnerability metrics like these?

    A. CSV

    B. NVD

    C. VSS

    D. CVSS

69. During a port scan of his network, Alex finds that a number of hosts respond on TCP ports 80, 443, 515, and 9100 in offices throughout his organization. What type of devices is Alex likely discovering?

    A. Web servers

    B. File servers

    C. Wireless access points

    D. Printers

70. Nikto, Burp Suite, and Wapiti are all examples of what type of tool?

    A. Web application vulnerability scanners

    B. Code review tools

    C. Vulnerability scanners

    D. Port scanners

71. During an nmap scan, what three potential statuses are provided for a port?

    A. Open, unknown, closed

    B. Open, closed, and filtered

    C. Available, denied, unknown

    D. Available, unavailable, filtered

72. Which of the following is not a method of synthetic transaction monitoring?

    A. Database monitoring

    B. Traffic capture and analysis

    C. User session monitoring

    D. Website performance monitoring

73. Susan needs to ensure that the interactions between the components of her e-commerce application are all handled properly. She intends to verify communications, error handling, and session management capabilities throughout her infrastructure. What type of testing is she planning to conduct?

    A. Misuse case testing

    B. Fuzzing

    C. Regression testing

    D. Interface testing

74. Jim is designing his organization's log management systems and knows that he needs to carefully plan to handle the organization's log data. Which of the following is not a factor that Jim should be concerned with?

    A. The volume of log data

    B. A lack of sufficient log sources

    C. Data storage security requirements

    D. Network bandwidth

75. Jim has contracted with a software testing organization that uses automated testing tools to validate software. He is concerned that they may not completely test all statements in his software. What measurement should he ask for in their report to provide information about this?

    A. A use case count

    B. A test coverage report

    C. A code coverage report

    D. A code review report

76. When a Windows system is rebooted, what type of log is generated?

    A. Error

    B. Warning

    C. Information

    D. Failure audit

77. During a review of access logs, Alex notices that Danielle logged into her workstation in New York at 8 a.m. daily, but that she was recorded as logging into her department's main web application shortly after 3 a.m. daily. What common logging issue has Alex likely encountered?

   A. Inconsistent log formatting

   B. Modified logs

   C. Inconsistent timestamps

   D. Multiple log sources

78. What type of vulnerability scan accesses configuration information from the systems it is run against as well as information that can be accessed via services available via the network?

   A. Authenticated scans

   B. Web application scans

   C. Unauthenticated scans

   D. Port scans

Ben's organization has begun to use STRIDE to assess their software, and has identified threat agents and the business impacts that these threats could have. Now they are working to identify appropriate controls for the issues they have identified. Use the STRIDE model to answer the following three questions.

79. Ben's development team needs to address an authorization issue, resulting in an elevation of privilege threat. Which of the following controls is most appropriate to this type of issue?

   A. Auditing and logging is enabled.

   B. RBAC is used for specific operations.

   C. Data type and format checks are enabled.

   D. User input is tested against a whitelist.

80. Ben's team is attempting to categorize a transaction identification issue that is caused by use of a symmetric key shared by multiple servers. What STRIDE category should this fall into?

   A. Information disclosure

   B. Denial of service

   C. Tampering

   D. Repudiation

81. Ben wants to prevent or detect tampering with data. Which of the following is not an appropriate solution?

   A. Hashes

   B. Digital signatures

   C. Filtering

   D. Authorization controls

82. Which NIST document covers the creation of an Information Security Continuous Monitoring (ISCM)?

    A. NIST SP 800-137

    B. NIST SP 800-53a

    C. NIST SP 800-145

    D. NIST SP 800-50

83. Which of the following is not an issue when using fuzzing to find program faults?

    A. They often find only simple faults.

    B. Fuzz testing bugs are often severe.

    C. Fuzzers may not fully cover the code.

    D. Fuzzers can't reproduce errors.

84. What term describes an evaluation of the effectiveness of security controls performed by a third party?

    A. A security assessment

    B. A penetration test

    C. A security audit

    D. A security test

During a port scan, Ben uses nmap's default settings and sees the following results. Use this information to answer the following three questions.

```
Nmap scan report for 192.168.184.130
Host is up (1.0s latency).
Not shown: 977 closed ports
PORT     STATE SERVICE
21/tcp   open  ftp
22/tcp   open  ssh
23/tcp   open  telnet
25/tcp   open  smtp
53/tcp   open  domain
80/tcp   open  http
111/tcp  open  rpcbind
139/tcp  open  netbios-ssn
445/tcp  open  microsoft-ds
512/tcp  open  exec
513/tcp  open  login
514/tcp  open  shell
1099/tcp open  rmiregistry
1524/tcp open  ingreslock
2049/tcp open  nfs
2121/tcp open  ccproxy-ftp
3306/tcp open  mysql
5432/tcp open  postgresql
5900/tcp open  vnc
6000/tcp open  X11
6667/tcp open  irc
8009/tcp open  ajp13
8180/tcp open  unknown

Nmap done: 1 IP address (1 host up) scanned in 54.69 seconds
```

85. If Ben is conducting a penetration test, what should his next step be after receiving these results?

    A. Connect to the web server using a web browser.

    B. Connect via Telnet to test for vulnerable accounts.

C. Identify interesting ports for further scanning.

D. Use sqlmap against the open databases.

86. Based on the scan results, what OS was the system that was scanned most likely running?

   A. Windows Desktop

   B. Linux

   C. Network device

   D. Windows Server

87. Ben's manager expresses concern about the coverage of his scan. Why might his manager have this concern?

   A. Ben did not test UDP services.

   B. Ben did not discover ports outside the "well-known ports."

   C. Ben did not perform OS fingerprinting.

   D. Ben tested only a limited number of ports.

88. What technique relies on reviewing code without running it?

   A. Fuzzing

   B. Black box analysis

   C. Static analysis

   D. Gray box analysis

89. Saria needs to write a request for proposal for code review and wants to ensure that the reviewers take the business logic behind her organization's applications into account. What type of code review should she specify in the RFP?

   A. Static

   B. Fuzzing

   C. Manual

   D. Dynamic

90. What type of diagram used in application threat modeling includes malicious users as well as descriptions like mitigates and threatens?

   A. Threat trees

   B. STRIDE charts

   C. Misuse case diagrams

   D. DREAD diagrams

91. What is the first step that should occur before a penetration test is performed?

   A. Data gathering

   B. Port scanning

   C. Getting permission

   D. Planning

92. What international framework was SSAE-16 based on?

    A. ISO27001

    B. SAS70

    C. SOX

    D. ISAE 3402

93. During a penetration test of her organization, Kathleen's IPS detects a port scan that has the URG, FIN, and PSH flags set and produces an alarm. What type of scan is the penetration tester attempting?

    A. A SYN scan

    B. A TCP flag scan

    C. An Xmas scan

    D. An ACK scan

94. Nmap is an example of what type of tool?

    A. Vulnerability scanner

    B. Web application fuzzer

    C. Network design and layout

    D. Port scanner

95. What type of vulnerabilities will not be found by a vulnerability scanner?

    A. Local vulnerabilities

    B. Service vulnerabilities

    C. Zero-day vulnerabilities

    D. Vulnerabilities that require authentication

96. MITRE's CVE database provides what type of information?

    A. Current versions of software

    B. Patching information for applications

    C. Vulnerability information

    D. A list of costs versus effort required for common processes

97. A zero-day vulnerability is announced for the popular Apache web server in the middle of a workday. In Jacob's role as an information security analyst, he needs to quickly scan his network to determine what servers are vulnerable to the issue. What is Jacob's best route to quickly identify vulnerable systems?

    A. Immediately run Nessus against all of the servers to identify which systems are vulnerable.

    B. Review the CVE database to find the vulnerability information and patch information.

    C. Create a custom IDS or IPS signature.

    D. Identify affected versions and check systems for that version number using an automated scanner.

NIST Special Publication 800-115, the Technical Guide to Information Security Testing and Assessment, provides NIST's process for penetration testing. Using this image as well as your knowledge of penetration testing, answer the following questions.

98. Which of the following is not a part of the discovery phase?

    A. Hostname and IP address information gathering

    B. Service information capture

    C. Dumpster diving

    D. Privilege escalation

99. NIST specifies four attack phase steps: gaining access, escalating privileges, system browsing, and installing additional tools. Once attackers install additional tools, what phase will a penetration tester typically return to?

    A. Discovery

    B. Gaining access

    C. Escalating privileges

    D. System browsing

100. Which of the following is not a typical part of a penetration test report?

    A. A list of identified vulnerabilities

    B. All sensitive data that was gathered during the test

    C. Risk ratings for each issue discovered

    D. Mitigation guidance for issues identified

Chapter
7

Security Operations
(Domain 7)

1. Referring to the figure below, what technology is shown that provides fault tolerance for the database servers?

    A. Failover cluster

    B. UPS

    C. Tape backup

    D. Cold site

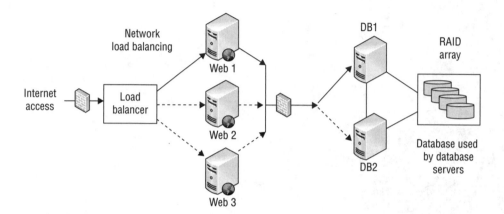

2. Joe is the security administrator for an ERP system. He is preparing to create accounts for several new employees. What default access should he give to all of the new employees as he creates the accounts?

    A. Read only

    B. Editor

    C. Administrator

    D. No access

3. Which one of the following is not a privileged administrative activity that should be automatically sent to a log of superuser actions?

    A. Purging log entries

    B. Restoring a system from backup

    C. Logging into a workstation

    D. Managing user accounts

4. Which one of the following individuals is most likely to lead a regulatory investigation?

    A. CISO

    B. CIO

    C. Government agent

    D. Private detective

5. What type of evidence consists entirely of tangible items that may be brought into a court of law?
   A. Documentary evidence
   B. Parol evidence
   C. Testimonial evidence
   D. Real evidence

6. Which one of the following trusted recovery types does not fail into a secure operating state?
   A. Manual recovery
   B. Automated recovery
   C. Automated recovery without undue loss
   D. Function recovery

7. Which one of the following might a security team use on a honeypot system to consume an attacker's time while alerting administrators?
   A. Honeynet
   B. Pseudoflaw
   C. Warning banner
   D. Darknet

8. Toni responds to the desk of a user who reports slow system activity. Upon checking outbound network connections from that system, Toni notices a large amount of social media traffic originating from the system. The user does not use social media, and when Toni checks the accounts in question, they contain strange messages that appear encrypted. What is the most likely cause of this traffic?
   A. Other users are relaying social media requests through Toni's computer.
   B. Toni's computer is part of a botnet.
   C. Toni is lying about her use of social media.
   D. Someone else is using Toni's computer when she is not present.

9. Under what virtualization model does the virtualization platform separate the network control plane from the data plane and replace complex network devices with simpler devices that simply receive instructions from the controller?
   A. Virtual machines
   B. VSAN
   C. VLAN
   D. SDN

10. Jim would like to identify compromised systems on his network that may be participating in a botnet. He plans to do this by watching for connections made to known command-and-control servers. Which one of the following techniques would be most likely to provide this information if Jim has access to a list of known servers?

    A. Netflow records

    B. IDS logs

    C. Authentication logs

    D. RFC logs

Questions 11–14 refer to the following scenario.

Gary was recently hired as the first chief information security officer (CISO) for a local government agency. The agency recently suffered a security breach and is attempting to build a new information security program. Gary would like to apply some best practices for security operations as he is designing this program.

11. As Gary decides what access permissions he should grant to each user, what principle should guide his decisions about default permissions?

    A. Separation of duties

    B. Least privilege

    C. Aggregation

    D. Separation of privileges

12. As Gary designs the program, he uses the matrix shown below. What principle of information security does this matrix most directly help enforce?

Roles/Tasks	Application Programmer	Security Administrator	Database Administrator	Database Server Administrator	Budget Analyst	Accounts Receivable	Accounts Payable	Deploy Patches	Verify Patches
Application Programmer	■	X	X	X					
Security Administrator	X	■	X	X	X	X	X	X	
Database Administrator	X	X	■	X					
Database Server Administrator	X	X	X	■					
Budget Analyst		X			■	X	X		
Accounts Receivable		X			X	■	X		
Accounts Payable		X			X	X	■		
Deploy Patches		X						■	X
Verify Patches								X	■
Potential Areas of Conflict									

    A. Segregation of duties

    B. Aggregation

    C. Two-person control

    D. Defense in depth

13. Gary is preparing to create an account for a new user and assign privileges to the HR database. What two elements of information must Gary verify before granting this access?

A. Credentials and need to know

B. Clearance and need to know

C. Password and clearance

D. Password and biometric scan

14. Gary is preparing to develop controls around access to root encryption keys and would like to apply a principle of security designed specifically for very sensitive operations. Which principle should he apply?

A. Least privilege

B. Defense in depth

C. Security through obscurity

D. Two-person control

15. When should an organization conduct a review of the privileged access that a user has to sensitive systems?

A. On a periodic basis

B. When a user leaves the organization

C. When a user changes roles

D. All of the above

16. Which one of the following terms is often used to describe a collection of unrelated patches released in a large collection?

A. Hotfix

B. Update

C. Security fix

D. Service pack

17. Which one of the following tasks is performed by a forensic disk controller?

A. Masking error conditions reported by the storage device

B. Transmitting write commands to the storage device

C. Intercepting and modifying or discarding commands sent to the storage device

D. Preventing data from being returned by a read operation sent to the device

18. Lydia is processing access control requests for her organization. She comes across a request where the user does have the required security clearance, but there is no business justification for the access. Lydia denies this request. What security principle is she following?

A. Need to know

B. Least privilege

C. Separation of duties

D. Two-person control

19. Which one of the following security tools consists of an unused network address space that may detect unauthorized activity?

   A. Honeypot

   B. Honeynet

   C. Psuedoflaw

   D. Darknet

20. Which one of the following mechanisms is not commonly seen as a deterrent to fraud?

   A. Job rotation

   B. Mandatory vacations

   C. Incident response

   D. Two-person control

21. Brian recently joined an organization that runs the majority of its services on a virtualization platform located in its own data center but also leverages an IaaS provider for hosting its web services and a SaaS email system. What term best describes the type of cloud environment this organization uses?

   A. Public cloud

   B. Dedicated cloud

   C. Private cloud

   D. Hybrid cloud

22. Tom is responding to a recent security incident and is seeking information on the approval process for a recent modification to a system's security settings. Where would he most likely find this information?

   A. Change log

   B. System log

   C. Security log

   D. Application log

23. Mark is considering replacing his organization's customer relationship management (CRM) solution with a new product that is available in the cloud. This new solution is completely managed by the vendor and Mark's company will not have to write any code or manage any physical resources. What type of cloud solution is Mark considering?

   A. IaaS

   B. CaaS

   C. PaaS

   D. SaaS

24. Which one of the following information sources is useful to security administrators seeking a list of information security vulnerabilities in applications, devices, and operating systems?

   A. OWASP

   B. Bugtraq

    C. Microsoft Security Bulletins

    D. CVE

25. Which of the following would normally be considered an example of a disaster when performing disaster recovery planning?

    I. Hacking incident

    II. Flood

    III. Fire

    IV. Terrorism

        A. II and III only

        B. I and IV only

        C. II, III, and IV only

        D. I, II, III, and IV

26. Glenda would like to conduct a disaster recovery test and is seeking a test that will allow a review of the plan with no disruption to normal information system activities and as minimal a commitment of time as possible. What type of test should she choose?

    A. Tabletop exercise

    B. Parallel test

    C. Full interruption test

    D. Checklist review

27. Which one of the following is not an example of a backup tape rotation scheme?

    A. Grandfather/Father/Son

    B. Meet in the middle

    C. Tower of Hanoi

    D. Six Cartridge Weekly

28. Helen is implementing a new security mechanism for granting employees administrative privileges in the accounting system. She designs the process so that both the employee's manager and the accounting manager must approve the request before the access is granted. What information security principle is Helen enforcing?

    A. Least privilege

    B. Two-person control

    C. Job rotation

    D. Separation of duties

29. Which one of the following is not a requirement for evidence to be admissible in court?

    A. The evidence must be relevant.

    B. The evidence must be material.

    C. The evidence must be tangible.

    D. The evidence must be competent.

30. In which cloud computing model does a customer share computing infrastructure with other customers of the cloud vendor where one customer may not know the other's identity?

    A. Public cloud

    B. Private cloud

    C. Community cloud

    D. Shared cloud

31. Which of the following organizations would be likely to have a representative on a CSIRT?

    I. Information security

    II. Legal counsel

    III. Senior management

    IV. Engineering

        A. I, III, and IV

        B. I, II, and III

        C. I, II, and IV

        D. All of the above

32. Sam is responsible for backing up his company's primary file server. He configured a backup schedule that performs full backups every Monday evening at 9 p.m. and differential backups on other days of the week at that same time. Files change according to the information shown in the figure below. How many files will be copied in Wednesday's backup?

    A. 2

    B. 3

    C. 5

    D. 6

File Modifications
Monday 8 a.m. - File 1 created
Monday 10 a.m. - File 2 created
Monday 11 a.m. - File 3 created
Monday 4 p.m. - File 1 modified
Monday 5 p.m. - File 4 created
Tuesday 8 a.m. - File 1 modified
Tuesday 9 a.m. - File 2 modified
Tuesday 10 a.m. - File 5 created
Wednesday 8 a.m. - File 3 modified
Wednesday 9 a.m. - File 6 created

33. Which one of the following security tools is not capable of generating an active response to a security event?

    A. IPS

    B. Firewall

   C. IDS

   D. Antivirus software

34. In virtualization platforms, what name is given to the module that is responsible for controlling access to physical resources by virtual resources?

   A. Guest machine

   B. SDN

   C. Kernel

   D. Hypervisor

35. What term is used to describe the default set of privileges assigned to a user when a new account is created?

   A. Aggregation

   B. Transitivity

   C. Baseline

   D. Entitlement

36. Which one of the following types of agreements is the most formal document that contains expectations about availability and other performance parameters between a service provider and a customer?

   A. Service-level agreement (SLA)

   B. Operations level agreement (OLA)

   C. Memorandum of understanding (MOU)

   D. Statement of work (SOW)

37. Which one of the following frameworks focuses on IT service management and includes topics such as change management, configuration management, and service-level agreements?

   A. ITIL

   B. PMBOK

   C. PCI DSS

   D. TOGAF

38. Richard is experiencing issues with the quality of network service on his organization's network. The primary symptom is that packets are consistently taking too long to travel from their source to their destination. What term describes the issue Richard is facing?

   A. Jitter

   B. Packet loss

   C. Interference

   D. Latency

39. Joe is an investigator with a law enforcement agency. He received a tip that a suspect is communicating sensitive information with a third party via a message board. After obtaining a warrant for the message, he obtained the contents and found that the message only contains the image shown in the figure below. If this is the sole content of the communication, what technique could the suspect have used to embed sensitive information in the message?

A. Steganography

B. Watermarking

C. Clipping

D. Sampling

40. Which one of the following is an example of a manmade disaster?

A. Hurricane

B. Flood

C. Mudslide

D. Transformer failure

41. Which of the following is not true about the (ISC)² code of ethics?

A. Adherence to the code is a condition of certification.

B. Failure to comply with the code may result in revocation of certification.

C. The code applies to all members of the information security profession.

D. Members who observe a breach of the code are required to report the possible violation.

42. Javier is verifying that only IT system administrators have the ability to log on to servers used for administrative purposes. What principle of information security is he enforcing?

   A. Need to know

   B. Least privilege

   C. Two person control

   D. Transitive trust

43. Which one of the following is not a basic preventative measure that you can take to protect your systems and applications against attack?

   A. Implement intrusion detection and prevention systems.

   B. Maintain current patch levels on all operating systems and applications.

   C. Remove unnecessary accounts and services.

   D. Conduct forensic imaging of all systems.

44. Tim is a forensic analyst who is attempting to retrieve information from a hard drive. It appears that the user attempted to erase the data, and Tim is trying to reconstruct it. What type of forensic analysis is Tim performing?

   A. Software analysis

   B. Media analysis

   C. Embedded device analysis

   D. Network analysis

45. Which one of the following is an example of a computer security incident?

   A. Completion of a backup schedule

   B. System access recorded in a log

   C. Unauthorized vulnerability scan of a file server

   D. Update of antivirus signatures

46. Which one of the following technologies would provide the most automation of an inventory control process in a cost-effective manner?

   A. IPS

   B. Wi-Fi

   C. RFID

   D. Ethernet

47. Connor's company recently experienced a denial of service attack that Connor believes came from an inside source. If true, what type of event has the company experienced?

   A. Espionage

   B. Confidentiality breach

   C. Sabotage

   D. Integrity breach

48. What type of attack is shown in the figure below?

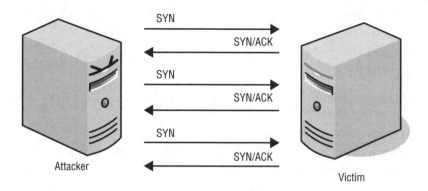

- **A.** SYN flood
- **B.** Ping flood
- **C.** Smurf
- **D.** Fraggle

49. Florian is building a disaster recovery plan for his organization and would like to determine the amount of time that a particular IT service may be down without causing serious damage to business operations. What variable is Florian calculating?

- **A.** RTO
- **B.** MTD
- **C.** RPO
- **D.** SLA

50. Which one of the following statements best describes a zero-day vulnerability?

- **A.** An attacker that is new to the world of hacking
- **B.** A database attack that places the date 00/00/0000 in data tables in an attempt to exploit flaws in business logic
- **C.** An attack previously unknown to the security community
- **D.** An attack that sets the operating system date and time to 00/00/0000 and 00:00:00

51. Which one of the following is not a canon of the (ISC)² code of ethics?

- **A.** Protect society, the common good, necessary public trust and confidence, and the infrastructure.
- **B.** Promptly report security vulnerabilities to relevant authorities.
- **C.** Act honorably, honestly, justly, responsibly, and legally.
- **D.** Provide diligent and competent service to principals.

52. During an incident investigation, investigators meet with a system administrator who may have information about the incident but is not a suspect. What type of conversation is taking place during this meeting?

A. Interview

B. Interrogation

C. Both an interview and an interrogation

D. Neither an interview nor an interrogation

53. Beth is selecting a disaster recovery facility for her organization. She would like to choose a facility that has appropriate environmental controls and power for her operations but wants to minimize costs. She is willing to accept a lengthy recovery time. What type of facility should she choose?

A. Hot site

B. Cold site

C. Warm site

D. Service bureau

54. What technique has been used to protect the intellectual property in the image shown below?

A. Steganography

B. Clipping

C. Sampling

D. Watermarking

55. You are working to evaluate the risk of flood to an area and consult the flood maps from the Federal Emergency Management Agency (FEMA). According to those maps, the area lies within a 200-year flood plain. What is the annualized rate of occurrence (ARO) of a flood in that region?

   A. 200

   B. 0.01

   C. 0.02

   D. 0.005

56. Which one of the following individuals poses the greatest risk to security in most well-defended organizations?

   A. Political activist

   B. Malicious insider

   C. Script kiddie

   D. Thrill attcker

57. Veronica is considering the implementation of a database recovery mechanism recommended by a consultant. In the recommended approach, an automated process will move database backups from the primary facility to an offsite location each night. What type of database recovery technique is the consultant describing?

   A. Remote journaling

   B. Remote mirroring

   C. Electronic vaulting

   D. Transaction logging

58. When designing an access control scheme, Hilda set up roles so that the same person does not have the ability to provision a new user account and assign superuser privileges to an account. What information security principle is Hilda following?

   A. Least privilege

   B. Separation of duties

   C. Job rotation

   D. Security through obscurity

59. Reggie recently received a letter from his company's internal auditors scheduling the kickoff meeting for an assessment of his group. Which of the following should Reggie not expect to learn during that meeting?

   A. Scope of the audit

   B. Purpose of the audit

   C. Expected timeframe

   D. Expected findings

60. Which one of the following events marks the completion of a disaster recovery process?

   A. Securing property and life safety

   B. Restoring operations in an alternate facility

   C. Restoring operations in the primary facility

   D. Standing down first responders

61. Melanie suspects that someone is using malicious software to steal computing cycles from her company. Which one of the following security tools would be in the best position to detect this type of incident?

   A. NIDS

   B. Firewall

   C. HIDS

   D. DLP

62. Brandon observes that an authorized user of a system on his network recently misused his account to exploit a system vulnerability against a shared server that allowed him to gain root access to that server. What type of attack took place?

   A. Denial of service

   B. Privilege escalation

   C. Reconaissance

   D. Brute force

63. Carla has worked for her company for 15 years and has held a variety of different positions. Each time she changed positions, she gained new privileges associated with that position, but no privileges were ever taken away. What concept describes the sets of privileges she has accumulated?

   A. Entitlement

   B. Aggregation

   C. Transitivity

   D. Isolation

64. During what phase of the incident response process do administrators take action to limit the effect or scope of an incident?

   A. Detection

   B. Response

   C. Mitigation

   D. Recovery

Questions 65–68 refer to the following scenario.

Ann is a security professional for a mid-sized business and typically handles log analysis and security monitoring tasks for her organization. One of her roles is to monitor alerts originating from the organization's intrusion detection system. The system typically generates several dozen alerts each day, and many of those alerts turn out to be false alarms after her investigation.

This morning, the intrusion detection system alerted because the network began to receive an unusually high volume of inbound traffic. Ann received this alert and began looking into the origin of the traffic.

65. At this point in the incident response process, what term best describes what has occurred in Ann's organization?

A. Security occurrence

B. Security incident

C. Security event

D. Security intrusion

66. Ann continues her investigation and realizes that the traffic generating the alert is abnormally high volumes of inbound UDP traffic on port 53. What service typically uses this port?

A. DNS

B. SSH/SCP

C. SSL/TLS

D. HTTP

67. As Ann analyzes the traffic further, she realizes that the traffic is coming from many different sources and has overwhelmed the network, preventing legitimate uses. The inbound packets are responses to queries that she does not see in outbound traffic. The responses are abnormally large for their type. What type of attack should Ann suspect?

A. Reconnaissance

B. Malicious code

C. System penetration

D. Denial of service

68. Now that Ann understands that an attack has taken place that violates her organization's security policy, what term best describes what has occurred in Ann's organization?

A. Security occurrence

B. Security incident

C. Security event

D. Security intrusion

69. Frank is seeking to introduce a hacker's laptop in court as evidence against the hacker. The laptop does contain logs that indicate the hacker committed the crime, but the court ruled that the search of the apartment that resulted in police finding the laptop was unconstitutional. What admissibility criteria prevents Frank from introducing the laptop as evidence?

A. Materiality

B. Relevance

C. Hearsay

D. Competence

70. Gordon suspects that a hacker has penetrated a system belonging to his company. The system does not contain any regulated information and Gordon wishes to conduct an investigation on behalf of his company. He has permission from his supervisor to conduct the investigation. Which of the following statements is true?

   A. Gordon is legally required to contact law enforcement before beginning the investigation.

   B. Gordon may not conduct his own investigation.

   C. Gordon's investigation may include examining the contents of hard disks, network traffic, and any other systems or information belonging to the company.

   D. Gordon may ethically perform "hack back" activities after identifying the perpetrator.

71. Which one of the following tools provides an organization with the greatest level of protection against a software vendor going out of business?

   A. Service-level agreement

   B. Escrow agreeement

   C. Mutual assistance agreement

   D. PCI DSS compliance agreement

72. Fran is considering new human resources policies for her bank that will deter fraud. She plans to implement a mandatory vacation policy. What is typically considered the shortest effective length of a mandatory vacation?

   A. Two days

   B. Four days

   C. One week

   D. One month

73. Which of the following events would constitute a security incident?

   1. An attempted network intrusion

   2. A successful database intrusion

   3. A malware infection

   4. A violation of a confidentiality policy

   5. An unsuccessful attempt to remove information from a secured area

      A. 2, 3, and 4

      B. 1, 2, and 3

      C. 4 and 5

      D. All of the above

74. Which one of the following traffic types should not be blocked by an organization's egress filtering policy?

   A. Traffic destined to a private IP address

   B. Traffic with a broadcast destination

    C. Traffic with a source address from an external network

    D. Traffic with a destination address on a external network

75. Allie is responsible for reviewing authentication logs on her organization's network. She does not have the time to review all logs, so she decides to choose only records where there have been four or more invalid authentication attempts. What technique is Allie using to reduce the size of the pool?

    A. Sampling

    B. Random selection

    C. Clipping

    D. Statistical analysis

76. You are performing an investigation into a potential bot infection on your network and wish to perform a forensic analysis of the information that passed between different systems on your network and those on the Internet. You believe that the information was likely encrypted. You are beginning your investigation after the activity concluded. What would be the best and easiest way to obtain the source of this information?

    A. Packet captures

    B. Netflow data

    C. Intrusion detection system logs

    D. Centralized authentication records

77. Which one of the following tools helps system administrators by providing a standard, secure template of configuration settings for operating systems and applications?

    A. Security guidelines

    B. Security policy

    C. Baseline configuration

    D. Running configuration

78. What type of disaster recovery test activates the alternate processing facility and uses it to conduct transactions but leaves the primary site up and running?

    A. Full interruption test

    B. Parallel test

    C. Checklist review

    D. Tabletop exercise

79. During which phase of the incident response process would an analyst receive an intrusion detection system alert and verify its accuracy?

    A. Response

    B. Mitigation

    C. Detection

    D. Reporting

80. In what virtualization model do full guest operating systems run on top of a virtualization platform?

    A. Virtual machines

    B. Software-defined networking

    C. Virtual SAN

    D. Application virtualization

81. What level of RAID is also known as disk mirroring?

    A. RAID-0

    B. RAID-1

    C. RAID-5

    D. RAID-10

82. Bruce is seeing quite a bit of suspicious activity on his network. It appears that an outside entity is attempting to connect to all of his systems using a TCP connection on port 22. What type of scanning is the outsider likely engaging in?

    A. FTP scanning

    B. Telnet scanning

    C. SSH scanning

    D. HTTP scanning

83. The historic ping of death attack is most similar to which of the following modern attack types?

    A. SQL injection

    B. Cross-site scripting

    C. Buffer overflow

    D. Brute force password cracking

84. Roger recently accepted a new position as a security professional at a company that runs its entire IT infrastructure within an IaaS environment. Which one of the following would most likely be the responsibility of Roger's firm?

    A. Configuring the network firewall

    B. Applying hypervisor updates

    C. Patching operating systems

    D. Wiping drives prior to disposal

85. What technique can application developers use to test applications in an isolated virtualized environment before allowing them on a production network?

    A. Penetration testing

    B. Sandboxing

    C. White box testing

    D. Black box testing

86. Gina is the firewall administrator for a small business and recently installed a new firewall. After seeing signs of unusually heavy network traffic, she checked the intrusion detection system, which reported that a fraggle attack was underway. What firewall configuration change can Gina make to most effectively prevent this attack?

  A. Block ICMP echo reply packets from entering the network.

  B. Block UDP port 7 and 19 traffic from entering the network.

  C. Block the source address of the attack.

  D. Block the destination address of the attack.

87. What type of trust relationship extends beyond the two domains participating in the trust to one or more of their subdomains?

  A. Transitive trust

  B. Inheritable trust

  C. Nontransitive trust

  D. Noninheritable trust

88. Renee is a software developer who writes code in Node.js for her organization. The company is considering moving from a self-hosted Node.js environment to one where Renee will run her code on application servers managed by a cloud vendor. What type of cloud solution is Renee's company considering?

  A. IaaS

  B. CaaS

  C. PaaS

  D. SaaS

89. Timber Industries recently got into a dispute with a customer. During a meeting with his account representative, the customer stood up and declared, "There is no other solution. We will have to take this matter to court." He then left the room. When does Timber Industries have an obligation to begin preserving evidence?

  A. Immediately

  B. Upon receipt of a notice of litigation from opposing attorneys

  C. Upon receipt of a subpoena

  D. Upon receipt of a court order

90. What legal protection prevents law enforcement agencies from searching a facility or electronic system without either probable cause or consent?

  A. First Amendment

  B. Fourth Amendment

  C. Fifth Amendment

  D. Fifteenth Amendment

91. Darcy is a computer security specialist who is assisting with the prosecution of a hacker. The prosecutor requests that Darcy give testimony in court about whether, in her opinion, the logs and other records in a case are indicative of a hacking attempt. What type of evidence is Darcy being asked to provide?

   A. Expert opinion

   B. Direct evidence

   C. Real evidence

   D. Documentary evidence

92. Which one of the following techniques is not commonly used to remove unwanted remnant data from magnetic tapes?

   A. Physical destruction

   B. Degaussing

   C. Overwriting

   D. Reformatting

93. What is the minimum number of disks required to implement RAID level 1?

   A. One

   B. Two

   C. Three

   D. Five

94. Jerome is conducting a forensic investigation and is reviewing database server logs to investigate query contents for evidence of SQL injection attacks. What type of analysis is he performing?

   A. Hardware analysis

   B. Software analysis

   C. Network analysis

   D. Media analysis

95. Quantum Computing regularly ships tapes of backup data across the country to a secondary facility. These tapes contain confidential information. What is the most important security control that Quantum can use to protect these tapes?

   A. Locked shipping containers

   B. Private couriers

   C. Data encryption

   D. Media rotation

96. Carolyn is concerned that users on her network may be storing sensitive information, such as Social Security numbers, on their hard drives without proper authorization or security controls. What technology can she use to best detect this activity?

   A. IDS

   B. IPS

    C. DLP

    D. TLS

97. Under what type of software license does the recipient of software have an unlimited right to copy, modify, distribute, or resell a software package?

    A. GNU Public License

    B. Freeware

    C. Open source

    D. Public domain

98. In what type of attack do attackers manage to insert themselves into a connection between a user and a legitimate website?

    A. Man-in-the-middle

    B. Fraggle

    C. Wardriving

    D. Meet-in-the-middle

99. Which one of the following techniques uses statistical methods to select a small number of records from a large pool for further analysis with the goal of choosing a set of records that is representative of the entire pool?

    A. Clipping

    B. Randomization

    C. Sampling

    D. Selection

100. Which one of the following controls protects an organization in the event of a sustained period of power loss?

    A. Redundant servers

    B. Uninterruptible power supply (UPS)

    C. Generator

    D. RAID

Chapter

8

Software Development Security (Domain 8)

1. When designing an object-oriented model, which of the following situations is ideal?

    A. High cohesion, high coupling

    B. High cohesion, low coupling

    C. Low cohesion, low coupling

    D. Low cohesion, high coupling

2. Which of the following is a common way that attackers leverage botnets?

    A. Sending spam messages

    B. Conducting brute-force attacks

    C. Scanning for vulnerable systems

    D. All of the above

3. Which one of the following statements is not true about code review?

    A. Code review should be a peer-driven process that includes multiple developers.

    B. Code review may be automated.

    C. Code review occurs during the design phase.

    D. Code reviewers may expect to review several hundred lines of code per hour.

4. Harold's company has a strong password policy that requires a minimum length of 12 characters and the use of both alphanumeric characters and symbols. What technique would be the most effective way for an attacker to compromise passwords in Harold's organization?

    A. Brute-force attack

    B. Dictionary attack

    C. Rainbow table attack

    D. Social engineering attack

5. Which process is responsible for ensuring that changes to software include acceptance testing?

    A. Request control

    B. Change control

    C. Release control

    D. Configuration control

6. Which one of the following attack types attempts to exploit the trust relationship that a user's browser has with other websites by forcing the submission of an authenticated request to a third-party site?

    A. XSS

    B. CSRF

    C. SQL injection

    D. Session hijacking

7. When using the SDLC, which one of these steps should you take before the others?

    A. Functional requirements determination

    B. Control specifications development

    C. Code review

    D. Design review

8. Jaime is a technical support analyst and is asked to visit a user whose computer is displaying the error message shown here. What state has this computer entered?

```
A problem has been detected and windows has been shut down to prevent damage
to your computer.

The problem seems to be caused by the following file: SPCMDCON.SYS

PAGE_FAULT_IN_NONPAGED_AREA

If this is the first time you've seen this stop error screen,
restart your computer. If this screen appears again, follow
these steps:

Check to make sure any new hardware or software is properly installed.
If this is a new installation, ask your hardware or software manufacturer
for any windows updates you might need.

If problems continue, disable or remove any newly installed hardware
or software. Disable BIOS memory options such as caching or shadowing.
If you need to use Safe Mode to remove or disable components, restart
your computer, press F8 to select Advanced Startup Options, and then
select Safe Mode.

Technical information:

*** STOP: 0x00000050 (0xFD3094C2,0x00000001,0xFBFE7617,0x00000000)

*** SPCMDCON.SYS - Address FBFE7617 base at FBFE5000, DateStamp 3d6dd67c
```

    A. Fail open

    B. Irrecoverable error

    C. Memory exhaustion

    D. Fail secure

9. Which one of the following is not a goal of software threat modeling?

    A. To reduce the number of security-related design flaws

    B. To reduce the number of security-related coding flaws

    C. To reduce the severity of non-security-related flaws

    D. To reduce the number of threat vectors

10. In the diagram shown here, which is an example of a method?

Account
Balance: currency = 0 Owner: string
AddFunds(deposit: currency) RemoveFunds (withdrawal: currency)

   A. Account

   B. Owner

   C. AddFunds

   D. None of the above

11. Which one of the following is considered primary storage?

   A. Memory

   B. Hard disk

   C. Flash drive

   D. DVD

12. Which one of the following testing methodologies typically works without access to source code?

   A. Dynamic testing

   B. Static testing

   C. White box testing

   D. Code review

13. What concept in object-oriented programming allows a subclass to access methods belonging to a superclass?

   A. Polymorphism

   B. Inheritance

   C. Coupling

   D. Cohesion

14. Bobby is investigating how an authorized database user is gaining access to information outside his normal clearance level. Bobby believes that the user is making use of a type of function that summarizes data. What term describes this type of function?

   A. Inference

   B. Polymorphic

   C. Aggregate

   D. Modular

15. Which one of the following controls would best protect an application against buffer overflow attacks?

    A. Encryption

    B. Input validation

    C. Firewall

    D. Intrusion prevention system

16. Berta is analyzing the logs of the Windows Firewall on one of her servers and comes across the entries shown in this figure. What type of attack do these entries indicate?

```
2016-04-21 05:14:52 DROP TCP 192.168.250.4 192.168.42.14 4004 21  - - - - - - - RECEIVE
2016-04-21 05:14:53 DROP TCP 192.168.250.4 192.168.42.14 4005 22  - - - - - - - RECEIVE
2016-04-21 05:14:54 DROP TCP 192.168.250.4 192.168.42.14 4006 23  - - - - - - - RECEIVE
2016-04-21 05:14:56 DROP TCP 192.168.250.4 192.168.42.14 4007 25  - - - - - - - RECEIVE
2016-04-21 05:14:59 DROP TCP 192.168.250.4 192.168.42.14 4008 53  - - - - - - - RECEIVE
2016-04-21 05:15:02 DROP TCP 192.168.250.4 192.168.42.14 4009 80  - - - - - - - RECEIVE
2016-04-21 05:15:03 DROP TCP 192.168.250.4 192.168.42.14 4010 110  - - - - - - - RECEIVE
2016-04-21 05:15:04 DROP TCP 192.168.250.4 192.168.42.14 4011 111  - - - -      - RECEIVE
```

    A. SQL injection

    B. Port scan

    C. Teardrop

    D. Land

Questions 17–20 refer to the following scenario:

Robert is a consultant who helps organizations create and develop mature software development practices. He prefers to use the Software Capability Maturity Model (SW-CMM) to evaluate the current and future status of organizations using both independent review and self-assessments. He is currently working with two different clients.

Acme Widgets is not very well organized with their software development practices. They have a dedicated team of developers who do "whatever it takes" to get software out the door, but they do not have any formal processes.

Beta Particles is a company with years of experience developing software using formal, documented software development processes. They use a standard model for software development but do not have quantitative management of those processes.

17. What phase of the SW-CMM should Robert report as the current status of Acme Widgets?

    A. Defined

    B. Repeatable

    C. Initial

    D. Managed

18. Robert is working with Acme Widgets on a strategy to advance their software development practices. What SW-CMM stage should be their next target milestone?

A. Defined

B. Repeatable

C. Initial

D. Managed

19. What phase of the SW-CMM should Robert report as the current status of Beta Particles?

A. Defined

B. Repeatable

C. Optimizing

D. Managed

20. Robert is also working with Beta Particles on a strategy to advance their software development practices. What SW-CMM stage should be their next target milestone?

A. Defined

B. Repeatable

C. Optimizing

D. Managed

21. Which one of the following database keys is used to enforce referential integrity relationships between tables?

A. Primary key

B. Candidate key

C. Foreign key

D. Master key

22. Which one of the following files is most likely to contain a macro virus?

A. `projections.doc`

B. `command.com`

C. `command.exe`

D. `loopmaster.exe`

23. Victor created a database table that contains information on his organization's employees. The table contains the employee's user ID, three different telephone number fields (home, work, and mobile), the employee's office location, and the employee's job title. There are 16 records in the table. What is the degree of this table?

A. 3

B. 4

C. 6

D. 16

24. Carrie is analyzing the application logs for her web-based application and comes across the following string:

`../../../../../../../../etc/passwd`

What type of attack was likely attempted against Carrie's application?

A. Command injection

B. Session hijacking

C. Directory traversal

D. Brute force

25. When should a design review take place when following an SDLC approach to software development?

A. After the code review

B. After user acceptance testing

C. After the development of functional requirements

D. After the completion of unit testing

26. Tracy is preparing to apply a patch to her organization's enterprise resource planning system. She is concerned that the patch may introduce flaws that did not exist in prior versions, so she plans to conduct a test that will compare previous responses to input with those produced by the newly patched application. What type of testing is Tracy planning?

A. Unit testing

B. Acceptance testing

C. Regression testing

D. Vulnerability testing

27. What term is used to describe the level of confidence that software is free from vulnerabilities, either intentionally designed into the software or accidentally inserted at any time during its life cycle, and that the software functions in the intended manner?

A. Validation

B. Accreditation

C. Confidence interval

D. Assurance

28. Victor recently took a new position at an online dating website and is responsible for leading a team of developers. He realized quickly that the developers are having issues with production code because they are working on different projects that result in conflicting modifications to the production code. What process should Victor invest in improving?

A. Request control

B. Release control

C. Change control

D. Configuration control

29. What type of database security issue exists when a collection of facts has a higher classification than the classification of any of those facts standing alone?

    A. Inference

    B. SQL injection

    C. Multilevel security

    D. Aggregation

30. What are the two types of covert channels that are commonly exploited by attackers seeking to surreptitiously exfiltrate information?

    A. Timing and storage

    B. Timing and firewall

    C. Storage and memory

    D. Firewall and storage

31. Vivian would like to hire a software tester to come in and evaluate a new web application from a user's perspective. Which of the following tests best simulates that perspective?

    A. Black box

    B. Gray box

    C. Blue box

    D. White box

32. Referring to the database transaction shown here, what would happen if no account exists in the Accounts table with account number 1001?

```
BEGIN TRANSACTION
UPDATE accounts
SET balance = balance + 250
WHERE account_number = 1001;

UPDATE accounts
SET balance = balance - 250
WHERE account_number = 2002;

END TRANSACTION
```

    A. The database would create a new account with this account number and give it a $250 balance.

    B. The database would ignore that command and still reduce the balance of the second account by $250.

    C. The database would roll back the transaction, ignoring the results of both commands.

    D. The database would generate an error message.

33. What type of malware is characterized by spreading from system to system under its own power by exploiting vulnerabilities that do not require user intervention?

    A. Trojan horse

    B. Virus

    C. Logic bomb

    D. Worm

34. Kim is troubleshooting an application firewall that serves as a supplement to the organization's network and host firewalls and intrusion prevention system, providing added protection against web-based attacks. The issue the organization is experiencing is that the firewall technology suffers somewhat frequent restarts that render it unavailable for 10 minutes at a time. What configuration might Kim consider to maintain availability during that period at the lowest cost to the company?

    A. High availability cluster

    B. Failover device

    C. Fail open

    D. Redundant disks

35. What type of security issue arises when an attacker can deduce a more sensitive piece of information by analyzing several pieces of information classified at a lower level?

    A. SQL injection

    B. Multilevel security

    C. Aggregation

    D. Inference

36. Greg is battling a malware outbreak in his organization. He used specialized malware analysis tools to capture samples of the malware from three different systems and noticed that the code is changing slightly from infection to infection. Greg believes that this is the reason that antivirus software is having a tough time defeating the outbreak. What type of malware should Greg suspect is responsible for this security incident?

    A. Stealth virus

    B. Polymorphic virus

    C. Multipartite virus

    D. Encrypted virus

Questions 37–40 refer to the following scenario:

Linda is reviewing posts to a user forum on her company's website and, when she browses a certain post, a message pops up in a dialog box on her screen reading "Alert." She reviews the source code for the post and finds the following code snippet:

```
<script>alert('Alert');</script>
```

37. What vulnerability definitely exists on Linda's message board?

    A. Cross-site scripting

    B. Cross-site request forgery

    C. SQL injection

    D. Improper authentication

38. What was the likely motivation of the user who posted the message on the forum containing this code?

    A. Reconnaissance

    B. Theft of sensitive information

    C. Credential stealing

    D. Social engineering

39. Linda communicates with the vendor and determines that no patch is available to correct this vulnerability. Which one of the following devices would best help her defend the application against further attack?

    A. VPN

    B. WAF

    C. DLP

    D. IDS

40. In further discussions with the vendor, Linda finds that they are willing to correct the issue but do not know how to update their software. What technique would be most effective in mitigating the vulnerability of the application to this type of attack?

    A. Bounds checking

    B. Peer review

    C. Input validation

    D. OS patching

41. What property of relational databases ensures that once a database transaction is committed to the database, it is preserved?

    A. Atomicity

    B. Consistency

    C. Durability

    D. Isolation

42. Which one of the following programming languages does not make use of a compiler?

    A. Java

    B. C++

    C. C

    D. JavaScript

43. Which one of the following is not a technique used by virus authors to hide the existence of their virus from antimalware software?

   A. Stealth

   B. Multipartitism

   C. Polymorphism

   D. Encryption

44. Which one of the following types of software testing usually occurs last and is executed against test scenarios?

   A. Unit testing

   B. Integration testing

   C. User acceptance testing

   D. System testing

45. What type of requirement specifies what software must do by describing the inputs, behavior, and outputs of software?

   A. Derived requirements

   B. Structural requirements

   C. Behavioral requirements

   D. Functional requirements

46. Which of the following organizations is widely considered as the definitive source for information on web-based attack vectors?

   A. (ISC)2

   B. ISACA

   C. OWASP

   D. Mozilla Foundation

47. In an object-oriented programming language, what does one object invoke in a second object to interact with the second object?

   A. Instance

   B. Method

   C. Behavior

   D. Class

48. Lisa is attempting to prevent her network from being targeted by IP spoofing attacks as well as preventing her network from being the source of those attacks. Which one of the following rules is NOT a best practice that Lisa can configure at her network border?

   A. Block packets with internal source addresses from entering the network.

   B. Block packets with external source addresses from leaving the network.

   C. Block packets with private IP addresses from exiting the network.

   D. Block packets with public IP addresses from entering the network.

49. What type of attack is demonstrated in the C programming language example below?

```
int myarray[10];
myarray[10] = 8;
```

    A. Mismatched data types

    B. Overflow

    C. SQL injection

    D. Covert channel

50. Which one of the following database issues occurs when one transaction writes a value to the database that overwrites a value that was needed by transactions with earlier precedence?

    A. Dirty read

    B. Incorrect summary

    C. Lost update

    D. SQL injection

51. Which one of the following is the most effective control against session hijacking attacks?

    A. TLS

    B. Complex session cookies

    C. SSL

    D. Expiring cookies frequently

52. Faith is looking at the /etc/passwd file on a system configured to use shadowed passwords. When she examines a line in the file for a user with interactive login permissions, what should she expect to see in the password field?

    A. Plaintext password

    B. Hashed password

    C. x

    D. *

53. What type of vulnerability does a TOC/TOU attack target?

    A. Lack of input validation

    B. Race condition

    C. Injection flaw

    D. Lack of encryption

54. While evaluating a potential security incident, Harry comes across a log entry from a web server request showing that a user entered the following input into a form field:

```
CARROT'&1=1;--
```

What type of attack was attempted?

- **A.** Buffer overflow
- **B.** Cross-site scripting
- **C.** SQL injection
- **D.** Cross-site request forgery

55. Which one of the following is not an effective control against SQL injection attacks?

- **A.** Escaping
- **B.** Client-side input validation
- **C.** Parameterization
- **D.** Limiting database permissions

56. What type of project management tool is shown in the figure?

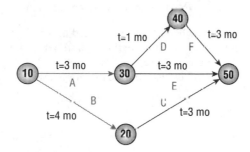

- **A.** WBS chart
- **B.** PERT chart
- **C.** Gantt chart
- **D.** Wireframe diagram

57. In what software testing technique does the evaluator retest a large number of scenarios each time that the software changes to verify that the results are consistent with a standard baseline?

- **A.** Orthogonal array testing
- **B.** Pattern testing
- **C.** Matrix testing
- **D.** Regression testing

58. Which one of the following conditions may make an application most vulnerable to a cross-site scripting (XSS) attack?

- **A.** Input validation
- **B.** Reflected input
- **C.** Unpatched server
- **D.** Promiscuous firewall rules

59. Roger is conducting a software test for a tax preparation application developed by his company. End users will access the application over the web, but Roger is conducting his test on the back end, evaluating the source code on the web server. What type of test is Roger conducting?

    A. White box

    B. Gray box

    C. Blue box

    D. Black box

60. Which of the following statements is true about heuristic-based antimalware software?

    A. It has a lower false positive rate than signature detection.

    B. It requires frequent definition updates to detect new malware.

    C. It has a higher likelihood of detecting zero-day exploits than signature detection.

    D. It monitors systems for files with content known to be viruses.

61. Martin is inspecting a system where the user reported unusual activity, including disk activity when the system is idle and abnormal CPU and network usage. He suspects that the machine is infected by a virus but scans come up clean. What malware technique might be in use here that would explain the clean scan results?

    A. File infector virus

    B. MBR virus

    C. Service injection virus

    D. Stealth virus

62. Tomas discovers a line in his application log that appears to correspond with an attempt to conduct a directory traversal attack. He believes the attack was conducted using URL encoding. The line reads:

```
%252E%252E%252F%252E%252E%252Fetc/passwd
```

What character is represented by the %252E value?

    A. .

    B. ,

    C. ;

    D. /

63. An attacker posted a message to a public discussion forum that contains an embedded malicious script that is not displayed to the user but executes on the user's system when read. What type of attack is this?

    A. Persistent XSRF

    B. Nonpersistent XSRF

    C. Persistent XSS

    D. Nonpersistent XSS

64. Which one of the following is not a principle of the Agile software development process?

   A. Welcome changing requirements, even late in the development process.

   B. Maximizing the amount of work not done is essential.

   C. Clear documentation is the primary measure of progress

   D. Build projects around motivated individuals.

65. Samantha is responsible for the development of three new code modules that will form part of a complex system that her company is developing. She is prepared to publish her code and runs a series of tests against each module to verify that it works as intended. What type of testing is Samantha conducting?

   A. Regression testing

   B. Integration testing

   C. Unit testing

   D. System testing

66. What are the two components of an expert system?

   A. Decision support system and neural network

   B. Inference engine and neural network

   C. Neural network and knowledge bank

   D. Knowledge bank and inference engine

67. Neal is working with a DynamoDB database. The database is not structured like a relational database but allows Neal to store data using a key-value store. What type of database is DynamoDB?

   A. Relational database

   B. Graph database

   C. Hierarchical database

   D. NoSQL database

68. In the transaction shown here, what would happen if the database failed in between the first and second update statement?

```
BEGIN TRANSACTION

UPDATE accounts
SET balance = balance + 250
WHERE account_number = 1001;

UPDATE accounts
SET balance = balance - 250
WHERE account_number = 2002;

COMMIT TRANSACTION
```

   A. The database would credit the first account with $250 in funds but then not reduce the balance of the second account.

    B. The database would ignore the first command and only reduce the balance of the second account by $250.

    C. The database would roll back the transaction, ignoring the results of both commands.

    D. The database would successfully execute both commands.

69. In the diagram shown here, which is an example of an attribute?

Account
Balance: currency = 0 Owner: string
AddFunds(deposit: currency) RemoveFunds (withdrawal: currency)

    A. Account

    B. Owner

    C. AddFunds

    D. None of the above

70. Which one of the following statements is true about software testing?

    A. Static testing works on runtime environments.

    B. Static testing performs code analysis.

    C. Dynamic testing uses automated tools but static testing does not.

    D. Static testing is a more important testing technique than dynamic testing.

71. David is working on developing a project schedule for a software development effort, and he comes across the chart shown here. What type of chart is this?

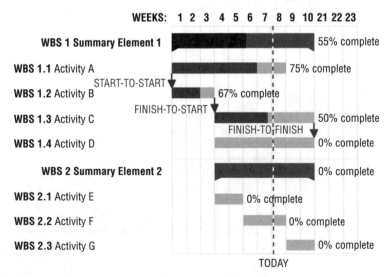

A. Work breakdown structure

B. Functional requirements

C. PERT chart

D. Gantt chart

72. Barry is a software tester who is working with a new gaming application developed by his company. He is playing the game on a smartphone to conduct his testing in an environment that best simulates a normal end user, but he is referencing the source code as he conducts his test. What type of test is Barry conducting?

A. White box

B. Black box

C. Blue box

D. Gray box

73. Miguel recently completed a penetration test of the applications that his organization uses to handle sensitive information. During his testing, he discovered a condition where an attacker can exploit a timing condition to manipulate software into allowing him to perform an unauthorized action. Which one of the following attack types fits this scenario?

A. SQL injection

B. Cross-site scripting

C. Pass the hash

D. TOC/TOU

74. In the diagram shown here, which is an example of a class?

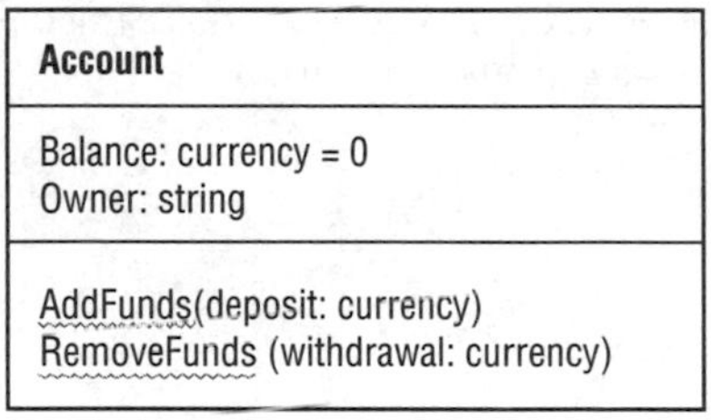

Account
Balance: currency = 0 Owner: string
AddFunds(deposit: currency) RemoveFunds (withdrawal: currency)

A. Account

B. Owner

C. AddFunds

D. None of the above

75. Gary is designing a database-driven application that relies on the use of aggregate functions. Which one of the following database concurrency issues might occur with aggregate functions and should be one of Gary's top concerns?

A. Lost updates

B. Incorrect summaries

C. SQL injections

D. Dirty reads

76. Which one of the following approaches to failure management is the most conservative from a security perspective?

A. Fail open

B. Fail mitigation

C. Fail clear

D. Fail closed

77. What software development model is shown in the figure?

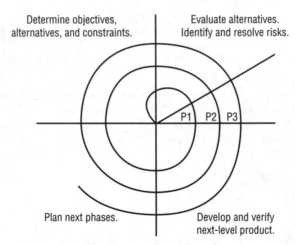

Image reprinted from *CISSP (ISC)² Certified Information Systems Security Professional Official Study Guide, 7th Edition* © John Wiley & Sons 2015, reprinted with permission.

A. Waterfall

B. Agile

C. Lean

D. Spiral

78. Which of the following database keys is used by an RDBMS to uniquely identify each row in a database table?

A. Foreign key

B. Primary key

C. Candidate key

D. Referential key

79. Which one of the following change management processes is initiated by users rather than developers?

A. Request control

B. Change control

    C. Release control

    D. Design review

80. Which one of the following techniques is an effective countermeasure against some inference attacks?

    A. Input validation

    B. Parameterization

    C. Polyinstantiation

    D. Server-side validation

81. Ursula is a government web developer who recently created a public application that offers property records. She would like to make it available for other developers to integrate into their applications. What can Ursula create to make it easiest for developers to call her code directly and integrate the output into their applications?

    A. Object model

    B. Data dictionary

    C. API

    D. Primary key

82. During what phase of the IDEAL model do organizations develop a specific plan of action for implementing change?

    A. Initiating

    B. Diagnosing

    C. Establishing

    D. Acting

83. TJ is inspecting a system where the user reported a strange error message and the inability to access files. He sees the window shown in this figure. What type of malware should TJ suspect?

    A. Service injection

    B. Encrypted virus

    C. SQL injection

    D. Ransomware

84. What function can be used to convert a string to a safe value for use in passing from a PHP application to a database?

    A. `bin2hex()`

    B. `hex2bin()`

    C. `dechex()`

    D. `hexdec()`

85. Which one of the following types of artificial intelligence attempts to use complex computations to replicate the partial function of the human mind?

    A. Decision support systems

    B. Expert systems

    C. Knowledge bank

    D. Neural networks

86. At which level of the Software Capability Maturity Model (SW-CMM) does an organization introduce basic life-cycle management processes?

    A. Initial

    B. Repeatable

    C. Defined

    D. Managed

87. Lucas runs the accounting systems for his company. The morning after a key employee was fired, systems began mysteriously losing information. Lucas suspects that the fired employee tampered with the systems prior to his departure. What type of attack should Lucas suspect?

    A. Privilege escalation

    B. SQL injection

    C. Logic bomb

    D. Remote code execution

88. Which one of the following principles would not be favored in an Agile approach to software development?

    A. Processes and tools over individuals and interactions

    B. Working software over comprehensive documentation

    C. Customer collaboration over contract negotiations

    D. Responding to change over following a plan

89. What technique do API developers most commonly use to limit access to an API to authorized individuals and applications?

   A. Encryption

   B. Input validation

   C. API keys

   D. IP filters

90. Which one of the following statements about malware is correct?

   A. Malware authors do not target Macintosh or Linux systems.

   B. The most reliable way to detect known malware is watching for unusual system activity.

   C. Signature detection is the most effective technique to combat known malware.

   D. APT attackers typically use malware designed to exploit vulnerabilities identified in security bulletins.

91. Which one of the following is the proper order of steps in the waterfall model of software development?

   A. Requirements, Design, Testing, Coding, Maintenance

   B. Requirements, Design, Coding, Testing, Maintenance

   C. Design, Requirements, Coding, Testing, Maintenance

   D. Design, Requirements, Testing, Coding, Maintenance

92. Which component of the database ACID model ensures that database transactions are an "all or nothing" affair?

   A. Atomicity

   B. Consistency

   C. Isolation

   D. Durability

93. Tom is writing a software program that calculates the sales tax for online orders placed from various jurisdictions. The application includes a user-defined field that allows the entry of the total sale amount. Tom would like to ensure that the data entered in this field is a properly formatted dollar amount. What technique should he use?

   A. Limit check

   B. Fail open

   C. Fail secure

   D. Input validation

94. Mal is eavesdropping on the unencrypted communication between the user of a website and the web server. She manages to intercept the cookies from a request header. What type of attack can she perform with these cookies?

   A. Session hijacking

   B. Cross-site scripting

    C. Cross-site request forgery

    D. SQL injection

95. Which of the following vulnerabilities might be discovered during a penetration test of a web-based application?

    A. Cross-site scripting

    B. Cross-site request forgery

    C. SQL injection

    D. All of the above

96. What approach to technology management integrates the three components of technology management shown in this illustration?

Image reprinted from *CISSP (ISC)² Certified Information Systems Security Professional Official Study Guide, 7th Edition* © John Wiley & Sons 2015, reprinted with permission.

    A. Agile

    B. Lean

    C. DevOps

    D. ITIL

97. Which one of the following tools might an attacker use to best identify vulnerabilities in a targeted system?

    A. nmap

    B. nessus

    C. ipconfig

    D. traceroute

98. Which one of the following database concurrency issues occurs when one transaction reads information that was written to a database by a second transaction that never committed?

   A. Lost update

   B. SQL injection

   C. Incorrect summary

   D. Dirty read

99. What type of virus works by altering the system boot process to redirect the BIOS to load malware before the operating system loads?

   A. File infector

   B. MBR

   C. Polymorphic

   D. Service injection

100. What type of virus is characterized by the use of two or more different propagation mechanisms to improve its likelihood of spreading between systems?

   A. Stealth virus

   B. Polymorphic virus

   C. Multipartite virus

   D. Encrypted virus

Chapter

9

Practice Test 1

1. NIST SP800-53 discusses a set of security controls as what type of security tool?

    A. A configuration list

    B. A threat management strategy

    C. A baseline

    D. The CIS standard

2. Ed has been tasked with identifying a service that will provide a low-latency, high-performance, and high-availability way to host content for his employer. What type of solution should he seek out to ensure that his employer's customers around the world can access their content quickly, easily, and reliably?

    A. A hot site

    B. A CDN

    C. Redundant servers

    D. A P2P CDN

3. Which one of the following is not a function of a forensic device controller?

    A. Preventing the modification of data on a storage device

    B. Returning data requested from the device

    C. Reporting errors sent by the device to the forensic host

    D. Blocking read commands sent to the device

4. Mike is building a fault-tolerant server and wishes to implement RAID 1. How many physical disks are required to build this solution?

    A. 1

    B. 2

    C. 3

    D. 5

5. Which Kerberos service generates a new ticket and session keys and sends them to the client?

    A. KDC

    B. TGT

    C. AS

    D. TGS

6. Communication systems that rely on start and stop flags or bits to manage data transmission are known as what type of communication?

    A. Analog

    B. Digital

    C. Synchronous

    D. Asynchronous

7. What type of motion detector uses high microwave frequency signal transmissions to identify potential intruders?

A. Infrared

B. Heat-based

C. Wave pattern

D. Capacitance

8. Susan sets up a firewall that keeps track of the status of the communication between two systems, and allows a remote system to respond to a local system after the local system starts communication. What type of firewall is Susan using?

A. A static packet filtering firewall

B. An application-level gateway firewall

C. A stateful packet inspection firewall

D. A circuit-level gateway firewall

Questions 9–11 refer to the following scenario:

Ben owns a coffeehouse and wants to provide wireless Internet service for his customers. Ben's network is simple and uses a single consumer grade wireless router and a cable modem connected via a commercial cable data contract. Using this information about Ben's network, answer the following questions.

9. How can Ben provide access control for his customers without having to provision user IDs before they connect while also gathering useful contact information for his business purposes?

A. WPA2 PSK

B. A captive portal

C. Require customers to use a publicly posted password like "BensCoffee."

D. Port security

10. Ben intends to run an open (unencrypted) wireless network. How should he connect his business devices?

A. Run WPA2 on the same SSID.

B. Set up a separate SSID using WPA2.

C. Run the open network in Enterprise mode.

D. Set up a separate wireless network using WEP.

11. After implementing the solution from the first question, Ben receives a complaint about users in his cafe hijacking other customers' web traffic, including using their usernames and passwords. How is this possible?

A. The password is shared by all users, making traffic vulnerable.

B. A malicious user has installed a Trojan on the router.

C. A user has ARP spoofed the router, making all traffic broadcast to all users.

D. Open networks are unencrypted, making traffic easily sniffable.

12. Which one of the following is not a mode of operation for the Data Encryption Standard?

    A. CBC

    B. CFB

    C. OFB

    D. AES

13. Tom is tuning his security monitoring tools in an attempt to reduce the number of alerts received by administrators without missing important security events. He decides to configure the system to only report failed login attempts if there are five failed attempts to access the same account within a one-hour period of time. What term best describes the technique that Tom is using?

    A. Thresholding

    B. Sampling

    C. Account lockout

    D. Clipping

14. Sally has been tasked with deploying an authentication, authorization, and accounting server for wireless network services in her organization, and needs to avoid using proprietary technology. What technology should she select?

    A. OAuth

    B. RADIUS

    C. XTACACS

    D. TACACS+

15. An accounting clerk for Christopher's Cheesecakes does not have access to the salary information for individual employees but wanted to know the salary of a new hire. He pulled total payroll expenses for the pay period before the new person was hired and then pulled the same expenses for the following pay period. He computed the difference between those two amounts to determine the individual's salary. What type of attack occurred?

    A. Aggregation

    B. Data diddling

    C. Inference

    D. Social engineering

16. Alice would like to have read permissions on an object and knows that Bob already has those rights and would like to give them to herself. Which one of the rules in the Take-Grant protection model would allow her to complete this operation if the relationship exists between Alice and Bob?

    A. Take rule

    B. Grant rule

    C. Create rule

    D. Remote rule

17. During a log review, Danielle discovers a series of logs that show login failures:

```
Jan 31 11:39:12 ip-10-0-0-2 sshd[29092]: Invalid user admin from remotehost
passwd=aaaaaaaa
Jan 31 11:39:20 ip-10-0-0-2 sshd[29098]: Invalid user admin from remotehost
passwd-aaaaaaab
Jan 31 11:39:23 ip-10-0-0-2 sshd[29100]: Invalid user admin from remotehost
passwd=aaaaaaac
Jan 31 11:39:31 ip-10-0-0-2 sshd[29106]: Invalid user admin from remotehost
passwd=aaaaaaad
Jan 31 20:40:53 ip-10-0-0-254 sshd[30520]: Invalid user admin from
remotehost passwd=aaaaaaad
```

What type of attack has Danielle discovered?

A. A pass-the-hash attack

B. A brute-force attack

C. A man-in-the-middle attack

D. A dictionary attack

18. What property of a relational database ensures that two executing transactions do not affect each other by storing interim results in the database?

A. Atomicity

B. Isolation

C. Consistency

D. Durability

19. Kim is the system administrator for a small business network that is experiencing security problems. She is in the office in the evening working on the problem and nobody else is there. As she is watching, she can see that systems on the other side of the office that were previously behaving normally are now exhibiting signs of infection. What type of malware is Kim likely dealing with?

A. Virus

B. Worm

C. Trojan horse

D. Logic bomb

20. Which one of the following attack types takes advantage of a vulnerability in the network fragmentation function of some operating systems?

A. Smurf

B. Land

C. Teardrop

D. Fraggle

21. Which of the following sequences properly describes the TCP 3-way handshake?

    A. SYN, ACK, SYN/ACK

    B. PSH, RST, ACK

    C. SYN, SYN/ACK, ACK

    D. SYN, RST, FIN

22. Which one of the following technologies is not normally a capability of Mobile Device Management (MDM) solutions?

    A. Remotely wiping the contents of a mobile device

    B. Assuming control of a nonregistered BYOD mobile device

    C. Enforcing the use of device encyrption

    D. Managing device backups

23. Jim is implementing an IDaaS solution for his organization. What type of technology is he putting in place?

    A. Identity as a Service

    B. Employee ID as a service

    C. Cloud based RADIUS

    D. OAuth

24. Gina recently took the CISSP certification exam and then wrote a blog post that included the text of many of the exam questions that she experienced. What aspect of the (ISC)² code of ethics is most directly violated in this situation?

    A. Advance and protect the profession.

    B. Act honorably, honestly, justly, responsibly, and legally.

    C. Protect society, the common good, necessary public trust and confidence, and the infrastructure.

    D. Provide diligent and competent service to principals.

25. Gordon is conducting a risk assessment for his organization and determined the amount of damage that flooding is expected to cause to his facilities each year. What metric has Gordon identified?

    A. ALE

    B. ARO

    C. SLE

    D. EF

26. Greg would like to implement application control technology in his organization. He would like to limit users to installing only approved software on their systems. What type of application control would be appropriate in this situation?

    A. Blacklisting

    B. Graylisting

   C. Whitelisting

   D. Bluelisting

27. Frank is the security administrator for a web server that provides news and information to people located around the world. His server received an unusually high volume of traffic that it could not handle and was forced to reject requests. Frank traced the source of the traffic back to a botnet. What type of attack took place?

   A. Denial of service

   B. Reconaissance

   C. Compromise

   D. Malicious insider

28. In the database table shown here, which column would be the best candidate for a primary key?

Company ID	Company Name	Address	City	State	ZIP Code	Telephone	Sales Rep
1	Acme Widgets	234 Main Street	Columbia	MD	21040	(301) 555-1212	14
2	Abrams Consulting	1024 Sample Street	Miami	FL	33131	(305) 555-1995	14
3	Dome Widgets	913 Sorin Street	South Bend	IN	46556	(574) 555-5863	26

   A. Company ID

   B. Company Name

   C. ZIP Code

   D. Sales Rep

29. Information about an individual like their name, Social Security number, date and place of birth, or their mother's maiden name is an example of what type of protected information?

   A. PHI

   B. Proprietary Data

   C. PII

   D. EDI

30. Bob is configuring egress filtering on his network, examining traffic destined for the Internet. His organization uses the public address range 12.8.195.0/24. Packets with which one of the following destination addresses should Bob permit to leave the network?

   A. 12.8.195.15

   B. 10.8.15.9

   C. 192.168.109.55

   D. 129.53.44.124

31. How many possible keys exist in a cryptographic algorithm that uses 6-bit encryption keys?

   A. 12

   B. 16

C. 32

D. 64

32. What problem drives the recommendation to physically destroy SSD drives to prevent data leaks when they are retired?

    A. Degaussing only partially wipes the data on SSDs.

    B. SSDs don't have data remanence.

    C. SSDs are unable to perform a zero fill.

    D. The built-in erase commands are not completely effective on some SSDs.

33. GAD Systems is concerned about the risk of hackers stealing sensitive information stored on a file server. They choose to pursue a risk mitigation strategy. Which one of the following actions would support that strategy?

    A. Encrypting the files

    B. Deleting the files

    C. Purchasing cyberliability insurance

    D. Taking no action

34. How should samples be generated when assessing account management practices?

    A. They should be generated by administrators.

    B. The last 180 days of accounts should be validated.

    C. Sampling should be conducted randomly.

    D. Sampling is not effective, and all accounts should be audited.

35. The International Safe Harbor Privacy Principles includes seven tenets. Which of the following lists correctly identifies all seven?

    A. Awareness, selection, control, security, data integrity, access, enforcement

    B. Notice, choice, onward transfer, security, data integrity, access, enforcement

    C. Privacy, security, control, notification, data integrity, access, enforcement

    D. Submission, editing, updates, confidential, integrity, security, access

36. In what type of software testing does the attacker have complete knowledge of the system implementation prior to beginning the test?

    A. Black box

    B. Blue box

    C. Gray box

    D. White box

37. What type of log is shown in the figure?

```
217.69.133.190 - - [11/Apr/2016:09:41:48 -0400] "GET /forum/viewtopic.php?f=4&t=25630 HTTP/1.1" 503 2009 "-
" "Mozilla/5.0 (compatible; Linux x86_64; Mail.RU_Bot/2.0; +http://go.mail.ru/help/robots)"
217.69.133.190 - - [11/Apr/2016:09:41:50 -0400] "GET /forum/viewtopic.php?f=7&t=28513 HTTP/1.1" 503 2009 "-
" "Mozilla/5.0 (compatible; Linux x86_64; Mail.RU_Bot/2.0; +http://go.mail.ru/help/robots)"
188.143.234.155 - - [11/Apr/2016:09:41:50 -0400] "GET /ask-a-pci-dss-question/ HTTP/1.1" 200 6501 "-"
"Mozilla/5.0 (Windows NT 6.1; WOW64; rv:41.0) Gecko/20100101 Firefox/41.0"
217.69.133.242 - - [11/Apr/2016:09:41:51 -0400] "GET /forum/viewtopic.php?f=5&t=27086 HTTP/1.1" 503 2009 "-
" "Mozilla/5.0 (compatible; Linux x86_64; Mail.RU_Bot/2.0; +http://go.mail.ru/help/robots)"
217.69.133.245 - - [11/Apr/2016:09:41:52 -0400] "GET /forum/viewtopic.php?f=6&t=28548 HTTP/1.1" 503 2009 "-
" "Mozilla/5.0 (compatible; Linux x86_64; Mail.RU_Bot/2.0; +http://go.mail.ru/help/robots)"
217.69.133.247 - - [11/Apr/2016:09:41:54 -0400] "GET /forum/viewtopic.php?f=3&t=26497 HTTP/1.1" 503 2009 "-
" "Mozilla/5.0 (compatible; Linux x86_64; Mail.RU_Bot/2.0; +http://go.mail.ru/help/robots)"
217.69.133.247 - - [11/Apr/2016:09:41:55 -0400] "GET /forum/viewtopic.php?f=3&t=27282 HTTP/1.1" 503 2009 "-
" "Mozilla/5.0 (compatible; Linux x86_64; Mail.RU_Bot/2.0; +http://go.mail.ru/help/robots)"
217.69.133.246 - - [11/Apr/2016:09:41:56 -0400] "GET /forum/viewtopic.php?f=6&t=33830 HTTP/1.1" 503 2009 "-
" "Mozilla/5.0 (compatible; Linux x86_64; Mail.RU_Bot/2.0; +http://go.mail.ru/help/robots)"
217.69.133.190 - - [11/Apr/2016:09:41:58 -0400] "GET /forum/viewtopic.php?f=6&t=26425 HTTP/1.1" 503 2009 "-
" "Mozilla/5.0 (compatible; Linux x86_64; Mail.RU_Bot/2.0; +http://go.mail.ru/help/robots)"
217.69.133.245 - - [11/Apr/2016:09:41:59 -0400] "GET /pci-dss/pci-dss-vulnerability-scanning-requirements/
HTTP/1.1" 301 - "-" "Mozilla/5.0 (compatible; Linux x86_64; Mail.RU_Bot/2.0;
+http://go.mail.ru/help/robots)"
217.69.133.247 - - [11/Apr/2016:09:42:01 -0400] "GET /forum/viewtopic.php?f=4&t=26035 HTTP/1.1" 503 2009 "-
" "Mozilla/5.0 (compatible; Linux x86_64; Mail.RU_Bot/2.0; +http://go.mail.ru/help/robots)"
217.69.133.190 - - [11/Apr/2016:09:42:02 -0400] "GET /vulnerability-scanning/pci-dss-vulnerability-
scanning-requirements/ HTTP/1.1" 200 11007 "http://www.pcidssguru.com/pci-dss/pci-dss-vulnerability-
scanning-requirements/" "Mozilla/5.0 (compatible; Linux x86_64; Mail.RU_Bot/2.0;
+http://go.mail.ru/help/robots)"
207.46.13.18 - - [11/Apr/2016:09:42:17 -0400] "GET /category/articles/page/3/ HTTP/1.1" 200 7583 "-"
"Mozilla/5.0 (compatible; bingbot/2.0; +http://www.bing.com/bingbot.htm)"
```

A. Firewall log

B. Change log

C. Application log

D. System log

38. Captain Crunch, famous phone phreak, was known for using a toy whistle to generate the 2600 Hz tones that phone trunk systems used to communicate. What is the common name for a phreaking tool with this capability?

A. A black box

B. A red box

C. A blue box

D. A white box

39. When an attacker calls an organization's help desk and persuades them to reset a password for them due to the help desk employee's trust and willingness to help, what type of attack succeeded?

A. A human Trojan

B. Social engineering

C. Phishing

D. Whaling

40. When a user attempts to log into their online account, Google sends a text message with a code to their cell phone. What type of verification is this?

A. Knowledge-based authentication

B. Dynamic knowledge–based authentication

C. Out-of-band identity proofing

D. Risk-based identity proofing

41. What mathematical operation, when substituted for the blank lines shown here, would make the equations correct?

$$8 \underline{\hspace{1cm}} 6 = 2$$
$$8 \underline{\hspace{1cm}} 4 = 0$$
$$10 \underline{\hspace{1cm}} 3 = 1$$
$$10 \underline{\hspace{1cm}} 2 = 0$$

A. MOD

B. XOR

C. NAND

D. DIV

Questions 42–44 refer to the following scenario:

The organization that Ben works for has a traditional onsite Active Directory environment that uses a manual provisioning process for each addition to their 350-employee company. As the company adopts new technologies, they are increasingly using Software as a Service applications to replace their internally developed software stack.

Ben has been tasked with designing an identity management implementation that will allow his company to use cloud services while supporting their existing systems. Using the logical diagram shown here, answer the following questions about the identity recommendations Ben should make.

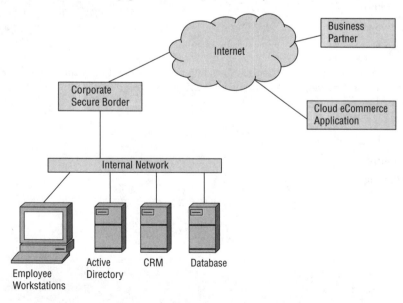

42. If availability of authentication services is the organization's biggest priority, what type of identity platform should Ben recommend?

    A. Onsite

    B. Cloud based

    C. Hybrid

    D. Outsourced

43. If Ben needs to share identity information with the business partner shown, what should he investigate?

    A. Single sign-on

    B. Multifactor authentication

    C. Federation

    D. IDaaS

44. What technology is likely to be involved when Ben's organization needs to provide authentication and authorization assertions to their e-commerce cloud partner?

    A. Active Directory

    B. SAML

    C. RADIUS

    D. SPML

45. Dave is responsible for password security in his organization and would like to strengthen the security of password files. He would like to defend his organization against the use of rainbow tables. Which one of the following techniques is specifically designed to frustrate the use of rainbow tables?

    A. Password expiration policies

    B. Salting

    C. User education

    D. Password complexity policies

46. Which one of the following is a single system designed to attract attackers because it seemingly contains sensitive information or other attractive resources?

    A. Honeynet

    B. Darknet

    C. Honeypot

    D. Pseudoflaw

47. When evaluating biometric devices, what is another term used to describe the equal error rate?

    A. FAR

    B. FRR

    C. CER

    D. ERR

48. A smart card is an example of what type of authentication factor?

   A. Type 1

   B. Type 2

   C. Type 3

   D. Type 4

49. Sean suspects that an individual in his company is smuggling out secret information despite his company's careful use of data loss prevention systems. He discovers that the suspect is posting photos, including the one shown here, to public Internet message boards. What type of technique may the individuals be using to hide messages inside this image?

   A. Watermarking

   B. VPN

   C. Steganography

   D. Covert timing channel

50. Roger is concerned that a third-party firm hired to develop code for an internal application will embed a backdoor in the code. The developer retains rights to the intellectual property and will only deliver the software in its final form. Which one of the following languages would be least susceptible to this type of attack because it would provide Roger with code that is human-readable in its final form?

   A. JavaScript

   B. C

   C. C++

   D. Java

51. Jesse is looking at the /etc/passwd file on a system configured to use shadowed passwords. What should she expect to see in the password field of this file?

   A. Plaintext passwords

   B. Encrypted passwords

C. Hashed passwords

D. x

52. Ping of Death, Smurf attacks, and ping floods all abuse features of what important protocol?

A. IGMP

B. UDP

C. IP

D. ICMP

53. What principle states that an individual should make every effort to complete his or her responsibilities in an accurate and timely manner?

A. Least privilege

B. Separation of duties

C. Due care

D. Due diligence

54. Cable modems, ISDN, and DSL are all examples of what type of technology?

A. Baseband

B. Broadband

C. Digital

D. Broadcast

55. What penetration testing technique can best help assess training and awareness issues?

A. Port scanning

B. Discovery

C. Social engineering

D. Vulnerability scanning

56. Bill implemented RAID level 5 on a server that he operates using a total of three disks. How many disks may fail without the loss of data?

A. 0

B. 1

C. 2

D. 3

57. Data is sent as bits at what layer of the OSI model?

A. Transport

B. Network

C. Data Link

D. Physical

58. Bert is considering the use of an infrastructure as a service cloud computing partner to provide virtual servers. Which one of the following would be a vendor responsibility in this scenario?

   A. Maintaining the hypervisor

   B. Managing operating system security settings

   C. Maintaining the host firewall

   D. Configuring server access control

59. When Ben records data, then replays it against his test website to verify how it performs based on a real production workload, what type of performance monitoring is he undertaking?

   A. Passive

   B. Proactive

   C. Reactive

   D. Replay

60. What technology ensures that an operating system allocates separate memory spaces used by each application on a system?

   A. Abstraction

   B. Layering

   C. Data hiding

   D. Process isolation

61. Alan is considering the use of new identification cards in his organization that will be used for physical access control. He comes across a sample card and is unsure of the technology. He breaks it open and sees the following internal construction. What type of card is this?

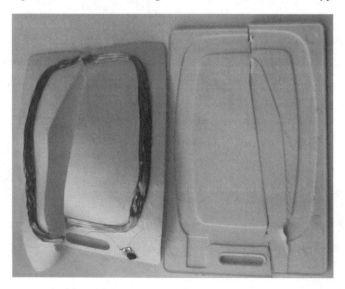

A. Smart card

B. Proximity card

C. Magnetic stripe

D. Phase-two card

62. Mark is planning a disaster recovery test for his organization. He would like to perform a live test of the disaster recovery facility but does not want to disrupt operations at the primary facility. What type of test should Mark choose?

A. Full interruption test

B. Checklist review

C. Parallel test

D. Tabletop exercise

63. Which one of the following is not a principle of the Agile approach to software development?

A. The best architecture, requirements, and designs emerge from self-organizing teams.

B. Deliver working software infrequently, with an emphasis on creating accurate code over longer timelines.

C. Welcome changing requirements, even late in the development process.

D. Simplicity is essential.

64. During a security audit, Susan discovers that the organization is using hand geometry scanners as the access control mechanism for their secure data center. What recommendation should Susan make about the use of hand geometry scanners?

A. They have a high FRR, and should be replaced.

B. A second factor should be added because they are not a good way to reliably distinguish individuals.

C. The hand geometry scanners provide appropriate security for the data center and should be considered for other high-security areas.

D. They may create accessibility concerns and an alternate biometric system should be considered.

65. Colleen is conducting a business impact assessment for her organization. What metric provides important information about the amount of time that the organization may be without a service before causing irreparable harm?

A. MTD

B. ALE

C. RPO

D. RTO

66. An attack that changes a symlink on a Linux system between the time that an account's rights to the file are verified and the file is accessed is an example of what type of attack?

    A. Unlinking

    B. Tick/tock

    C. setuid

    D. TOC/TOU

67. An authentication factor that is "something you have," and that typically includes a microprocessor and one or more certificates, is what type of authenticator?

    A. A smart card

    B. A token

    C. A Type I validator

    D. A Type III authenticator

68. What term best describes an attack that relies on stolen or falsified authentication credentials to bypass an authentication mechanism?

    A. Spoofing

    B. Replay

    C. Masquerading

    D. Modification

69. What speed is a T1 line?

    A. 64 Kbps

    B. 128 Kbps

    C. 1.544 Mbps

    D. 44.736 Mbps

70. Owen recently designed a security access control structure that prevents a single user from simultaneously holding the role required to create a new vendor and the role required to issue a check. What principle is Owen enforcing?

    A. Two-person control

    B. Least privilege

    C. Separation of duties

    D. Job rotation

71. Denise is preparing for a trial relating to a contract dispute between her company and a software vendor. The vendor is claiming that Denise made a verbal agreement that amended their written contract. What rule of evidence should Denise raise in her defense?

    A. Real evidence rule

    B. Best evidence rule

C. Parol evidence rule

D. Testimonial evidence rule

72. While Lauren is monitoring traffic on two ends of a network connection, she sees traffic that is inbound to a public IP address show up inside of the production network bound for an internal host that uses an RFC 1918 reserved address. What technology should she expect is in use at the network border?

    A. NAT

    B. VLANs

    C. S/NAT

    D. BGP

73. Which of the following statements about SSAE-16 is not true?

    A. It mandates a specific control set.

    B. It is an attestation standard.

    C. It is used for external audits.

    D. It uses a framework, including SOC 1, SOC 2, and SOC 3 reports.

74. What does a constrained user interface do?

    A. It prevents unauthorized users from logging in.

    B. It limits the data visible in an interface based on the content.

    C. It limits the access a user is provided based on what activity they are performing.

    D. It limits what users can do or see based on privileges.

75. Greg is building a disaster recovery plan for his organization and would like to determine the amount of time that it should take to restore a particular IT service after an outage. What variable is Greg calculating?

    A. MTD

    B. RTO

    C. RPO

    D. SLA

76. In object-oriented programming, what type of variable exists only once and shares the same value across all instances of an object?

    A. Instance variable

    B. Member variable

    C. Class variable

    D. Global variable

77. What type of fire extinguisher is useful against liquid-based fires?

   A. Class A

   B. Class B

   C. Class C

   D. Class D

78. The company Chris works for has notifications posted at each door reminding employees to be careful to not allow people to enter when they do. Which type of controls best describes this?

   A. Detective

   B. Physical

   C. Preventive

   D. Directive

79. Which one of the following principles is not included in the International Safe Harbor Provisions?

   A. Access

   B. Security

   C. Enforcement

   D. Nonrepudiation

80. What group is eligible to receive safe harbor protection under the terms of the Digital Millennium Copyright Act (DMCA)?

   A. Music producers

   B. Book publishers

   C. Internet service providers

   D. Banks

81. Alex is the system owner for the HR system at a major university. According to NIST SP 800-18, what action should he take when a significant change occurs in the system?

   A. He should develop a data confidentiality plan.

   B. He should update the system security plan.

   C. He should classify the data the system contains.

   D. He should select custodians to handle day-to-day operational tasks.

Questions 82–84 refer to the following scenario:

Alex has been with the university he works at for over 10 years. During that time, he has been a system administrator and a database administrator, and he has worked in the university's help desk. He is now a manager for the team that runs the university's web applications. Using the provisioning diagram shown here, answer the following questions.

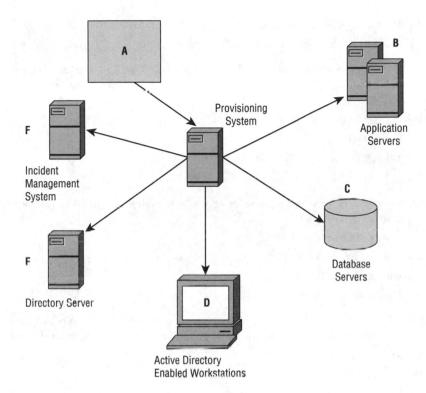

82. If Alex hires a new employee and the employee's account is provisioned after HR manually inputs information into the provisioning system based on data Alex provides via a series of forms, what type of provisioning has occurred?

A. Discretionary account provisioning

B. Workflow-based account provisioning

C. Automated account provisioning

D. Self-service account provisioning

83. Alex has access to B, C, and D. What concern should he raise to the university's identity management team?

A. The provisioning process did not give him the rights he needs.

B. He has excessive privileges.

C. Privilege creep may be taking place.

D. Logging is not properly enabled.

84. When Alex changes roles, what should occur?

A. He should be de-provisioned and a new account should be created.

B. He should have his new rights added to his existing account.

C. He should be provisioned for only the rights that match his role.

D. He should have his rights set to match those of the person he is replacing.

85. Robert is reviewing a system that has been assigned the EAL2 evaluation assurance level under the Common Criteria. What is the highest level of assurance that he may have about the system?

    A. It has been functionally tested.

    B. It has been structurally tested.

    C. It has been formally verified, designed, and tested.

    D. It has been semiformally designed and tested.

86. Adam is processing an access request for an end user. What two items should he verify before granting the access?

    A. Separation and need to know

    B. Clearance and endorsement

    C. Clearance and need to know

    D. Second factor and clearance

87. During what phase of the electronic discovery reference model does an organization ensure that potentially discoverable information is protected against alteration or deletion?

    A. Identification

    B. Preservation

    C. Collection

    D. Production

88. Nessus, OpenVAS, and SAINT are all examples of what type of tool?

    A. Port scanners

    B. Patch management suites

    C. Port mappers

    D. Vulnerability scanners

89. Harry would like to access a document owned by Sally stored on a file server. Applying the subject/object model to this scenario, who or what is the object of the resource request?

    A. Harry

    B. Sally

    C. File server

    D. Document

90. What is the process that occurs when the session layer removes the header from data sent by the transport layer?

    A. Encapsulation

    B. Packet unwrapping

    C. De-encapsulation

    D. Payloading

91. Which of the following tools is best suited to testing known exploits against a system?

    A. Nikto

    B. Ettercap

    C. Metasploit

    D. THC Hydra

92. What markup language uses the concepts of a Requesting Authority, a Provisioning Service Point, and a Provisioning Service Target to handle its core functionality?

    A. SAML

    B. SAMPL

    C. SPML

    D. XACML

93. What type of risk assessment uses tools such as the one shown here?

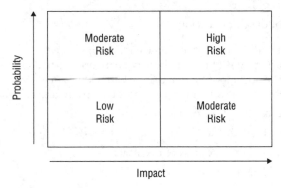

    A. Quantitative

    B. Loss expectancy

    C. Financial

    D. Qualitative

94. MAC models use three types of environments. Which of the following is not a mandatory access control design?

    A. Hierarchical

    B. Bracketed

    C. Compartmentalized

    D. Hybrid

95. What level of RAID is also called disk striping with parity?

    A. RAID 0

    B. RAID 1

    C. RAID 5

    D. RAID 10

96. Sally is wiring a gigabit Ethernet network. What cabling choices should she make to ensure she can use her network at the full 1000 Mbps she wants to provide to her users?

    A. Cat 5 and Cat 6

    B. Cat 5e and Cat 6

    C. Cat 4e and Cat 5e

    D. Cat 6 and Cat 7

97. Which one of the following is typically considered a business continuity task?

    A. Business impact assessment

    B. Alternate facility selection

    C. Activation of cold sites

    D. Restoration of data from backup

98. Robert is the network administrator for a small business and recently installed a new firewall. After seeing signs of unusually heavy network traffic, he checked his intrusion detection system, which reported that a Smurf attack was under way. What firewall configuration change can Robert make to most effectively prevent this attack.

    A. Block the source IP address of the attack.

    B. Block inbound UDP traffic.

    C. Block the destination IP address of the attack.

    D. Block inbound ICMP traffic.

99. Which one of the following types of firewalls does not have the ability to track connection status between different packets?

    A. Stateful inspection

    B. Application proxy

    C. Packet filter

    D. Next generation

100. Which of the following is used only to encrypt data in transit over a network and cannot be used to encrypt data at rest?

    A. TKIP

    B. AES

    C. 3DES

    D. RSA

101. What type of fuzzing is known as intelligent fuzzing?

    A. Zzuf

    B. Mutation

    C. Generational

    D. Code based

102. Matthew is experiencing issues with the quality of network service on his organization's network. The primary symptom is that packets are occasionally taking too long to travel from their source to their destination. The length of this delay changes for individual packets. What term describes the issue Matthew is facing?

    A. Latency

    B. Jitter

    C. Packet loss

    D. Interference

103. Which of the following multifactor authentication technologies provides both low management overhead and flexibility?

    A. Biometrics

    B. Software tokens

    C. Synchronous hardware tokens

    D. Asynchronous hardware tokens

104. What type of testing would validate support for all the web browsers that are supported by a web application?

    A. Regression testing

    B. Interface testing

    C. Fuzzing

    D. White box testing

105. Kathleen is implementing an access control system for her organization and builds the following array:

Reviewers: update files, delete files

Submitters: upload files

Editors: upload files, update files

Archivists: delete files

What type of access control system has Kathleen implemented?

    A. Role-based access control

    B. Task-based access control

    C. Rule-based access control

    D. Discretionary access control

106. Alan is installing a fire suppression system that will kick in after a fire breaks out and protect the equipment in the data center from extensive damage. What metric is Alan attempting to lower?

A. Likelihood

B. RTO

C. RPO

D. Impact

107. Alan's Wrenches recently developed a new manufacturing process for its product. They plan to use this technology internally and not share it with others. They would like it to remain protected for as long as possible. What type of intellectual property protection is best suited for this situation?

A. Patent

B. Copyright

C. Trademark

D. Trade secret

108. Ben wants to interface with the National Vulnerability Database using a standardized protocol. What option should he use to ensure that the tools he builds work with the data contained in the NVD?

A. XACML

B. SCML

C. VSML

D. SCAP

109. Which of the following is not one of the three components of the DevOps model?

A. Software development

B. Change management

C. Quality assurance

D. Operations

110. In the figure shown here, Harry's request to read the data file is blocked. Harry has a Secret security clearance and the data file has a Top Secret classification. What principle of the Bell-LaPadula model blocked this request?

A. Simple Security Property

B. Simple Integrity Property

C. *-Security Property

D. Discretionary Security Property

111. Norm is starting a new software project with a vendor that uses an SDLC approach to development. When he arrives on the job, he receives a document that has the sections shown here. What type of planning document is this?

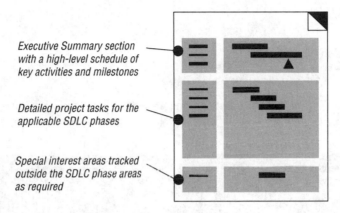

Executive Summary section with a high-level schedule of key activities and milestones

Detailed project tasks for the applicable SDLC phases

Special interest areas tracked outside the SDLC phase areas as required

A. Functional requirements

B. Work breakdown structure

C. Test analysis report

D. Project plan

112. Kolin is searching for a network security solution that will allow him to help reduce zero-day attacks while using identities to enforce a security policy on systems before they connect to the network. What type of solution should Kolin implement?

A. A firewall

B. An NAC system

C. An intrusion detection system

D. Port security

113. Gwen comes across an application that is running under a service account on a web server. The service account has full administrative rights to the server. What principle of information security does this violate?

A. Need to know

B. Separation of duties

C. Least privilege

D. Job rotation

114. Which of the following is not a type of structural coverage?

A. Statement

B. Trace

    C. Loop

    D. Data flow

115. Which of the following tools is best suited to the information gathering phase of a penetration test?

    A. Whois

    B. zzuf

    C. Nessus

    D. Metasploit

Questions 116–118 refer to the following scenario:

During a web application vulnerability scanning test, Steve runs Nikto against a web server he believes may be vulnerable to attacks. Using the Nikto output shown here, answer the following questions.

```
- Nikto v2.1.4
---------------------------------------------------------------------
+ Target IP:          192.168.184.130
+ Target Hostname:    192.168.184.130
+ Target Port:        80
+ Start Time:         2016-02-15 18:40:54
---------------------------------------------------------------------
+ Server: Apache/2.2.8 (Ubuntu) DAV/2
+ Retrieved x-powered-by header: PHP/5.2.4-2ubuntu5.10
+ Apache/2.2.8 appears to be outdated (current is at least Apache/2.2.19). Apache 1.3.
42 (final release) and 2.0.64 are also current.
+ DEBUG HTTP verb may show server debugging information. See http://msdn.microsoft.com
/en-us/library/e8z01xdh%28VS.80%29.aspx for details.
+ OSVDB-877: HTTP TRACE method is active, suggesting the host is vulnerable to XST
+ OSVDB-3233: /phpinfo.php: Contains PHP configuration information
+ OSVDB-3268: /doc/: Directory indexing found.
+ OSVDB-48: /doc/: The /doc/ directory is browsable. This may be /usr/doc.
+ OSVDB-12184: /index.php?=PHPB8B5F2A0-3C92-11d3-A3A9-4C7B08C10000: PHP reveals potent
ially sensitive information via certain HTTP requests that contain specific QUERY stri
ngs.
+ OSVDB-3092: /phpMyAdmin/changelog.php: phpMyAdmin is for managing MySQL databases, a
nd should be protected or limited to authorized hosts.
+ OSVDB-3092: /phpMyAdmin/: phpMyAdmin is for managing MySQL databases, and should be
protected or limited to authorized hosts.
+ OSVDB-3268: /test/: Directory indexing found.
+ OSVDB-3092: /test/: This might be interesting...
+ OSVDB-3268: /icons/: Directory indexing found.
+ OSVDB-3233: /icons/README: Apache default file found.
+ /phpMyAdmin/: phpMyAdmin directory found
+ 6456 items checked: 1 error(s) and 15 item(s) reported on remote host
+ End Time:            2016-02-15 18:41:36 (42 seconds)
---------------------------------------------------------------------
+ 1 host(s) tested
```

116. Why does Nikto flag the /test directory?

    A. The /test directory allows administrative access to PHP.

    B. It is used to store sensitive data.

    C. Test directories often contain scripts that can be misused.

    D. It indicates a potential compromise.

117. Why does Nikto identify directory indexing as an issue?

    A. It lists files in a directory.

    B. It may allow for XDRF.

C. Directory indexing can result in a denial-of-service attack.

D. Directory indexing is off by default, potentially indicating compromise.

118. Nikto lists OSVDB-877, noting that the system may be vulnerable to XST. What would this type of attack allow an attacker to do?

   A. Use cross-site targeting.

   B. Steal a user's cookies.

   C. Counter SQL tracing.

   D. Modify a user's TRACE information.

119. Which one of the following memory types is considered volatile memory?

   A. Flash

   B. EEPROM

   C. EPROM

   D. RAM

120. Ursula believes that many individuals in her organization are storing sensitive information on their laptops in a manner that is unsafe and potentially violates the organization's security policy. What control can she use to identify the presence of these files?

   A. Network DLP

   B. Network IPS

   C. Endpoint DLP

   D. Endpoint IPS

121. In what cloud computing model does the customer build a cloud computing environment in his or her own data center or build an environment in another data center that is for the customer's exclusive use?

   A. Public cloud

   B. Private cloud

   C. Hybrid cloud

   D. Shared cloud

122. Which one of the following technologies is designed to prevent a hard drive from becoming a single point of failure in a system?

   A. Load balancing

   B. Dual-power supplies

   C. IPS

   D. RAID

123. Alice wants to send Bob a message with the confidence that Bob will know the message was not altered while in transit. What goal of cryptography is Alice trying to achieve?

   A. Confidentiality

   B. Nonrepudiation

    C. Authentication

    D. Integrity

124. What network topology is shown here?

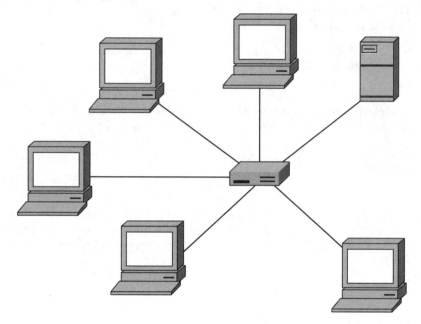

    A. A ring

    B. A bus

    C. A star

    D. A mesh

125. Monica is developing a software application that calculates an individual's body mass index for use in medical planning. She would like to include a control on the field where the physician enters an individual's weight to ensure that the weight falls within an expected range. What type of control should Monica use?

    A. Fail open

    B. Fail secure

    C. Limit check

    D. Buffer bounds

126. Fred's data role requires him to maintain system security plans and to ensure that system users and support staff get the training they need about security practices and acceptable use. What is the role that Fred is most likely to hold in the organization?

    A. Data owner

    B. System owner

   C. User

   D. Custodian

127. Sally is using IPSec's ESP component in transport mode. What important information should she be aware of about transport mode?

   A. Transport mode provides full encryption of the entire IP packet.

   B. Transport mode adds a new, unencrypted header to ensure that packets reach their destination.

   C. Transport mode does not encrypt the header of the packet.

   D. Transport mode provides no encryption, only tunnel mode provides encryption.

128. Which one of the following is not a key process area for the Repeatable phase of the Software Capability Maturity Model (SW-CMM)?

   A. Software Project Planning

   B. Software Quality Management

   C. Software Project Tracking

   D. Software Subcontract Management

129. Ben wants to provide predictive information about his organization's risk exposure in an automated way as part of an ongoing organizational risk management plan. What should he use to do this?

   A. KRIs

   B. Quantitative risk assessments

   C. KPIs

   D. Penetration tests

130. In the image shown here, what does system B send to system A at step 2 of the three-way TCP handshake?

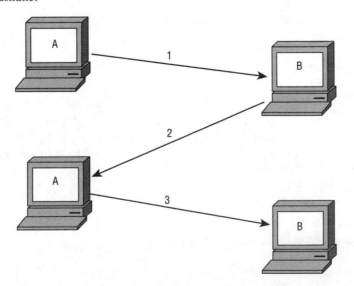

    A. SYN

    B. ACK

    C. FIN/ACK

    D. SYN/ACK

131. Chris is conducting reconnaissance on a remote target and discovers that pings are allowed through his target's border firewall. What can he learn by using ping to probe the remote network?

    A. Which systems respond to ping, a rough network topology, and potentially the location of additional firewalls

    B. A list of all of the systems behind the target's firewall

    C. The hostnames and time to live (TTL) for each pingable system, and the ICMP types allowed through the firewall

    D. Router advertisements, echo request responses, and potentially which hosts are tarpitted

132. What access management concept defines what rights or privileges a user has?

    A. Identification

    B. Accountability

    C. Authorization

    D. Authentication

133. Which one of the following is not a classification level commonly found in commercial data classification schemes?

    A. Secret

    B. Sensitive

    C. Confidential

    D. Public

134. Files, databases, computers, programs, processes, devices, and media are all examples of what?

    A. Subjects

    B. Objects

    C. File stores

    D. Users

135. Danielle is testing tax software, and part of her testing process requires her to input a variety of actual tax forms to verify that the software produces the right answers. What type of testing is Danielle performing?

    A. Use case testing

    B. Dynamic testing

    C. Fuzzing

    D. Misuse testing

136. What is the standard term of protection for a copyrighted work by a known author?

    A. 95 years

    B. 120 years

    C. 70 years from the death of the author

    D. 100 years from the death of the author

137. IP addresses like 10.10.10.10 and 172.19.24.21 are both examples of what type of IP address?

    A. Public IP addresses

    B. Prohibited IP addresses

    C. Private IP addresses

    D. Class B IP ranges

138. What flaw is a concern with preset questions for cognitive passwords?

    A. It prevents the use of tokens.

    B. The question's answer may be easy to find on the Internet.

    C. Cognitive passwords require users to think to answer the question, and not all users may be able to solve the problems presented.

    D. Cognitive passwords don't support long passwords.

139. In the Clark-Wilson integrity model, what type of process is authorized to modify constrained items?

    A. CDI

    B. UDI

    C. IVP

    D. TP

140. Kay is selecting an application management approach for her organization. Employees need the flexibility to install software on their systems, but Kay wants to prevent them from installing certain prohibited packages. What type of approach should she use?

    A. Antivirus

    B. Whitelist

    C. Blacklist

    D. Heuristic

141. Data relating to the past, present, or future payment for the provision of healthcare to an individual is what type of data per HIPAA?

    A. PCI

    B. Personal billing data

    C. PHI

    D. Personally identifiable information (PII)

142. Yagis, panel, cantennas, and parabolic antennas are all examples of what type of antenna?

    A. Omnidirectional

    B. Rubber duck or base antenna

    C. Signal boosting

    D. Directional

143. Function, statement, branch, and condition are all types of what?

    A. Penetration testing methodologies

    B. Fuzzing techniques

    C. Code coverage measures

    D. Synthetic transaction analysis

144. What is the minimum number of people who should be trained on any specific business continuity plan implementation task?

    A. 1

    B. 2

    C. 3

    D. 5

145. Cameron is responsible for backing up his company's primary file server. He configured a backup schedule that performs full backups every Monday evening at 9:00 and incremental backups on other days of the week at that same time. How many files will be copied in Wednesday's backup?

    File Modifications
    Monday 8AM - File 1 created
    Monday 10AM - File 2 created
    Monday 11AM - File 3 created
    Monday 4PM - File 1 modified
    Monday 5PM - File 4 created
    Tuesday 8AM - File 1 modified
    Tuesday 9AM - File 2 modified
    Tuesday 10AM - File 5 created
    Wednesday 8AM - File 3 modified
    Wednesday 9AM - File 6 created

    A. 1

    B. 2

    C. 5

    D. 6

146. Susan uses a span port to monitor traffic to her production website, and uses a monitoring tool to identify performance issues in real time. What type of monitoring is she conducting?

    A. Passive monitoring

    B. Active monitoring

C. Synthetic monitoring

D. Signature-based monitoring

147. The type of access granted to an object, and the actions that you can take on or with the object, are examples of what?

    A. Permissions

    B. Rights

    C. Priviliges

    D. Roles

148. Which one of the following would be considered an example of Infrastructure as a Service cloud computing?

    A. Payroll system managed by a vendor and delivered over the web

    B. Application platform managed by a vendor that runs customer code

    C. Servers provisioned by customers on a vendor-managed virtualization platform

    D. Web-based email service provided by a vendor

Questions 149–151 refer to the following scenario.

Darcy is an information security risk analyst for Roscommon Agricultural Products. She is currently trying to decide whether the company should purchase an upgraded fire suppression system for their primary data center. The data center facility has a replacement cost of $2 million.

After consulting with actuaries, data center managers, and fire subject matter experts, Darcy determined that a typical fire would likely require the replacement of all equipment inside the building but not cause significant structural damage. Together, they estimated that recovering from the fire would cost $750,000. They also determined that the company can expect a fire of this magnitude once every 50 years.

149. Based on the information in this scenario, what is the exposure factor for the effect of a fire on the Roscommon Agricultural Products data center?

    A. 7.5%

    B. 15.0%

    C. 27.5%

    D. 37.5%

150. Based on the information in this scenario, what is the annualized rate of occurrence for a fire at the Roscommon Agricultural Products data center?

    A. 0.002

    B. 0.005

    C. 0.02

    D. 0.05

151. Based on the information in this scenario, what is the annualized loss expectancy for a fire at the Roscommon Agricultural Products data center?

  A. $15,000

  B. $25,000

  C. $75,000

  D. $750,000

152. Two TCP header flags are rarely used. Which two are you unlikely to see in use in a modern network?

  A. CWR and ECE

  B. URG and FIN

  C. ECE and RST

  D. CWR and URG

153. Which one of the following is not a tape rotation strategy commonly used in disaster recovery plans?

  A. Tower of Hanoi

  B. Key Rotation

  C. Grandfather, Father, Son

  D. First In, First Out

154. Fran is a web developer who works for an online retailer. Her boss asked her to create a way that customers can easily integrate themselves with Fran's company's site. They need to be able to check inventory in real time, place orders, and check order status programatically without having to access the web page. What can Fran create to most directly facilitate this interaction?

  A. API

  B. Web scraper

  C. Data dictionary

  D. Call center

155. What type of power issue occurs when a facility experiences a momentary loss of power?

  A. Fault

  B. Blackout

  C. Sag

  D. Brownout

156. Lauren's team of system administrators each deal with hundreds of systems with varying levels of security requirements and find it difficult to handle the multitude of usernames and passwords they each have. What type of solution should she recommend to ensure that passwords are properly handled and that features like logging and password rotation occur?

    A. A credential management system

    B. A strong password policy

    C. Separation of duties

    D. Single sign-on

157. Ed's Windows system can't connect to the network and `ipconfig` shows the following:

```
Ethernet adapter Local Area Connection:

    Connection-specific DNS Suffix  . :
    Link-local IPv6 Address . . . . . : fe80::90f1:e9f0:c0f5:b0bax11
    IPv4 Address. . . . . . . . . . . : 169.254.19.21
    Subnet Mask . . . . . . . . . . . : 255.255.0.0
    Default Gateway . . . . . . . . . :
```

What has occurred on the system?

    A. The system has been assigned in invalid IP address by its DHCP server.

    B. The system has a manually assigned IP address.

    C. The system has failed to get a DHCP address and has assigned itself an address.

    D. The subnet mask is set incorrectly and the system cannot communicate with the gateway.

158. What term is commonly used to describe initial creation of a user account in the provisioning process?

    A. Enrollment

    B. Clearance verification

    C. Background checks

    D. Initialization

159. As part of her ongoing duties related to her company's security program, Susan's reports to management include the number of repeated audit findings. This information is an example of what type of useful measure?

    A. Key risk indicator

    B. Safeguard metrics

    C. Key performance indicator

    D. Audit tracking indicators

160. There is a significant conflict between the drive for profit and the security requirements that Olivia's organization has standardized. Olivia's role means that decreased usability and loss of profit due to her staff's inability to use the system is her major concern. What is the most likely role that Olivia plays in her organization?

    A. Business manager

    B. Information security analyst

    C. Data processor

    D. Mission owner

161. Tom believes that a customer of his Internet service provider has been exploiting a vulner-ability in his system to read the email messages of other customers. If true, what law did the customer most likely violate?

A. ECPA

B. CALEA

C. HITECH

D. Privacy Act

162. In the ring protection model shown here, what ring contains user programs and applications?

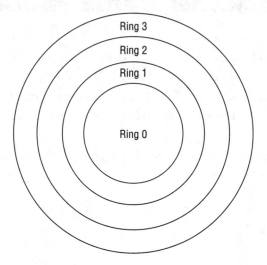

A. Ring 0

B. Ring 1

C. Ring 2

D. Ring 3

163. Metrics like the attack vector, complexity, exploit maturity, and how much user interaction is required are all found in what scoring system?

A. CVE

B. CVSS

C. CNA

D. NVD

164. In which of the following circumstances does an individual not have a reasonable expectation of privacy?

A. Placing a telephone call on your cell phone

B. Sending a letter through the U.S. mail

    C. Sending an email at work

    D. Retrieving your personal voicemail

165. During which of the following disaster recovery tests does the team sit together and discuss the response to a scenario but not actually activate any disaster recovery controls?

    A. Checklist review

    B. Full interruption test

    C. Parallel test

    D. Tabletop exercise

166. Susan wants to integrate her website to allow users to use accounts from sites like Google. What technology should she adopt?

    A. Kerberos

    B. LDAP

    C. OpenID

    D. SESAME

167. Tom is conducting a business continuity planning effort for Orange Blossoms, a fruit orchard located in Central Florida. During the assessment process, the committee determined that there is a small risk of snow in the region but that the cost of implementing controls to reduce the impact of that risk is not warranted. They elect to not take any specific action in response to the risk. What risk management strategy is Orange Blossoms pursuing?

    A. Risk mitigation

    B. Risk transference

    C. Risk avoidance

    D. Risk acceptance

168. Fred needs to run a network cable for over a kilometer. What wiring option should he choose to ensure that he doesn't encounter issues?

    A. 10Base5

    B. 10BaseT

    C. STP

    D. Fiber optic

169. Jack's organization is a multinational nonprofit that has small offices in many developing countries throughout the world. They need to implement an access control system that allows flexibility and which can work despite poor Internet connectivity at their locations. What is the best type of access control design for Jack's organization?

    A. Centralized access control

    B. Mandatory access control

    C. Decentralized access control

    D. Rule-based access control

170. What U.S. government classification label is applied to information that, if disclosed, could cause serious damage to national security, and also requires that the damage that would be caused is able to be described or identified by the classification authority?

A. Classified

B. Secret

C. Confidential

D. Top Secret

Questions 171–174 refer to the following scenario.

Mike and Renee would like to use an asymmetric cryptosystem to communicate with each other. They are located in different parts of the country but have exchanged encryption keys by using digital certificates signed by a mutually trusted certificate authority.

171. When the certificate authority (CA) created Renee's digital certificate, what key was contained within the body of the certificate?

A. Renee's public key

B. Renee's private key

C. CA's public key

D. CA's private key

172. When the certificate authority created Renee's digital certificate, what key did it use to digitally sign the completed certificate?

A. Renee's public key

B. Renee's private key

C. CA's public key

D. CA's private key

173. When Mike receives Renee's digital certificate, what key does he use to verify the authenticity of the certificate?

A. Renee's public key

B. Renee's private key

C. CA's public key

D. CA's private key

174. Mike would like to send Renee a private message using the information gained during this exchange. What key should he use to encrypt the message?

A. Renee's public key

B. Renee's private key

C. CA's public key

D. CA's private key

175. Which one of the following tools may be used to directly violate the confidentiality of communications on an unencrypted VoIP network?

   A. Nmap

   B. Nessus

   C. Wireshark

   D. Nikto

176. How does single sign-on increase security?

   A. It decreases the number of accounts required for a subject.

   B. It helps decrease the likelihood users will write down their passwords.

   C. It provides logging for each system that it is connected to.

   D. It provides better encryption for authentication data.

177. Which one of the following cryptographic algorithms supports the goal of nonrepudiation?

   A. Blowfish

   B. DES

   C. AES

   D. RSA

178. Microsoft's STRIDE threat assessment framework uses six categories for threats: Spoofing, Tampering, Repudiation, Information Disclosure, Denial of Service, and Elevation of Privilege. If a penetration tester is able to modify audit logs, what STRIDE categories best describe this issue?

   A. Tampering and information disclosure

   B. Elevation of privilege and tampering

   C. Repudiation and denial of service

   D. Repudiation and tampering

179. RIP, OSPF, and BGP are all examples of protocols associated with what type of network device?

   A. Switches

   B. Bridges

   C. Routers

   D. Gateways

180. AES-based CCMP and 802.1x replaced what security protocol that was designed as part of WPA to help fix the significant security issues found in WEP?

   A. TLS

   B. TKIP

   C. EAP

   D. PEAP

181. The government agency that Ben works at installed a new access control system. The system uses information such as Ben's identity, department, normal working hours, job category, and location to make authorization What type of access control system did Ben's employer adopt?

    A. Role-based access control

    B. Attribute-based access control

    C. Administrative access control

    D. System discretionary access control

182. The Low Orbit Ion Cannon (LOIC) attack tool used by Anonymous leverages a multitude of home PCs to attack its chosen targets. This is an example of what type of network attack?

    A. DDoS

    B. Ionization

    C. Zombie horde

    D. Teardrop

183. Andrew believes that a digital certificate belonging to his organization was compromised and would like to add it to a Certificate Revocation List. Who must add the certificate to the CRL?

    A. Andrew

    B. The root authority for the top-level domain

    C. The CA that issued the certificate

    D. The revocation authority for the top-level domain

184. Amanda is considering the implementation of a database recovery mechanism recommended by a consultant. In the recommended approach, an automated process will move records of transactions from the primary site to a backup site on an hourly basis. What type of database recovery technique is the consultant describing?

    A. Electronic vaulting

    B. Transaction logging

    C. Remote mirroring

    D. Remote journaling

185. A process on a system needs access to a file that is currently in use by another process. What state will the process scheduler place this process in until the file becomes available?

    A. Running

    B. Ready

    C. Waiting

    D. Stopped

186. Which one of the following investigation types has the loosest standards for the collection and preservation of information?

A. Civil investigation

B. Operational investigation

C. Criminal investigation

D. Regulatory investigation

187. Sue was required to sign an NDA when she took a job at her new company. Why did the company require her to sign it?

A. To protect the confidentiality of their data

B. To ensure that Sue did not delete their data

C. To prevent Sue from directly competing with them in the future

D. To require Sue to ensure the availability for their data as part of her job

188. Susan is concerned about the FAR associated with her biometric technology. What is the best method to deal with the FAR?

A. Adjust the CER.

B. Change the sensitivity of the system to lower the FRR.

C. Add a second factor.

D. Replace the biometric system.

189. What length of time does an SOC 2 report typically cover?

A. Point in time

B. 6 months

C. 12 months

D. 3 months

190. Which of the following is not a code review process?

A. Email pass-around

B. Over the shoulder

C. Pair programming

D. IDE forcing

191. Which one of the following attack types depends on precise timing?

A. TOC/TOU

B. SQL injection

C. Pass the hash

D. Cross-site scripting

192. What process adds a header and a footer to data received at each layer of the OSI model?

A. Attribution

B. Encapsulation

C. TCP wrapping

D. Data hiding

193. Attackers who compromise websites often acquire databases of hashed passwords. What technique can best protect these passwords against automated password cracking attacks that use precomputed values?

A. Using the MD5 hashing algorithm

B. Using the SHA-1 hashing algorithm

C. Salting

D. Double-hashing

194. Jim starts a new job as a system engineer and his boss provides him with a document entitled "Forensic Response Guidelines." Which one of the following statements is not true?

A. Jim must comply with the information in this document.

B. The document contains information about forensic examinations.

C. Jim should read the document thoroughly.

D. The document is likely based on industry best practices.

195. Which one of the following tools is most often used for identification purposes and is not suitable for use as an authenticator?

A. Password

B. Retinal scan

C. Username

D. Token

196. Ben needs to verify that the most recent patch for his organization's critical application did not introduce issues elsewhere. What type of testing does Ben need to conduct to ensure this?

A. Unit testing

B. White box

C. Regression testing

D. Black box

197. Tamara recently decided to purchase cyberliability insurance to cover her company's costs in the event of a data breach. What risk management strategy is she pursuing?

A. Risk acceptance

B. Risk mitigation

C. Risk transference

D. Risk avoidance

198. Which of the following is not one of the four canons of the (ISC)² code of ethics?

A. Avoid conflicts of interest that may jeopardize impartiality.

B. Protect society, the common good, necessary public trust and confidence, and the infrastructure.

C. Act honorably, honestly, justly, responsibly, and legally.

D. Provide diligent and competent service to principals.

199. Jim wants to allow a partner organization's Active Directory forest (B) to access his domain forest's (A)'s resources but doesn't want to allow users in his domain to access B's resources. He also does not want the trust to flow upward through the domain tree as it is formed. What should he do?

- **A.** Set up a two-way transitive trust.
- **B.** Set up a one-way transitive trust.
- **C.** Set up a one-way nontransitive trust.
- **D.** Set up a two-way nontransitive trust.

200. Susan's team is performing code analysis by manually reviewing the code for flaws. What type of analysis are they performing?

- **A.** Gray box
- **B.** Static
- **C.** Dynamic
- **D.** Fuzzing

201. The IP address 201.19.7.45 is what type of address?

- **A.** A public IP address
- **B.** An RFC 1918 address
- **C.** An APIPA address
- **D.** A loopback address

202. Sam is a security risk analyst for an insurance company. He is currently examining a scenario where a hacker might use a SQL injection attack to deface a web server due to a missing patch in the company's web application. In this scenario, what is the vulnerability?

- **A.** Unpatched web application
- **B.** Web defacement
- **C.** Hacker
- **D.** Operating system

203. Which one of the following categories of secure data removal techniques would include degaussing?

- **A.** Clear
- **B.** Shrink
- **C.** Purge
- **D.** Destroy

204. What type of alternate processing facility includes all of the hardware and data necessary to restore operations in a matter of minutes or seconds?

- **A.** Hot site
- **B.** Warm site
- **C.** Cold site
- **D.** Mobile site

205. What UDP port is typically used by the syslog service?

    A. 443

    B. 514

    C. 515

    D. 445

206. Fred finds a packet that his protocol analyzer shows with both PSH and URG set. What type of packet is he looking at, and what do the flags mean?

    A. A UDP packet; PSH and URG are used to indicate that the data should be sent at high speed

    B. A TCP packet; PSH and URG are used to clear the buffer and indicate that the data is urgent

    C. A TCP packet; PSH and URG are used to preset the header and indicate that the speed of the network is unregulated

    D. A UDP packet; PSH and URG are used to indicate that the UDP buffer should be cleared and that the data is urgent

207. What code review process is shown here?

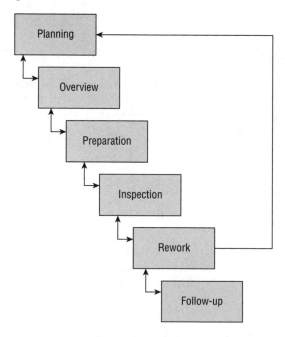

    A. Static inspection

    B. Fagan inspection

    C. Dynamic inspectiom

    D. Interface testing

208. During a log review, Karen discovers that the system she needs to gather logs from has the log setting shown here. What problem is Karen likely to encounter?

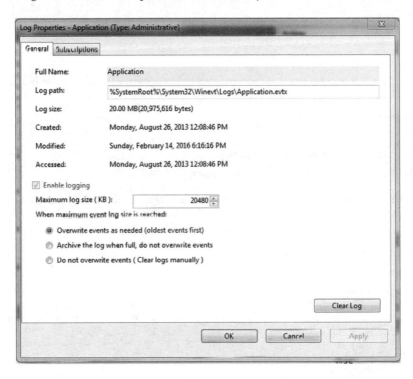

A. Too much log data will be stored on the system.

B. The system is automatically purging archived logs.

C. The logs will not contain the information needed.

D. The logs will only contain the most recent 20 MB of log data.

209. The ESP component of IPSec provides what two functions?

A. Authentication and integrity

B. Confidentiality and authentication

C. Nonrepudiation and authentication

D. Confidentiality and availability

Questions 210–212 refer to the following scenario.

Alejandro is an incident response analyst for a large corporation. He is on the midnight shift when an intrusion detection system alerts him to a potential brute-force password attack against one of the company's critical information systems. He performs an initial triage of the event before taking any additional action.

210. What stage of the incident response process is Alejandro currently conducting?
    A. Detection
    B. Response
    C. Recovery
    D. Mitigation

211. If Alejandro's initial investigation determines that a security incident is likely taking place, what should be his next step?
    A. Investigate the root cause.
    B. File a written report.
    C. Activate the incident response team.
    D. Attempt to restore the system to normal operations.

212. As the incident response progresses, during which stage should the team conduct a root cause analysis?
    A. Response
    B. Reporting
    C. Remediation
    D. Lessons Learned

213. Barry recently received a message from Melody that Melody encrypted using symmetric cryptography. What key should Barry use to decrypt the message?
    A. Barry's public key
    B. Barry's private key
    C. Melody's public key
    D. Shared secret key

214. After you do automated functional testing with 100 percent coverage of an application, what type of error is most likely to remain?
    A. Business logic errors
    B. Input validation errors
    C. Runtime errors
    D. Error handling errors

215. During what phase of the incident response process would security professionals analyze the process itself to determine whether any improvements are warranted?
    A. Lessons Learned
    B. Remediation
    C. Recovery
    D. Reporting

216. What law prevents the removal of protection mechanisms placed on a copyrighted work by the copyright holder?

A. HIPAA

B. DMCA

C. GLBA

D. ECPA

217. Linda is selecting a disaster recovery facility for her organization, and she wishes to retain independence from other organizations as much as possible. She would like to choose a facility that balances cost and recovery time, allowing activation in about one week after a disaster is declared. What type of facility should she choose?

A. Cold site

B. Warm site

C. Mutual assistance agreement

D. Hot site

218. What term is used to describe two-way communications in which only one direction can send at a time?

A. Duplex

B. Half-duplex

C. Simplex

D. Suplex

219. What type of penetration testing provides detail on the scope of a penetration test—including items like what systems would be targeted—but does not provide full visibility into the configuration or other details of the systems or networks the penetration tester must test?

A. Crystal box

B. White box

C. Black box

D. Gray box

220. Test coverage is computed using which of the following formulas?

A. Number of use cases tested/total number of use cases

B. Number of lines of code tested/total number of lines of code

C. Number of functions tested/total number of functions

D. Number of conditional branches tested/Total number of testable branches

221. TCP and UDP both operate at what layer of the OSI model?

A. Layer 2

B. Layer 3

    C. Layer 4

    D. Layer 5

222. Which one of the following goals of physical security environments occurs first in the functional order of controls?

    A. Delay

    B. Detection

    C. Deterrence

    D. Denial

223. In what type of trusted recovery process is the system able to recover without administrator intervention but the system may suffer some loss of data?

    A. Automated recovery

    B. Manual recovery

    C. Automated recovery without undue data loss

    D. Function recovery

224. Skip needs to transfer files from his PC to a remote server. What protocol should he use instead of FTP?

    A. SCP

    B. SSH

    C. HTTP

    D. Telnet

225. Ben's New York–based commercial web service collects personal information from California residents. What does the California Online Privacy Protection Act require Ben to do to be compliant?

    A. Ben must encrypt all personal data he receives.

    B. Ben must comply with the EU DPD.

    C. Ben must have a conspicuously posted privacy policy on his site.

    D. Ben must provide notice and choice for users of his website.

226. What process is used to verify that a dial-up user is connecting from the phone number they are preauthorized to use in a way that avoids spoofing?

    A. CallerID

    B. Callback

    C. CHAP

    D. PPP

227. In the diagram shown here of security boundaries within a computer system, what component's name has been replaced with XXX?

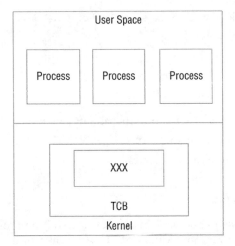

A. Reference monitor

B. Privileged core

C. Security perimeter

D. User kernel

228. Why are iris scans preferable to most other types of biometric factors?

A. Iris scanners are harder to deceive.

B. Irises don't change as much as other factors.

C. Iris scanners are cheaper than other factors.

D. Iris scans cannot be easily replicated.

229. Alex would like to ask all of his staff to sign an agreement that they will not share his organization's intellectual property with unauthorized individuals. What type of agreement should Alex ask employees to sign?

A. SLA

B. NDA

C. OLA

D. DLP

230. Matthew, Richard, and Christopher would like to exchange messages with each other using symmetric cryptography. They want to ensure that each individual can privately send a message to another individual without the third person being able to read the message. How many keys do they need?

A. 1

B. 2

C. 3

D. 6

231. Which one of the following is not an example of criminal law?

   A. Gramm Leach Bliley Act

   B. Computer Fraud and Abuse Act

   C. Electronic Communications Privacy Act

   D. Identity Theft and Assumption Deterrence Act

232. What is the best way to ensure email confidentiality in motion?

   A. Use TLS between the client and server.

   B. Use SSL between the client and server.

   C. Encrypt the email content.

   D. Use a digital signature.

233. Brenda is analyzing the web server logs after a successful compromise of her organization's web-based order processing application. She finds an entry in the log file showing that a user entered the following information as his last name when placing an order:

```
Smith';DROP TABLE orders;--
```

What type of attack was attempted?

   A. Buffer overflow

   B. Cross-site scripting

   C. Cross-site request forgery

   D. SQL injection

234. What type of policy describes how long data is kept before destruction?

   A. Classification

   B. Audit

   C. Record retention

   D. Availability

235. What is the goal of the BCP process?

   A. RTO<MTD

   B. MTD<RTO

   C. RPO<MTD

   D. MTD<RPO

236. During which phase of the incident response process would administrators design new security controls intended to prevent a recurrence of the incident?

   A. Reporting

   B. Recovery

   C. Remediation

   D. Lessons Learned

237. Bethany received an email from one of her colleagues with an unusual attachment named `smime.p7s`. She does not recognize the attachment and is unsure what to do. What is the most likely scenario?

    A. This is an encrypted email message.

    B. This is a phishing attack.

    C. This is embedded malware.

    D. This is a spoofing attack.

Questions 238–241 refer to the following scenario.

Kim is the database security administrator for Aircraft Systems, Inc. (ASI). ASI is a military contractor engaged in the design and analysis of aircraft avionics systems and regularly handles classified information on behalf of the government and other government contractors. Kim is concerned about ensuring the security of information stored in ASI databases.

Kim's database is a multilevel security database, and different ASI employees have different security clearances. The database contains information on the location of military aircraft containing ASI systems to allow ASI staff to monitor those systems.

238. Kim learned that the military is planning a classified mission that involves some ASI aircraft. She is concerned that employees not cleared for the mission may learn of it by noticing the movement of many aircraft to the region. Individual employees are cleared to know about the movement of an individual aircraft but they are not cleared to know about the overall mission. What type of attack is Kim concerned about?

    A. Aggregation

    B. SQL injection

    C. Inference

    D. Multilevel security

239. What technique can Kim employ to prevent employees not cleared for the mission from learning the true location of the aircraft?

    A. Input validation

    B. Polyinstantiation

    C. Parameterization

    D. Server-side validation

240. Kim's database uniquely identifies aircraft by using their tail number. Which one of the following terms would not necessarily accurately describe the tail number?

    A. Database field

    B. Foreign key

    C. Primary key

    D. Candidate key

241. Kim would like to create a key that enforces referential integrity for the database. What type of key does she need to create?

A. Primary key

B. Foreign key

C. Candidate key

D. Master key

242. Doug is choosing a software development life-cycle model for use in a project he is leading to develop a new business application. He has very clearly defined requirements and would like to choose an approach that places an early emphasis on developing comprehensive documentation. He does not have a need for the production of rapid prototypes or iterative improvement. Which model is most appropriate for this scenario?

A. Agile

B. Waterfall

C. Spiral

D. DevOps

243. Which individual bears the ultimate responsibility for data protection tasks?

A. Data owner

B. Data custodian

C. User

D. Auditor

244. What should be true for salts used in password hashes?

A. A single salt should be set so passwords can be de-hashed as needed.

B. A single salt should be used so the original salt can be used to check passwords against their hash.

C. Unique salts should be stored for each user.

D. Unique salts should be created every time a user logs in.

245. What type of assessment methods are associated with mechanisms and activities based on the recommendations of NIST SP800-53A, the Guide for Assessing Security Controls in Federal Information Systems?

A. Examine and interview

B. Test and assess

C. Test and interview

D. Examine and test

246. Which one of the following controls would be most effective in detecting zero-day attack attempts?

A. Signature-based intrusion detection

B. Anomaly-based intrusion detection

C. Strong patch management

D. Full-disk encryption

247. The ability to store and generate passwords, provide logging and auditing capabilities, and allow password check-in and check-out are all features of what type of system?

    A. AAA

    B. Credential management

    C. Two-factor authentication

    D. Kerberos

248. Which one of the following components should be included in an organization's emergency response guidelines?

    A. Secondary response procedures for first responders

    B. Long-term business continuity protocols

    C. Activation procedures for the organization's cold sites

    D. Contact information for ordering equipment

249. When Jim enters his organization's data center, he has to use a smart card and code to enter, and is allowed through one set of doors. The first set of doors closes, and he must then use his card again to get through a second set, which locks behind him. What type of control is this, and what is it called?

    A. A physical control; a one-way trapdoor

    B. A logical control; dual-swipe authorization

    C. A directive control; one-way access corridor

    D. A preventive access control; a mantrap

250. What security control may be used to implement a concept known as two-person control?

    A. Mandatory vacation

    B. Separation of duties

    C. Least privilege

    D. Defense in depth

Chapter 10

Practice Test 2

1. James is building a disaster recovery plan for his organization and would like to determine the amount of acceptable data loss after an outage. What variable is James determining?

    A. SLA

    B. RTO

    C. MTD

    D. RPO

2. Fred needs to deploy a network device that can connect his network to other networks while controlling traffic on his network. What type of device is Fred's best choice?

    A. A switch

    B. A bridge

    C. A gateway

    D. A router

3. Alex is preparing to solicit bids for a penetration test of his company's network and systems. He wants to maximize the effectiveness of the testing rather than the realism of the test. What type of penetration test should he require in his bidding process?

    A. Black box

    B. Crystal box

    C. Gray box

    D. Zero box

4. Application banner information is typically recorded during what penetration testing phase?

    A. Planning

    B. Attack

    C. Reporting

    D. Discovery

5. What is the default subnet mask for a Class B network?

    A. 255.0.0.0

    B. 255.255.0.0

    C. 255.254.0.0

    D. 255.255.255.0

6. Jim has been asked to individually identify devices that users are bringing to work as part of a new BYOD policy. The devices will not be joined to a central management system like Active Directory, but he still needs to uniquely identify the systems. Which of the following options will provide Jim with the best means of reliably identifying each unique device?

    A. Record the MAC address of each system.

    B. Require users to fill out a form to register each system.

    C. Scan each system using a port scanner.

    D. Use device fingerprinting via a web-based registration system.

7. David works in an organization that uses a formal data governance program. He is consulting with an employee working on a project that created an entirely new class of data and wants to work with the appropriate individual to assign a classification level to that information. Who is responsible for the assignment of information to a classification level?

    A. Data creator

    B. Data owner

    C. CISO

    D. Data custodian

8. What type of inbound packet is characteristic of a ping flood attack?

    A. ICMP echo request

    B. ICMP echo reply

    C. ICMP destination unreachable

    D. ICMP route changed

9. Gabe is concerned about the security of passwords used as a cornerstone of his organization's information security program. Which one of the following controls would provide the greatest improvement in Gabe's ability to authenticate users?

    A. More complex passwords

    B. User education against social engineering

    C. Multifactor authentication

    D. Addition of security questions based on personal knowledge

10. The separation of network infrastructure from the control layer, combined with the ability to centrally program a network design in a vendor-neutral, standards-based implementation, is an example of what important concept?

    A. MPLS, a way to replace long network addresses with shorter labels and support a wide range of protocols

    B. FCoE, a converged protocol that allows common applications over Ethernet

    C. SDN, a converged protocol that allows network virtualization

    D. CDN, a converged protocol that makes common network designs accessible

11. Susan is preparing to decommission her organization's archival DVD-ROMs that contain Top Secret data. How should she ensure that the data cannot be exposed?

    A. Degauss

    B. Zero wipe

    C. Pulverize

    D. Secure erase

12. What is the final stage of the Software Capability Maturity Model (SW-CMM)?

    A. Repeatable

    B. Defined

    C. Managed

    D. Optimizing

13. Angie is configuring egress monitoring on her network to provide added security. Which one of the following packet types should Angie allow to leave the network headed for the Internet?

    A. Packets with a source address from Angie's public IP address block

    B. Packets with a destination address from Angie's public IP address block

    C. Packets with a source address outside of Angie's address block

    D. Packets with a source address from Angie's private address block

14. Matt is conducting a penetration test against a Linux server and successfully gained access to an administrative account. He would now like to obtain the password hashes for use in a brute-force attack. Where is he likely to find the hashes, assuming the system is configured to modern security standards?

    A. /etc/passwd

    B. /etc/hash

    C. /etc/secure

    D. /etc/shadow

15. Theresa is implementing a new access control system and wants to ensure that developers do not have the ability to move code from development systems into the production environment. What information security principle is she most directly enforcing?

    A. Separation of duties

    B. Two-person control

    C. Least privilege

    D. Job rotation

16. Which one of the following tools may be used to achieve the goal of nonrepudiation?

    A. Digital signature

    B. Symmetric encryption

    C. Firewall

    D. IDS

17. In the diagram of the TCP three-way handshake here, what should system A send to system B in step 3?

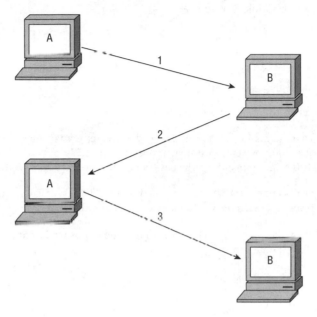

A. ACK

B. SYN

C. FIN

D. RST

18. What RADIUS alternative is commonly used for Cisco network gear and supports two-factor authentication?

A. RADIUS+

B. TACACS+

C. XTACACS

D. Kerberos

19. What two types of attacks are VoIP call managers and VoIP phones most likely to be susceptible to?

A. DoS and malware

B. Worms and Trojans

C. DoS and host OS attacks

D. Host OS attacks and buffer overflows

20. Vivian works for a chain of retail stores and would like to use a software product that restricts the software used on point-of-sale terminals to those packages on a preapproved list. What approach should Vivian use?

   A. Antivirus

   B. Heuristic

   C. Whitelist

   D. Blacklist

Questions 21–23 refer to the following scenario.

Hunter is the facilities manager for DataTech, a large data center management firm. He is evaluating the installation of a flood prevention system at one of DataTech's facilities. The facility and contents are valued at $100 million. Installing the new flood prevention system would cost $10 million.

Hunter consulted with flood experts and determined that the facility lies within a 200-year flood plain and that, if a flood occurred, it would likely cause $20 million in damage to the facility.

21. Based on the information in this scenario, what is the exposure factor for the effect of a flood on DataTech's data center?

   A. 2%

   B. 20%

   C. 100%

   D. 200%

22. Based on the information in this scenario, what is the annualized rate of occurrence for a flood at DataTech's data center?

   A. 0.002

   B. 0.005

   C. 0.02

   D. 0.05

23. Based on the information in this scenario, what is the annualized loss expectancy for a flood at DataTech's data center?

   A. $40,000

   B. $100,000

   C. $400,000

   D. $1,000,000

24. Which accounts are typically assessed during an account management assessment?

   A. A random sample

   B. Highly privileged accounts

   C. Recently generated accounts

   D. Accounts that have existed for long periods of time

25. In the shared responsibility model, under which tier of cloud computing does the customer take responsibility for securing server operating systems?

   A. IaaS

   B. PaaS

   C. SaaS

   D. TaaS

26. What type of error occurs when a valid subject using a biometric authenticator is not authenticated?

   A. A Type 1 error

   B. A Type 2 error

   C. A Type 3 error

   D. A Type 4 error

27. Jackie is creating a database that contains the Customers table, shown here. She is designing a new table to contain Orders and plans to use the Company ID in that table to uniquely identify the customer associated with each order. What role does the Company ID field play in the Orders table?

Company ID	Company Name	Address	City	State	ZIP Code	Telephone	Sales Rep
1	Acme Widgets	234 Main Street	Columbia	MD	21040	(301) 555-1212	14
2	Abrams Consulting	1024 Sample Street	Miami	FL	33131	(305) 555-1995	14
3	Dome Widgets	913 Sorin Street	South Bend	IN	46556	(574) 555-5863	26

   A. Primary key

   B. Foreign key

   C. Candidate key

   D. Referential key

28. What three types of interfaces are typically tested during software testing?

   A. Network, physical, and application interfaces

   B. APIs, UIs, and physical interfaces

   C. Network interfaces, APIs, and UIs

   D. Application, programmatic, and user interfaces

29. George is assisting a prosecutor with a case against a hacker who attempted to break into George's company's computer systems. He provides system logs to the prosecutor for use as evidence but the prosecutor insists that George testify in court about how he gathered the logs. What rule of evidence requires George's testimony?

   A. Testimonial evidence rule

   B. Parol evidence rule

   C. Best evidence rule

   D. Hearsay rule

30. Which of the following is not a valid use for key risk indicators?

    A. Provide warnings before issues occur.

    B. Provide real-time incident response information.

    C. Provide historical views of past risks.

    D. Provide insight into risk tolerance for the organization.

31. Which one of the following malware types uses built-in propagation mechanisms that exploit system vulnerabilities to spread?

    A. Trojan horse

    B. Worm

    C. Logic bomb

    D. Virus

32. Don's company is considering the use of an object-based storage system where data is placed in a vendor-managed storage environment through the use of API calls. What type of cloud computing service is in use?

    A. IaaS

    B. PaaS

    C. CaaS

    D. SaaS

33. In what model of cloud computing do two or more organizations collaborate to build a shared cloud computing environment that is for their own use?

    A. Public cloud

    B. Private cloud

    C. Community cloud

    D. Shared cloud

34. Which one of the following is not a principle of the Agile approach to software development?

    A. The most efficient method of conveying information is electronic.

    B. Working software is the primary measure of progress.

    C. Simplicity is essential.

    D. Business people and developers must work together daily.

35. Harry is concerned that accountants within his organization will use data diddling attacks to cover up fraudulent activity in accounts that they normally access. Which one of the following controls would best defend against this type of attack?

    A. Encryption

    B. Access controls

    C. Integrity verification

    D. Firewalls

36. What class of fire extinguisher is capable of fighting electrical fires?

  A. Class A

  B. Class B

  C. Class C

  D. Class D

37. What important factor differentiates Frame Relay from X.25?

  A. Frame Relay supports multiple PVCs over a single WAN carrier connection.

  B. Frame Relay is a cell switching technology instead of a packet switching technology like X.25.

  C. Frame Relay does not provide a Committed Information Rate (CIR).

  D. Frame Relay only requires a DTE on the provider side.

Using the following table, and your knowledge of the auditing process, answer questions 38–40.

	Report Content	Audience
SOC 1	Internal controls for financial reporting	Users and auditors
SOC 2	Confidentiality, integrity, availability, security, and privacy controls	Auditors, regulators, management, partners, and others under NDA
SOC 3	Confidentiality, integrity, availability, security, and privacy controls	Publicly available, often used for a website seal

38. As they prepare to migrate their data center to an Infrastructure as a Service (IaaS) provider, Susan's company wants to understand the effectiveness of their new provider's security, integrity, and availability controls. What SOC report would provide them with the most detail?

  A. SOC 1

  B. SOC 2

  C. SOC 3

  D. None of the SOC reports are suited to this, and they should request another form of report.

39. Susan wants to ensure that the audit report that her organization requested includes input from an external auditor. What type of report should she request?

  A. SOC 2, Type 1

  B. SOC 3, Type 1

  C. SOC 2, Type 2

  D. SOC 3, Type 2

40. When Susan requests a SOC2 report, they receive a SAS70 report. What issue should Susan raise?

A. SAS 70 does not include Type 2 reports, so control evaluation is only point in time.

B. SAS 70 has been replaced.

C. SAS 70 is a financial reporting standard and does not cover data centers.

D. SAS 70 only uses a 3-month period for testing.

41. What two logical network topologies can be physically implemented as a star topology?

A. A bus and a mesh

B. A ring and a mesh

C. A bus and a ring

D. It is not possible to implement other topologies as a star.

42. Bell-LaPadula is an example of what type of access control model?

A. DAC

B. RBAC

C. MAC

D. ABAC

43. Martha is the information security officer for a small college and is responsible for safeguarding the privacy of student records. What law most directly applies to her situation?

A. HIPAA

B. HITECH

C. COPPA

D. FERPA

44. What U.S. law mandates the protection of Protected Health Information?

A. FERPA

B. SAFE Act

C. GLBA

D. HIPAA

45. What type of Windows audit record describes events like an OS shutdown or a service being stopped?

A. An application log

B. A security log

C. A system log

D. A setup log

46. Susan is configuring her network devices to use syslog. What should she set to ensure that she is notified about issues but does not receive normal operational issue messages?

    A. The facility code

    B. The log priority

    C. The security level

    D. The severity level

47. What RAID level is also known as disk mirroring?

    A. RAID 0

    B. RAID 1

    C. RAID 3

    D. RAID 5

48. What type of firewall uses multiple proxy servers that filter traffic based on analysis of the protocols used for each service?

    A. A static packet filtering firewall

    B. An application-level gateway firewall

    C. A circuit-level gateway firewall

    D. A stateful inspection firewall

49. Surveys, interviews, and audits are all examples of ways to measure what important part of an organization's security posture?

    A. Code quality

    B. Service vulnerabilities

    C. Awareness

    D. Attack surface

50. Tom is the general counsel for an Internet service provider and he recently received notice of a lawsuit against the firm because of copyrighted content illegally transmitted over the provider's circuits by a customer. What law protects Tom's company in this case?

    A. Computer Fraud and Abuse Act

    B. Digital Millennium Copyright Act

    C. Wiretap Act

    D. Copyright Code

51. A Type 2 authentication factor that generates dynamic passwords based on a time- or algorithm-based system is what type of authenticator?

    A. A PIV

    B. A smart card

    C. A token

    D. A CAC

52. Fred's new employer has hired him for a position with access to their trade secrets and confidential internal data. What legal tool should they use to help protect their data if he chooses to leave to work at a competitor?

A. A stop-loss order

B. An NDA

C. An AUP

D. Encryption

53. Which one of the following computing models allows the execution of multiple processes on a single processor by having the operating system switch between them without requiring modification to the applications?

A. Multitasking

B. Multiprocessing

C. Multiprogramming

D. Multithreading

54. How many possible keys exist when using a cryptographic algorithm that has an 8-bit binary encryption key?

A. 16

B. 128

C. 256

D. 512

55. What activity is being performed when you apply security controls based on the specific needs of the IT system that they will be applied to?

A. Standardizing

B. Baselining

C. Scoping

D. Tailoring

56. During what phase of the electronic discovery process does an organization perform a rough cut of the information gathered to discard irrelevant information?

A. Preservation

B. Identification

C. Collection

D. Processing

57. Ben's job is to ensure that data is labeled with the appropriate sensitivity label. Since Ben works for the US government, he has to apply the labels Unclassified, Confidential, Secret, and Top Secret to systems and media. If Ben is asked to label a system that handles Secret, Confidential, and Unclassified information, how should he label it?

A. Mixed classification

B. Confidential

C. Top Secret

D. Secret

58. Susan has discovered that the smart card-based locks used to keep the facility she works at secure are not effective because staff members are propping the doors open. She places signs on the doors reminding staff that leaving the door open creates a security issue, and adds alarms that will sound if the doors are left open for more than five minutes. What type of controls has she put into place?

A. Physical

B. Administrative

C. Compensation

D. Recovery

59. Ben is concerned about password cracking attacks against his system. He would like to implement controls that prevent an attacker who has obtained those hashes from easily cracking them. What two controls would best meet this objective?

A. Longer passwords and salting

B. Over-the-wire encryption and use of SHA1 instead of MD5

C. Salting and use of MD5

D. Using shadow passwords and salting

60. Which group is best suited to evaluate and report on the effectiveness of administrative controls an organization has put in place to a third party?

A. Internal auditors

B. Penetration testers

C. External auditors

D. Employees who design, implement, and monitor the controls

61. Renee is using encryption to safeguard sensitive business secrets when in transit over the Internet. What risk metric is she attempting to lower?

A. Likelihood

B. RTO

C. MTO

D. Impact

62. As part of hiring a new employee, Kathleen's identity management team creates a new user object and ensures that the user object is available in the directories and systems where it is needed. What is this process called?

A. Registration

B. Provisioning

C. Population

D. Authenticator loading

63. Ricky would like to access a remote file server through a VPN connection. He begins this process by connecting to the VPN and attempting to log in. Applying the subject/object model to this request, what is the subject of Ricky's login attempt?

    A. Ricky

    B. VPN

    C. Remote file server

    D. Files contained on the remote server

64. Alice is designing a cryptosystem for use by six users and would like to use a symmetric encryption algorithm. She wants any two users to be able to communicate with each other without worrying about eavesdropping by a third user. How many symmetric encryption keys will she need to generate?

    A. 6

    B. 12

    C. 15

    D. 30

65. Which one of the following intellectual property protection mechanisms has the shortest duration?

    A. Copyright

    B. Patent

    C. Trademark

    D. Trade secret

66. Gordon is developing a business continuity plan for a manufacturing company's IT operations. The company is located in North Dakota and they are currently evaluating the risk of earthquake. They choose to pursue a risk acceptance strategy. Which one of the following actions is consistent with that strategy?

    A. Purchasing earthquake insurance

    B. Relocating the data center to a safer area

    C. Documenting the decision-making process

    D. Reengineering the facility to withstand the shock of an earthquake

67. Carol would like to implement a control that protects her organization from the momentary loss of power to the data center. Which control is most appropriate for her needs?

    A. Redundant servers

    B. RAID

    C. UPS

    D. Generator

68. Ben has encountered problems with users in his organization reusing passwords, despite a requirement that they change passwords every 30 days. What type of password setting should Ben employ to help prevent this issue?

A. Longer minimum age

B. Increased password complexity

C. Implement password history

D. Implement password length requirements

69. Chris is conducting a risk assessment for his organization and determined the amount of damage that a single flood could be expected to cause to his facilities. What metric has Chris identified?

A. ALE

B. SLE

C. ARO

D. AV

70. The removal of a hard drive from a PC before it is retired and sold as surplus is an example of what type of action?

A. Purging

B. Sanitization

C. Degaussing

D. Destruction

71. During which phase of the incident response process would an organization determine whether it is required to notify law enforcement officials or other regulators of the incident?

A. Detection

B. Recovery

C. Remediation

D. Reporting

72. What OASIS standard markup language is used to generate provisioning requests both within organizations and with third parties?

A. SAML

B. SPML

C. XACML

D. SOA

73. Michelle is in charge of her organization's mobile device management efforts, and handles lost and stolen devices. Which of the following recommendations will provide the most assurance to her organization that data will not be lost if a device is stolen?

A. Mandatory passcodes and application management

B. Full device encryption and mandatory passcodes

    C. Remote wipe and GPS tracking

    D. Enabling GPS tracking and full device encryption

74. Susan's SMTP server does not authenticate senders before accepting and relaying email. What is this security configuration issue known as?

    A. An email gateway

    B. An SMTP relay

    C. An X.400-compliant gateway

    D. An open relay

The large business that Jack works for has been using noncentralized logging for years. They have recently started to implement centralized logging, however, and as they reviewed logs they discovered a breach that appeared to have involved a malicious insider. Use this scenario to answer questions 75 through 77 about logging environments.

75. When the breach was discovered and the logs were reviewed, it was discovered that the attacker had purged the logs on the system that they compromised. How can this be prevented in the future?

    A. Encrypt local logs

    B. Require administrative access to change logs

    C. Enable log rotation

    D. Send logs to a bastion host

76. How can Jack detect issues like this using his organization's new centralized logging?

    A. Deploy and use an IDS

    B. Send logs to a central logging server

    C. Deploy and use a SIEM

    D. Use syslog

77. How can Jack best ensure accountability for actions taken on systems in his environment?

    A. Log review and require digital signatures for each log.

    B. Require authentication for all actions taken and capture logs centrally.

    C. Log the use of administrative credentials and encrypt log data in transit.

    D. Require authorization and capture logs centrally.

78. Ed's organization has 5 IP addresses allocated to them by their ISP, but needs to connect over 100 computers and network devices to the Internet. What technology can he use to connect his entire network via the limited set of IP addresses he can use?

    A. IPSec

    B. PAT

    C. SDN

    D. IPX

79. What type of attack would the following precautions help prevent?

- Requesting proof of identity
- Requiring callback authorizations on voice-only requests
- Not changing passwords via voice communications

A. DoS attacks

B. Worms

C. Social engineering

D. Shoulder surfing

80. Fred's organization needs to use a non-IP protocol on their VPN. Which of the common VPN protocols should he select to natively handle non-IP protocols?

A. PPTP

B. L2F

C. L2TP

D. IPSec

81. Residual data is another term for what type of data left after attempts have been made to erase it?

A. Leftover data

B. MBR

C. Bitrot

D. Remnant data

82. Which one of the following disaster recovery test types involves the actual activation of the disaster recovery facility?

A. Simulation test

B. Tabletop exercise

C. Parallel test

D. Checklist review

83. What access control system lets owners decide who has access to the objects they own?

A. Role-based access control

B. Task-based access control

C. Discretionary access control

D. Rule-based access control

84. Using a trusted channel and link encryption are both ways to prevent what type of access control attack?

A. Brute force

B. Spoofed login screens

    C. Man-in-the-middle attacks

    D. Dictionary attacks

85. Which one of the following is not one of the canons of the (ISC)² Code of Ethics?

    A. Protect society, the common good, necessary public trust and confidence, and the infrastructure.

    B. Act honorably, honestly, justly, responsibly, and legally.

    C. Provide diligent and competent service to principals.

    D. Maintain competent records of all investigations and assessments.

86. Which one of the following components should be included in an organization's emergency response guidelines?

    A. Immediate response procedures

    B. Long-term business continuity protocols

    C. Activation procedures for the organization's cold sites

    D. Contact information for ordering equipment

87. Ben is working on integrating a federated identity management system and needs to exchange authentication and authorization information for browser-based single sign-on. What technology is his best option?

    A. HTML

    B. XACML

    C. SAML

    D. SPML

88. What is the minimum interval at which an organization should conduct business continuity plan refresher training for those with specific business continuity roles?

    A. Weekly

    B. Monthly

    C. Semi-annually

    D. Annually

89. What is the minimum number of cryptographic keys necessary to achieve strong security when using the 3DES algorithm?

    A. 1

    B. 2

    C. 3

    D. 4

90. What type of address is 10.11.45.170?

    A. A public IP address

    B. An RFC 1918 address

   C. An APIPA address

   D. A loopback address

91. Lauren wants to monitor her LDAP servers to identify what types of queries are causing problems. What type of monitoring should she use if she wants to be able to use the production servers and actual traffic for her testing?

   A. Active

   B. Real-time

   C. Passive

   D. Replay

92. Steve is developing an input validation routine that will protect the database supporting a web application from SQL injection attack. Where should Steve place the input validation code?

   A. JavaScript embedded in the web pages

   B. Backend code on the web server

   C. Stored procedure on the database

   D. Code on the user's web browser

93. Ben is selecting an encryption algorithm for use in an organization with 10,000 employees. He must facilitate communication between any two employees within the organization. Which one of the following algorithms would allow him to meet this goal with the least time dedicated to key management?

   A. RSA

   B. IDEA

   C. 3DES

   D. Skipjack

94. Grace is considering the use of new identification cards in her organization that will be used for physical access control. She comes across the sample card shown here and is unsure of the technology it uses. What type of card is this?

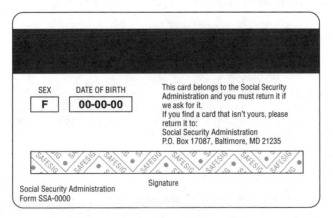

    A. Smart card

    B. Phase-two card

    C. Proximity card

    D. Magnetic stripe card

95. What type of log file is shown in this figure?

```
2015-08-09 16:39:01 ALLOW UDP 172.30.0.64 172.30.0.2 62166 53 0 - - - - - - - SEND
2015-08-09 16:39:01 ALLOW UDP 172.30.0.64 172.30.0.2 62167 53 0 - - - - - - - SEND
2015-08-09 16:39:01 ALLOW UDP 172.30.0.64 172.30.0.2 62168 53 0 - - - - - - - SEND
2015-08-09 16:39:01 ALLOW UDP 172.30.0.64 172.30.0.2 62169 53 0 - - - - - - - SEND
2015-08-09 16:39:01 ALLOW UDP 172.30.0.64 172.30.0.2 62170 53 0 - - - - - - - SEND
2015-08-09 16:39:01 ALLOW UDP 172.30.0.64 172.30.0.2 62171 53 0 - - - - - - - SEND
2015-08-09 16:39:01 ALLOW UDP 172.30.0.64 172.30.0.2 62172 53 0 - - - - - - - SEND
2015-08-09 16:39:01 ALLOW UDP 172.30.0.64 172.30.0.2 62173 53 0 - - - - - - - SEND
2015-08-09 16:39:01 ALLOW UDP 172.30.0.64 172.30.0.2 62174 53 0 - - - - - - - SEND
2015-08-09 16:39:01 ALLOW UDP 172.30.0.64 172.30.0.2 62175 53 0 - - - - - - - SEND
2015-08-09 16:39:01 ALLOW UDP 172.30.0.64 172.30.0.2 62176 53 0 - - - - - - - SEND
2015-08-09 16:39:39 ALLOW TCP 54.172.251.189 172.30.0.64 53355 80 0 - 0 0 0 - - - RECEIVE
2015-08-09 16:39:44 ALLOW TCP 54.172.251.189 172.30.0.64 53356 80 0 - 0 0 0 - - - RECEIVE
2015-08-09 16:39:44 ALLOW TCP 127.0.0.1 127.0.0.1 49178 47001 0 - 0 0 0 - - - SEND
2015-08-09 16:39:44 ALLOW TCP 127.0.0.1 127.0.0.1 49178 47001 0 - 0 0 0 - - - RECEIVE
2015-08-09 16:39:47 ALLOW TCP 172.30.0.64 169.254.169.254 49179 80 0 - 0 0 0 - - - SEND
2015-08-09 16:40:37 ALLOW TCP 54.172.251.189 172.30.0.64 53362 80 0 - 0 0 0 - - - RECEIVE
2015-08-09 16:40:47 ALLOW TCP 172.30.0.64 169.254.169.254 49180 80 0 - 0 0 0 - - - SEND
2015-08-09 16:40:55 ALLOW UDP fe80::11ef:7f4f:afb5:7f70 ff02::1:2 546 547 0 - - - - - - - SEND
```

    A. Application

    B. Web server

    C. System

    D. Firewall

96. Which one of the following activities transforms a zero-day vulnerability into a less dangerous attack vector?

    A. Discovery of the vulnerability

    B. Implementation of transport-layer encryption

    C. Reconfiguration of a firewall

    D. Release of a security patch

97. Which one of the following is an example of a hardening provision that might strengthen an organization's existing physical facilities and avoid implementation of a business continuity plan?

    A. Patching a leaky roof

    B. Reviewing and updating firewall access control lists

    C. Upgrading operating systems

    D. Deploying a network intrusion detection system

98. Susan wants to monitor traffic between systems in a VMWare environment. What solution would be her best option to monitor that traffic?

    A. Use a traditional hardware-based IPS.

    B. Install Wireshark on each virtual system.

Practice Test 2 **257**

   C. Set up a virtual span port and capture data using a VM IDS.

   D. Use netcat to capture all traffic sent between VMs.

Questions 99–102 refer to the following scenario.

Matthew and Richard are friends located in different physical locations who would like to begin communicating with each other using cryptography to protect the confidentiality of their communications. They exchange digital certificates to begin this process and plan to use an asymmetric encryption algorithm for the secure exchange of email messages.

99. When Matthew sends Richard a message, what key should he use to encrypt the message?

   A. Matthew's public key

   B. Matthew's private key

   C. Richard's public key

   D. Richard's private key

100. When Richard receives the message from Matthew, what key should he use to decrypt the message?

   A. Matthew's public key

   B. Matthew's private key

   C. Richard's public key

   D. Richard's private key

101. Matthew would like to enhance the security of his communication by adding a digital signature to the message. What goal of cryptography are digital signatures intended to enforce?

   A. Secrecy

   B. Availability

   C. Confidentiality

   D. Nonrepudiation

102. When Matthew goes to add the digital signature to the message, what encryption key does he use to create the digital signature?

   A. Matthew's public key

   B. Matthew's private key

   C. Richard's public key

   D. Richard's private key

103. When Jim logs into a system, his password is compared to a hashed value stored in a database. What is this process?

   A. Identification

   B. Hashing

   C. Tokenization

   D. Authentication

104. What is the primary advantage of decentralized access control?

   A. It provides better redundancy.

   B. It provides control of access to people closer to the resources.

   C. It is less expensive.

   D. It provides more granular control of access.

105. Which of the following types of controls does not describe a mantrap?

   A. Deterrent

   B. Preventive

   C. Compensating

   D. Physical

106. Sally's organization needs to be able to prove that certain staff members sent emails, and she wants to adopt a technology that will provide that capability without changing their existing email system. What is the technical term for the capability Sally needs to implement as the owner of the email system, and what tool could she use to do it?

   A. Integrity; IMAP

   B. Repudiation; encryption

   C. Nonrepudiation; digital signatures

   D. Authentication; DKIM

107. Which one of the following background checks is not normally performed during normal pre-hire activities?

   A. Credit check

   B. Reference verification

   C. Criminal records check

   D. Medical records check

108. Margot is investigating suspicious activity on her network and uses a protocol analyzer to sniff inbound and outbound traffic. She notices an unusual packet that has identical source and destination IP addresses. What type of attack uses this packet type?

   A. Fraggle

   B. Smurf

   C. Land

   D. Teardrop

109. Jim wants to perform an audit that will generate an industry recognized report on the design and suitability of his organization's controls as they stand at the time of the report. If this is his only goal, what type of report should he provide?

   A. An SSAE-16 Type I

   B. An SAS70 Type I

   C. An SSAE-16 Type II

   D. An SAS-70 Type II

110. In the OSI model, when a packet changes from a datastream to a segment or a datagram, what layer has it traversed?

   A. The Transport layer

   B. The Application layer

   C. The Data Link layer

   D. The Physical layer

111. Tommy handles access control requests for his organization. A user approaches him and explains that he needs access to the human resources database in order to complete a headcount analysis requested by the CFO. What has the user demonstrated successfully to Tommy?

   A. Clearance

   B. Separation of duties

   C. Need to know

   D. Isolation

112. Kathleen wants to set up a service to provide information about her organization's users and services using a central, open, vendor-neutral, standards-based system that can be easily queried. Which of the following technologies is her best choice?

   A. RADIUS

   B. LDAP

   C. Kerberos

   D. Active Directory

113. What type of firewall is capable of inspecting traffic at layer 7 and performing protocol-specific analysis for malicious traffic?

   A. Application firewall

   B. Stateful inspection firewall

   C. Packet filtering firewall

   D. Bastion host

114. Alice would like to add another object to a security model and grant herself rights to that object. Which one of the rules in the Take-Grant protection model would allow her to complete this operation?

  A. Take rule

  B. Grant rule

  C. Create rule

  D. Remove rule

115. Which of the following concerns should not be on Lauren's list of potential issues when penetration testers suggest using Metasploit during their testing?

  A. Metasploit can only test vulnerabilities it has plug-ins for.

  B. Penetration testing only covers a point-in-time view of the organization's security.

  C. Tools like Metasploit can cause denial-of-service issues.

  D. Penetration testing cannot test process and policy.

116. Colin is reviewing a system that has been assigned the EAL7 evaluation assurance level under the Common Criteria. What is the highest level of assurance that he may have about the system?

  A. It has been functionally tested.

  B. It has been methodically tested and checked.

  C. It has been methodically designed, tested, and reviewed.

  D. It has been formally verified, designed, and tested.

117. Which ITU-T standard should Alex expect to see in use when he uses his smart card to provide a certificate to an upstream authentication service?

  A. X.500

  B. SPML

  C. X.509

  D. SAML

118. What type of websites are regulated under the terms of COPPA?

  A. Financial websites not run by financial institutions

  B. Healthcare websites that collect personal information

  C. Websites that collect information from children

  D. Financial websites run by financial institutions

119. Tracy recently accepted an IT compliance position at a federal government agency that works very closely with the Defense Department on classified government matters. Which one of the following laws is least likely to pertain to Tracy's agency?

  A. HIPAA

  B. FISMA

C. HSA

D. CFAA

120. Referring to the figure shown here, what is the name of the security control indicated by the arrow?

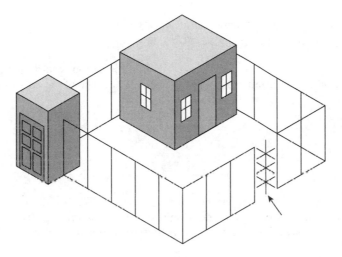

A. Mantrap

B. Intrusion prevention system

C. Turnstile

D. Portal

121. What two important factors does accountability for access control rely on?

A. Identification and authorization

B. Authentication and authorization

C. Identification and authentication

D. Accountability and authentication

122. What key assumption made by EAP can be remedied by using PEAP?

A. EAP assumes that LEAP will replace TKIP, ensuring authentication will occur.

B. EAP originally assumed the use of physically isolated channels and is usually not encrypted.

C. There are no TLS implementations available using EAP.

D. EAP does not allow additional authentication methods, and PEAP adds additional methods.

123. Scott's organization has configured their external IP address to be 192.168.1.25. When traffic is sent to their ISP, it never reaches its destination. What problem is Scott's organization encountering?

    A. BGP is not set up properly.

    B. They have not registered their IP with their ISP.

    C. The IP address is a private, non-routable address.

    D. 192.168.1.25 is a reserved address for home routers.

124. Jennifer needs to measure the effectiveness of her information security program as she works toward her organization's long-term goals. What type of measures should she select?

    A. Metrics

    B. KPIs

    C. SLAs

    D. OKRs

125. Sue's organization recently failed a security assessment because their network was a single flat broadcast domain, and sniffing traffic was possible between different functional groups. What solution should she recommend to help prevent the issues that were identified?

    A. Use VLANs.

    B. Change the subnet mask for all systems.

    C. Deploy gateways.

    D. Turn on port security.

126. Susan is setting up the network for a local coffee house and wants to ensure that users have to authenticate using an email address and agree to the coffee house's acceptable use policy before being allowed on the network. What technology should she use to do this?

    A. 802.11

    B. NAC

    C. A captive portal

    D. A wireless gateway

127. What is another term for active monitoring?

    A. Synthetic

    B. Passive

    C. Reactive

    D. Span-based

128. The TCP header is made up of elements such as the source port, destination port, sequence number, and others. How many bytes long is the TCP header?

A. 8 bytes

B. 20–60 bytes

C. 64 bytes

D. 64–128 bytes

The company that Fred works for is reviewing the security of their company issued cell phones. They issue 4G capable smartphones running Android and iOS, and use a mobile device management solution to deploy company software to the phones. The mobile device management software also allows the company to remotely wipe the phones if they are lost. Use this information, as well as your knowledge of cellular technology, to answer questions 129–131.

129. What security considerations should Fred's company require for sending sensitive data over the cellular network?

A. They should use the same requirements as data over any public network.

B. Cellular provider networks are private networks and should not require special consideration.

C. Encrypt all traffic to ensure confidentiality.

D. Require the use of WAP for all data sent from the phone.

130. Fred intends to attend a major hacker conference this year. What should he do when connecting to his cellular provider's 4G network while at the conference?

A. Continue normal usage.

B. Discontinue all usage; towers can be spoofed.

C. Only use trusted Wi-Fi networks.

D. Connect to his company's encrypted VPN service.

131. What are the most likely circumstances that would cause a remote wipe of a mobile phone to fail?

A. The phone has a passcode on it.

B. The phone cannot contact a network.

C. The provider has not unlocked the phone.

D. The phone is in use.

132. Elaine is developing a business continuity plan for her organization. What value should she seek to minimize?

A. AV

B. SSL

C. RTO

D. MTO

133. NIST Special Publication 800-53, revision 4, describes two measures of assurance. Which measure of developmental assurance is best described as measuring "the rigor, level of detail, and formality of the artifacts produced during the design and development of the hardware, software, and firmware components of information systems (e.g., functional specifications, high-level design, low-level design, source code)"?

A. Coverage

B. Suitability

C. Affirmation

D. Depth

134. Which one of the following disaster recovery test types does not involve the actual use of any technical disaster recovery controls?

A. Simulation test

B. Parallel test

C. Structured walk-through

D. Full interruption test

135. Chris is experiencing issues with the quality of network service on his organization's network. The primary symptom is that packets are becoming corrupted as they travel from their source to their destination. What term describes the issue Chris is facing?

A. Latency

B. Jitter

C. Interference

D. Packet loss

136. Kathleen has been asked to choose a highly formalized code review process for her software quality assurance team to use. Which of the following software testing processes is the most rigorous and formal?

A. Fagan

B. Fuzzing

C. Over the shoulder

D. Pair programming

137. Frank is attempting to protect his web application against cross-site scripting attacks. Users do not need to provide input containing scripts, so he decided the most effective way to filter would be to write a filter on the server that watches for the <SCRIPT> tag and removes it. What is the issue with Frank's approach?

A. Validation should always be performed on the client side.

B. Attackers may use XSS filter evasion techniques against this approach.

C. Server-side validation requires removing all HTML tags, not just the <SCRIPT> tag.

D. There is no problem with Frank's approach.

138. Which one of the following is not an object-oriented programming language?

    A. C++

    B. Java

    C. Fortran

    D. C#

139. Uptown Records Management recently entered into a contract with a hospital for the secure storage of medical records. The hospital is a HIPAA-covered entity. What type of agreement must the two organizations sign to remain compliant with HIPAA?

    A. NDA

    B. NCA

    C. BAA

    D. SLA

140. Norm would like to conduct a disaster recovery test for his organization and wants to choose the most thorough type of test, recognizing that it may be quite disruptive. What type of test should Norm choose?

    A. Full interruption test

    B. Parallel test

    C. Tabletop exercise

    D. Checklist review

141. Ed is building a network that supports IPv6 but needs to connect it to an IPv4 network. What type of device should Ed place between the networks?

    A. A switch

    B. A router

    C. A bridge

    D. A gateway

142. What encryption standard won the competition for certification as the Advanced Encryption Standard?

    A. Blowfish

    B. Twofish

    C. Rijndael

    D. Skipjack

143. Which law can be summarized through these seven key principles: notice, choice, onward transfer, security, data integrity, access, enforcement?

    A. COPA

    B. NY SAFE Act

    C. The EU Data Protection Directive

    D. FISMA

144. Which one of the following actions is not required under the EU Data Protection Directive?

    A. Organizations must allow individuals to opt out of information sharing.

    B. Organizations must provide individuals with lists of employees with access to information.

    C. Organizations must use proper mechanisms to protect data against unauthorized disclosure.

    D. Organizations must have a dispute resolution process for privacy issues.

145. Tammy is selecting a disaster recovery facility for her organization. She would like to choose a facility that balances the time required to recover operations with the cost involved. What type of facility should she choose?

    A. Hot site

    B. Warm site

    C. Cold site

    D. Red site

146. What layer of the OSI model is associated with datagrams?

    A. Session

    B. Transport

    C. Network

    D. Data Link

147. Which one of the following is not a valid key length for the Advanced Encryption Standard?

    A. 128 bits

    B. 192 bits

    C. 256 bits

    D. 384 bits

148. Which one of the following technologies provides a function interface that allows developers to directly interact with systems without knowing the implementation details of that system?

    A. Data dictionary

    B. Object model

    C. Source code

    D. API

149. What email encryption technique is illustrated in this figure?

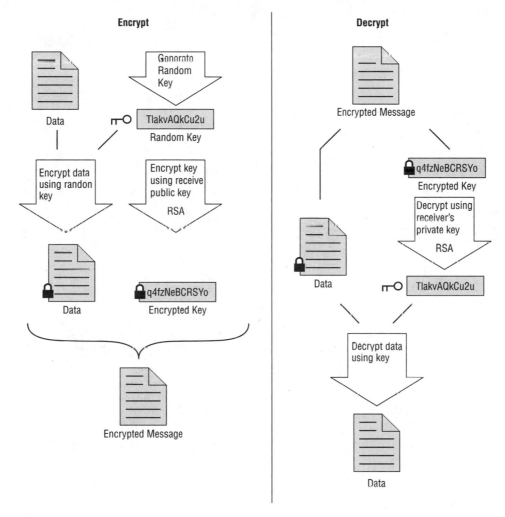

A. MD5

B. Thunderbird

C. S/MIME

D. PGP

150. When Ben lists the files on a Linux system, he sees a set of attributes as shown in the following image.

```
[demo@ip-10-0-0-254 ~]$ ls -l
total 8
-rw-r--r-- 1 demo demo 93 Apr 11 23:38 example.txt
-rw-rw-r-- 1 demo demo 15 Apr 11 23:37 index.html
[demo@ip-10-0-0-254 ~]$ 
```

This letters rwx indicate different levels of what?

    A. Identification

    B. Authorization

    C. Authentication

    D. Accountability

151. What type of access control is intended to discover unwanted or unauthorized activity by providing information after the event has occurred?

    A. Preventive

    B. Corrective

    C. Detective

    D. Directive

152. Which one of the following presents the most complex decoy environment for an attacker to explore during an intrusion attempt?

    A. Honeypot

    B. Darknet

    C. Honeynet

    D. Pseudo flaw

Ben's organization is adopting biometric authentication for their high-security building's access control system. Using this chart, answer questions 153–155 about their adoption of the technology.

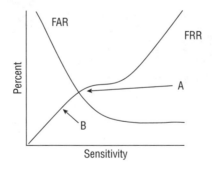

153. Ben's company is considering configuring their systems to work at the level shown by point A on the diagram. What level are they setting the sensitivity to?

    A. The FRR crossover

    B. The FAR point

    C. The CER

    D. The CFR

154. At point B, what problem is likely to occur?

    A. False acceptance will be very high.

    B. False rejection will be very high.

C. False rejection will be very low.

D. False acceptance will be very low.

155. What should Ben do if the FAR and FRR shown in this diagram does not provide an acceptable performance level for his organization's needs?

A. Adjust the sensitivity of the biometric devices.

B. Assess other biometric systems to compare them.

C. Move the CER.

D. Adjust the FRR settings in software.

156. Ed is tasked with protecting information about his organization's customers, including their name, Social Security number, birthdate and place of birth, as well as a variety of other information. What is this information known as?

A. PHI

B. PII

C. Personal Protected Data

D. PID

157. What software development life-cycle model is shown in the following illustration?

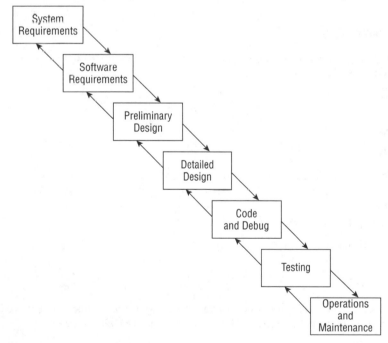

A. Spiral

B. Agile

C. Boehm

D. Waterfall

158. Encapsulation is the core concept that enables what type of protocol?

   A. Bridging

   B. Multilayer

   C. Hashing

   D. Storage

159. Which one of the following is not a key principle of the COBIT framework for IT security control objectives?

   A. Meeting stakeholder needs

   B. Performing exhaustive analysis

   C. Covering the enterprise end-to-end

   D. Separating governance from management

160. Roscommon Enterprises is an Irish company that handles personal information. They exchange information with many other countries. Which of the following countries would trigger the onward transfer provisions of the International Safe Harbor Privacy Principles?

   A. United States

   B. United Kingdom

   C. Italy

   D. Germany

161. What important protocol is responsible for providing human-readable addresses instead of numerical IP addresses?

   A. TCP

   B. IP

   C. DNS

   D. ARP

162. NIST Special Publication 800-53A describes four types of objects that can be assessed. If Ben is reviewing a password standard, which of the four types of objects is he assessing?

   A. A mechanism

   B. A specification

   C. An activity

   D. An individual

163. What process is typically used to ensure data security for workstations that are being removed from service, but which will be resold or otherwise reused?

   A. Destruction

   B. Erasing

    C. Sanitization

    D. Clearing

164. Colleen is conducting a software test that is evaluating code for both security flaws and usability issues. She is working with the application from an end-user perspective and referencing the source code as she works her way through the product. What type of testing is Colleen conducting?

    A. White box

    B. Blue box

    C. Gray box

    D. Black box

165. Harold is looking for a software development methodology that will help with a major issue he is seeing in his organization. Currently, developers and operations staff do not work together and are often seen as taking problems and "throwing them over the fence" to the other team. What technology management approach is designed to alleviate this problem?

    A. ITIL

    B. Lean

    C. ITSM

    D. DevOps

166. NIST Special Publication 800-92, the Guide to Computer Security Log Management, describes four types of common challenges to log management:

- Many log sources
- Inconsistent log content
- Inconsistent timestamps
- Inconsistent log formats

Which of the following solutions is best suited to solving these issues?

    A. Implement SNMP for all logging devices.

    B. Implement a SIEM.

    C. Standardize on the Windows event log format for all devices and use NTP.

    D. Ensure logging is enabled on all endpoints using their native logging formats and set their local time correctly.

167. Mike has a flash memory card that he would like to reuse. The card contains sensitive information. What technique can he use to securely remove data from the card and allow its reuse?

    A. Degaussing

    B. Physical destruction

    C. Overwriting

    D. Reformatting

168. Carlos is investigating the compromise of sensitive information in his organization. He believes that attackers managed to retrieve personnel information on all employees from the database and finds the following user-supplied input in a log entry for a web-based personnel management system:

```
Collins'&1=1;--
```

What type of attack took place?

   A. SQL injection

   B. Buffer overflow

   C. Cross-site scripting

   D. Cross-site request forgery

169. Which one of the following is a detailed, step-by-step document that describes the exact actions that individuals must complete?

   A. Policy

   B. Standard

   C. Guideline

   D. Procedure

170. What principle of relational databases ensures the permanency of transactions that have successfully completed?

   A. Atomicity

   B. Consistency

   C. Isolation

   D. Durability

171. Bryan has a set of sensitive documents that he would like to protect from public disclosure. He would like to use a control that, if the documents appear in a public forum, may be used to trace the leak back to the person who was originally given the document copy. What security control would best fulfill this purpose?

   A. Digital signature

   B. Document staining

   C. Hashing

   D. Watermarking

172. Carlos is planning a design for a data center that will be constructed within a new four-story corporate headquarters. The building consists of a basement and three above-ground floors. What is the best location for the data center?

   A. Basement

   B. First floor

   C. Second floor

   D. Third floor

173. Chris is an information security professional for a major corporation and, as he is walking into the building, he notices that the door to a secure area has been left ajar. Physical security does not fall under his responsibility, but he takes immediate action by closing the door and informing the physical security team of his action. What principle is Chris demonstrating?

　　A. Due care

　　B. Due diligence

　　C. Separation of duties

　　D. Informed consent

174. Which one of the following investigation types always uses the beyond a reasonable doubt standard of proof?

　　A. Civil investigation

　　B. Criminal investigation

　　C. Operational investigation

　　D. Regulatory investigation

175. Which one of the following backup types does not alter the status of the archive bit on a file?

　　A. Full backup

　　B. Incremental backup

　　C. Partial backup

　　D. Differential backup

176. What type of alternate processing facility contains the hardware necessary to restore operations but does not have a current copy of data?

　　A. Hot site

　　B. Warm site

　　C. Cold site

　　D. Mobile site

177. Which one of the following terms describes a period of momentary high voltage?

　　A. Sag

　　B. Brownout

　　C. Spike

　　D. Surge

178. A web application accesses information in a database to retrieve user information. What is the web application acting as?

　　A. A subject

　　B. An object

　　C. A user

　　D. A token

179. The Open Shortest Path First (OSPF) protocol is a routing protocol that keeps a map of all connected remote networks and uses that map to select the shortest path to a remote destination. What type of routing protocol is OSPF?

   A. Link state

   B. Shortest path first

   C. Link mapping

   D. Distance vector

180. Which one of the following categories consists of first-generation programming languages?

   A. Machine languages

   B. Assembly languages

   C. Compiled languages

   D. Natural language

Questions 181–185 refer to the following scenario.

Concho Controls is a mid-sized business focusing on building automation systems. They host a set of local file servers in their on-premises data center that store customer proposals, building plans, product information, and other data that is critical to their business operations.

Tara works in the Concho Controls IT department and is responsible for designing and implementing the organization's backup strategy, among other tasks. She currently conducts full backups every Sunday evening at 8 p.m. and differential backups on Monday through Friday at noon.

Concho experiences a server failure at 3 p.m. on Wednesday. Tara rebuilds the server and wants to restore data from the backups.

181. What backup should Tara apply to the server first?

   A. Sunday's full backup

   B. Monday's differential backup

   C. Tuesday's differential backup

   D. Wednesday's differential backup

182. How many backups in total must Tara apply to the system to make the data it contains as current as possible?

   A. 1

   B. 2

   C. 3

   D. 4

183. In this backup approach, some data may be irretrievably lost. How long is the time period where any changes made will have been lost?

   A. 3 hours

   B. 5 hours

C. 8 hours

D. No data will be lost.

184. If Tara followed the same schedule but switched the differential backups to incremental backups, how many backups in total would she need to apply to the system to make the data it contains as current as possible?

A. 1

B. 2

C. 3

D. 4

185. If Tara made the change from differential to incremental backups and we assume that the same amount of information changes each day, which one of the following files would be the largest?

A. Monday's incremental backup

B. Tuesday's incremental backup

C. Wednesday's incremental backup

D. All three will be the same size.

186. Susan is conducting a STRIDE threat assessment by placing threats into one or more of the following categories: Spoofing, Tampering, Repudiation, Information Disclosure, Denial of Service, and Elevation of Privilege. As part of her assessment, she has discovered an issue that allows transactions to be modified between a web browser and the application server that it accesses. What STRIDE categorization(s) best fit this issue?

A. Tampering and Information Disclosure

B. Spoofing and Tampering

C. Tampering and Repudiation

D. Information Disclosure and Elevation of Privilege

187. Bob has been tasked with writing a policy that describes how long data should be kept and when it should be purged. What concept does this policy deal with?

A. Data remanence

B. Record retention

C. Data redaction

D. Audit logging

188. Which component of IPSec provides authentication, integrity, and nonrepudiation?

A. L2TP

B. Encapsulating Security Payload

C. Encryption Security Header

D. Authentication Header

189. Renee notices that a system on her network recently received connection attempts on all 65,536 TCP ports from a single system during a short period of time. What type of attack did Renee most likely experience?

   A. Denial of service

   B. Reconnaissance

   C. Malicious insider

   D. Compromise

190. Which one of the following techniques can an attacker use to exploit a TOC/TOU vulnerability?

   A. File locking

   B. Exception handling

   C. Algorithmic complexity

   D. Concurrency control

191. In the ring protection model shown here, what ring does not run in privileged mode?

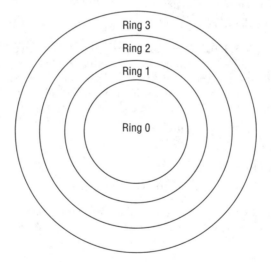

   A. Ring 0

   B. Ring 1

   C. Ring 2

   D. Ring 3

192. What level of RAID is also known as disk striping?

   A. RAID 0

   B. RAID 1

   C. RAID 5

   D. RAID 10

193. Jacob executes an attack against a system using a valid but low privilege user account by accessing a file pointer that the account has access to. After the access check, but before the file is opened, he quickly switches the file pointer to point to a file that the user account does not have access to. What type of attack is this?

    A. TOC/TOU

    B. Permissions creep

    C. Impersonation

    D. Link swap

194. What is the minimum number of disks required to implement RAID level 0?

    A. 1

    B. 2

    C. 3

    D. 5

195. Fred's company wants to ensure the integrity of email messages sent via their central email servers. If the confidentiality of the messages is not critical, what solution should Fred suggest?

    A. Digitally sign and encrypt all messages to ensure integrity.

    B. Digitally sign but don't encrypt all messages.

    C. Use TLS to protect messages, ensuring their integrity.

    D. Use a hashing algorithm to provide a hash in each message to prove that it hasn't changed.

196. The leadership at Susan's company has asked her to implement an access control system that can support rule declarations like "Only allow access to salespeople from managed devices on the wireless network between 8 a.m. and 6 p.m." What type of access control system would be Susan's best choice?

    A. ABAC

    B. RBAC

    C. DAC

    D. MAC

197. What type of communications rely on a timing mechanism using either an independent clock or a time stamp embedded in the communications?

    A. Analog

    B. Digital

    C. Synchronous

    D. Asynchronous

198. Chris is deploying a gigabit Ethernet network using Category 6 cable between two buildings. What is the maximum distance he can run the cable according to the Category 6 standard?

    A. 50 meters

    B. 100 meters

    C. 200 meters

    D. 300 meters

199. Howard is a security analyst working with an experienced computer forensics investigator. The investigator asks him to retrieve a forensic drive controller, but Howard cannot locate a device in the storage room with this name. What is another name for a forensic drive controller?

    A. RAID controller

    B. Write blocker

    C. SCSI terminator

    D. Forensic device analyzer

200. The web application that Saria's development team is working on needs to provide secure session management that can prevent hijacking of sessions using the cookies that the application relies on. Which of the following techniques would be the best for her to recommend to prevent this?

    A. Set the Secure attribute for the cookies, thus forcing TLS.

    B. Set the Domain cookie attribute to example.com to limit cookie access to servers in the same domain.

    C. Set the Expires cookie attribute to less than a week.

    D. Set the HTTPOnly attribute to require only unencrypted sessions.

201. Ben's company has recently retired their fleet of multifunction printers. Their information security team has expressed concerns that the printers contain hard drives and that they may still have data from scans and print jobs. What is the technical term for this issue?

    A. Data pooling

    B. Failed clearing

    C. Data permanence

    D. Data remanence

202. What access control scheme labels subjects and objects, and allows subjects to access objects when the labels match?

    A. DAC

    B. MAC

    C. Rule BAC

    D. Role BAC

203. A cloud-based service that provides account provisioning, management, authentication, authorization, reporting, and monitoring capabilities is known as what type of service?

    A. PaaS

    B. IDaaS

    C. IaaS

    D. SaaS

204. Sally wants to secure her organization's VOIP systems. Which of the following attacks is one that she shouldn't have to worry about?

    A. Eavesdropping

    B. Denial of service

C. Blackboxing

D. Caller ID spoofing

205. Marty discovers that the access restrictions in his organization allow any user to log into the workstation assigned to any other user, even if they are from completely different department ments. This type of access most directly violates which information security principle?

A. Separation of duties

B. Two-person control

C. Need to know

D. Least privilege

206. Fred needs to transfer files between two servers on an untrusted network. Since he knows the network isn't trusted, he needs to select an encrypted protocol that can ensure his data remains secure. What protocol should he choose?

A. SSH

B. TCP

C. SFTP

D. IPSec

207. Chris uses a packet sniffer to capture traffic from a TACACS+ server. What protocol should he monitor, and what data should he expect to be readable?

A. UDP; none—TACACS+ encrypts the full session

B. TCP; none—TACACS+ encrypts the full session

C. UDP; all but the username and password, which are encrypted

D. TCP; all but the username and password, which are encrypted

Use your knowledge of Kerberos authentication and authorization as well as the following diagram to answer questions 208–210.

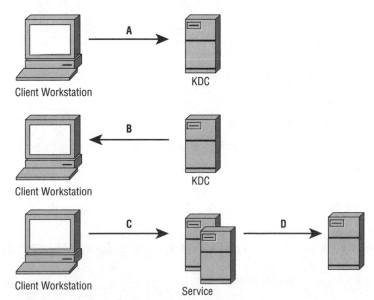

208. If the client has already authenticated to the KDC, what does the client workstation send to the KDC at point A when it wants to access a resource?

   A. It re-sends the password.

   B. A TGR

   C. Its TGT

   D. A service ticket

209. What occurs between steps A and B?

   A. The KDC verifies the validity of the TGT and whether the user has the right privileges for the requested resource.

   B. The KDC updates its access control list based on the data in the TGT.

   C. The KDC checks its service listing and prepares an updated TGT based on the service request.

   D. The KDC generates a service ticket to issue to the client.

210. What system or systems does the service that is being accessed use to validate the ticket?

   A. The KDC

   B. The client workstation and the KDC

   C. The client workstation supplies it in the form of a client-to-server ticket and an authenticator.

   D. The KVS

211. What does a service ticket (ST) provide in Kerberos authentication?

   A. It serves as the authentication host.

   B. It provides proof that the subject is authorized to access an object.

   C. It provides proof that a subject has authenticated through a KDC and can request tickets to access other objects.

   D. It provides ticket granting services.

212. A password that requires users to answer a series of questions like "What is your mother's maiden name?" or "What is your favorite color?" is known as what type of password?

   A. A passphrase

   B. Multifactor passwords

   C. Cognitive passwords

   D. Password reset questions

213. CDMA, GSM, and IDEN are all examples of what generation of cellular technology?

   A. 1G

   B. 2G

   C. 3G

   D. 4G

214. Which one of the following fire suppression systems poses the greatest risk of accidental discharge that damages equipment in a data center?

   A. Closed head

   B. Dry pipe

   C. Deluge

   D. Preaction

215. Lauren's healthcare provider maintains such data as details about her health, treatments, and medical billing. What type of data is this?

   A. Protected Health Information

   B. Personally Identifiable Information

   C. Protected Health Insurance

   D. Individual Protected Data

216. What type of code review is best suited to identifying business logic flaws?

   A. Mutational fuzzing

   B. Manual

   C. Generational fuzzing

   D. Interface testing

217. Something you know is an example of what type of authentication factor?

   A. Type 1

   B. Type 2

   C. Type 3

   D. Type 4

218. Saria is the system owner for a healthcare organization. What responsibilities does she have related to the data that resides on or is processed by the systems she owns?

   A. She has to classify the data.

   B. She has to make sure that appropriate security controls are in place to protect the data.

   C. She has to grant appropriate access to personnel.

   D. She bears sole responsibility for ensuring that data is protected at rest, in transit, and in use.

219. During software testing, Jack diagrams how a hacker might approach the application he is reviewing and determines what requirements the hacker might have. He then tests how the system would respond to the attacker's likely behavior. What type of testing is Jack conducting?

   A. Misuse case testing

   B. Use case testing

   C. Hacker use case testing

   D. Static code analysis

220. When a vendor develops a product that they wish to submit for Common Criteria evaluation, what do they complete to describe the claims of security for their product?

  A. PP

  B. ITSEC

  C. TCSEC

  D. ST

221. Chris has been assigned to scan a system on all of its possible TCP and UDP ports. How many ports of each type must he scan to complete his assignment?

  A. 65,536 TCP ports and 32,768 UDP ports

  B. 1024 common TCP ports and 32,768 ephemeral UDP ports

  C. 65,536 TCP and 65,536 UDP ports

  D. 16,384 TCP ports, and 16,384 UDP ports

222. CVE and the NVD both provide information about what?

  A. Vulnerabilities

  B. Markup languages

  C. Vulnerability assessment tools

  D. Penetration testing methodologies

223. What is the highest level of the military classification scheme?

  A. Secret

  B. Confidential

  C. SBU

  D. Top Secret

224. In what type of trusted recovery process does the system recover against one or more failure types without administrator intervention while protecting itself against data loss?

  A. Automated recovery

  B. Manual recovery

  C. Function recovery

  D. Automated recovery without undue data loss

225. What three important items should be considered if you are attempting to control the strength of signal for a wireless network as well as where it is accessible?

  A. Antenna placement, antenna type, and antenna power levels

  B. Antenna design, power levels, use of a captive portal

  C. Antenna placement, antenna design, use of a captive portal

  D. Power levels, antenna placement, FCC minimum strength requirements

226. What is the best way to ensure that data is unrecoverable from a SSD?

  A. Use the built-in erase commands

  B. Use a random pattern wipe of 1s and 0s

    C. Physically destroy the drive

    D. Degauss the drive

227. Alice sends a message to Bob and wants to ensure that Mal, a third party, does not read the contents of the message while in transit. What goal of cryptography is Alice attempting to achieve?

    A. Confidentiality

    B. Integrity

    C. Authentication

    D. Nonrepudiation

228. Which one of the following metrics specifies the amount of time that business continuity planners believe it will take to restore a service when it goes down?

    A. MTD

    B. RTO

    C. RPO

    D. MTO

229. Gary would like to examine the text of a criminal law on computer fraud to determine whether it applies to a recent act of hacking against his company. Where should he go to read the text of the law?

    A. Code of Federal Regulations

    B. Supreme Court rulings

    C. Compendium of Laws

    D. United States Code

230. James has opted to implement an NAC solution that uses a post-admission philosophy for its control of network connectivity. What type of issues can't a strictly post-admission policy handle?

    A. Out-of-band monitoring

    B. Preventing an unpatched laptop from being exploited immediately after connecting to the network

    C. Denying access when user behavior doesn't match an authorization matrix

    D. Allowing user access when user behavior is allowed based on an authorization matrix

231. Ben has built an access control list that lists the objects that his users are allowed to access. When users attempt to access an object that they don't have rights to, they are denied access, even though there isn't a specific rule that prevents it. What access control principle is key to this behavior?

    A. Least privilege

    B. Implicit deny

    C. Explicit deny

    D. Final rule fall-through

232. Mary is a security risk analyst for an insurance company. She is currently examining a scenario where a hacker might use a SQL injection attack to deface a web server due to a missing patch in the company's web application. In this scenario, what is the risk?

   A. Unpatched web application

   B. Web defacement

   C. Hacker

   D. Operating system

233. In the diagram shown here of security boundaries within a computer system, what component's name has been replaced with XXX?

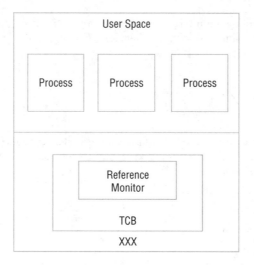

   A. Kernel

   B. Privileged core

   C. User monitor

   D. Security perimeter

234. Val is attempting to review security logs but is overwhelmed by the sheer volume of records maintained in her organization's central log repository. What technique can she use to select a representative set of records for further review?

   A. Statistical sampling

   B. Clipping

   C. Choose the first 5% of records from each day.

   D. Choose 5% of records from the middle of the day.

235. In Jen's job as the network administrator for an industrial production facility, she is tasked with ensuring that the network is not susceptible to electromagnetic interference due to the large motors and other devices running on the production floor. What type of network cabling should she choose if this concern is more important than cost and difficulty of installation?

A. 10Base2

B. 100BaseT

C. 1000BaseT

D. Fiber-optic

Questions 236–239 refer to the following scenario.

Jasper Diamonds is a jewelry manufacturer that markets and sells custom jewelry through their website. Bethany is the manager of Jasper's software development organization, and she is working to bring the company into line with industry standard practices. She is developing a new change management process for the organization and wishes to follow commonly accepted approaches.

236. Bethany would like to put in place controls that provide an organized framework for company employees to suggest new website features that her team will develop. What change management process facilitates this?

A. Configuration control

B. Change control

C. Release control

D. Request control

237. Bethany would also like to create a process that helps multiple developers work on code at the same time. What change management process facilitates this?

A. Configuration control

B. Change control

C. Release control

D. Request control

238. Bethany is working with her colleagues to conduct user acceptance testing. What change management process includes this task?

A. Configuration control

B. Change control

C. Release control

D. Request control

239. Bethany noticed that some problems arise when system administrators update libraries without informing developers. What change management process can assist with this problem?

A. Configuration control

B. Change control

C. Release control

D. Request control

240. Ben has written the password hashing system for the web application he is building. His hashing code function for passwords results in the following process for a series of passwords:

```
hash (password1 + 07C98BFE4CF67B0BFE2643B5B22E2D7D) =
10B222970537B97919DB36EC757370D2
hash (password2 + 07C98BFE4CF67B0BFE2643B5B22E2D7D) =
F1F16683F3E0208131B46D37A79C8921
```

What flaw has Ben introduced with his hashing implementation?

A. Plaintext salting

B. Salt reuse

C. Use of a short salt

D. Poor salt algorithm selection

241. Which one of the following is an example of risk transference?

A. Building a guard shack

B. Purchasing insurance

C. Erecting fences

D. Relocating facilities

242. What protocol takes the place of certificate revocation lists and adds real-time status verification?

A. RTCP

B. RTVP

C. OCSP

D. CSRTP

243. Jim performs both lexical analysis on a program and produces control flow graphs. What type of software testing is he performing?

A. Dynamic

B. Fuzzing

C. Manual

D. Static

244. What process makes TCP a connection-oriented protocol?

A. It works via network connections.

B. It uses a handshake.

C. It monitors for dropped connections.

D. It uses a complex header.

245. What LDAP operation includes authentication to the LDAP server?

A. Bind

B. Auth

C. StartLDAP

D. AuthDN

246. You are conducting a qualitative risk assessment for your organization. The two important risk elements that should weigh most heavily in your analysis of risk are probability and
_____.

A. Likelihood

B. History

C. Impact

D. Cost

247. Using the OSI model, what format does the Data link Layer use to format messages received from higher up the stack?

A. A datastream

B. A frame

C. A segment

D. A datagram

248. What is the maximum penalty that may be imposed by an (ISC)² peer review board when considering a potential ethics violation?

A. Revocation of certification

B. Termination of employment

C. Financial penalty

D. Suspension of certification

249. Which one of the following statements about the SDLC is correct?

A. The SDLC requires the use of an iterative approach to software development.

B. The SDLC requires the use of a sequential approach to software development.

C. The SDLC does not include training for end users and support staff.

D. The waterfall methodology is compatible with the SDLC.

250. In the scenario shown here, Harry is prevented from reading a file at a higher classification level than his security clearance. What security model prevents this behavior?

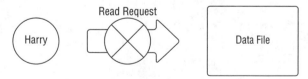

A. Bell-LaPadula

B. Biba

C. Clark-Wilson

D. Brewer-Nash

Appendix

Answers to Review Questions

Chapter 1: Security and Risk Management (Domain 1)

1. D. The final step of a quantitative risk analysis is conducting a cost/benefit analysis to determine whether the organization should implement proposed countermeasure(s).

2. A. Spoofing attacks use falsified identities. Spoofing attacks may use false IP addresses, email addresses, names, or, in the case of an evil twin attack, SSIDs.

3. C. The DMCA states that providers are not responsible for the transitory activities of their users. Transmission of information over a network would qualify for this exemption. The other activities listed are all nontransitory actions that require remediation by the provider.

4. A. The Notice principle says that organizations must inform individuals of the information the organization collects about individuals and how the organization will use it. These principles are based upon the Safe Harbor Privacy Principles issued by the US Department of Commerce in 2000 to help US companies comply with EU and Swiss privacy laws when collecting, storing, processing or transmitting data on EU or Swiss citizens.

5. D. The three common threat modeling techniques are focused on attackers, software, and assets. Social engineering is a subset of attackers.

6. A. Most state data breach notification laws are modeled after California's law, which covers Social Security number, driver's license number, state identification card number, credit/debit card numbers, bank account numbers (in conjunction with a PIN or password), medical records, and health insurance information.

7. C. The prudent man rule requires that senior executives take personal responsibility for ensuring the due care that ordinary, prudent individuals would exercise in the same situation. The rule originally applied to financial matters, but the Federal Sentencing Guidelines applied them to information security matters in 1991.

8. D. A fingerprint scan is an example of a "something you are" factor, which would be appropriate for pairing with a "something you know" password to achieve multifactor authentication. A username is not an authentication factor. PINs and security questions are both "something you know," which would not achieve multifactor authentication when paired with a password because both methods would come from the same category, failing the requirement for multifactor authentication.

9. D. The US Department of Commerce is responsible for implementing the EU-US Safe Harbor agreement. The validity of this agreement was in legal question in the wake of the NSA surveillance disclosures.

10. A. The Gramm-Leach-Bliley Act (GLBA) contains provisions regulating the privacy of customer financial information. It applies specifically to financial institutions.

11. A. The Federal Information Security Management Act (FISMA) specifically applies to government contractors. The Government Information Security Reform Act (GISRA) was the precursor to FISMA and expired in November 2002. HIPAA and PCI DSS apply to healthcare and credit card information, respectively.

12. D. The export of encryption software to certain countries is regulated under US export control laws.

13. D. In an elevation of privilege attack, the attacker transforms a limited user account into an account with greater privileges, powers, and/or access to the system. Spoofing attacks falsify an identity, while repudiation attacks attempt to deny accountability for an action. Tampering attacks attempt to violate the integrity of information or resources.

14. D. Whenever you choose to accept a risk, you should maintain detailed documentation of the risk acceptance process to satisfy auditors in the future. This should happen before implementing security controls, designing a disaster recovery plan, or repeating the business impact analysis (BIA).

15. B. A fence does not have the ability to detect intrusions. It does, however, have the ability to prevent and deter an intrusion. Fences are an example of a physical control.

16. D. Tony would see the best results by combining elements of quantitative and qualitative risk assessment. Quantitative risk assessment excels at analyzing financial risk, while qualitative risk assessment is a good tool for intangible risks. Combining the two techniques provides a well rounded risk picture.

17. D. The Economic Espionage Act imposes fines and jail sentences on anyone found guilty of stealing trade secrets from a US corporation. It gives true teeth to the intellectual property rights of trade secret owners.

18. C. The due care principle states that an individual should react in a situation using the same level of care that would be expected from any reasonable person. It is a very broad standard. The due diligence principle is a more specific component of due care that states that an individual assigned a responsibility should exercise due care to complete it accurately and in a timely manner.

19. C. RAID level 5, disk striping with parity, requires a minimum of three physical hard disks to operate.

20. B. Awareness training is an example of an administrative control. Firewalls and intrusion detection systems are technical controls. Security guards are physical controls.

21. A. Patents and trade secrets can both protect intellectual property related to a manufacturing process. Trade secrets are appropriate only when the details can be tightly controlled within an organization, so a patent is the appropriate solution in this case.

22. B. RAID technology provides fault tolerance for hard drive failures and is an example of a business continuity action. Restoring from backup tapes, relocating to a cold site, and restarting business operations are all disaster recovery actions.

23. C. After developing a list of assets, the business impact analysis team should assign values to each asset.

24. C. Risk mitigation strategies attempt to lower the probability and/or impact of a risk occurring. Intrusion prevention systems attempt to reduce the probability of a successful attack and are, therefore, examples of risk mitigation.

25. D. Fire suppression systems protect infrastructure from physical damage. Along with uninterruptible power supplies, fire suppression systems are good examples of technology used to harden physical infrastructure. Antivirus software, hardware firewalls, and two-factor authentication are all examples of logical controls.

26. A. Access control lists are used for determining a user's authorization level. Usernames are identification tools. Passwords and tokens are authentication tools.

27. D. Trademark protection extends to words and symbols used to represent an organization, product, or service in the marketplace.

28. A. The message displayed is an example of ransomware, which encrypts the contents of a user's computer to prevent legitimate use. This is an example of an availability attack.

29. B. HIPAA regulates three types of entities—healthcare providers, health information clearinghouses, and health insurance plans—as well as the business associates of any of those covered entities.

30. A. A Smurf attack is an example of a denial of service attack, which jeopardizes the availability of a targeted network.

31. D. Strategic plans have a long-term planning horizon of up to five years in most cases. Operational and tactical plans have shorter horizons of a year or less.

32. A. The United States Patent and Trademark Office (USPTO) bears responsibility for the registration of trademarks.

33. B. When following the separation of duties principle, organizations divide critical tasks into discrete components and ensure that no one individual has the ability to perform both actions. This prevents a single rogue individual from performing that task in an unauthorized manner.

34. B. The Federal Information Security Management Act (FISMA) applies to federal government agencies and contractors. Of the entities listed, a defense contractor is the most likely to have government contracts subject to FISMA.

35. B. The Payment Card Industry Data Security Standard (PCI DSS) governs the storage, processing, and transmission of credit card information.

36. A. The data custodian role is assigned to an individual who is responsible for implementing the security controls defined by policy and senior management. The data owner does bear ultimate responsibility for these tasks, but the data owner is typically a senior leader who delegates operational responsibility to a data custodian.

37. B. Written works, such as website content, are normally protected by copyright law. Trade secret status would not be appropriate here because the content is online and available outside the company. Patents protect inventions and trademarks protect words and symbols used to represent a brand, neither of which is relevant in this scenario.

38. C. The Code of Federal Regulations (CFR) contains the text of all administrative laws promulgated by federal agencies. The United States Code contains criminal and civil law. Supreme Court rulings contain interpretations of law and are not laws themselves. The Compendium of Laws does not exist.

39. D. Installing a device that will block attacks is an attempt to lower risk by reducing the likelihood of a successful application attack.

40. B. The owner of information security programs may be different from the individuals responsible for implementing the controls. This person should be as senior an individual as possible who is able to focus on the management of the security program. The president and CEO would not be an appropriate choice because an executive at this level is unlikely to have the time necessary to focus on security. Of the remaining choices, the CIO is the most senior position who would be the strongest advocate at the executive level.

41. A. Senior managers play several business continuity planning roles. These include setting priorities, obtaining resources, and arbitrating disputes among team members.

42. D. The Service Organizations Control audit program includes business continuity controls in a Type 2, but not Type 1, audit. Although FISMA and PCI DSS may audit business continuity, they would not apply to an email service used by a hospital.

43. A. Repudiation threats allow an attacker to deny having performed an action or activity without the other party being able to prove differently.

44. A. Integrity controls, such as the one Beth is implementing in this example, are designed to prevent the unauthorized modification of information.

45. A. SLAs do not normally address issues of data confidentiality. Those provisions are normally included in a non-disclosure agreement (NDA).

46. A. Trademarks protect words and images that represent a product or service and would not protect computer software.

47. B. Virtual private networks (VPNs) provide secure communications channels over otherwise insecure networks (such as the Internet) using encryption. If you establish a VPN connection between the two offices, users in one office could securely access content located on the other office's server over the Internet. Digital signatures are used to provide nonrepudiation, not confidentiality. Virtual LANs (VLANs) provide network segmentation on local networks but do not cross the Internet. Digital content management solutions are designed to manage web content, not access shared files located on a file server.

48. C. Redundant Array of Inexpensive Disks (RAID) uses additional hard drives to protect the server against the failure of a single device. Load balancing and server clustering do add robustness but require the addition of a server. Scheduled backups protect against data loss but do not provide immediate access to data in the event of a hard drive failure.

49. A. Hashing allows you to computationally verify that a file has not been modified between hash evaluations. ACLs and read-only attributes are useful controls that may help you prevent unauthorized modification, but they cannot verify that files were not modified. Firewalls are network security controls and do not verify file integrity.

50. B. The Fourth Amendment directly prohibits government agents from searching private property without a warrant and probable cause. The courts have expanded the interpretation of the Fourth Amendment to include protections against other invasions of privacy.

51. A. Business continuity plan documentation normally includes the continuity planning goals, a statement of importance, statement of priorities, statement of organizational responsibility, statement of urgency and timing, risk assessment and risk acceptance and mitigation documentation, a vital records program, emergency response guidelines, and documentation for maintaining and testing the plan.

52. D. Mandatory vacation programs require that employees take continuous periods of time off each year and revoke their system privileges during that time. This will hopefully disrupt any attempt to engage in the cover-up actions necessary to hide fraud and result in exposing the threat. Separation of duties, least privilege, and defense in depth controls all may help prevent the fraud in the first place but are unlikely to speed the detection of fraud that has already occurred.

53. C. Electronic vaulting is a data backup task that is part of disaster recovery, not business continuity, efforts.

54. C. Denial of service (DoS) and distributed denial of service (DDoS) attacks try to disrupt the availability of information systems and networks by flooding a victim with traffic or otherwise disrupting service.

55. B. Baselines provide the minimum level of security that every system throughout the organization must meet.

56. C. Everyone in the organization should receive a basic awareness training for the business continuity program. Those with specific roles, such as first responders and senior executives, should also receive detailed, role-specific training.

57. C. If the organization's primary concern is the cost of rebuilding the data center, James should use the replacement cost method to determine the current market price for equivalent servers.

58. D. The Computer Security Act of 1987 gave the National Institute of Standards and Technology (NIST) responsibility for developing standards and guidelines for federal computer systems. For this purpose, NIST draws upon the technical advice and assistance of the National Security Agency where appropriate.

59. B. There is no requirement that patents be for inventions made by American citizens. Patentable inventions must, on the other hand, be new, nonobvious, and useful.

60. A. Keyloggers monitor the keystrokes of an individual and report them back to an attacker. They are designed to steal sensitive information, a disruption of the goal of confidentiality.

61. A. Risks exist when there is an intersection of a threat and a vulnerability. This is described using the equation Risk = Threat * Vulnerability.

62. A. The fourth step of the NIST risk management framework is assessing security controls.

63. D. HAL Systems decided to stop offering the service because of the risk. This is an example of a risk avoidance strategy. The company altered its operations in a manner that eliminates the risk of NTP misuse.

64. C. Confidentiality controls prevent the disclosure of sensitive information to unauthorized individuals. Limiting the likelihood of a data breach is an attempt to prevent unauthorized disclosure.

65. A. The emergency response guidelines should include the immediate steps an organization should follow in response to an emergency situation. These include immediate response procedures, a list of individuals who should be notified of the emergency and secondary response procedures for first responders. They do not include long-term actions such as activating business continuity protocols, ordering equipment, or activating DR sites.

66. B. Although the CEO will not normally serve on a BCP team, it is best to obtain top-level management approval for your plan to increase the likelihood of successful adoption.

67. D. The project scope and planning phase includes four actions: a structured analysis of the organization, the creation of a BCP team, an assessment of available resources, and an analysis of the legal and regulatory landscape.

68. D. Keeping a server up and running is an example of an availability control because it increases the likelihood that a server will remain available to answer user requests.

69. A. A cold site includes the basic capabilities required for data center operations: space, power, HVAC, and communications, but it does not include any of the hardware required to restore operations.

70. C. The Computer Fraud and Abuse Act (CFAA) makes it a federal crime to maliciously cause damage in excess of $5,000 to a federal computer system during any one-year period.

71. B. ISO 27002 is an international standard focused on information security and titled "Information technology – Security techniques – Code of practice for information security management." The IT Infrastructure Library (ITIL) does contain security management practices, but it is not the sole focus of the document and the ITIL security section is derived from ISO 27002. The Capability Maturity Model (CMM) is focused on software development, and the Project Management Body of Knowledge (PMBOK) Guide focuses on project management.

72. B. The Communications Assistance to Law Enforcement Act (CALEA) requires that all communications carriers make wiretaps possible for law enforcement officials who have an appropriate court order.

73. B. The Gramm-Leach-Bliley Act (GLBA) places strict privacy regulations on financial institutions, including providing written notice of privacy practices to customers.

74. C. Non-disclosure agreements (NDAs) typically require either mutual or one-way confidentiality in a business relationship. Service-level agreements (SLAs) specify service uptime and other performance measures. Non-compete agreements (NCAs) limit the future employment possibilities of employees. Recovery time objectives (RTOs) are used in business continuity planning.

75. D. Router ACLs, encryption, and firewall rules are all examples of technical controls. Data classification is an administrative control.

76. C. While senior management should be represented on the BCP team, it would be highly unusual for the CEO to fill this role personally.

77. D. Nonrepudiation allows a recipient to prove to a third party that a message came from a purported source. Authentication would provide proof to Ben that the sender was authentic, but Ben would not be able to prove this to a third party.

78. C. Defense in depth states that organizations should have overlapping security controls designed to meet the same security objectives whenever possible. This approach provides security in the event of a single control failure.

79. D. Stakeholders should be informed of changes before, not after, they occur. The other items listed are goals of change management programs.

80. B. Ben should encrypt the data to provide an additional layer of protection as a compensating control. The organization has already made a policy exception, so he should not react by objecting to the exception or removing the data without authorization. Purchasing insurance may transfer some of the risk but is not a mitigating control.

81. A. The risk assessment team should pay the most immediate attention to those risks that appear in quadrant I. These are the risks with a high probability of occurring and a high impact on the organization if they do occur.

82. D. Electronic access to company resources must be carefully coordinated. An employee who retains access after being terminated may use that access to take retaliatory action. On the other hand, if access is terminated too early, the employee may figure out that he or she is about to be terminated.

83. D. In a risk acceptance strategy, the organization decides that taking no action is the most beneficial route to managing a risk.

84. A. COPPA requires that websites obtain advance parental consent for the collection of personal information from children under the age of 13.

85. D. The annualized rate of occurrence (ARO) is the frequency at which you should expect a risk to materialize each year. In a 100-year flood plain, risk analysts expect a flood to occur once every 100 years, or 0.01 times per year.

86. D. Wireshark is a protocol analyzer and may be used to eavesdrop on network connections. Eavesdropping is an attack against confidentiality.

87. C. In reduction analysis, the security professional breaks the system down into five key elements: trust boundaries, data flow paths, input points, privileged operations, and details about security controls.

88. D. The Sarbanes-Oxley Act (SOX) governs the financial reporting of publicly traded companies and includes requirements for security controls that ensure the integrity of that information.

89. D. Of the states listed, Florida is the only one that is not shaded to indicate a serious risk of a major earthquake.

90. C. Usernames are an identification tool. They are not secret, so they are not suitable for use as a password.

91. B. Qualitative tools are often used in business impact assessment to capture the impact on intangible factors such as customer confidence, employee morale, and reputation.

92. A. An organization pursuing a vital records management program should begin by identifying all of the documentation that qualifies as a vital business record. This should include all of the records necessary to restart the business in a new location should the organization invoke its business continuity plan.

93. B. Security training is designed to provide employees with the specific knowledge they need to fulfill their job functions. It is usually designed for individuals with similar job functions.

94. D. Awareness establishes a minimum standard of information security understanding. It is designed to accommodate all personnel in an organization, regardless of their assigned tasks.

95. C. Risks are the combination of a threat and a vulnerability. Threats are the external forces seeking to undermine security, such as the hacker in this case. Vulnerabilities are the internal weaknesses that might allow a threat to succeed. In this case, the missing patch is the vulnerability. In this scenario, if the hacker (threat) attempts a SQL injection attack against the unpatched server (vulnerability), the result is website defacement.

96. C. The exposure factor is the percentage of the facility that risk managers expect will be damaged if a risk materializes. It is calculated by dividing the amount of damage by the asset value. In this case, that is $5 million in damage divided by the $10 million facility value, or 50%.

97. B. The annualized rate of occurrence is the number of times that risk analysts expect a risk to happen in any given year. In this case, the analysts expect tornados once every 200 years, or 0.005 times per year.

98. A. The annualized loss expectancy is calculated by multiplying the single loss expectancy (SLE) by the annualized rate of occurrence (ARO). In this case, the SLE is $5,000,000 and the ARO is 0.005. Multiplying these numbers together gives you the ALE of $25,000.

99. C. Information disclosure attacks rely upon the revelation of private, confidential, or controlled information. Programming comments embedded in HTML code are an example of this type of attack.

100. B. Non-disclosure agreements (NDAs) protect the confidentiality of sensitive information by requiring that employees and affiliates not share confidential information with third parties. NDAs normally remain in force after an employee leaves the company.

Chapter 2: Asset Security (Domain 2)

1. C. Encryption is often used to protect traffic like bank transactions from sniffing. While packet injection and man-in-the-middle attacks are possible, they are far less likely to occur, and if a VPN were used, it would be used to provide encryption. TEMPEST is a specification for techniques used to prevent spying using electromagnetic emissions and wouldn't be used to stop attacks at any normal bank.

2. A. Business owners have to balance the need to provide value with regulatory, security, and other requirements. This makes the adoption of a common framework like COBIT attractive. Data owners are more likely to ask that those responsible for control selection identify a standard to use. Data processors are required to perform specific actions under regulations like the EU DPD. Finally, in many organizations, data stewards are internal roles that oversee how data is used.

3. B. A baseline is used to ensure a minimum security standard. A policy is the foundation that a standard may point to for authority, and a configuration guide may be built from a baseline to help staff who need to implement it to accomplish their task. An outline is helpful, but *outline* isn't the term you're looking for here.

4. B. Media is typically labeled with the highest classification level of data it contains. This prevents the data from being handled or accessible at a lower classification level. Data integrity requirements may be part of a classification process but don't independently drive labeling in a classification scheme.

5. A. The need to protect sensitive data drives information classification. This allows organizations to focus on data that needs to be protected rather than spending effort on less important data. Remanence describes data left on media after an attempt is made to remove the data. Transmitting data isn't a driver for an administrative process to protect sensitive data, and clearing is a technical process for removing data from media.

6. A. A data retention policy can help to ensure that outdated data is purged, removing potential additional costs for discovery. Many organizations have aggressive retention policies to both reduce the cost of storage and limit the amount of data that is kept on hand and discoverable.

    Data retention policies are not designed to destroy incriminating data, and legal requirements for data retention must still be met.

7. D. Custodians are delegated the role of handling day-to-day tasks by managing and overseeing how data is handled, stored, and protected. Data processors are systems used to process data. Business owners are typically project or system owners who are tasked with making sure systems provide value to their users or customers.

8. D. Safe Harbor compliance helps US companies meet the EU Data Protection Directive. Yearly assessments may be useful, but they aren't required. HIPAA is a US law that applies specifically to healthcare and related organizations, and encrypting all data all the time is impossible (at least if you want to use the data!).

9. C. Security baselines provide a starting point to scope and tailor security controls to your organization's needs. They aren't always appropriate to specific organizational needs, they cannot ensure that systems are always in a secure state, nor do they prevent liability.

10. A. *Clearing* describes preparing media for reuse. When media is cleared, unclassified data is written over all addressable locations on the media. Once that's completed, the media can be reused. Erasing is the deletion of files or media. Purging is a more intensive form of clearing for reuse in lower security areas, and sanitization is a series of processes that removes data from a system or media while ensuring that the data is unrecoverable by any means.

11. C. The US government uses the label Confidential for data that could cause damage if it was disclosed without authorization. Exposure of Top Secret data is considered to potentially cause grave damage, while Secret data could cause serious damage. Classified is not a level in the US government classification scheme.

12. D. Spare sectors, bad sectors, and space provided for wear leveling on SSDs (overprovisioned space) may all contain data that was written to the space that will not be cleared when the drive is wiped. Most wiping utilities only deal with currently addressable space on the drive. SSDs cannot be degaussed, and wear leveling space cannot be reliably used to hide data. These spaces are still addressable by the drive, although they may not be seen by the operating system.

13. B. *Data remanence* is a term used to describe data left after attempts to erase or remove data. Slack space describes unused space in a disk cluster, zero fill is a wiping methodology that replaces all data bits with zeroes, and *residual bytes* is a made-up term.

14. C. Information shared with customers is public, internal business could be sensitive or private, and trade secrets are proprietary. Thus public, sensitive, proprietary matches this most closely. Confidential is a military classification, which removes two of the remaining options, and trade secrets are more damaging to lose than a private classification would allow.

15. C. A watermark is used to digitally label data and can be used to indicate ownership. Encryption would have prevented the data from being accessed if it was lost, while classification is part of the set of security practices that can help make sure the right controls are in place. Finally, metadata is used to label data and might help a data loss prevention system flag it before it leaves your organization.

16. B. AES is a strong modern symmetric encryption algorithm that is appropriate for encrypting data at rest. TLS is frequently used to secure data when it is in transit. A virtual private network is not necessarily an encrypted connection and would be used for data in motion, while DES is an outdated algorithm and should not be used for data that needs strong security.

17. A. Data loss prevention (DLP) systems can use labels on data to determine the appropriate controls to apply to the data. DLP systems won't modify labels in real time and typically don't work directly with firewalls to stop traffic. Deleting unlabeled data would cause big problems for organizations that haven't labeled every piece of data!

18. B. The value of the data contained on media often exceeds the cost of the media, making more expensive media that may have a longer life span or additional capabilities like encryption support a good choice. While expensive media may be less likely to fail, the reason it makes sense is the value of the data, not just that it is less likely to fail. In general, the cost of the media doesn't have anything to do with the ease of encryption, and data integrity isn't ensured by better media.

19. C. Sanitization is a combination of processes that ensure that data from a system cannot be recovered by any means.

Erasing and clearing are both prone to mistakes and technical problems that can result in remnant data and don't make sense for systems that handled proprietary information. Destruction is the most complete method of ensuring that data cannot be exposed, and some organizations opt to destroy the entire workstation, but that is not a typical solution due to the cost involved.

20. A. The US government's classification levels from least to most sensitive are Confidential, Secret, and Top Secret.

21. C. Data at rest is inactive data that is physically stored. Data in an IPsec tunnel or part of an e-commerce transaction is data in motion. Data in RAM is ephemeral and is not inactive

22. C. PCI DSS, the Payment Card Industry Data Security Standard, provides the set of requirements for credit card processing systems. The Microsoft, NSA, and CIS baseline are all useful for building a Windows 10 security standard, but they aren't as good of an answer as the PCI DSS standard itself.

23. D. The CIS benchmarks are an example of a security baseline. A risk assessment would help identify which controls were needed, and proper system ownership is an important part of making sure baselines are implemented and maintained. Data labeling can help ensure that controls are applied to the right systems and data.

24. B. Scoping involves selecting only the controls that are appropriate for your IT systems, while tailoring matches your organization's mission and the controls from a selected baseline. Baselining is the process of configuring a system or software to match a baseline, or building a baseline itself. *Selection* isn't a technical term used for any of these processes.

25. B. The controls implemented from a security baseline should match the data classification of the data used or stored on the system. Custodians are trusted to ensure the day-to-day security of the data and should do so by ensuring that the baseline is met and maintained. Business owners often have a conflict of interest between functionality and data security, and of course, applying the same controls everywhere is expensive and may not meet business needs or be a responsible use of resources.

26. B. FTP and Telnet do not provide encryption for the data they transmit and should not be used if they can be avoided. SFTP and SSH provide encryption to protect both the data they send and the credentials that are used to log in via both utilities.

27. B. Many organizations require the destruction of media that contains data at higher levels of classification. Often the cost of the media is lower than the potential costs of data exposure, and it is difficult to guarantee that reused media doesn't contain remnant data. Tapes can be erased by degaussing, but degaussing is not always fully effective. Bitrot describes the slow loss of data on aging media, while *data permanence* is a term sometimes used to describe the life span of data and media.

28. A. NIST Special Publication 800-122 defines PII as any information that can be used to distinguish or trace an individual's identity, such as name, Social Security number, date and place of birth, mother's maiden name, biometric records, and other information that is linked or linkable to an individual such as medical, educational, financial, and employment information. PHI is health-related information about a specific person, Social Security numbers are issued to individuals in the United States, and *SII* is a made-up term.

29. B. The biggest threat to data at rest is typically a data breach. Data at rest with a high level of sensitivity is often encrypted to help prevent this. Decryption is not as significant of a threat if strong encryption is used and encryption keys are well secured. Data integrity issues could occur, but proper backups can help prevent this, and of course data could be improperly classified, but this is not the primary threat to the data.

30. B. Full disk encryption only protects data at rest. Since it encrypts the full disk, it does not distinguish between labeled and unlabeled data.

31. B. One way to use an IPsec VPN is to create a private, encrypted network (or tunnel) via a public network, allowing users to be a virtual part of their employer's internal network. IPsec is distinct from TLS, provides encryption for confidentiality and integrity, and of course, in this scenario Sue is connecting to her employer's network rather than the employer connecting to hers.

32. D. Classification identifies the value of data to an organization. This can often help drive IT expenditure prioritization and could help with rough cost estimates if a breach occurred, but that's not the primary purpose. Finally, most breach laws call out specific data types for notification rather than requiring organizations to classify data themselves.

33. B. Downgrading systems and media is rare due to the difficulty of ensuring that sanitization is complete. The need to completely wipe (or destroy) the media that systems use means that the cost of reuse is often significant and may exceed the cost of purchasing a new system or media. The goal of purging is to ensure that no data remains, so commingling data should not be a concern, nor should the exposure of the data; only staff with the proper clearance should handle the systems! Finally, a DLP system should flag data based on labels, not on the system it comes from.

34. A. Classification should be conducted based on the value of the data to the organization, its sensitivity, and the amount of harm that could result from exposure of the data. Cost should be considered when implementing controls and is weighed against the damage that exposure would create.

35. C. Erasing, which describes a typical deletion process in many operating systems, typically removes only the link to the file, and leaves the data that makes up the file itself. The data will remain in place but not indexed until the space is needed and it is overwritten. Degaussing works only on magnetic media, but it can be quite effective on it. Purging and clearing both describe more elaborate removal processes.

36. D. Safe Harbor is a framework intended to bridge the different privacy protection laws between the United States and the European Union and is run by the US Department of Commerce. At the time of this writing, Safe Harbor had been declared "invalid" by the European Court of Justice, although the US Department of Commerce has stated that it will continue the Safe Harbor program.

Both the GDPR and NIS are pending EU regulations, and there is no EU CyberSafe Act.

37. C. TLS is a modern encryption method used to encrypt and protect data in transit. AES256 is a symmetric cipher often used to protect data at rest. DES and SSL are both outdated encryption methods and should not be used for data that requires high levels of security.

38. C. We know that the data classification will not be the top level classification, "Confidential" because the loss of the data would not cause severe damage. This means we have to choose between private (PHI) and sensitive (confidential). Calling this private due to the patient's personal health information fits the classification scheme, giving us the correct answer.

39. A. A data loss prevention (DLP) system or software is designed to identify labeled data or data that fits specific patterns and descriptions to help prevent it from leaving the organization. An IDS is designed to identify intrusions. Although some IDS systems can detect specific types of sensitive data using pattern matching, they have no ability to stop traffic. A firewall uses rules to control traffic routing, while UDP is a network protocol.

40. A. When data is stored in a mixed classification environment, it is typically classified based on the highest classification of data included. In this case, the US government's highest classification is Top Secret. Mixed classification is not a valid classification in this scheme.

41. B. A non-disclosure agreement, or NDA, is a legal agreement that prevents employees from sharing proprietary data with their new employers. Purging is used on media, while classification is used on data. Encryption can help secure data, but it doesn't stop employees who can decrypt or copy the data from sharing it.

42. C. By default, BitLocker and Microsoft's Encrypting File System (EFS) both use AES (Advanced Encryption Standard), which is the NIST-approved replacement for DES (Data Encryption Standard). Serpent was a competitor of AES, and 3DES was created as a possible replacement for DES.

43. B. Group Policy provides the ability to monitor and apply settings in a security baseline. Manual checks by users or using startup scripts provide fewer reviews and may be prone to failure, while periodic review of the baseline won't result in compliance being checked.

44. B. A baseline is a set of security configurations that can be adopted and modified to fit an organization's security needs. A security policy is written to describe an organization's approach to security, while DSS is the second half of the Payment Card Industry Data Security Standard. The NIST SP-800 series of documents address computer security in a variety of areas.

45. C. Record retention policies describe how long an organization should retain data and may also specify how and when destruction should occur. Classification policies describe how and why classification should occur and who is responsible, while availability and audit policies may be created for specific purposes.

46. A. The POODLE (or Padding Oracle On Downgraded Legacy Encryption) attack helped force the move from SSL 3.0 to TLS because it allowed attackers to easily access SSL encrypted messages. Stuxnet was a worm aimed at the Iranian nuclear program, while CRIME and BEAST were earlier attacks against SSL.

47. D. Using strong encryption, like AES256, can help ensure that loss of removable media like tapes doesn't result in a data breach. Security labels may help with handling processes, but they won't help once the media is stolen or lost. Having multiple copies will ensure that you can still access the data but won't increase the security of the media. Finally, using hard drives instead of tape only changes the media type and not the risk from theft or loss.

48. D. Electronic signatures, as used in this rule, prove that the signature was provided by the intended signer. Electronic signatures as part of the FDA code are intended to ensure that electronic records are "trustworthy, reliable, and generally equivalent to paper records and handwritten signatures executed on paper." Signatures cannot provide confidentiality, or integrity, and don't ensure that someone has reviewed the data.

49. D. Secure Shell (SSH) is an encrypted protocol for remote login and command-line access. SCP and SFTP are both secure file transfer protocols, while WDS is the acronym for Windows Deployment Services, which provides remote installation capabilities for Windows operating systems.

50. B. Degaussing uses strong magnetic fields to erase magnetic media. *Magwipe* is a made-up term. Sanitization is a combination of processes used to remove data from a system or media to ensure that it cannot be recovered. Purging is a form of clearing used on media that will be reused in a lower classification or lower security environment.

51. D. Personnel retention deals with the knowledge that employees gain while employed. Issues related to the knowledge they may leave with and share are often handled with non-disclosure agreements. Knowledge gained after employment, as well as how soon (or how late) employees leave the organization, is not central to this issue.

52. C. One of the most important parts of labeling the data is ensuring that it receives a mark or label that provides the classification of the data. Digital rights management (DRM) tools provide ways to control how data is used, while encrypting it can help maintain the confidentiality and integrity of the data. Classifying the data is necessary to label it, but it doesn't automatically place a label on the data.

53. D. The NIST SP 800-88 process for sanitization and disposition shows that media that will be reused and was classified at a moderate level should be purged and then that purge should be validated. Finally, it should be documented.

54. D. Data in transit is data that is traversing a network or is otherwise in motion. TLS, VPNs, and IPsec tunnels are all techniques used to protect data in transit. AES, Serpent, and IDEA are all symmetric algorithms, while Telnet, ISDN, and UDP are all protocols. Encrypting your storage media before it is transported is a good practice, but transporting media isn't the type of transit that is meant by the phrase.

55. C. The data owner has ultimate responsibility for data belonging to an organization and is typically the CEO, president, or another senior employee. Business and mission owners typically own processes or programs. System owners own a system that processes sensitive data.

56. D. The U.S. Department of Commerce oversees Safe Harbor. Only U.S. organizations subject to the jurisdiction of the Federal Trade Commission (FTC) or U.S. air carriers and ticket agents subject to the jurisdiction of the Department of Transportation (DOT) are permitted to participate in Safe Harbor.

57. A. Chris is most likely to be responsible for classifying the data that he owns as well as assisting with or advising the system owners on security requirements and control selection. In an organization with multiple data owners, Chris is unlikely to set criteria for classifying data on his own. As a data owner, Chris will also not typically have direct responsibility for scoping, tailoring, applying, or enforcing those controls.

58. B. The system administrators are acting in the roles of data administrators who grant access and will also act as custodians who are tasked with the day-to-day application of security controls. They are not acting as data owners who own the data itself. Typically, system administrators are delegated authority by system owners, such as a department head, and of course they are tasked with providing access to users.

59. C. According to the European Union's Data Protection Directive, third-party organizations that process personal data on behalf of a data controller are known as data processors. The organization that they are contracting with would act in the role of the business or mission owners, and others within Chris's organization would have the role of data administrators, granting access as needed to the data based on their operational procedures and data classification.

60. B. The European Data Protection Directive has seven primary tenets:

- Notice
- Choice
- Onward transfer
- Security
- Data integrity
- Access
- Enforcement

Reason is not included in this list.

61. B. Under the EU's DPD, data processors like the third-party company in this question bear responsibility for ensuring that the data is not used for anything other than the purpose for which it is intended. Ben's company is the data controller, while the third party is the data processor, leaving the third party with that role.

62. D. The US government specifies Secret as the classification level for information that, if disclosed, could cause serious harm to national security. Top Secret is reserved for information that could cause exceptionally grave harm, while confidential data could be expected to cause less harm. Unclassified is not an actual classification but only indicates that the data may be released to unclassified individuals. Organizations may still restrict access to unclassified information.

63. A. Sanitization is the combination of processes used to remove data from a system or media. When a PC is disposed of, sanitization includes the removal or destruction of drives, media, and any other storage devices it may have. Purging, destruction, and declassification are all other handling methods.

64. D. Bcrypt is based on Blowfish (the *b* is a key hint here). AES and 3DES are both replacements for DES, while Diffie-Hellman is a protocol for key exchange.

65. B. Requiring all media to have a label means that when unlabeled media is found, it should immediately be considered suspicious. This helps to prevent mistakes that might leave sensitive data un-labeled. Prelabeled media is not necessarily cheaper (nor may it make sense to buy!), while reusing public media simply means that it must be classified based on the data it now contains. HIPAA does not have specific media labeling requirements.

66. B. Data in use is data that is in a temporary storage location while an application or process is using it. Thus, data in memory is best described as data in use or ephemeral data. Data at rest is in storage, while data in transit is traveling over a network or other channel. *Data at large* is a made-up term.

67. C. Validation processes are conducted to ensure that the sanitization process was completed, avoiding data remanence. A form like this one helps to ensure that each device has been checked and that it was properly wiped, purged, or sanitized. This can allow reuse, does not prevent destruction, and does not help with attribution, which is a concept used with encryption to prove who created or sent a file.

68. C. Ensuring that data cannot be recovered is difficult, and the time and effort required to securely and completely wipe media as part of declassification can exceed the cost of new media. Sanitization, purging, and clearing may be part of declassification, but they are not reasons that it is not frequently chosen as an option for organizations with data security concerns.

69. B. In the NIST SP 800-60 diagram, the process determines appropriate categorization levels resulting in security categorization and then uses that as an input to determine controls. Standard selection would occur at an organizational level, while baselining occurs when systems are configured to meet a baseline. Sanitization would require the intentional removal of data from machines or media.

70. C. A and E can both be expected to have data at rest. C, the Internet, is an unknown, and the data can't be guaranteed to be at rest. B, D, and F are all data in transit across network links.

71. C. B, D, and F all show network links. Of the answers provided, Transport Layer Security (TLS) provides the best security for data in motion. AES256 and 3DES are both symmetric ciphers and are more likely to be used for data at rest. SSL has been replaced with TLS and should not be a preferred solution.

72. B. Sending a file that is encrypted before it leaves means that exposure of the file in transit will not result in a confidentiality breach and the file will remain secure until decrypted at location E. Since answers A, C, and D do not provide any information about what happens at point C, they should be considered insecure, as the file may be at rest at point C in an unencrypted form.

73. D. Destruction is the final stage in the life cycle of media and can be done via disintegration, incineration, or a variety of other methods that result in the media and data being nonrecoverable. Sanitization is a combination of processes used when data is being removed from a system or media. Purging is an intense form of clearing, and degaussing uses strong magnetic fields to wipe data from magnetic media.

74. B. The Data Protection Directive's principles do not address data retention time periods. The seven principles are notice, purpose, consent, security, disclosure, access, and accountability.

75. D. Visual indicators like a distinctive screen background can help employees remember what level of classification they are dealing with and thus the handling requirements that they are expected to follow.

76. C. If an organization allows media to be downgraded, the purging process should be followed, and then the media should be relabeled. Degaussing may be used for magnetic media but won't handle all types of media. Pulverizing would destroy the media, preventing reuse, while relabeling first could lead to mistakes that result in media that hasn't been purged entering use.

77. B. The data owner sets the rules for use and protection of data. The remaining options all describe tasks for the system owner, including implementation of security controls.

78. C. Encrypting and labeling sensitive email will ensure that it remains confidential and can be identified. Performing these actions only on sensitive email will reduce the cost and effort of encrypting all email, allowing only sensitive email to be the focus of the organization's efforts. Only encrypting highly sensitive email not only skips labeling but might expose other classifications of email that shouldn't be exposed.

79. D. Scoping is performed when you match baseline controls to the IT system you're working to secure. Creation of standards is part of the configuration process and may involve the use of baselines. Baselining can mean the process of creating a security baseline or configuring systems to meet the baseline. CIS, the Center for Internet Security, provides a variety of security baselines.

80. C. Systems used to process data are data processors. Data owners are typically CEOs or other very senior staff, custodians are granted rights to perform day-to-day tasks when handling data, and mission owners are typically program or information system owners.

81. A. The EU GDPR is slated to replace the EU DPD, with adoption starting in 2015 and 2016 and full enforcement occurring in 2017 and 2018. NIST standards and special publications apply to the United States, while COBIT is an IT management framework. There is no EU Personal Data Protection Regulation.

82. B. Protected health information, or PHI, includes a variety of data in multiple formats, including oral and recorded data, such as that created or received by healthcare providers, employers, and life insurance providers. PHI must be protected by HIPAA. PII is personally identifiable information. SHI and HPHI are both made-up acronyms.

83. C. AES is a strong symmetric cipher that is appropriate for use with data at rest. SHA1 is a cryptographic hash, while TLS is appropriate for data in motion. DES is an outdated and insecure symmetric encryption method.

84. B. The principle of data integrity states that data should be reliable and that information should not be used for purposes other than those that users are made aware of by notice and that they have accepted through choice.

Enforcement is aimed at ensuring that compliance with principles is assured. Access allows individuals to correct, change, or delete their information, while onward transfer limits transfers to other organizations that comply with the principles of notice and choice.

85. C. Due to problems with remnant data, the US National Security Agency requires physical destruction of SSDs. This process, known as disintegration, results in very small fragments via a shredding process. Zero fill wipes a drive by replacing data with zeros, degaussing uses magnets to wipe magnetic media, and clearing is the process of preparing media for reuse.

86. A. The data owner bears responsibility for categorizing information systems and delegates selection of controls to system owners, while custodians implement the controls. Users don't perform any of these actions, while business owners are tasked with ensuring that systems are fulfilling their business purpose.

87. B. PCI DSS provides a set of required security controls and standards. Step 2 would be guided by the requirements of PCI DSS. PCI DSS will not greatly influence step 1 because all of the systems handle credit card information, making PCI DSS apply to all systems covered. Steps 3 and 4 will be conducted after PCI DSS has guided the decisions in step 2.

88. C. Custodians are tasked with the day-to-day monitoring of the integrity and security of data. Step 5 requires monitoring, which is a custodial task. A data owner may grant rights to custodians but will not be responsible for conducting monitoring. Data processors process data on behalf of the data controller, and a user simply uses the data via a computing system.

89. B. Susan's organization is limiting its risk by sending drives that have been sanitized before they are destroyed. This limits the possibility of a data breach if drives are mishandled by the third party, allowing them to be stolen, resold, or simply copied. The destruction of the drives will handle any issues with data remanence, while classification mistakes are not important if the drives have been destroyed. Data permanence and the life span of the data are not important on a destroyed drive.

90. C. A digital watermark is used to identify the owner of a file or to otherwise label it. A copyright notice provides information about the copyright asserted on the file, while data loss prevention (DLP) is a solution designed to prevent data loss. Steganography is the science of hiding information, often in images or files.

91. D. Record retention is the process of retaining and maintaining information for as long as it is needed. A data storage policy describes how and why data is stored, while data storage is the process of actually keeping the data. Asset maintenance is a non-information-security-related process for maintaining physical assets.

92. C. The cost of the data is not directly included in the classification process. Instead, the impact to the organization if the data were exposed or breached is considered. Who can access the data and what regulatory or compliance requirements cover the data are also important considerations.

93. B. Symmetric encryption like AES is typically used for data at rest. Asymmetric encryption is often used during transactions or communications when the ability to have public and private keys is necessary. DES is an outdated encryption standard, and OTP is the acronym for *one-time password*.

94. D. Administrators have the rights to assign permissions to access and handle data. Custodians are trusted to handle day-to-day data handling tasks. Business owners are typically system or project owners, and data processors are systems used to process data.

95. B. The California Online Privacy Protection Act (COPPA) requires that operators of commercial websites and services post a prominently displayed privacy policy if they collect personal information on California residents.

The Personal Information Protection and Electronic Documents Act is a Canadian privacy law, while California Civil Code 1798.82 is part of the set of California codes that requires breach notification. The California Online Web Privacy Act does not exist.

96. A. Tapes are frequently exposed due to theft or loss in transit. That means that tapes that are leaving their normal storage facility should be handled according to the organization's classification schemes and handling requirements. Purging the tapes would cause the loss of data, while increasing the classification level of the tapes or encrypting them may create extra work that isn't required by the classification level of the tapes.

97. A. The correct answer is the tape that is being shipped to a storage facility. You might think that the tape in shipment is "in motion," but the key concept is that the data is not being accessed and is instead in storage. Data in a TCP packet, in an e-commerce transaction, or in local RAM is in motion and is actively being used.

98. D. When the value of data changes due to legal, compliance, or business reasons, reviewing classifications and reclassifying the data is an appropriate response. Once the review is complete, data can be reclassified and handled according to its classification level. Simply relabeling the data avoids the classification process and may not result in the data being handled appropriately. Similarly, selecting a new baseline or simply encrypting the data may not handle all of the needs that the changes affecting the data create.

99. C. PGP, or Pretty Good Privacy (or its open-source alternative, GPG) provide strong encryption of files, which can then be sent via email. Email traverses multiple servers and will be unencrypted at rest at multiple points along its path as it is stored and forwarded to its destination.

100. A. While many non-government organizations create their own classification schemes, a common model with levels that align with the U.S. government's classification labels is shown below. In the given options, B and D do not match the US government's Top Secret, Secret, Confidential scheme, and C incorrectly matches business proprietary data with confidential data as well as Top Secret data with business sensitive data. Business internal is often another term for business sensitive, meaning that it is used to match two classifications!

US Government Classification	DAMAGE DESCRIPTION	CIVILIAN CLASSIFICATION
Top Secret	Exceptionally grave damage	Confidential/Proprietary
Secret	Serious damage	Private
Confidential	Damage	Sensitive

Chapter 3: Security Engineering (Domain 3)

1. D. The Brewer-Nash model allows access controls to change dynamically based upon a user's actions. It is often used in environments like Matthew's to implement a "Chinese wall" between data belonging to different clients.

2. A. Fires may be detected as early as the incipient stage. During this stage, air ionization takes place and specialized incipient fire detection systems can identify these changes to provide early warning of a fire.

3. A. Closed circuit television (CCTV) systems act as a secondary verification mechanism for physical presence because they allow security officials to view the interior of the facility when a motion alarm sounds to determine the current occupants and their activities.

4. B. In an m of n control system, at least m of n possible escrow agents must collaborate to retrieve an encryption key from the escrow database.

5. A. This is an example of a vendor offering a fully functional application as a web-based service. Therefore, it fits under the definition of Software as a Service (SaaS). In Infrastructure as a Service (IaaS), Compute as a Service (CaaS), and Platform as a Service (PaaS) approaches, the customer provides their own software. In this example, the vendor is providing the email software, so none of those choices are appropriate.

6. B. The Digital Signature Standard approves three encryption algorithms for use in digital signatures: the Digital Signature Algorithm (DSA); the Rivest, Shamir, Adleman (RSA) algorithm; and the Elliptic Curve DSA (ECDSA) algorithm. HAVAL is a hash function, not an encryption algorithm. While hash functions are used as part of the digital signature process, they do not provide encryption.

7. A. In the subject/object model of access control, the user or process making the request for a resource is the subject of that request. In this example, Harry is requesting resource access and is, therefore, the subject.

8. C. Michael should conduct his investigation, but there is a pressing business need to bring the website back online. The most reasonable course of action would be to take a snapshot of the compromised system and use the snapshot for the investigation, restoring the website to operation as quickly as possible while using the results of the investigation to improve the security of the site.

9. C. The use of a sandbox is an example of confinement, where the system restricts the access of a particular process to limit its ability to affect other processes running on the same system.

10. D. Assurance is the degree of confidence that an organization has that its security controls are correctly implemented. It must be continually monitored and re-verified.

11. A. Maintenance hooks, otherwise known as backdoors, provide developers with easy access to a system, bypassing normal security controls. If not removed prior to finalizing code, they pose a significant security vulnerability if an attacker discovers the maintenance hook.

12. B. The Simple Integrity Property states that an individual may not read a file classified at a lower security level than the individual's security clearance.

13. B. Supervisory control and data acquisition (SCADA) systems are used to control and gather data from industrial processes. They are commonly found in power plants and other industrial environments.

14. B. The Trusted Platform Module (TPM) is a hardware security technique that stores an encryption key on a chip on the motherboard and prevents someone from accessing an encrypted drive by installing it in another computer.

15. B. Running DES three times produces a strong encryption standard known as Triple DES, or 3DES. In order for this to provide additional security, DES must also be run using at least two different keys. NIST recommends use of three independent keys for the strongest version.

16. C. In an asymmetric cryptosystem, the sender of a message always encrypts the message using the recipient's public key.

17. D. When Bob receives the message, he uses his own private key to decrypt it. Since he is the only one with his private key, he is theB.

18. B. Each user retains their private key as secret information. In this scenario, Bob would only have access to his own private key and would not have access to the private key of Alice or any other user.

19. B. Alice creates the digital signature using her own private key. Then Bob, or any other user, can verify the digital signature using Alice's public key.

20. B. The salt is a random value added to a password before it is hashed by the operating system. The salt is then stored in a password file with the hashed password. This increases the complexity of cryptanalytic attacks by negating the usefulness of attacks that use pre-computed hash values, such as rainbow tables.

21. A. Hash functions do not include any element of secrecy and, therefore, do not require a cryptographic key.

22. D. A preaction fire suppression system activates in two steps. The pipes fill with water once the early signs of a fire are detected. The system does not dispense water until heat sensors on the sprinkler heads trigger the second phase.

23. B. The Encapsulating Security Payload (ESP) protocol provides confidentiality and integrity for packet contents. It encrypts packet payloads and provides limited authentication and protection against replay attacks.

24. D. The greatest risk when a device is lost or stolen is that sensitive data contained on the device will fall into the wrong hands. Confidentiality protects against this risk.

25. C. The exclusive or (XOR) operation is true when one and only one of the input values is true.

26. A. DES uses a 64-bit encryption key but only 56 of those bits are actually used as keying material in the encryption operation. The remaining 8 bits are used to detect tampering or corruption of the key.

27. C. The *-Security Property states that an individual may not write to a file at a lower classification level than that of the individual. This is also known as the confinement property.

28. B. The Diffie-Hellman algorithm allows for the secure exchange of symmetric encryption keys over a public network.

29. C. Protection Profiles (PPs) specify the security requirements and protections that must be in place for a product to be accepted under the Common Criteria.

30. A. Hash functions must be able to work on any variable-length input and produce a fixed-length output from that input, regardless of the length of the input.

31. C. Binary keyspaces contain a number of keys equal to two raised to the power of the number of bits. Two to the fifth power is 32, so a 5-bit keyspace contains 32 possible keys.

32. B. Kerchoff's principle says that a cryptographic system should be secure even if everything about the system, except the key, is public knowledge.

33. A. Mantraps use a double set of doors to prevent piggybacking by allowing only a single individual to enter a facility at a time.

34. A. While it would be ideal to have wiring closets in a location where they are monitored by security staff, this is not feasible in most environments. Wiring closets must be distributed geographically in multiple locations across each building used by an organization.

35. D. The *-Integrity Property states that a subject cannot modify an object at a higher security level than that possessed by the subject.

36. C. Companies with BYOD environments often require nonintrusive security controls, such as remote wiping capability, device passcodes, and full device encryption. They do not normally use application control to restrict applications because users object to the use of this technology to personally owned devices.

37. B. In the Fair Cryptosystem approach to key escrow, the secret keys used in communications are divided into two or more pieces, each of which is given to an independent third party.

38. A. The Ready state is used when a process is prepared to execute but the CPU is not available. The Running state is used when a process is executing on the CPU. The Waiting state is used when a process is blocked waiting for an external event. The Stopped state is used when a process terminates.

39. A. EAL1 assurance applies when the system in question has been functionally tested. It is the lowest level of assurance under the Common Criteria.

40. A. Administrators and processes may attach security labels to objects that provide information on an object's attributes. Labels are commonly used to apply classifications in a mandatory access control system.

41. B. Open-source software exposes the source code to public inspection and modification. The open-source community includes major software packages, including the Linux operating system.

42. A. Adam created a list of individual users that may access the file. This is an access control list, which consists of multiple access control entries. It includes the names of users, so it is not role-based, and Adam was able to modify the list, so it is not mandatory access control.

43. C. Parameter checking, or input validation, is used to ensure that input provided by users to an application matches the expected parameters for the application. Developers may use parameter checking to ensure that input does not exceed the expected length, preventing a buffer overflow attack.

44. A. *Kernel mode, supervisory mode,* and *system mode* are all terms used to describe privileged modes of system operation. User mode is an unprivileged mode.

45. D. Multistate systems are certified to handle data from different security classifications simultaneously by implementing protection mechanisms that segregate data appropriately.

46. C. For systems running in System High mode, the user must have a valid security clearance for all information processed by the system, access approval for all information processed by the system, and a valid need to know for some, but not necessarily all, information processed by the system.

47. B. Steganography is the art of using cryptographic techniques to embed secret messages within other content. Some steganographic algorithms work by making alterations to the least significant bits of the many bits that make up image files.

48. C. The Caesar cipher is a shift cipher that works on a stream of text and is also a substitution cipher. It is not a block cipher or a transposition cipher. It is extremely weak as a cryptographic algorithm.

49. A. The kernel lies within the central ring, Ring 0. Conceptually, Ring 1 contains other operating system components. Ring 2 is used for drivers and protocols. User-level programs and applications run at Ring 3. Rings 0 through 2 run in privileged mode while Ring 3 runs in user mode. It is important to note that many modern operating systems do not fully implement this model.

50. D. In an Infrastructure as a Service environment, security duties follow a shared responsibility model. Since the vendor is responsible for managing the storage hardware, the vendor would retain responsibility for destroying or wiping drives as they are taken out of service. However, it is still the customer's responsibility to validate that the vendor's sanitization procedures meet their requirements prior to utilizing the vendor's storage services.

51. B. The major difference between a code and a cipher is that ciphers alter messages at the character or bit level, not at the word level. DES, shift ciphers, and word scrambles all work at the character or bit level and are ciphers. "One if by land; two if by sea" is a message with hidden meaning in the words and is an example of a code.

52. C. The verification process is similar to the certification process in that it validates security controls. Verification may go a step further by involving a third-party testing service and compiling results that may be trusted by many different organizations. Accreditation is the act of management formally accepting an evaluating system, not evaluating the system itself.

53. B. When a process is confined within certain access bounds, that process runs in isolation. Isolation protects the operating environment, the operating system kernel, and other processes running on the system.

54. B. The mean time to failure (MTTF) provides the average amount of time before a device of that particular specification fails.

55. A. Class A fire extinguishers are useful only against common combustible materials. They use water or soda acid as their suppressant. Class B extinguishers are for liquid fires. Class C extinguishers are for electrical fires, and Class D fire extinguishers are for combustible metals.

56. A. Mobile Device Management (MDM) products provide a consistent, centralized interface for applying security configuration settings to mobile devices.

57. C. Nonrepudiation occurs when the recipient of a message is able to demonstrate to a third party that the message came from the purported sender.

58. A. The card shown in the image has a smart chip underneath the American flag. Therefore, it is an example of a smart card. This is the most secure type of identification card technology.

59. D. The TEMPEST program creates technology that is not susceptible to Van Eck phreaking attacks because it reduces or suppresses natural electromagnetic emanations.

60. B. The Trusted Computing Base (TCB) is a small subset of the system contained within the kernel that carries out critical system activities.

61. A. The MD5 hash algorithm has known collisions and, as of 2005, is no longer considered secure for use in modern environments.

62. B. Encrypting data on SSD drives does protect against wear leveling. Disk formatting does not effectively remove data from any device. Degaussing is only effective for magnetic media. Physically destroying the drive would not permit reuse.

63. C. In a known plaintext attack, the attacker has a copy of the encrypted message along with the plaintext message used to generate that ciphertext.

64. B. In a Time of Check/Time of Use (TOCTOU) attack, the attacker exploits the difference in time between when a security control is verified and the data protected by the control is actually used.

65. A. The X.509 standard, developed by the International Telecommunications Union, contains the specification for digital certificates.

66. D. Fences designed to deter more than the casual intruder should be at least 6 feet high. If a physical security system is designed to deter even determined intruders, it should be at least 8 feet high and topped with three strands of barbed wire.

67. C. In an aggregation attack, individual(s) use their access to specific pieces of information to piece together a larger picture that they are not authorized to access.

68. D. While all of the controls mentioned protect against unwanted electromagnetic emanations, only white noise is an active control. White noise generates false emanations that effectively "jam" the true emanations from electronic equipment.

69. B. In a Software as a service environment, the customer has no access to any underlying infrastructure, so firewall management is a vendor responsibility under the cloud computing shared responsibility model.

70. C. The grant rule allows a subject to grant rights that it possesses on an object to another subject.

71. A. In a phlashing attack, the attacker introduces a custom, malicious BIOS that grants the attacker some level of control over the attacked system.

72. D. Multithreading permits multiple tasks to execute concurrently within a single process. These tasks are known as threads and may be alternated between without switching processes.

73. C. This message was most likely encrypted with a transposition cipher. The use of a substitution cipher, a category that includes AES and 3DES, would change the frequency distribution so that it did not mirror that of the English language.

74. D. The meet-in-the-middle attack uses a known plaintext message and uses both encryption of the plaintext and decryption of the ciphertext simultaneously in a brute force manner to identify the encryption key in approximately double the time of a brute force attack against the basic DES algorithm.

75. A. The blacklisting approach to application control allows users to install any software they wish except for packages specifically identified by the administrator as prohibited. This would be an appropriate approach in a scenario where users should be able to install any nonmalicious software they wish to use.

76. A. Heartbeat sensors send periodic status messages from the alarm system to the monitoring center. The monitoring center triggers an alarm if it does not receive a status message for a prolonged period of time, indicating that communications were disrupted.

77. B. In a zero-knowledge proof, one individual demonstrates to another that they can achieve a result that requires sensitive information without actually disclosing the sensitive information.

78. A. Blowfish allows the user to select any key length between 32 and 448 bits.

79. B. Soda acid and other dry powder extinguishers work to remove the fuel supply. Water suppresses temperature, while halon and carbon dioxide remove the oxygen supply from a fire.

80. A. Digital signatures are possible only when using an asymmetric encryption algorithm. Of the algorithms listed, only RSA is asymmetric and supports digital signature capabilities.

81. C. The Open Web Application Security Project (OWASP) produces an annual list of the top ten web application security issues that developers and security professionals around the world rely upon for education and training purposes. The OWASP vulnerabilities form the basis for many web application security testing products.

82. A. The information flow model applies state machines to the flow of information. The Bell-LaPadula model applies the information flow model to confidentiality while the Biba model applies it to integrity.

83. D. Each process that runs on a system is assigned certain physical or logical bounds for resource access, such as memory.

84. C. Capacitance motion detectors monitor the electromagnetic field in a monitored area, sensing disturbances that correspond to motion.

85. D. Halon fire suppression systems use a chlorofluorocarbon (CFC) suppressant material that was banned in the Montreal Protocol because it depletes the ozone layer.

86. D. The Biba model focuses only on protecting integrity and does not provide protection against confidentiality or availability threats. It also does not provide protection against covert channel attacks. The Biba model focuses on external threats and assumes that internal threats are addressed programatically.

87. A. In TLS, both the server and the client first communicate using an ephemeral symmetric session key. They exchange this key using asymmetric cryptography, but all encrypted content is protected using symmetric cryptography.

88. B. A Faraday cage is a metal skin that prevents electromagnetic emanations from exiting. It is a rarely used technology because it is unwieldy and expensive, but it is quite effective at blocking unwanted radiation.

89. B. The hypervisor is responsible for coordinating access to physical hardware and enforcing isolation between different virtual machines running on the same physical platform.

90. B. Cloud computing systems where the customer only provides application code for execution on a vendor-supplied computing platform are examples of Platform as a Service (PaaS) computing.

91. B. The feedback model of composition theory occurs when one system provides input for a second system and then the second system provides input for the first system. This is a specialized case of the cascading model, so the feedback model is the most appropriate answer.

92. B. UPSes are designed to protect against short-term power losses, such as power faults. When they conduct power conditioning, they are also able to protect against sags and noise. UPSes have limited-life batteries and are not able to maintain continuous operating during a sustained blackout.

93. D. Data center humidity should be maintained between 40% and 60%. Values below this range increase the risk of static electricity, while values above this range may generate moisture that damages equipment.

94. C. Asymmetric cryptosystems use a pair of keys for each user. In this case, with 1,000 users, the system will require 2,000 keys.

95. B. Accreditation is the formal approval by a DAA that an IT system may operate in a described risk environment.

96. B. Abstraction uses a black box approach to hide the implementation details of an object from the users of that object.

97. A. The certificate revocation list contains the serial numbers of digital certificates issued by a certificate authority that have later been revoked.

98. A. The point of the digital certificate is to prove to Alison that the server belongs to the bank, so she does not need to have this trust in advance. To trust the certificate, she must verify the CA's digital signature on the certificate, trust the CA, verify that the certificate is not listed on a CRL, and verify that the certificate contains the name of the bank.

99. C. Covert channels use surreptitious communications' paths. Covert timing channels alter the use of a resource in a measurable fashion to exfiltrate information. If a user types using a specific rhythm of Morse code, this is an example of a covert timing channel. Someone watching or listening to the keystrokes could receive a secret message with no trace of the message left in logs.

100. C. Self-signed digital certificates should only be used for internal-facing applications, where the user base trusts the internally generated digital certificate.

Chapter 4: Communication and Network Security (Domain 4)

1. A. Frame Relay supports multiple private virtual circuits (PVCs), unlike X.25. It is a packet-switching technology that provides a Committed Information Rate (CIR), which is a minimum bandwidth guarantee provided by the service provider to customers. Finally, Frame Relay requires a DTE/DCE at each connection point, with the DTE providing access to the Frame Relay network, and a provider-supplied DCE, which transmits the data over the network.

2. B. LEAP, the Lightweight Extensible Authentication Protocol. is a Cisco proprietary protocol designed to handle problems with TKIP. Unfortunately, LEAP has significant security issues as well and should not be used. Any modern hardware should support WPA2 and technologies like PEAP or EAP-TLS. Using WEP, the predecessor to WPA and WPA2, would be a major step back in security for any network.

3. C. Ben is using ad hoc mode, which directly connects two clients. It can be easy to confuse this with stand-alone mode, which connects clients using a wireless access point, but not to wired resources like a central network. Infrastructure mode connects endpoints to a central network, not directly to each other. Finally, wired extension mode uses a wireless access point to link wireless clients to a wired network.

4. C. A collision domain is the set of systems that could cause a collision if they transmitted at the same time. Systems outside of a collision domain cannot cause a collision if they send at the same time. This is important, as the number of systems in a collision domain increases the likelihood of network congestion due to an increase in collisions. A broadcast domain is the set of systems that can receive a broadcast from each other. A subnet is a logical division of a network, while a supernet is made up of two or more networks.

5. D. The RST flag is used to reset or disconnect a session. It can be resumed by restarting the connection via a new three-way handshake.

6. C. He should choose 802.11n, which supports 200+ Mbps in the 2.4 GHz or the 5 GHz frequency range. 802.11a and 802.11ac are both 5 GHz only, while 802.11g is only capable of 54 Mbps.

7. C. These common ports are important to know, although some of the protocols are becoming less common. TCP 23 is used for Telnet; TCP 25 is used for SMTP (the Simple Mail Transfer Protocol); 143 is used for IMAP, the Internet Message Access Protocol; and 515 is associated with LPD, the Line Printer Daemon protocol used to send print jobs to printers.

POP3 operates on TCP 110, SSH operates on TCP 22 (and SFTP operates over SSH), and X Windows operates on a range of ports between 6000 and 6063.

8. A. The File Transfer Protocol (FTP) operates on TCP ports 20 and 21. UDP port 69 is used for the Trivial File Transfer Protocol, or TFTP, while UDP port 21 is not used for any common file transfer protocol.

9. B. Frequency Hopping Spread Spectrum (FHSS), Direct Sequence Spread Spectrum (DSSS), and Orthogonal Frequency-Division Multiplexing (OFDM) all use spread spectrum techniques to transmit on more than one frequency at the same time. Neither FHSS nor DHSS uses orthogonal modulation, while multiplexing describes combining multiple signals over a shared medium of any sort. Wi-Fi may receive interference from FHSS systems but doesn't use it.

10. B. The Challenge-Handshake Authentication Protocol, or CHAP, is used by PPP servers to authenticate remote clients. It encrypts both the username and password and performs periodic reauthentication while connected using techniques to prevent replay attacks. LEAP provides reauthentication but was designed for WEP, while PAP sends passwords unencrypted. EAP is extensible and was used for PPP connections, but it doesn't directly address the listed items.

11. C. SSID broadcast is typically disabled for secure networks. While this won't stop a determined attacker, it will stop casual attempts to connect. Separating the network from other wired networks, turning on the highest level of encryption supported (like WPA2), and using MAC filtering for small groups of clients that can reasonably be managed by hand are all common best practices for wireless networks.

12. A. A ring connects all systems like points on a circle. A ring topology was used with Token Ring networks, and a token was passed between systems around the ring to allow each system to communicate. More modern networks may be described as a ring but are only physically a ring and not logically using a ring topology.

13. B. The firewall in the diagram has two protected zones behind it, making it a two-tier firewall design.

14. D. Remote PCs that connect to a protected network need to comply with security settings and standards that match those required for the internal network. The VPN concentrator logically places remote users in the protected zone behind the firewall, but that means that user workstations (and users) must be trusted in the same way that local workstations are.

15. C. An intrusion protection system can scan traffic and stop both known and unknown attacks. A web application firewall, or WAF, is also a suitable technology, but placing it at location C would only protect from attacks via the organization's VPN, which should only be used by trusted users. A firewall typically won't have the ability to identify and stop cross-site scripting attacks, and IDS systems only monitor and don't stop attacks.

16. D. Distance-vector protocols use metrics including the direction and distance in hops to remote networks to make decisions. A link-state routing protocol considers the shortest distance to a remote network. Destination metric and link-distance protocols don't exist.

17. B. Disabling SSID broadcast can help prevent unauthorized personnel from attempting to connect to the network. Since the SSID is still active, it can be discovered by using a wireless sniffer. Encryption keys are not related to SSID broadcast, beacon frames are used to broadcast the SSID, and it is possible to have multiple networks with the same SSID.

18. B. A proxy is a form of gateway that provide clients with a filtering, caching, or other service that protects their information from remote systems. A router connects networks, while a firewall uses rules to limit traffic permitted through it. A gateway translates between protocols.

19. B. DNS poisoning occurs when an attacker changes the domain name to IP address mappings of a system to redirect traffic to alternate systems. DNS spoofing occurs when an attacker sends false replies to a requesting system, beating valid replies from the actual DNS server. ARP spoofing provides a false hardware address in response to queries about an IP, and Cain & Abel is a powerful Windows hacking tool, but a Cain attack is not a specific type of attack.

20. B. Screen scrapers copy the actual screen displayed and display it at a remote location. RDP provides terminal sessions without doing screen scraping, remote node operation is the same as dial-up access, and remote control is a means of controlling a remote system (screen scraping is a specialized subset of remote control).

21. A. S/MIME supports both signed messages and a secure envelope method. While the functionality of S/MIME can be replicated with other tools, the secure envelope is an S/MIME-specific concept. MOSS, or MIME Object Security Services, and PEM can also both provide authentication, confidentiality, integrity, and nonrepudiation, while DKIM, or Domain Keys Identified Mail, is a domain validation tool.

22. A. Multilayer protocols like DNP3 allow SCADA and other systems to use TCP/IP-based networks to communicate. Many SCADA devices were never designed to be exposed to a network, and adding them to a potentially insecure network can create significant risks. TLS or other encryption can be used on TCP packets, meaning that even serial data can be protected. Serial data can be carried via TCP packets because TCP packets don't care about their content; it is simply another payload. Finally, TCP/IP does not have a specific throughput as designed, so issues with throughput are device-level issues.

23. C. WEP has a very weak security model that relies on a single, predefined, shared static key. This means that modern attacks can break WEP encryption in less than a minute.

24. B. A denial of service attack is an attack that causes a service to fail or to be unavailable. Exhausting a system's resources to cause a service to fail is a common form of denial of service attack. A worm is a self-replicating form of malware that propagates via a network, a virus is a type of malware that can copy itself to spread, and a Smurf attack is a distributed denial of service attack (DDoS) that spoofs a victim's IP address to systems using an IP broadcast, resulting in traffic from all of those systems to the target.

25. C. 802.11n can operate at speeds over 200 Mbps, and it can operate on both the 2.4 and 5 GHz frequency range. 802.11g operates at 54 Mbps using the 2.4 GHz frequency range, and 802.11ac is capable of 1 Gbps using the 5 GHz range. 802.11a and b are both outdated and are unlikely to be encountered in modern network installations.

26. B. ARP and RARP operate at the Data Link layer, the second layer of the OSI model. Both protocols deal with physical hardware addresses, which are used above the Physical layer (layer 1) and below the Network layer (layer 3), thus falling at the Data Link layer.

27. D. iSCSI is a converged protocol that allows location-independent file services over traditional network technologies. It costs less than traditional Fibre Channel. VoIP is Voice over IP, SDN is Software-defined networking, and MPLS is Multiprotocol Label Switching, a technology that uses path labels instead of network addresses.

28. A. A repeater or concentrator will amplify the signal, ensuring that the 100-meter distance limitation of 1000Base-T is not an issue. A gateway would be useful if network protocols were changing, while Cat7 cable is appropriate for a 10Gbps network at much shorter distances. STP cable is limited to 155 Mbps and 100 meters, which would leave Chris with network problems.

29. B. TCP 80 is typically HTTP.

30. C. HTTP traffic is typically sent via TCP 80. Unencrypted HTTP traffic can be easily captured at any point between A and B, meaning that the instant messaging solution chosen does not provide confidentiality for the organization's corporate communications.

31. B. If a business need requires instant messaging, using a local instant messaging server is the best option. This prevents traffic from traveling to a third-party server and can offer additional benefits such as logging, archiving, and control of security options like the use of encryption.

32. B. Multilayer protocols create three primary concerns for security practitioners: They can conceal covert channels (and thus covert channels are allowed), filters can be bypassed by traffic concealed in layered protocols, and the logical boundaries put in place by network segments can be bypassed under some circumstances. Multilayer protocols allow encryption at various layers and support a range of protocols at higher layers.

33. C. A bus can be linear or tree-shaped and connects each system to trunk or backbone cable. Ethernet networks operate on a bus topology.

34. B. When a workstation or other device is connected simultaneously to both a secure and a nonsecure network like the Internet, it may act as a bridge, bypassing the security protections located at the edge of a corporate network. It is unlikely that traffic will be routed improperly leading to the exposure of sensitive data, as traffic headed to internal systems and networks is unlikely to be routed to the external network. Reflected DDoS attacks are used to hide identities rather than to connect through to an internal network, and security administrators of managed systems should be able to determine both the local and wireless IP addresses his system uses.

35. A. Wardriving and warwalking are both processes used to locate wireless networks, but are not typically as detailed and thorough as a site survey, and design map is a made-up term.

36. C. The DARPA TCP/IP model was used to create the OSI model, and the designers of the OSI model made sure to map the OSI model layers to it. The Application layer of the TCP model maps to the Application, Presentation, and Session layers, while the TCP and OSI models both have a distinct Transport layer.

37. B. ARP cache poisoning occurs when false ARP data is inserted into a system's ARP cache, allowing the attacker to modify its behavior. *RARP flooding*, *denial of ARP attacks*, and *ARP buffer blasting* are all made-up terms.

38. C. The process of using a fake MAC (Media Access Control) address is called spoofing, and spoofing a MAC address already in use on the network can lead to an address collision, preventing traffic from reaching one or both systems. Tokens are used in token ring networks, which are outdated, and EUI refers to an *Extended Unique Identifier*, another term for *MAC address*, but token loss is still not the key issue. *Broadcast domains* refers to the set of machines a host can send traffic to via a broadcast message.

39. D. Direct Inward System Access uses access codes assigned to users to add a control layer for external access and control of the PBX. If the codes are compromised, attackers can make calls through the PBX or even control it. Not updating a PBX can lead to a range of issues, but this question is looking for a DISA issue. Allowing only local calls and using unpublished numbers are both security controls and might help keep the PBX more secure.

40. D. Application-specific protocols are handled at layer 7, the Application layer of the OSI model.

41. D. Ping uses ICMP, the Internet Control Message Protocol, to determine whether a system responds and how many hops there are between the originating system and the remote system. Lauren simply needs to filter out ICMP to not see her pings.

42. D. 802.1x provides port-based authentication and can be used with technologies like EAP, the Extensible Authentication Protocol. 802.11a is a wireless standard, 802.3 is the standard for Ethernet, and 802.15.1 was the original Bluetooth IEEE standard.

43. D. 1000Base-T is capable of a 100 meter run according to its specifications. For longer distances, a fiber-optic cable is typically used in modern networks.

44. C. PRI, or Primary Rate Interface, can use between 2 and 23 64 Kbps channels, with a maximum potential bandwidth of 1.544 Mbps. Actual speeds will be lower due to the D channel, which can't be used for actual data transmission, but PRI beats BRI's two B channels paired with a D channel for 144 Kbps of bandwidth.

45. C. SPIT stands for Spam over Internet Telephony and targets VoIP systems.

46. D. Bluesnarfing targets the data or information on Bluetooth-enabled devices. Bluejacking occurs when attackers send unsolicited messages via Bluetooth.

47. C. Layer 6, the Presentation layer, transforms data from the Application layer into formats that other systems can understand by formatting and standardizing the data. That means that standards like JPEG, ASCII, and MIDI are used at the Presentation layer for data. TCP, UDP, and TLS are used at the Transport layer; NFS, SQL, and RPC operate at the Session layer; and HTTP, FTP, and SMTP are Application layer protocols.

48. D. Fully connected mesh networks provide each system with a direct physical link to every other system in the mesh. This is very expensive but can provide performance advantages for specific types of computational work.

49. C. PPTp, L2F, L2TP, and IPsec are the most common VPN protocols. TLS is also used for an increasingly large percentage of VPN connections and may appear at some point in the CISSP exam. PPP is a dial-up protocol, LTP is not a protocol, and SPAP is the Shiva Password Authentication Protocol sometimes used with PPTP.

50. C. FDDI, or Fiber Distributed Data Interface, is a token-passing network that uses a pair of rings with traffic flowing in opposite directions. It can bypass broken segments by dropping the broken point and using the second, unbroken ring to continue to function. Token Ring also uses tokens, but it does not use a dual loop. SONET is a protocol for sending multiple optical streams over fiber, and a ring topology is a design, not a technology.

51. C. The Physical Layer includes electrical specifications, protocols, and standards that allow control of throughput, handling line noise, and a variety of other electrical interface and signaling requirements. The OSI layer doesn't have a Device layer. The Transport layer connects the Network and Session layers, and the Data Link layer packages packets from the network layer for transmission and receipt by devices operating on the Physical layer.

52. A. WPA2, the replacement for WPA, does not suffer from the security issues that WEP, the original wireless security protocol, and WPA, its successor, both suffer from. AES is used in WPA2 but is not specifically a wireless security standard.

53. A. User awareness is one of the most important tools when dealing with attachments. Attachments are often used as a vector for malware, and aware users can help prevent successful attacks by not opening the attachments. Anti-malware tools, including antivirus software, can help detect known threats before users even see the attachments. Encryption, including tools like S/MIME, won't help prevent attachment-based security problems, and removing ZIP file attachments will only stop malware that is sent via those ZIP files.

54. A. The Transport layer provides logical connections between devices, including end-to-end transport services to ensure that data is delivered. Transport layer protocols include TCP, UDP, SSL, and TLS.

55. B. Machine Access Control (MAC) addresses are the hardware address the machine uses for layer 2 communications. The MAC addresses include an organizationally unique identifier (OUI), which identifies the manufacturer. MAC addresses can be changed, so this is not a guarantee of accuracy, but under normal circumstances you can tell what manufacturer made the device by using the MAC address.

56. D. PEAP provides encryption for EAP methods and can provide authentication. It does not implement CCMP, which was included in the WPA2 standard. LEAP is dangerously insecure and should not be used due to attack tools that have been available since the early 2000s.

57. C. Double NATing isn't possible with the same IP range; the same IP addresses cannot appear inside and outside of a NAT router. RFC 1918 addresses are reserved, but only so they are not used and routable on the Internet, and changing to PAT would not fix the issue.

58. B. A Class B network holds 2^16 systems, and its default network mask is 255.255.0.0.

59. C. Traditional private branch exchange (PBX) systems are vulnerable to eavesdropping because voice communications are carried directly over copper wires. Since standard telephones don't provide encryption (and you're unlikely to add encrypted phones unless you're the NSA), physically securing access to the lines and central connection points is the best strategy available.

60. A. Most cordless phones don't use encryption, and even modern phones that use DECT (which does provide encryption) have already been cracked. This means that a determined attacker can almost always eavesdrop on cordless phones, and makes them a security risk if they're used for confidential communication.

61. A. VLAN hopping between the voice and computer VLANs can be accomplished when devices share the same switch infrastructure. Using physically separate switches can prevent this attack. Encryption won't help with VLAN hopping because it relies on header data that the switch needs to read (and this is unencrypted), while Caller ID spoofing is an inherent problem with VoIP systems. A denial of service is always a possibility, but it isn't specifically a VoIP issue and a firewall may not stop the problem if it's on a port that must be allowed through.

62. A. A static packet filtering firewall is only aware of the information contained in the message header of packets: the source, destination, and port it is sent from and headed to. This means that they're not particularly smart, unlike Application layer firewalls that proxy traffic based on the service they support or stateful inspection firewalls (also known as dynamic packet inspection firewalls) that understand the relationship between systems and their communications.

63. A. Black boxes are designed to steal long-distance service by manipulating line voltages. Red boxes simulate tones of coins being deposited into payphones; blue boxes were tone generators used to simulate the tones used for telephone networks; and white boxes included a dual tone, multifrequency generator to control phone systems.

64. A. Data streams are associated with the Application, Presentation, and Session layers. Once they reach the Transport layer, they become segments (TCP) or datagrams (UDP). From there, they are converted to packets at the Network layer, frames at the Data Link layer, and bits at the Physical layer.

65. C. A three-tier design separates three distinct protected zones and can be accomplished with a single firewall that has multiple interfaces. Single- and two-tier designs don't support the number of protected networks needed in this scenario, while a four-tier design would provide a tier that isn't needed.

66. C. Software-defined networking provides a network architecture than can be defined and configured as code or software. This will allow Lauren's team to quickly change the network based on organizational requirements. The 5-4-3 rule is an old design rule for networks that relied on repeaters or hubs. A converged network carries multiple types of traffic like voice, video, and data. A hypervisor-based network may be software defined, but it could also use traditional network devices running as virtual machines.

67. B. Sensitive information contained in faxes should not be left in a public area. Disabling automatic printing will help prevent unintended viewing of the faxes. Purging local memory after the faxes are printed will ensure that unauthorized individuals can't make additional copies of faxes. Encryption would help keep the fax secure during transmission but won't help with the public location and accessibility of the fax machine itself, and of course, enabling automatic printing will only make casual access easier.

68. B. ISDN, cable modems, DSL, and T1 and T3 lines are all examples of broadband technology that can support multiple simultaneous signals. They are analog, not digital, and are not broadcast technologies.

69. A. A single-tier firewall deployment is very simple and does not offer useful design options like a DMZ or separate transaction subnets.

70. D. Network segmentation can reduce issues with performance as well as diminish the chance of broadcast storms by limiting the number of systems in a segment. This decreases broadcast traffic visible to each system and can reduce congestion. Segmentation can also help provide security by separating functional groups who don't need to be able to access each other's systems. Installing a firewall at the border would only help with inbound and outbound traffic, not cross-network traffic. Spanning tree loop prevention helps prevent loops in Ethernet networks (for example, when you plug a switch into a switch via two ports on each), but it won't solve broadcast storms that aren't caused by a loop or security issues. Encryption might help prevent some problems between functional groups, but it won't stop them from scanning other systems, and it definitely won't stop a broadcast storm!

71. C. ICMP, RIP, and network address translation all occur at layer 3, the Network layer.

72. C. One of the visibility risks of virtualization is that communication between servers and systems using virtual interfaces can occur "inside" of the virtual environment. This means that visibility into traffic in the virtualization environment has to be purpose built as part of its design. Option D is correct but incomplete because inter-hypervisor traffic isn't the only traffic the IDS will see.

73. B. Cut and paste between virtual machines can bypass normal network-based data loss prevention tools and monitoring tools like an IDS or IPS. Thus, it can act as a covert channel, allowing the transport of data between security zones. So far, cut and paste has not been used as a method for malware spread in virtual environments and has not been associated with denial of service attacks. Cut and paste requires users to be logged in and does not bypass authentication requirements.

74. A. While virtual machine escape has only been demonstrated in laboratory environments, the threat is best dealt with by limiting what access to the underlying hypervisor can prove to a successful tracker. Segmenting by data types or access levels can limit the potential impact of a hypervisor compromise. If attackers can access the underlying system, restricting the breach to only similar data types or systems will limit the impact. Escape detection tools are not available on the market, restoring machines to their original snapshots will not prevent the exploit from occuring again, and Tripwire detects file changes and is unlikely to catch exploits that escape the virtual machines themselves.

75. C. WPA2's CCMP encryption scheme is based on AES. As of the writing of this book, there have not been any practical real-world attacks against WPA2.

DES has been successfully broken, and neither 3DES nor TLS is used for WPA2.

76. B. Ethernet networks use Carrier-Sense Multiple Access with Collision Detection (CSMA/CD) technology. When a collision is detected and a jam signal is sent, hosts wait a random period of time before attempting retransmission.

77. C. IPX, AppleTalk, and NetBEUI are all examples of non-IP protocols. TCP and UDP are both IP protocols, while routing protocols are used to send information about how traffic should be routed through networks.

78. C. A T3 (DS-3) line is capable of 44.736 Mbps. This is often referred to as 45 Mbps. A T1 is 1.544 Mbps, ATM is 155 Mbps, and ISDN is often 64 or 128 Kbps.

79. B. A two-tier firewall uses a firewall with multiple interfaces or multiple firewalls in series. This image shows a firewall with two protected interfaces, with one used for a DMZ and one used for a protected network. This allows traffic to be filtered between each of the zones (Internet, DMZ, and private network).

80. B. Endpoint security solutions face challenges due to the sheer volume of data that they can create. When each workstation is generating data about events, this can be a massive amount of data. Endpoint security solutions should reduce the number of compromises when properly implemented, and they can also help by monitoring traffic after it is decrypted on the local host. Finally, non-TCP protocols are relatively uncommon on modern networks, making this a relatively rare concern for endpoint security system implementations.

81. D. The IP address 127.0.0.1 is a loopback address and will resolve to the local machine. Public addresses are non-RFC 1918, non-reserved addresses. RFC 1918 addresses are reserved and include ranges like 10.x.x.x. An APIPA address is a self-assigned address used when a DHCP server cannot be found.

82. B. Since Bluetooth doesn't provide strong encryption, it should only be used for activities that are not confidential. Bluetooth PINs are four-digit codes that often default to 0000. Turning it off and ensuring that your devices are not in discovery mode can help prevent Bluetooth attacks.

83. C. Stateful packet inspection firewalls are known as second-generation firewalls. UTM, or Unified Threat Management is a concept used in next generation firewalls, packet filters are called first generation firewalls, and application level gateway firewalls are known as third generation firewalls.

84. B. Fiber Channel over Ethernet allows Fiber Channel communications over Ethernet networks, allowing existing high-speed networks to be used to carry storage traffic. This avoids the cost of a custom cable plant for a Fiber Channel implementation. MPLS, or Multiprotocol label Switching, is used for high performance networking; VoIP is Voice over IP; and SDN is Software-Defined Networking.

85. D. A modem (MOdulator/DEModulator) modulates between an analog carrier like a phone line and digital communications like those used between computers. While modems aren't in heavy use in most areas, they are still in place for system control and remote system contact and in areas where phone lines are available but other forms of communication are too expensive or not available.

86. D. The OSI layers in order are Application, Presentation, Session, Transport, Network, Data Link, and Physical.

87. B. A teardrop attack uses fragmented packets to target a flaw in how the TCP stack on a system handles fragment reassembly. If the attack is successful, the TCP stack fails, resulting in a denial of service. Christmas tree attacks set all of the possible TCP flags on a packet, thus "lighting it up like a Christmas tree." Stack killer and frag grenade attacks are made-up answers.

88. D. The Point-to-Point Protocol (PPP) is used for dial-up connections for modems, IDSN, Frame Relay, and other technologies. It replaced SLIP in almost all cases. PPTP is the Point-to-Point Tunneling Protocol used for VPNs, and SLAP is not protocol at all!

89. B. While non-IP protocols like IPX/SPX, NetBEUI, and AppleTalk are rare in modern networks, they can present a challenge because many firewalls are not capable of filtering them. This can create risks when they are necessary for an application or system's function because they may have to be passed without any inspection. Christmas tree attacks set all of the possible flags on a TCP packet (and are thus related to an IP protocol), IPX is not an IP-based protocol, and while these protocols are outdated, there are ways to make even modern PCs understand them.

90. C. Of the three answers, PEAP is the best solution. It encapsulates EAP in a TLS tunnel, providing strong encryption. LEAP is a Cisco proprietary protocol that was originally designed to help deal with problems in WEP. LEAP's protections have been defeated, making it a poor choice.

91. A. L2TP can use IPsec to provide encryption of traffic, ensuring confidentiality of the traffic carried via an L2TP VPN. PPTP sends the initial packets of a session in plaintext, potentially including usernames and hashed passwords. PPTP does support EAP and was designed to encapsulate PPP packets. All VPNs are point to point, and multipoint issues are not a VPN problem.

92. C. A full mesh topology directly connects each machine to every other machine on the network. For five systems, this means four connections per system.

93. D. Ethernet uses a bus topology. While devices may be physically connected to a switch in a physical topology that looks like a star, systems using Ethernet can all transmit on the bus simultaneously, possibly leading to collisions.

94. D. ARP spoofing is often done to replace a target's cache entry for a destination IP, allowing the attacker to conduct a man-in-the-middle attack. A denial of service attack would be aimed at disrupting services rather than spoofing an ARP response, a replay attack will involve existing sessions, and a Trojan is malware that is disguised in a way that makes it look harmless.

95. B. Category 3 UTP cable is primarily used for phone cables and was also used for early Ethernet networks where it provided 10 Mbps of throughput. Cat 5 cable provides 100 Mbps (and 1000 Mbps if it is Cat 5e). Cat 6 cable can also provide 1000 Mbps.

96. B. Crosstalk occurs when data transmitted on one set of wires is picked up on another set of wires. Interference like this is electromagnetic rather than simply magnetic, *transmission absorption* is a made-up term, and amplitude modulation is how AM radio works.

97. B. WEP's implementation of RC4 is weakened by its use of a static common key and a limited number of initialization vectors. It does not use asymmetric encryption, and clients do not select encryption algorithms.

98. B. VLANs can be used to logically separate groups of network ports while still providing access to an uplink. Per-room VPNs would create significant overhead for support as well as create additional expenses. Port security is used to limit what systems can connect to ports, but it doesn't provide network security between systems. Finally, while firewalls might work, they would add additional expense and complexity without adding any benefits over a VLAN solution.

99. D. MAC addresses and their organizationally unique identifiers are used at the Data Link layer to identify systems on a network. The Application and Session layers don't care about physical addresses, while the Physical layer involves electrical connectivity and handling physical interfaces rather than addressing.

100. C. Domain Keys Identified Mail, or DKIM, is designed to allow assertions of domain identity to validate email. S/MIME, PEM, and MOSS are all solutions that can provide authentication, integrity, nonrepudiation, and confidentiality, depending on how they are used.

Chapter 5: Identity and Access Management (Domain 5)

1. C. Capability tables list the privileges assigned to subjects and identify the objects that subjects can access. Access control lists are object-focused rather than subject-focused. Implicit deny is a principle that states that anything that is not explicitly allowed is denied, and a rights management matrix is not an access control model.

2. B. Since Jim's organization is using a cloud-based Identity as a Service solution, a third party, on-premise identity service can provide the ability to integrate with the IDaaS solution, and the company's use of Active Directory is widely supported by third-party vendors. OAuth is used to log into third-party websites using existing credentials and would not meet the needs described. SAML is a markup language and would not meet the full set of AAA needs. Since the organization is using Active Directory, a custom in-house solution is unlikely to be as effective as a preexisting third-party solution and may take far more time and expense to implement.

3. C. Kerberos encrypts messages using secret keys, providing protection for authentication traffic. The KDC is both a single point of failure and can cause problems if compromised because keys are stored on the KDC that would allow attackers to impersonate any user. Like many authentication methods, Kerberos can be susceptible to password guessing.

4. C. Voice pattern recognition is "something you are," a Type 3 authentication factor. Type 1 factors are "something you know," and Type 2 factors are "something you have." Type 4 is made up and is not a valid type of authentication factor.

5. B. Susan has used two distinct types of factors: the PIN and password are both Type 1 factors, and the retina scan is a Type 3 factor. Her username is not a factor.

6. B. Menus, shells, and database views are all commonly used for constrained interfaces. A keyboard is not typically a constrained interface, although physically constrained interfaces like those found on ATMs, card readers, and other devices are common.

7. C. Dictionary attacks use a dictionary or list of common passwords as well as variations of those words to attempt to log in as an authorized user. This attack shows a variety of passwords based on a similar base word, which is often a good indicator of a dictionary attack. A brute force attack will typically show simple iteration of passwords, while a man-in-the-middle attack would not be visible in the authentication log. A rainbow table attack is used when attackers already have password hashes in their possession and would also not show up in logs.

8. D. The Common Criteria defines trusted paths as a way to protect data between users and a security component. This includes attacks like replacing login windows for systems and is the reason Windows uses Ctrl+Alt_Del as a login sequence. Man-in-the-middle attacks can be prevented by using a trusted channel, which is often implemented with encryption and certificates. Brute force and dictionary attacks are often discouraged by using a back-off algorithm to slow down or prevent attacks.

9. B. Decentralized access control can result in less consistency because the individuals tasked with control may interpret policies and requirements differently and may perform their roles in different ways. Access outages, overly granular control, and training costs may occur, depending on specific implementations, but they are not commonly identified issues with decentralized access control.

10. B. A callback to a home phone number is an example of a "somewhere you are" factor. This could potentially be spoofed by call forwarding or using a VoIP system. Type 1 factors are "something you know," Type 3 factors are biometric, and geographic factors are typically based on IP addresses or access to a GPS.

11. D. Kerberos uses realms, and the proper type of trust to set up for an Active Directory environment that needs to connect to a K5 domain is a realm trust. A shortcut trust is a transitive trust between parts of a domain tree or forest that shortens the trust path, a forest trust is a transitive trust between two forest root domains, and an external trust is a non-transitive trust between AD domains in separate forests.

12. B. TACACS+ is the only modern protocol on the list. It provides advantages of both TACACS and XTACACS as well as some benefits over RADIUS, including encryption of all authentication information. Super TACACS is not an actual protocol.

13. D. Kerberos, Active Directory Federation Services (ADFS), and Central Authentication Services (CAS) are all SSO implementations. RADIUS is not a single-sign on implementation, although some vendors use it behind the scenes to provide authentication for proprietary SSO.

14. C. Interface restrictions based on user privileges is an example of a constrained interface. Least privilege describes the idea of providing users with only the rights they need to accomplish their job, while need to know limits access based on whether a subject needs to know the information to accomplish an assigned task. Separation of duties focuses on preventing fraud or mistakes by splitting tasks between multiple subjects.

15. D. When the owner of a file makes the decisions about who has rights or access privileges to it, they are using discretionary access control. Role-based access controls would grant accessed based on a subject's role, while rule-based controls would base the decision on a set of rules or requirements. Non-discretionary access controls apply a fixed set of rules to an environment to manage access. Non-discretionary access controls include rule-, role-, and lattice-based access controls.

16. D. Need to know is applied when subjects like Alex have access to only the data they need to accomplish their job. Separation of duties is used to limit fraud and abuse by having multiple employees perform parts of a task. Constrained interfaces restrict what a user can see or do and would be a reasonable answer if need to know did not describe his access more completely in this scenario. Context-dependent control relies on the activity being performed to apply controls, and this question does not specify a work-flow or process.

17. D. The client in Kerberos logins uses AES to encrypt the username and password prior to sending it to the KDC.

18. C. The KDC uses the user's password to generate a hash and then uses that hash to encrypt a symmetric key. It transmits both the encrypted symmetric key and an encrypted time-stamped TGT to the client.

19. B. The client needs to install the TGT for use until it expires, and must also decrypt the symmetric key using a hash of the user's password.

20. A. Retina scans can reveal additional information, including high blood pressure and pregnancy, causing privacy concerns. Newer retina scans don't require a puff of air, and retina scanners are not the most expensive biometric factor. Their false positive rate can typically be adjusted in software, allowing administrators to adjust their acceptance rate as needed to balance usability and security.

21. C. Mandatory access control systems are based on a lattice-based model. Lattice-based models use a matrix of classification labels to compartmentalize data. Discretionary access models allow object owners to determine access to the objects they control, role-based access controls are often group based, and rule-based access controls like firewall ACLs apply rules to all subjects they apply to.

22. C. Dictionary, brute force, and man-in-the-middle attacks are all types of attacks that are frequently aimed at access controls. Teardrop attacks are a type of denial of service attack.

23. A. Logging systems can provide accountability for identity systems by tracking the actions, changes, and other activities a user or account performs.

24. B. As an employee's role changes, they often experience privilege creep, which is the accu-mulation of old rights and roles. Account review is the process of reviewing accounts and ensuring that their rights match their owners' role and job requirements. Account revoca-tion removes accounts, while re-provisioning might occur if an employee was terminated and returned or took a leave of absence and returned.

25. A. Biba uses a lattice to control access and is a form of the mandatory access control (MAC) model. It does not use rules, roles, or attributes, nor does it allow user discretion. Users can create content at their level or lower but cannot decide who gets access, levels are not roles, and attributes are not used to make decisions on access control.

26. C. RADIUS is an AAA protocol used to provide authentication and authorization; it's often used for modems, wireless networks, and network devices. It uses network access servers to send access requests to central RADIUS servers. Kerberos is a ticket-based authentication protocol; OAuth is an open standard for authentication allowing the use of credentials from one site on third-party sites; and EAP is the Extensible Authentication Protocol, an authentication framework often used for wireless networks.

27. A. Resource-based access controls match permissions to resources like a storage volume. Resource-based access controls are becoming increasingly common in cloud-based Infrastructure as a Service environments. The lack of roles, rules, or a classification system indicate that role-based, rule-based, and mandatory access controls are not in use here.

28. C. By default, RADIUS uses UDP and only encrypts passwords. RADIUS supports TCP and TLS, but this is not a default setting.

29. D. A key distribution center (KDC) provides authentication services, and ticket-granting tickets (TGTs) provide proof that a subject has authenticated and can request tickets to access objects. Authentication services (ASs) are part of the KDC. There is no TS in a Kerberos infrastructure.

30. D. Authorization provides a user with capabilities or rights. Roles and group management are both methods that could be used to match users with rights. Logins are used to validate a user.

31. C. Privilege creep occurs when users retain from roles they held previously rights they do not need to accomplish their current job. Unauthorized access occurs when an unauthorized user accesses files. *Excessive provisioning* is not a term used to describe permissions issues, and account review would help find issues like this.

32. B. Phishing is not an attack against an access control mechanism. While phishing can result in stolen credentials, the attack itself is not against the control system and is instead against the person being phished. Dictionary attacks and man-in-the-middle attacks both target access control systems.

33. B. Race conditions occur when two or more processes need to access the same resource in the right order. If an attacker can disrupt this order, they may be able to affect the normal operations of the system and gain unauthorized access or improper rights. Collisions occur when two different files produce the same result from a hashing operation, out-of-order execution is a CPU architecture feature that allows the use of otherwise unused cycles, and *determinism* is a philosophical term rather than something you should see on the CISSP exam!

34. C. Mandatory access controls use a lattice to describe how classification labels relate to each other. In this image, classification levels are set for each of the labels shown. A discretionary access control (DAC) system would show how the owner of the objects allows access. RBAC could be either rule- or role-based access control and would either use system-wide rules or roles. Task-based access control (TBAC) would list tasks for users.

35. C. LDAP distinguished names are made up of zero or more comma-separate components known as relative distinguished names. cn=ben,ou=example; ends with a semicolon and is not a valid DN. It is possible to have additional values in the same RDN by using a plus sign between then.

36. B. The process of a subject claiming or professing an identity is known as identification. Authorization verifies the identity of a subject by checking a factor like a password. Logins typically include both identification and authorization, and token presentation is a type of authentication.

37. D. Dogs, guards, and fences are all examples of physical controls. While dogs and guards might detect a problem, fences cannot, so they are not all examples of detective controls. None of these controls would help repair or restore functionality after an issue, and thus none are recovery controls, nor are they administrative controls that involve policy or procedures, although the guards might refer to them when performing their duties.

38. B. Password complexity is driven by length, and a longer password will be more effective against brute force attacks than a shorter password. Each character of additional length increases the difficulty by the size of the potential character set (for example, a single lowercase character makes the passwords 26 times more difficult to crack). While each of the other settings is useful for a strong password policy, they won't have the same impact on brute force attacks.

39. A. The stored sample of a biometric factor is called a reference profile or a reference template. None of the other answers are common terms used for biometric systems.

40. A. Organizations that have very strict security requirements that don't have a tolerance for false acceptance want to lower the false acceptance rate, or FAR, to be as near to zero as possible. That often means that the false rejection rate, or FRR, increases. Different biometric technologies or a better registration method can help improve biometric performance, but false rejections due to data quality are not typically a concern with modern biometric systems. In this case, knowing the crossover error rate, or CER, or having a very high CER doesn't help the decision.

41. B. The complexity of brute forcing a password increases based on both the number of potential characters and the number of letters added. In this case, there are 26 lowercase letters, 26 uppercase letters, and 10 possible digits. That creates 62 possibilities. Since we added only a single letter of length, we get 62^1, or 62 possibilities, and thus, the new passwords would be 62 times harder to brute force on average.

42. B. Biometric systems can face major usability challenges if the time to enroll is long (over a couple of minutes) and if the speed at which the biometric system is able to scan and accept or reject the user is too slow. FAR and FRR may be important in the design decisions made by administrators or designers, but they aren't typically visible to users. CER and ERR are the same and are the point where FAR and FRR meet. Reference profile requirements are a system requirement, not a user requirement.

43. C. TLS provides message confidentiality and integrity, which can prevent eavesdropping. When paired with digital signatures, which provide integrity and authentication, forged assertions can also be defeated. SAML does not have a security mode and relies on TLS and digital signatures to ensure security if needed. Message hashing without a signature would help prevent modification of the message but won't necessarily provide authentication.

44. B. Integration with cloud-based third parties that rely on local authentication can fail if the local organization's Internet connectivity or servers are offline. Adopting a hybrid cloud and local authentication system can ensure that Internet or server outages are handled, allowing authentication to work regardless of where the user is or if their home organization is online. Using encrypted and signed communication does not address availability, redirects are a configuration issue with the third party, and a local gateway won't handle remote users. Also, host files don't help with availability issues with services other than DNS.

45. A. While many solutions are technical, if a trusted third party redirects to an unexpected authentication site, awareness is often the best defense. Using TLS would keep the transaction confidential but would not prevent the redirect. Handling redirects locally only works for locally hosted sites, and using a third-party service requires offsite redirects. An IPS might detect an attacker's redirect, but tracking the multitude of load-balanced servers most large providers use can be challenging, if not impossible. In addition, an IPS relies on visibility into the traffic, and SAML integrations should be encrypted for security, which would require a man-in-the-middle type of IPS to be configured.

46. B. Discretionary access control (DAC) can provide greater scalability by leveraging many administrators, and those administrators can add flexibility by making decisions about access to their objects without fitting into an inflexible mandatory access control system (MAC). MAC is more secure due to the strong set of controls it provides, but it does not scale as well as DAC and is relatively inflexible in comparison.

47. C. While signature-based detection is used to detect attacks, review of provisioning processes typically involves checking logs, reviewing the audit trail, or performing a manual review of permissions granted during the provisioning process.

48. C. Service Provisioning Markup Language, or SPML is an XML-based language designed to allow platforms to generate and respond to provisioning requests. SAML is used to make authorization and authentication data, while XACML is used to describe access controls. SOAP, or Simple Object Access Protocol, is a messaging protocol and could be used for any XML messaging, but is not a markup language itself.

49. C. Rainbow tables are databases of prehashed passwords paired with high-speed lookup functions. Since they can quickly compare known hashes against those in a file, using rainbow tables is the fastest way to quickly determine passwords from hashes. A brute force attack may eventually succeed but will be very slow against most hashes. Pass-the-hash attacks rely on sniffed or otherwise acquired NTLM or LanMan hashes being sent to a system to avoid the need to know a user's password. Salts are data added to a hash to avoid the use of tools like rainbow tables. A salt added to a password means the hash won't match a rainbow table generated without the same salt.

50. B. Google's federation with other applications and organizations allows single-sign on as well as management of their electronic identity and its related attributes. While this is an example of SSO, it goes beyond simple single-sign on. Provisioning provides accounts and rights, and a public key infrastructure is used for certificate management.

51. D. When users have more rights than they need to accomplish their job, they have excessive privileges. This is a violation of the concept of least privilege. Unlike creeping privileges, this is a provisioning or rights management issue rather than a problem of retention of rights the user needed but no longer requires. *Rights collision* is a made-up term, and thus is not an issue here.

52. B. Registration is the process of adding a user to an identity management system. This includes creating their unique identifier and adding any attribute information that is associated with their identity. Proofing occurs when the user provides information to prove who they are. Directories are managed to maintain lists of users, services, and other items. Session management tracks application and user sessions.

53. A. Port 636 is the default port for LDAP-S, which provides LDAP over SSL or TLS, thus indicating that the server supports encrypted connections. Since neither port 3268 nor 3269 is mentioned, we do not know if the server provides support for a global catalog.

54. D. The X.500 series of standards covers directory services. Kerberos is described in RFCs; biometric systems are covered by a variety of standards, including ISO standards; and provisioning standards include SCIM, SPML, and others.

55. B. Active Directory Domain Services is based on LDAP, the Lightweight Directory Access Protocol. Active Directory also uses Kerberos for authentication.

56. C. Identity proofing can be done by comparing user information that the organization already has, like account numbers or personal information. Requiring users to create unique questions can help with future support by providing a way for them to do password resets. Using a phone call only verifies that the individual who created the account has the phone that they registered and won't prove their identity. In-person verification would not fit the business needs of most websites.

57. A. By default, OpenLDAP stored the userPassword attribute in the clear. This means that ensuring that the password is provided to OpenLDAP in a secure format is the responsibility of the administrator or programmer who builds its provisioning system.

58. C. Type 2 errors occur in biometric systems when an invalid subject is incorrectly authenticated as a valid user. In this case, nobody except the actual customer should be validated when fingerprints are scanned. Type 1 errors occur when a valid subject is not authenticated; if the existing customer was rejected, it would be a Type 1 error. Registration is the process of adding users, but registration errors and time of use, method of use errors are not specific biometric authentication terms.

59. B. Firewalls use rule-based access control, or Rule-BAC, in their access control lists and apply rules created by administrators to all traffic that pass through them. DAC, or discretionary access control, allows owners to determine who can access objects they control, while task-based access control lists tasks for users. MAC, or mandatory access control, uses classifications to determine access.

60. C. When you input a username and password, you are authenticating yourself by providing a unique identifier and a verification that you are the person who should have that identifier (the password). Authorization is the process of determining what a user is allowed to do. Validation and login both describe elements of what is happening in the process; however, they aren't the most important identity and access management activity.

61. C. Kathleen should implement a biometric factor. The cards and keys are an example of a Type 2 factor, or "something you have." Using a smart card replaces this with another

Type 2 factor, but the cards could still be loaned out or stolen. Adding a PIN suffers from the same problem: A PIN can be stolen. Adding cameras doesn't prevent access to the facility and thus doesn't solve the immediate problem (but it is a good idea!).

62. D. Kerberos is an authentication protocol that uses tickets, and provides secure communications between the client, key distribution center (KDC), ticket granting service (TGS), authentication server (AS), and endpoint services. RADIUS does not provide the same level of security by default, SAML is a markup language, and OAuth is designed to allow third-party websites to rely on credentials from other sites like Google or Microsoft.

63. D. Administrative access controls are procedures and the policies from which they derive. They are based on regulations, requirements, and the organization's own policies. Corrective access controls return an environment to its original status after an issue, while logical controls are technical access controls that rely on hardware or software to protect systems and data. Compensating controls are used in addition to or as an alternative to other controls.

64. A. When clients perform a client service authorization, they send a TGT and the ID of the requested service to the TGS, and the TGS responds with a client-to-server ticket and session key back to the client if the request is validated. An AS is an authentication server and the SS is a service server, neither of which can be sent.

65. C. In a mandatory access control system, all subjects and objects have a label. Compartments may or may not be used, but there is not a specific requirement for either subjects or objects to be compartmentalized. The specific labels of Confidential, Secret, and Top Secret are not required by MAC.

66. D. Passwords are never stored for web applications in a well-designed environment. Instead, salted hashes are stored and compared to passwords after they are salted and hashed. If the hashes match, the user is authenticated.

67. C. When a third-party site integrates via OAuth 2.0, authentication is handled by the service provider's servers. In this case, Google is acting as the service provider for user authentication. Authentication for local users who create their own accounts would occur in the e-commerce application (or a related server), but that is not the question that is asked here.

68. B. The anti-forgery state token exchanged during OAuth sessions is intended to prevent cross-site request forgery. This makes sure that the unique session token with the authentication response from Google's OAuth service is available to verify that the user, not an attacker, is making a request. XSS attacks focus on scripting and would have script tags involved, SQL injection would have SQL code included, and XACML is the eXtensible Access Control Markup Language, not a type of attack.

69. A. Knowledge-based authentication relies on preset questions "What is your pet's name?" and the answers. It can be susceptible to attacks due to the availability of the answers on social media or other sites. Dynamic knowledge based authentication relies on facts or data that the user already knows which can be used to create questions they can answer on an as needed basis (for example, a previous address, or a school they attended).

Out-of-band identity proofing relies on an alternate channel like a phone call or text message. Finally, Type 3 authentication factors are biometric, or "something you are," rather than knowledge based.

70. C. An access control matrix is a table that lists objects, subjects, and their privileges. Access control lists focus on objects and which subjects can access them. Capability tables list subjects and what objects they can access. Subject/object rights management systems are not based on an access control model.

71. C. Self-service password reset tools typically have a significant impact on the number of password reset contacts that a help desk has. Two-factor and biometric authentication both add additional complexity and may actually increase the number of contacts. Passphrases can be easier to remember than traditional complex passwords and may decrease calls, but they don't have the same impact that a self-service system does.

72. C. RADIUS supports TLS over TCP. RADIUS does not have a supported TLS mode over UDP. AES pre-shared symmetric ciphers are not a supported solution and would be very difficult to both implement and maintain in a large environment, and the built-in encryption in RADIUS only protects passwords.

73. B. OAuth provides the ability to access resources from another service and would meet Jim's needs. OpenID would allow him to use an account from another service with his application, and Kerberos and LDAP are used more frequently for in-house services.

74. B. Since physical access to the workstations is part of the problem, setting application time-outs and password-protected screensavers with relatively short inactivity time-outs can help prevent unauthorized access. Using session IDs for all applications and verifying system IP addresses would be helpful for online attacks against applications.

75. C. Firewalls, routers, and passwords are all examples of technical access controls and are software or hardware systems used to manage and protect access. RAID-5 is an example of a recovery control. If you're questioning why routers are a technical access control, remember that router access control lists (ACLs) are quite often used to control network access or traffic flows.

76. A. Verifying information that an individual should know about themselves using third-party factual information (a Type 1 authentication factor) is sometimes known as dynamic knowledge-based authentication and is a type of identity proofing. Out-of-band identity proofing would use another means of contacting the user, like a text message or phone call, and password verification requires a password.

77. C. The US government's Common Access Card is a smart card. The US government also issues PIV cards, or personal identity verification cards.

78. C. OpenID Connect is a RESTful, JSON-based authentication protocol that, when paired with OAuth, can provide identity verification and basic profile information. SAML is the Security Assertion Markup Language, Shibboleth is a federated identity solution designed to allow web-based SSO, and Higgins is an open-source project designed to provide users with control over the release of their identity information.

79. C. In a mandatory access control system, classifications do not have to include rights to lower levels. This means that the only label we can be sure Jim has rights to is Secret. Despite the fact that it is unclassified, Unclassified data remains a different label, and Jim may not be authorized to access it.

80. B. Time-based controls are an example of context-dependent controls. A constrained interface would limit what Susan was able to do in an application or system interface, while content-dependent control would limit her access to content based on her role or rights. Least privilege is used to ensure that subjects only receive the rights they need to perform their role.

81. C. A Type 3 authentication factor is: something you are: like a biometric identifier. A Type 1 authentication factor is "something you know." A Type 2 factor is "something you have," like a smart card or hardware token. There is not a Type 4 authentication factor.

82. B. Policy is a subset of the administrative layer of access controls. Administrative, technical, and physical access controls all play an important role in security.

83. C. Google Authenticator's constantly changing codes are part of a synchronous token that uses a time-based algorithm to generate codes. Asynchronous tokens typically require a challenge to be entered on the token to allow it to calculate a response, which the server compares to the response it expects. Smart cards typically present a certificate but may have other token capabilities built in. Static tokens are physical devices that can contain credentials and include smart cards and memory cards.

84. A. Asynchronous tokens use a challenge/response process in which the system sends a challenge and the user responds with a PIN and a calculated response to the challenge. The server performs the same calculations, and if both match, it authenticates the user. Synchronous tokens use a time-based calculation to generate codes. Smart cards are paired with readers and don't need to have challenges entered, and RFID devices are not used for challenge/response tokens.

85. C. The crossover error rate is the point where false acceptance rate and false rejection rate cross over and is a standard assessment used to compare the accuracy of biometric devices.

86. A. At point B, the false acceptance rate, or FAR, is quite high, while the false rejection rate, or FRR, is relatively low. This may be acceptable in some circumstances, but in organizations where a false acceptance can cause a major problem, it is likely that they should instead choose a point to the right of pointA.

87. B. CER is a standard used to assess biometric devices. If the CER for this device does not fit the needs of the organization, Ben should assess other biometric systems to find one with a lower CER. Sensitivity is already accounted for in CER charts, and moving the CER isn't something Ben can do. FRR is not a setting in software, so Ben can't use that as an option either.

88. B. The Simple Authentication and Security Layer (SASL) for LDAP provides support for a range of authentication types, including secure methods. Anonymous authentication does not require or provide security, and simple authentication can be tunneled over SSL or TLS but does not provide security by itself. S-LDAP is not an LDAP protocol.

89. C. Palm scans compare the vein patterns in the palm to a database to authenticate a user. Vein patterns are unique, and this method is a better single-factor authentication method than voice pattern recognition, hand geometry, and pulse patterns, each of which can be more difficult to uniquely identify between individuals or can be fooled more easily.

90. B. Allowing the relying party to provide the redirect to the OpenID provider could allow a phishing attack by directing clients to a fake OpenID provider that can capture valid credentials. Since the OpenID provider URL is provided by the client, the relying party cannot select the wrong provider. The relying party never receives the user's password, which means that they can't steal it. Finally, the relying party receives the signed assertion but does not send one.

91. A. IDaaS, or Identity as a Service, provides an identity platform as a third-party service. This can provide benefits including integration with cloud services and removing overhead for maintenance of traditional on-premise identity systems, but it can also create risk due to third-party control of identity services and reliance on an offsite identity infrastructure.

92. B. Drives in a RAID-5 array are intended to handle failure of a drive. This is an example of a recovery control, which is used to return operations to normal function after a failure. Administrative controls are policies and procedures. Compensation controls help cover for issues with primary controls or improve them. Logical controls are software and hardware mechanisms used to protect resources and systems.

93. D. The Linux filesystem allows the owners of objects to determine the access rights that subjects have to them. This means that it is a discretionary access control. If the system enforced a role-based access control, Alex wouldn't set the controls; they would be set based on the roles assigned to each subject. A rule-based access control system would apply rules throughout the system, and a mandatory access control system uses classification labels.

94. D. Diameter was designed to provide enhanced, modern features to replace RADIUS. Diameter provides better reliability and a broad range of improved functionality. RADIUS-NG does not exist, Kerberos is not a direct competitor for RADIUS, and TACACS is not an open protocol.

95. A. In this example, uid=ben,ou=sales,dc=example,dc=com, the items proceed from most specific to least specific (broadest) from left to right, as required by a DN.

96. D. Kerberos relies on properly synchronized time on each end of a connection to function. If the local system time is more than 5 minutes out of sync, otherwise valid TGTs will be invalid and the system won't receive any new tickets.

97. A. Kerberos, KryptoKnight, and SESAME are all single sign-on, or SSO, systems. PKI systems are public key infrastructure systems, CMS systems are content management systems, and LDAP and other directory servers provide information about services, resources, and individuals.

98. B. Locks can be preventative access controls by stopping unwanted access, can deter potential intruders by making access difficult, and are physical access controls. They are not directive controls because they don't control the actions of subjects.

99. B. Windows uses Kerberos for authentication. RADIUS is typically used for wireless networks, modems, and network devices, while OAuth is primarily used for web applications. TACACS+ is used for network devices.

100. C. The default ports for SSL/TLS LDAP directory information and global catalog services are 636 and 3269, respectively. Unsecure LDAP uses 389, and unsecure global directory services use 3268.

Chapter 6: Security Assessment and Testing (Domain 6)

1. B. TCP and UDP ports 137-139 are used for NetBIOS services, whereas 445 is used for Active Directory. TCP 1433 is the default port for Microsoft SQL, indicating that this is probably a Windows server providing SQL services.

2. D. Mutation testing modifies a program in small ways, and then tests that mutant to determine if it behaves as it should or if it fails. This technique is used to design and test software tests through mutation. Static code analysis and regression testing are both means of testing code, whereas code auditing is an analysis of source code rather than a means of designing and testing software tests.

3. B. TCP port 443 normally indicates an HTTPS server. Nikto is useful for vulnerability scanning web servers and applications and is the best choice listed for a web server. Metasploit includes some scanning functionality but is not a purpose-built tool for vulnerability scanning. zzuf is a fuzzing tool and isn't relevant for vulnerability scans, whereas sqlmap is a SQL injection testing tool.

4. A. Syslog is a widely used protocol for event and message logging. Eventlog, netlog, and Remote Log Protocol are all made-up terms.

5. C. Fuzzers are tools that are designed to provide invalid or unexpected input to applications, testing for vulnerabilities like format string vulnerabilities, buffer overflow issues, and other problems. A static analysis relies on examining code without running the application or code, and thus would not fill forms as part of a web application. Brute-force tools attempt to bypass security by trying every possible combination for passwords or other values. A black box is a type of penetration test where the testers do not know anything about the environment.

6. B. OpenVAS is an open source vulnerability scanning tool that will provide Susan with a report of the vulnerabilities that it can identify from a remote, network-based scan. Nmap is an open source port scanner. Both the Microsoft Baseline Security Analyzer (MBSA) and Nessus are closed source tools, although Nessus was originally open source.

7. B. An IPS is an example of a mechanism like a hardware-, software-, or firmware-based control or system. Specifications are document-based artifacts like policies or designs, activities are actions that support an information system that involves people, and an individual is one or more people applying specifications, mechanisms, or activities.

8. C. Jim has agreed to a black box penetration test, which provides no information about the organization, its systems, or its defenses. A crystal or white box penetration test provides all of the information an attacker needs, whereas a gray box penetration test provides some, but not all, information.

9. A. A vulnerability scanner that has a test (sometimes called a signature or plugin) that provides a detection method for CVE-2014-0160, also known as the Heartbleed bug, a vulnerability in OpenSSL will detect and report on the issue on any system it can connect to. Port scanners do not determine whether services are vulnerable, and Heartbleed was not a vulnerability in the Apache web server—but even without knowing this, the CVE number is a better indicator of whether the issue will be found than a generic detect for a service.

10. C. Service Organization Control (SOC) reports replaced SAS-70 reports in 2010. A Type 1 report only covers a point in time, so Susan needs an SOC Type 2 report to have the information she requires to make a design and operating effectiveness decision based on the report.

11. B. WPA2 enterprise uses RADIUS authentication for users rather than a preshared key. This means a password attack is more likely to fail as password attempts for a given user may result in account lock-out. WPA2 encryption will not stop a password attack, and WPA2's preshared key mode is specifically targeted by password attacks that attempt to find the key. Not only is WEP encryption outdated, but it can also frequently be cracked quickly by tools like aircrack-ng.

12. C. SOC 3 reports are intended to be shared with a broad community, often with a website seal, and support the organization's claims about their ability to provide integrity, availability, and confidentiality. SOC 1 reports report on controls over financial reporting, whereas SOC 2 reports cover security, availability, integrity, and privacy for business partners, regulators, and other similar organizations in detail that would not typically be provided to a broad audience.

13. C. Interface testing is used to ensure that software modules properly meet interface specifications and thus will properly exchange data. Dynamic testing tests software in a running environment, whereas fuzzing is a type of dynamic testing that feeds invalid input to running software to test error and input handling. API checksums are not a testing technique.

14. B. Not only should active scanning be expected to cause wireless IPS alarms, but they may actually be desired if the test is done to test responses. Accidently scanning guests, neighbors, or misidentifying devices belonging to third parties are all potential problems with active scanning and require the security assessor to carefully verify the systems that she is scanning.

15. C. Generational fuzzing relies on models for application input and conducts fuzzing attacks based on that information. Mutation based fuzzers are sometimes called "dumb" fuzzers because they simply mutate or modify existing data samples to create new test samples. Neither parametric nor derivative is a term used to describe types of fuzzers.

16. B. Flows, also often called network flows, are captured to provide insight into network traffic for security, troubleshooting, and performance management. Audit logging provides information about events on the routers, route logging is not a common network logging function, and trace logs are used in troubleshooting specific software packages as they perform their functions.

17. D. The IP addresses that his clients have provided are RFC 1918 non-routable IP addresses, and Jim will not be able to scan them from offsite. To succeed in his penetration test, he will either have to first penetrate their network border or place a machine inside their network to scan from the inside. IP addresses overlapping is not a real concern for scanning, and the ranges can easily be handled by current scanning systems.

18. B. Karen can't use MTD verification because MTD is the Maximum Tolerable Downtime. Verifying it will only tell her how long systems can be offline without significant business impact. Reviewing logs, using hashing to verify that the logs are intact, and performing periodic tests are all valid ways to verify that the backups are working properly.

19. B. Group Policy enforced by Active Directory can ensure consistent logging settings and can provide regular enforcement of policy on systems. Periodic configuration audits won't catch changes made between audits, and local policies can drift due to local changes or differences in deployments. A Windows syslog client will enable the Windows systems to send syslog to the SIEM appliance but won't ensure consistent logging of events.

20. B. Windows systems generate logs in the Windows native logging format. To send syslog events, Windows systems require a helper application or tool. Enterprise wireless access points, firewalls, and Linux systems all typically support syslog.

21. B. Network Time Protocol (NTP) can ensure that systems are using the same time, allowing time sequencing for logs throughout a centralized logging infrastructure. Syslog is a way for systems to send logs to a logging server and won't address time sequencing. Neither logsync nor SNAP is an industry term.

22. A. When a tester does not have raw packet creation privileges, such as when they have not escalated privileges on a compromised host, a TCP connect scan can be used. TCP SYN scans require elevated privileges on most Linux systems due to the need to write raw packets. A UDP scan will miss most services that are provided via TCP, and an ICMP is merely a ping sweep of systems that respond to pings and won't identify services at all.

23. B. Joseph may be surprised to discover FTP (TCP port 21) and Telnet (TCP port 23) open on his network since both services are unencrypted and have been largely replaced by SSH, and SCP or SFTP. SSH uses port 22, SMTP uses port 25, and POP3 uses port 110.

24. D. Black box testing is the most realistic type of penetration test because it does not provide the penetration tester with inside information about the configuration or design of systems, software, or networks. A gray box test provides some information, whereas a white or crystal box test provides significant or full detail.

25. A. A test coverage analysis is often used to provide insight into how well testing covered the set of use cases that an application is being tested for. Source code reviews look at the code of a program for bugs, not necessarily at a use case analysis, whereas fuzzing tests invalid inputs. A code review report might be generated as part of a source code review.

26. C. Testing how a system could be misused, or misuse testing, focuses on behaviors that are not what the organization desires or that are counter to the proper function of a system or application. Use case testing is used to verify whether a desired functionality works. Dynamic testing is used to determine how code handles variables that change over time, whereas manual testing is just what it implies: testing code by hand.

27. B. Synthetic monitoring uses emulated or recorded transactions to monitor for performance changes in response time, functionality, or other performance monitors. Passive monitoring uses a span port or other method to copy traffic and monitor it in real time. Log analysis is typically performed against actual log data but can be performed on simulated traffic to identify issues. Simulated transaction analysis is not an industry term.

28. C. Path disclosures, local file inclusions, and buffer overflows are all vulnerabilities that may be found by a web vulnerability scanner, but race conditions that take advantage of timing issues tend to be found either by code analysis or using automated tools that specifically test for race conditions as part of software testing.

29. C. Vulnerability scanners that do not have administrative rights to access a machine or that are not using an agent scan remote machines to gather information, including fingerprints from responses to queries and connections, banner information from services, and related data. CVE information is Common Vulnerability and Exposure information, or vulnerability information. A port scanner gathers information about what service ports are open, although some port scanners blur the line between port and vulnerability scanners. Patch management tools typically run as an agent on a system to allow them to both monitor patch levels and update the system as needed. Service validation typically involves testing the functionality of a service, not its banner and response patterns.

30. B. Emily is using synthetic transactions, which can use recorded or generated transactions, and is conducting use case testing to verify that the application responds properly to actual use cases. Neither actual data nor dynamic monitoring is an industry term. Fuzzing involves sending unexpected inputs to a program to see how it responds. Passive monitoring uses a network tap or other capture technology to allow monitoring of actual traffic to a system or application.

31. B. Real user monitoring (RUM) is a passive monitoring technique that records user interaction with an application or system to ensure performance and proper application behavior. RUM is often used as part of a predeployment process using the actual user interface. The other answers are all made up—synthetic monitoring uses simulated behavior, but synthetic user monitoring is not a testing method. Similarly, passive monitoring monitors actual traffic, but passive user recording is not an industry term or technique. Client/server testing merely describes one possible architecture.

32. B. Jim should ask the information security team to flag the issue as resolved if he is sure the patch was installed. Many vulnerability scanners rely on version information or banner information, and may flag patched versions if the software provider does not update the information they see. Uninstalling and reinstalling the patch will not change this. Changing the version information may not change all of the details that are being flagged

by the scanner, and may cause issues at a later date. Reviewing the vulnerability information for a workaround may be a good idea but should not be necessary if the proper patch is installed; it can create maintenance issues later.

33. B. zzuf is the only fuzzer on the list, and zzuf is specifically designed to work with tools like web browsers, image viewers, and similar software by modifying network and file input to application. Nmap is a port scanner, Nessus is a vulnerability scanner, and Nikto is a web server scanner.

34. C. An important part of application threat modeling is threat categorization. It helps to assess attacker goals that influence the controls that should be put in place. The other answers all involve topics that are not directly part of application threat modeling.

35. A. Passive scanning can help identify rogue devices by capturing MAC address vendor IDs that do not match deployed devices, by verifying that systems match inventories of organizationally owned hardware by hardware address, and by monitoring for rogue SSIDs or connections.

Scripted attacks are part of active scanning rather than passive scanning, and active scanning is useful for testing IDS or IPS systems, whereas passive scanning will not be detected by detection systems. Finally, a shorter dwell time can actually miss troublesome traffic, so balancing dwell time versus coverage is necessary for passive wireless scanning efforts.

36. D. Bluetooth active scans can determine both the strength of the PIN and what security mode the device is operating in. Unfortunately, Bluetooth scans can be challenging due to the limited range of Bluetooth and the prevalence of personally owned Bluetooth enabled devices. Passive Bluetooth scanning only detects active connections and typically requires multiple visits to have a chance of identifying all devices.

37. D. Regression testing, which is a type of functional or unit testing, tests to ensure that changes have not introduced new issues. Nonregression testing checks to see if a change has had the effect it was supposed to, smoke testing focuses on simple problems with impact on critical functionality, and evolution testing is not a software testing technique.

38. D. Nmap, Nessus, and Nikto all have OS fingerprinting or other operating system identification capabilities. sqlmap is designed to perform automated detection and testing of SQL injection flaws, and does not provide OS detection.

39. C. Key risk indicators are used to tell those in charge of risk management how risky an activity is and how much impact changes are having on that risk profile. Identifying key risk indicators and monitoring them can help to identify high-risk areas earlier in their life cycle. Yearly risk assessments may be a good idea, but only provide a point in time view, whereas penetration tests may miss out on risks that are not directly security related. Monitoring logs and events using a SIEM device can help detect issues as they occur but won't necessarily show trends in risk.

40. C. Passive monitoring only works after issues have occurred because it requires actual traffic. Synthetic monitoring uses simulated or recorded traffic, and thus can be used to proactively identify problems. Both synthetic and passive monitoring can be used to detect functionality issues.

41. B. Getting authorization is the most critical element in the planning phase. Permission, and the "get out of jail free card" that demonstrates that organizational leadership is aware of the issues that a penetration test could cause, is the first step in any penetration test. Gathering tools and building a lab, as well as determining what type of test will be conducted, are all important, but nothing should happen without permission.

42. C. Discovery can include both active and passive discovery. Port scanning is commonly done during discovery to assess what services the target provides, and nmap is one of the most popular tools used for this purpose. Nessus and Nikto might be used during the vulnerability scanning phase, and john, a password cracker, can be used to recover passwords during the exploitation phase.

43. B. Penetration test reports often include information that could result in additional exposure if they were accidently released or stolen. Therefore, determining how vulnerability data should be stored and sent is critical. Problems with off-limits targets are more likely to result in issues during the vulnerability assessment and exploitation phase, and reports should not be limited in length but should be as long as they need to be to accomplish the goals of the test.

44. B. Code coverage testing most frequently requires that every function has been called, that each statement has been executed, that all branches have been fully explored, and that each condition has been evaluated for all possibilities. API, input, and loop testing are not common types of code coverage testing measures.

45. B. Time to remediate a vulnerability is a commonly used key performance indicator for security teams. Time to live measures how long a packet can exist in hops, business criticality is a measure used to determine how important a service or system is to an organization, and coverage rates are used to measure how effective code testing is.

46. D. Unique user IDs provide accountability when paired with auditable logs to provide that a specific user took any given action. Confidentiality, availability, and integrity can be provided through other means like encryption, systems design, and digital signatures.

47. B. Application programming interfaces (APIs), user interfaces (UIs), and physical interfaces are all important to test when performing software testing. Network interfaces are not a part of the typical list of interfaces tested in software testing.

48. C. The Security Content Automation Protocol (SCAP) is a community sourced specification for security flaw and security configuration information and is defined in NIST SP 800-126. SVML, VSCAP, and VML are not information security–related terms.

49. B. Security vulnerabilities can be created by misconfiguration, logical or functional design or implementation issues, or poor programming practices. Fuzzing is a method of software testing and is not a type of issue. Buffer overflows and race conditions are both caused by logical or programming flaws, but they are not typically caused by misconfiguration or functional issues.

50. C. Simply updating the version that an application provides may stop the vulnerability scanner from flagging it, but it won't fix the underlying issue. Patching, using workarounds, or installing an application layer firewall or IPS can all help to remediate or limit the impact of the vulnerability.

51. C. Saria's social-engineering attack succeeded in persuading a staff member at the help desk to change a password for someone who they not only couldn't see, but who they couldn't verify actually needed their password reset. Black box and zero knowledge are both terms describing penetration tests without information about the organization or system, and help desk spoofing is not an industry term.

52. D. The menu shown will archive logs when they reach the maximum size allowed (20 MB). These archives will be retained, which could fill the disk. Log data will not be overwritten, and log data should not be lost when the data is archived. The question does not include enough information to determine if needed information may not be logged.

53. C. Penetration tests are intended to help identify vulnerabilities, and exploiting them is part of the process rather than a hazard. Application crashes; denial of service due to system, network, or application failures; and even data corruption can all be hazards of penetration tests.

54. B. NIST SP 800-53A is titled "Assessing Security and Privacy Controls in Federal Information Systems and Organizations: Building Effective Assessment Plans," and covers methods for assessing and measuring controls.

NIST 800-12 is an introduction to computer security, 800-34 covers contingency planning, and 800-86 is the "Guide to Integrating Forensic Techniques into Incident Response."

55. C. TCP SYN scans only open a connection halfway; they do not complete the TCP connection with an ACK, thus leaving the connection open. TCP Connect scans complete the connection, whereas TCP ACK scans attempt to appear like an open connection. Xmas, or Christmas tree, scans set the FIN, PSH, and URG flags, thereby "lighting up" the TCP packet.

56. C. SOC 1 reports are prepared according to the Statement on Standards for Attestation Engagements, or SSAE number 16 (typically shortened to SSAE-16). An SOC 1 Type I report validates policies and procedures at a point in time, whereas SOC 1 Type II reports cover a period of time of at least six months. SOC 1 reports replaced SAS 70 reports in 2011, meaning that a current report should be an SSAE-16 SOC 1 report.

57. B. Metasploit is an exploitation package that is designed to assist penetration testers. A tester using Metasploit can exploit known vulnerabilities for which an exploit has been created or can create their own exploits using the tool. While Metasploit provides built-in access to some vulnerability scanning functionality, a tester using Metasploit should primarily be expected to perform actual tests of exploitable vulnerabilities. Similarly, Metasploit supports creating buffer overflow attacks, but it is not a purpose-built buffer overflow testing tool, and of course testing systems for zero-day exploits doesn't work unless they have been released.

58. C. The audit finding indicates that the backup administrator may not be monitoring backup logs and taking appropriate action based on what they report, thus resulting in potentially unusable backups. Issues with review, logging, or being aware of the success or failure of backups are less important than not having usable backups.

59. C. ITIL, which originally stood for IT Infrastructure Library, is a set of practices for IT service management, and is not typically used for auditing. COBIT, or the Control Objectives for Information and Related Technology, ISO 27002, and SSAE-16, or the Statement on Standards for Attestation Engagements number 16, are all used for auditing.

60. A. NIST SP 800-137 outlines the process for organizations that are establishing, implementing, and maintaining an ICSM as define, establish, implement, analyze and report, respond, review, and update. Prepare, detect and analyze, contain, respond, recover, report is an incident response plan, and the others do not match the NIST process.

61. B. Lauren's team is using regression testing, which is intended to prevent the recurrence of issues. This means that measuring the rate of defect recurrence is an appropriate measure for their work. Time to remediate vulnerabilities is associated with activities like patching, rather than preparing the patch, whereas a weighted risk trend is used to measure risk over time to an organization. Finally, specific coverage may be useful to determine if they are fully testing their effort, but regression testing is more specifically covered by defect recurrence rates.

62. C. Static program reviews are typically performed by an automated tool. Program understanding, program comprehension, code review, software inspections and software walkthroughs are all human-centric methods for reviewing code.

63. A. In order to fully test code, a white box test is required. Without full visibility of the code, error conditions or other code could be missed, making a gray box or black box test an inappropriate solution. Using dynamic testing that runs against live code could also result in some conditions being missed due to sections of code not being exposed to typical usage.

64. A. A test coverage report measures how many of the test cases have been completed and is used as a way to provide test metrics when using test cases. A penetration test report is provided when a penetration test is conducted—this is not a penetration test. A code coverage report covers how much of the code has been tested, and a line coverage report is a type of code coverage report.

65. C. The changes from a testing environment with instrumentation inserted into the code and the production environment for the code can mask timing-related issues like race conditions. Bounds checking, input validation, and pointer manipulation are all related to coding issues rather than environmental issues and are more likely to be discoverable in a test environment.

66. D. Once a vulnerability scanner identifies a potential problem, validation is necessary to verify that the issue exists. Reporting, patching, or other remediation actions can be conducted once the vulnerability has been confirmed.

67. B. Fagan testing is a detailed code review that steps through planning, overview, preparation, inspection, rework, and follow-up phases. Dynamic tests test the code in a real runtime environment, whereas fuzzing is a type of dynamic testing that feeds invalid inputs to software to test its exception-handling capabilities. Roth-Parker reviews were made up for this question.

68. D. The Common Vulnerability Scoring System (CVSS) includes metrics and calculation tools for exploitability, impact, how mature exploit code is, and how vulnerabilities can be remediated, as well as a means to score vulnerabilities against users' unique requirements. NVD is the National Vulnerability Database, CSV is short for Comma-Separated Values, and VSS is a made-up term.

69. D. Network-enabled printers often provided services via TCP 515 and 9100, and have both nonsecure and secure web-enabled management interfaces on TCP 80 and 443. Web servers, access points, and file servers would not typically provide service on the LPR and LPD ports (515 and 9100).

70. A. Nikto, Burp Suite, and Wapiti are all web application vulnerability scanners, tools designed specifically to scan web servers and applications. While they share some functionality with broader vulnerability scanners and port scanning tools, they have a narrower focus and typically have deeper capabilities than vulnerability scanners.

71. B. Nmap reports one of three statuses: Open, which means that the port is open and that an application responds; Closed, which means that the port is accessible but there is no application response; and Filtered, which means that a firewall is not allowing nmap to determine if the port is open or closed.

72. C. User session monitoring is not a means of conducting synthetic performance monitoring. Synthetic performance monitoring uses scripted or recorded data, not actual user sessions. Traffic capture, database performance monitoring, and website performance monitoring can all be used during synthetic performance monitoring efforts.

73. D. Susan is conducting interface testing. Interface testing involves testing system or application components to ensure that they work properly together. Misuse case testing focuses on how an attacker might misuse the application and would not test normal cases. Fuzzing attempts to send unexpected input and might be involved in interface testing, but it won't cover the full set of concerns. Regression testing is conducted when testing changes and is used to ensure that the application or system functions as it did before the update or change.

74. B. Not having enough log sources is not a key consideration in log management system design, although it may be a worry for security managers who can't capture the data they need. Log management system designs must take into account the volume of log data and the network bandwidth it consumes, the security of the data, and the amount of effort required to analyze the data.

75. C. Jim should ask for a code coverage report, which provides information on the functions, statements, branches, and conditions or other elements that were covered in the testing. Use cases are used as part of a test coverage calculation that divides the tested use cases by the total use cases, but use cases may not cover all possible functions or branches. A code review report would be generated if the organization was manually reviewing the application's source code.

76. C. Rebooting a Windows machine results in an information log entry. Windows defines five types of events: errors, which indicate a significant problem; warnings, which may indicate future problems; information, which describes successful operation; success audits, which record successful security accesses; and failure audits, which record failed security access attempts.

77. C. Inconsistent timestamps are a common problem, often caused by improperly set time zones or due to differences in how system clocks are set. In this case, a consistent time difference often indicates that one system uses local time, and the other is using Greenwich Mean Time (GMT). Logs from multiple sources tend to cause problems with centralization and collection, whereas different log formats can create challenges in parsing log data. Finally, modified logs are often a sign of intrusion or malicious intent.

78. A. Authenticated scans use a read-only account to access configuration files, allowing more accurate testing of vulnerabilities. Web application, unauthenticated scans, and port scans don't have access to configuration files unless they are inadvertently exposed.

Microsoft's STRIDE threat assessment model places threats into one of six categories:

- Spoofing—threats that involve user credentials and authentication, or falsifying legitimate communications
- Tampering—threats that involve the malicious modification of data
- Repudiation—threats that cause actions to occur that cannot be denied by a user
- Information disclosure—threats that involve exposure of data to unauthorized individuals
- Denial of service—threats that deny service to legitimate users
- Elevation of privilege—threats that provide higher privileges to unauthorized users

79. B. Using role-based access controls (RBACs) for specific operations will help to ensure that users cannot perform actions that they should not be able to. Auditing and logging can help detect abuse but won't prevent it, and data type, format checks, and whitelisting are all useful for preventing attacks like SQL injection and buffer overflow attacks but are not as directly aimed at authorization issues.

80. D. Since a shared symmetric key could be used by any of the servers, transaction identification problems caused by a shared key are likely to involve a repudiation issue. If encrypted transactions cannot be uniquely identified by server, they cannot be proved to have come from a specific server.

81. C. Filtering is useful for preventing denial of service attacks but won't prevent tampering with data. Hashes and digital signatures can both be used to verify the integrity of data, and authorization controls can help ensure that only those with the proper rights can modify the data.

82. A. NIST SP 800-137 is titled "Information Security Continuous Monitoring (ISCM) for Federal Systems and Organizations" and describes the process of building and maintaining an ISCM. NIST SP 800-145 defines cloud computing, whereas NIST SP 800-53A covers assessing security and privacy controls for federal systems and organizations. NIST SP 800-50 focuses on information security awareness programs.

83. B. Finding severe bugs is not a fault—in fact, fuzzing often finds important issues that would otherwise have been exploitable. Fuzzers can reproduce errors (and thus, "fuzzers can't reproduce errors" is not an issue), but typically don't fully cover the code—code coverage tools are usually paired with fuzzers to validate how much coverage was possible. Fuzzers are often limited to simple errors because they won't handle business logic or attacks that require knowledge from the application user.

84. C. Security audits are security assessments performed by third parties and are intended to evaluate the effectiveness of security controls. Security assessments are conducted by internal staff, and security tests are used to verify that a control is functioning effectively. Penetration tests can be conducted by internal or external staff and test systems by using actual exploitation techniques.

85. C. After scanning for open ports using a port scanning tool like nmap, penetration testers will identify interesting ports and then conduct vulnerability scans to determine what services may be vulnerable. This will perform many of the same activities that connecting via a web server will, and will typically be more useful than trying to manually test for vulnerable accounts via Telnet. sqlmap would typically be used after a vulnerability scanner identifies additional information about services, and the vulnerability scanner will normally provide a wider range of useful information.

86. B. The system is likely a Linux system. The system shows X11, as well as login, shell, and nfs ports, all of which are more commonly found on Linux systems than Windows systems or network devices. This system is also very poorly secured; many of the services running on it should not be exposed in a modern secure network.

87. D. Nmap only scans 1000 TCP and UDP ports by default, including ports outside of the 0–1024 range of "well-known" ports. By using the defaults for nmap, Ben missed 64,535 ports. OS fingerprinting won't cover more ports but would have provided a best guess of the OS running on the scanned system.

88. C. Static analysis is the process of reviewing code without running it. It relies on techniques like data flow analysis to review what the code does if it was run with a given set of inputs. Black and gray box analyses are not types of code review, although black box and gray box both describe types of penetration testing. Fuzzing provides unexpected or invalid data inputs to test how software responds.

89. C. A manual code review, which is performed by humans who review code line by line, is the best option when it is important to understand the context and business logic in the code. Fuzzing, dynamic, and static code review can all find bugs that manual code review might not, but won't take the intent of the programmers into account.

90. C. Misuse case diagrams use language beyond typical use case diagrams, including threatens and mitigates. Threat trees are used to map threats but don't use specialized languages like threatens and mitigates. STRIDE is a mnemonic and model used in threat modeling, and DREAD is a risk assessment model.

91. C. The most important first step for a penetration test is getting permission. Once permission has been received, planning, data gathering, and then elements of the actual test like port scanning can commence.

92. D. SSAE-16 is based on ISAE 3402, the International Standard on Assurance Engagements. It differs in a number of ways, including how it handles purposeful acts by service organizational personnel as well as anomalies, but the two share many elements. SAS-70 has been replaced by SSAE-16, whereas ISO27001 is a formal specification for an information security management system (ISMS). SOX is the Sarbanes–Oxley Act, a U.S. law that impacts accounting and investor protection.

93. C. A TCP scan that sets all or most of the possible TCP flags is called a Christmas tree, or Xmas, scan since it is said to "light up like a Christmas tree" with the flags. A SYN scan would attempt to open TCP connections, whereas an ACK scan sends packets with the ACK flag set. There is no such type of scan known as a TCP flag scan.

94. D. Nmap is a very popular open source port scanner. Nmap is not a vulnerability scanner, nor is it a web application fuzzer. While port scanners can be used to partially map a network, and its name stands for Network Mapper, it is not a network design tool.

95. C. Vulnerability scanners cannot detect vulnerabilities for which they do not have a test, plug-in, or signature. Signatures often include version numbers, service fingerprints, or configuration data. They can detect local vulnerabilities as well as those that require authentication if they are provided with credentials, and of course, they can detect service vulnerabilities.

96. C. The Common Vulnerabilities and Exposures (CVE) dictionary provides a central repository of security vulnerabilities and issues. Patching information for applications and software versions are sometimes managed using central patch management tools, but a single central database is not available for free or public use. Costs versus effort is also not what CVE stands for.

97. D. In many cases when an exploit is initially reported, there are no prebuilt signatures or detections for vulnerability scanners, and the CVE database may not have information about the attack immediately. Jacob's best option is to quickly gather information and review potentially vulnerable servers based on their current configuration. As more information becomes available, signatures and CVE information are likely to be published. Unfortunately for Jacob, IDS and IPS signatures will only detect attacks, and won't detect whether systems are vulnerable unless he sees the systems being exploited.

98. D. Privilege escalation occurs during the attack phase of a penetration test. Host and service information gathering, as well as activities like dumpster diving that can provide information about the organization, its systems, and security, are all part of the discovery phase.

99. B. Once additional tools have been installed, penetration testers will typically use them to gain additional access. From there they can further escalate privileges, search for new targets or data, and once again, install more tools to allow them to pivot further into infrastructure or systems.

100. B. Penetration testing reports often do not include the specific data captured during the assessment, as the readers of the report may not be authorized to access all of the data, and exposure of the report could result in additional problems for the organization. A listing of the issues discovered, risk ratings, and remediation guidance are all common parts of a penetration test report.

Chapter 7: Security Operations (Domain 7)

1. A. The illustration shows an example of a failover cluster, where DB1 and DB2 are both configured as database servers. At any given time, only one will function as the active database server, while the other remains ready to assume responsibility if the first one fails. While the environment may use UPS, tape backup, and cold sites as disaster recovery and business continuity controls, they are not shown in the diagram.

2. D. The principle of least privilege should guide Joe in this case. He should apply no access permissions by default and then give each user the necessary permissions to perform their job responsibilities. Read only, editor, and administrator permissions may be necessary for one or more of these users, but those permissions should be assigned based upon business need and not by default.

3. C. While most organizations would want to log attempts to log in to a workstation, this is not considered a privileged administrative activity and would go through normal logging processes.

4. C. Regulatory investigations attempt to uncover whether an individual or organization has violated administrative law. These investigations are almost always conducted by government agents.

5. D. Real evidence consists of things that may actually be brought into a courtroom as evidence. For example, real evidence includes hard disks, weapons, and items containing fingerprints. Documentary evidence consists of written items that may or may not be in tangible form. Testimonial evidence is verbal testimony given by witnesses with relevant information. The parol evidence rule says that when an agreement is put into written form, the written document is assumed to contain all the terms of the agreement.

6. A. In a manual recovery approach, the system does not fail into a secure state but requires an administrator to manually restore operations. In an automated recovery, the system can recover itself against one or more failure types. In an automated recovery without undue loss, the system can recover itself against one or more failure types and also preserve data against loss. In function recovery, the system can restore functional processes automatically.

7. B. A pseudoflaw is a false vulnerability in a system that may attract an attacker. A honeynet is a network of multiple honeypots that creates a more sophisticated environment for intruders to explore. A darknet is a segment of unused network address space that should have no network activity and, therefore, may be easily used to monitor for illicit activity. A warning banner is a legal tool used to notify intruders that they are not authorized to access a system.

8. B. Social media is commonly used as a command-and-control system for botnet activity. The most likely scenario here is that Toni's computer was infected with malware and joined to a botnet. This accounts for both the unusual social media traffic and the slow system activity.

9. D. Software-defined networking separates the control plane from the data plane. Network devices then do not contain complex logic themselves but receive instructions from the SDN.

10. A. Netflow records contain an entry for every network communication session that took place on a network and can be compared to a list of known malicious hosts. IDS logs may contain a relevant record but it is less likely because they would only create log entries if the traffic triggers the IDS, as opposed to netflow records which encompass all communications. Authentication logs and RFC logs would not have records of any network traffic.

11. B. Gary should follow the least privilege principle and assign users only the permissions they need to perform their job responsibilities. *Aggregation* is a term used to describe the unintentional accumulation of privileges over time, also known as privilege creep. Separation of duties and separation of privileges are principles used to secure sensitive processes.

12. A. The matrix shown in the figure is known as a segregation of duties matrix. It is used to ensure that one person does not obtain two privileges that would create a potential conflict. *Aggregation* is a term used to describe the unintentional accumulation of privileges over time, also known as privilege creep. Two-person control is used when two people must work together to perform a sensitive action. Defense in depth is a general security principle used to describe a philosophy of overlapping security controls.

13. B. Before granting access, Gary should verify that the user has a valid security clearance and a business need to know the information. Gary is performing an authorization task, so he does not need to verify the user's credentials, such as a password or biometric scan.

14. D. Gary should follow the principle of two-person control by requiring simultaneous action by two separate authorized individuals to gain access to the encryption keys. He should also apply the principles of least privilege and defense in depth, but these principles apply to all operations and are not specific to sensitive operations. Gary should avoid the security through obscurity principle, the reliance upon the secrecy of security mechanisms to provide security for a system or process.

15. D. Privileged access reviews are one of the most critical components of an organization's security program because they ensure that only authorized users have access to perform the most sensitive operations. They should take place whenever a user with privileged access leaves the organization or changes roles as well as on a regular, recurring basis.

16. D. Hotfixes, updates, and security fixes are all synonyms for single patches designed to correct a single problem. Service packs are collections of many different updates that serve as a major update to an operating system or application.

17. C. A forensic disk controller performs four functions. One of those, write blocking, intercepts write commands sent to the device and prevents them from modifying data on the device. The other three functions include returning data requested by a read operation, returning access-significant information from the device, and reporting errors from the device back to the forensic host.

18. A. Lydia is following the need to know principle. While the user may have the appropriate security clearance to access this information, there is no business justification provided, so she does not know that the user has an appropriate need to know the information.

19. D. A darknet is a segment of unused network address space that should have no network activity and, therefore, may be easily used to monitor for illicit activity. A honeypot is a decoy computer system used to bait intruders into attacking. A honeynet is a network of multiple honeypots that creates a more sophisticated environment for intruders to explore. A pseudoflaw is a false vulnerability in a system that may attract an attacker.

20. C. Job rotation and mandatory vacations deter fraud by increasing the likelihood that it will be detected. Two-person control deters fraud by requiring collusion between two employees. Incident response does not normally serve as a deterrent mechanism.

21. D. The scenario describes a mix of public cloud and private cloud services. This is an example of a hybrid cloud environment.

22. A. The change log contains information about approved changes and the change management process. While other logs may contain details about the change's effect, the audit trail for change management would be found in the change log.

23. D. In a Software as a Service solution, the vendor manages both the physical infrastructure and the complete application stack, providing the customer with access to a fully managed application.

24. D. The Common Vulnerability and Exposures (CVE) dictionary contains standardized information on many different security issues. The Open Web Application Security Project (OWASP) contains general guidance on web application security issues but does not track specific vulnerabilities or go beyond web applications. The Bugtraq mailing list and Microsoft Security Bulletins are good sources of vulnerability information but are not comprehensive databases of known issues.

25. D. A disaster is any event that can disrupt normal IT operations and can be either natural or manmade. Hacking and terrorism are examples of manmade disasters, while flooding and fire are examples of natural disasters.

26. D. The checklist review is the least disruptive type of disaster recovery test. During a checklist review, team members each review the contents of their disaster recovery checklists on their own and suggest any necessary changes. During a tabletop exercise, team members come together and walk through a scenario without making any changes to information systems. During a parallel test, the team actually activates the disaster recovery site for testing, but the primary site remains operational. During a full interruption test, the team takes down the primary site and confirms that the disaster recovery site is capable of handling regular operations. The full interruption test is the most thorough test but also the most disruptive.

27. B. The Grandfather/Father/Son, Tower of Hanoi, and Six Cartridge Weekly schemes are all different approaches to rotating backup media that balance reuse of media with data retention concerns. Meet-in-the-middle is a cryptographic attack against 2DES encryption.

28. B. In this scenario, Helen designed a process that requires the concurrence of two people to perform a sensitive action. This is an example of two-person control.

29. C. Evidence provided in court must be relevant to determining a fact in question, material to the case at hand, and competently obtained. Evidence does not need to be tangible. Witness testimony is an example of intangible evidence that may be offered in court.

30. A. In the public cloud computing model, the vendor builds a single platform that is shared among many different customers. This is also known as the shared tenancy model.

31. D. CSIRT representation normally includes at least representatives of senior management, information security professionals, legal representatives, public affairs staff, and engineering/technical staff.

32. C. In this scenario, all of the files on the server will be backed up on Monday evening during the full backup. The differential backup on Wednesday will then copy all files modified since the last full backup. These include files 1, 2, 3, 5, and 6: a total of five files.

File Modifications
Monday 8 a.m. - File 1 created
Monday 10 a.m. - File 2 created
Monday 11 a.m. - File 3 created
Monday 4 p.m. - File 1 modified
Monday 5 p.m. - File 4 created
Tuesday 8 a.m. - File 1 modified
Tuesday 9 a.m. - File 2 modified
Tuesday 10 a.m. - File 5 created
Wednesday 8 a.m. - File 3 modified
Wednesday 9 a.m. - File 6 created

33. C. Intrusion detection systems (IDSs) provide only passive responses, such as alerting administrators to a suspected attack. Intrusion prevention systems and firewalls, on the other hand, may take action to block an attack attempt. Antivirus software also may engage in active response by quarantining suspect files.

34. D. The hypervisor runs within the virtualization platform and serves as the moderator between virtual resources and physical resources.

35. D. *Entitlement* refers to the privileges granted to users when an account is first provisioned.

36. A. The service-level agreement (SLA) is between a service provider and a customer and documents in a formal manner expectations around availability, performance, and other parameters. An MOU may cover the same items but is not as formal a document. An OLA is between internal service organizations and does not involve customers. An SOW is an addendum to a contract describing work to be performed.

37. A. The IT Infrastructure Library (ITIL) framework focuses on IT service management. The Project Management Body of Knowledge (PMBOK) provides a common core of project management expertise. The Payment Card Industry Data Security Standard (PCI DSS) contains regulations for credit card security. The Open Group Architecture Framework (TOGAF) focuses on IT architecture issues.

38. D. Latency is a delay in the delivery of packets from their source to their destination. Jitter is a variation in the latency for different packets. Packet loss is the disappearance of packets in transit that requires retransmission. Interference is electrical noise or other disruptions that corrupt the contents of packets.

39. A. Steganography is a technique used to hide information in an otherwise innocuous-seeming file. The suspect may have used this technique to embed hidden information in the image file. Watermarking also manipulates images but does so in an attempt to protect intellectual property. Clipping and sampling are techniques used to reduce a large set of data to a small quantity that may be used for analysis.

40. D. A transformer failure is a failure of a manmade electrical component. Flooding, mudslides, and hurricanes are all examples of natural disasters.

41. C. The (ISC)² code of ethics applies only to information security professionals who are members of (ISC)². Adherence to the code is a condition of certification, and individuals found in violation of the code may have their certifications revoked. (ISC)^2 members who observe a breach of the code are required to report the possible violation by following the ethics complaint procedures.

42. B. The principle of least privilege says that an individual should only have the privileges necessary to complete their job functions. Removing administrative privileges from non-administrative users is an example of least privilege.

43. D. There is no need to conduct forensic imaging as a preventative measure. Rather, forensic imaging should be used during the incident response process. Maintaining patch levels, implementing intrusion detection/prevention, and removing unnecessary services and accounts are all basic preventative measures.

44. B. The scrutiny of hard drives for forensic purposes is an example of media analysis. Embedded device analysis looks at the computers included in other large systems, such as automobiles or security systems. Software analysis analyzes applications and their logs. Network analysis looks at network traffic and logs.

45. C. Security incidents negatively affect the confidentiality, integrity, or availability of information or assets and/or violate a security policy. The unauthorized vulnerability scan of a server does violate security policy and may negatively affect the security of that system, so it qualifies as a security incident. The completion of a backup schedule, logging of system access, and update of antivirus signatures are all routine actions that do not violate policy or jeopardize security, so they are all events rather than incidents.

46. C. Radio Frequency IDentification (RFID) technology is a cost-effective way to track items around a facility. While Wi-Fi could be used for the same purpose, it would be much more expensive to implement.

47. C. An attack committed against an organization by an insider, such as an employee, is known as sabotage. Espionage and confidentiality breaches involve the theft of sensitive information, which is not alleged to have occurred in this case. Integrity breaches involve the unauthorized modification of information, which is not described in this scenario.

48. A. In a SYN flood attack, the attacker sends a large number of SYN packets to a system but does not respond to the SYN/ACK packets, attempting to overwhelm the attacked system's connection state table with half-open connections.

49. B. The maximum tolerable downtime (MTD) is the longest amount of time that an IT service or component may be unavailable without causing serious damage to the organization. The recovery time objective (RTO) is the amount of time expected to return an IT service or component to operation after a failure. The recovery point objective (RPO) identifies the maximum amount of data, measured in time, that may be lost during a recovery effort. Service-level agreements (SLAs) are written contracts that document service expectations.

50. C. Zero-day attacks are those that are previously unknown to the security community and, therefore, have no available patch. These are especially dangerous attacks because they may be highly effective until a solution becomes available.

51. B. The four canons of the (ISC)^2 code of ethics are to protect society, the common good, necessary public trust and confidence and the infrastructure; act honorably, honestly, justly, responsibly and legally; provide diligent and competent service to principals; and advance and protect the profession.

52. A. Interviews occur when investigators meet with an individual who may have information relevant to their investigation but is not a suspect. If the individual is a suspect, then the meeting is an interrogation.

53. B. Beth should choose a cold site. This type of facility meets her requirements for environmental controls and power but, does not have the equipment or data found in a warm site, hot site, or service bureau. However, it does have the lowest cost of the four options.

54. D. The image clearly contains the watermark of the US Geological Survey (USGS), which ensures that anyone seeing the image knows its origin. It is not possible to tell from looking at the image whether steganography was used. Sampling and clipping are data analysis techniques and are not used to protect images.

55. D. The annualized rate of occurrence (ARO) is the expected number of times an incident will occur each year. In the case of a 200-year flood plain, planners should expect a flood once every 200 years. This is equivalent to a 1/200 chance of a flood in any given year, or 0.005 floods per year.

56. B. While all hackers with malicious intent pose a risk to the organization, the malicious insider poses the greatest risk to security because they likely have legitimate access to sensitive systems that may be used as a launching point for an attack. Other attackers do not begin with this advantage.

57. C. In an electronic vaulting approach, automated technology moves database backups from the primary database server to a remote site on a scheduled basis, typically daily. Transaction logging is not a recovery technique alone; it is a process for generating the logs used in remote journaling. Remote journaling transfers transaction logs to a remote site on a more frequent basis than electronic vaulting, typically hourly. Remote mirroring maintains a live database server at the backup site and mirrors all transactions at the primary site on the server at the backup site.

58. B. Hilda's design follows the principle of separation of duties. Giving one user the ability to both create new accounts and grant administrative privileges combines two actions that would result in a significant security change that should be divided among two users.

59. D. An audit kickoff meeting should clearly describe the scope and purpose of the audit as well as the expected timeframe. Auditors should never approach an audit with any expectations about what they will discover because the findings should only be developed based upon the results of audit examinations.

60. C. The end goal of the disaster recovery process is restoring normal business operations in the primary facility. All of the other actions listed may take place during the disaster recovery process but the process is not complete until the organization is once again functioning normally in its primary facilities.

61. C. A host-based intrusion detection system (HIDS) may be able to detect unauthorized processes running on a system. The other controls mentioned, network intrusion detection systems (NIDSs), firewalls, and DLP systems, are network-based and may not notice rogue processes.

62. B. The scenario describes a privilege escalation attack where a malicious insider with authorized access to a system misused that access to gain privileged credentials.

63. B. Carla's account has experienced aggregation, where privileges accumulated over time. This condition is also known as privilege creep and likely constitutes a violation of the least privilege principle.

64. C. The Mitigation phase of incident response focuses on actions that can contain the damage incurred during an incident. This includes limiting the scope and or effectiveness of the incident.

65. C. At this point in the process, Ann has no reason to believe that any actual security compromise or policy violation took place, so this situation does not meet the criteria for a security incident or intrusion. Rather, the alert generated by the intrusion detection system is simply a security event requiring further investigation. *Security occurrence* is not a term commonly used in incident handling.

66. A. DNS traffic commonly uses port 53 for both TCP and UDP communications. SSH and SCP use TCP port 22. SSL and TLS do not have ports assigned to them but are commonly used for HTTPS traffic on port 443. Unencrypted web traffic over HTTP often uses port 80.

67. D. The attack described in this scenario has all of the hallmarks of a denial of service attack. More specifically, Ann's organization is likely experiencing a DNS amplification attack where an attacker sends false requests to third-party DNS servers with a forged source IP address belonging to the targeted system. Because the attack uses UDP requests, there is no three-way handshake. The attack packets are carefully crafted to elicit a lengthy response from a short query. The purpose of these queries is to generate responses headed to the target system that are sufficiently large and numerous enough to overwhelm the targeted network or system.

68. B. Now that Ann suspects an attack against her organization, she has sufficient evidence to declare a security incident. The attack underway seems to have undermined the availability of her network, meeting one of the criteria for a security incident. This is an escalation beyond a security event but does not reach the level of an intrusion because there is no evidence that the attacker has even attempted to gain access to systems on Ann's network. *Security occurrence* is not a term commonly used in incident handling.

69. D. To be admissible, evidence must be relevant, material, and competent. The laptop in this case is clearly material because it contains logs related to the crime in question. It is also relevant because it provides evidence that ties the hacker to the crime. It is not competent because the evidence was not legally obtained.

70. C. Gordon may conduct his investigation as he wishes and use any information that is legally available to him, including information and systems belonging to his employer.

There is no obligation to contact law enforcement. However, Gordon may not perform "hack back" activities because those may constitute violations of the law and/or (ISC)² Code of Ethics.

71. B. Software escrow agreements place a copy of the source code for a software package in the hands of an independent third party who will turn the code over to the customer if the vendor ceases business operations. Service-level agreements, mutual assistance agreements, and compliance agreements all lose some or all of their effectiveness if the vendor goes out of business.

72. C. Most security professionals recommend at least one, and preferably two, weeks of vacation to deter fraud. The idea is that fraudulent schemes will be uncovered during the time that the employee is away and does not have the access required to perpetuate a cover-up.

73. D. Any attempt to undermine the security of an organization or violation of a security policy is a security incident. Each of the events described meets this definition and should be treated as an incident.

74. D. Egress filtering scans outbound traffic for potential security policy violations. This includes traffic with a private IP address as the destination, traffic with a broadcast address as the destination, and traffic that has a falsified source address not belonging to the organization.

75. C. The two main methods of choosing records from a large pool for further analysis are sampling and clipping. Sampling uses statistical techniques to choose a sample that is representative of the entire pool, while clipping uses threshold values to select those records that exceed a predefined threshold because they may be of most interest to analysts.

76. B. Netflow data contains information on the source, destination, and size of all network communications and is routinely saved as a matter of normal activity. Packet capture data would provide relevant information, but it must be captured during the suspicious activity and cannot be re-created after the fact unless the organization is already conducting 100 percent packet capture, which is very rare. Additionally, the use of encryption limits the effectiveness of packet capture. Intrusion detection system logs would not likely contain relevant information because the encrypted traffic would probably not match intrusion signatures. Centralized authentication records would not contain information about network traffic.

77. C. Baseline configurations serve as the starting point for configuring secure systems and applications. They contain the security settings necessary to comply with an organization's security policy and may then be customized to meet the specific needs of an implementation. While security policies and guidelines may contain information needed to secure a system, they do not contain a set of configuration settings that may be applied to a system. The running configuration of a system is the set of currently applied settings, which may or may not be secure.

78. B. During a parallel test, the team actually activates the disaster recovery site for testing but the primary site remains operational. During a full interruption test, the team takes down the primary site and confirms that the disaster recovery site is capable of handling regular operations. The full interruption test is the most thorough test but also the most disruptive. The checklist review is the least disruptive type of disaster recovery test. During a checklist review, team members each review the contents of their disaster recovery checklists on their own and suggest any necessary changes. During a tabletop exercise, team members come together and walk through a scenario without making any changes to information systems.

79. C. Both the receipt of alerts and the verification of their accuracy occurs during the Detection phase of the incident response process.

80. A. Virtual machines run full guest operating systems on top of a host platform known as the hypervisor.

81. B. RAID level 1 is also known as disk mirroring. RAID-0 is called disk striping. RAID-5 is called disk striping with parity. RAID-10 is known as a stripe of mirrors.

82. C. SSH uses TCP port 22, so this attack is likely an attempt to scan for open or weakly secured SSH servers. FTP uses ports 20 and 21. Telnet uses port 23, and HTTP uses port 80.

83. C. The ping of death attack placed more data than allowed by the specification in the payload of an ICMP echo request packet. This is similar to the modern-day buffer overflow attack where attackers attempt to place more data in a targeted system's memory that consumes more space than is allocated for that data.

84. C. In an Infrastructure as a Service environment, the vendor is responsible for hardware- and network-related responsibilities. These include configuring network firewalls, maintaining the hypervisor, and managing physical equipment. The customer retains responsibility for patching operating systems on its virtual machine instances.

85. B. Sandboxing is a technique where application developers (or the recipients of an untrusted application) may test the code in a virtualized environment that is isolated from production systems. White box testing, black box testing, and penetration testing are all common software testing techniques but do not require the use of an isolated system.

86. B. Fraggle attacks use a distributed attack approach to send UDP traffic at a targeted system from many different source addresses on ports 7 and 19. The most effective way to block this attack would be to block inbound UDP traffic on those ports. Blocking the source addresses is not feasible because the attacker would likely simply change the source addresses. Blocking destination addresses would likely disrupt normal activity. The fraggle attack does not use ICMP, so blocking that traffic would have no effect.

87. A. Transitive trusts go beyond the two domains directly involved in the trust relationship and extend to their subdomains.

88. C. In a Platform as a Service solution, the customer supplies application code that the vendor then executes on its own infrastructure.

89. A. Companies have an obligation to preserve evidence whenever they believe that the threat of litigation is imminent. The statement made by this customer that "we will have to take this matter to court" is a clear threat of litigation and should trigger the preservation of any related documents and records.

90. B. The Fourth Amendment states, in part, that "the right of the people to be secure in their persons, houses, papers and effects, against unreasonable searches and seizures, shall not be violated, and no Warrants shall issue, but upon probable cause, supported by Oath or affirmation, and particularly describing the place to be searched, and the persons or things to be seized." The First Amendment contains protections related to freedom of speech. The Fifth Amendment ensures that no person will be required to serve as a witness against themselves. The Fifteenth Amendment protects the voting rights of citizens.

91. A. Expert opinion evidence allows individuals to offer their opinion based upon the facts in evidence and their personal knowledge. Expert opinion evidence may be offered only if the court accepts the witness as an expert in a particular field. Direct evidence is when witnesses testify about their direct observations. Real evidence consists of tangible items brought into court as evidence. Documentary evidence consists of written records used as evidence in court.

92. D. The standard methods for clearing magnetic tapes, according to the NIST Guidelines for Media Sanitization, are overwriting the tape with nonsensitive data, degaussing, and physical destruction via shredding or incineration. Reformatting a tape does not remove remnant data.

93. B. RAID level 1, also known as disk mirroring, uses two disks that contain identical information. If one disk fails, the other contains the data needed for the system to continue operation.

94. B. The analysis of application logs is one of the core tasks of software analysis because SQL injection attacks are application attacks.

95. C. Quantum may choose to use any or all of these security controls, but data encryption is, by far, the most important control. It protects the confidentiality of data stored on the tapes, which are most vulnerable to theft while in transit between two secure locations.

96. C. Data loss prevention (DLP) systems may identify sensitive information stored on end-point systems or in transit over a network. This is their primary purpose. Intrusion detection and prevention systems (IDS/IPS) may be used to identify some sensitive information using signatures built for that purpose, but this is not the primary role of those tools and they would not be as effective as DLP systems at this task. TLS is a network encryption protocol that may be used to protect sensitive information, but it does not have any ability to identify sensitive information.

97. D. If software is released into the public domain, anyone may use it for any purpose, without restriction. All other license types contain at least some level of restriction.

98. A. In a man-in-the-middle attack, attackers manage to insert themselves into a connection between a user and a legitimate website, relaying traffic between the two parties while eavesdropping on the connection. Although similarly named, the meet-in-the-middle attack is a cryptographic attack that does not necessarily involve connection tampering. Fraggle is a network-based denial of service attack using UDP packets. Wardriving is a reconnaissance technique for discovering open or weakly secured wireless networks.

99. C. The two main methods of choosing records from a large pool for further analysis are sampling and clipping. Sampling uses statistical techniques to choose a sample that is representative of the entire pool, while clipping uses threshold values to select those records that exceed a predefined threshold because they may be of most interest to analysts.

100. C. Generators are capable of providing backup power for a sustained period of time in the event of a power loss, but they take time to activate. Uninterruptible power supplies (UPS) provide immediate, battery-driven power for a short period of time to cover momentary losses of power, which would not cover a sustained period of power loss. RAID and redundant servers are high availability controls but do not cover power loss scenarios.

Chapter 8: Software Development Security (Domain 8)

1. B. Coupling is a description of the level of interaction between objects. Cohesion is the strength of the relationship between the purposes of methods within the same class. When you are developing an object-oriented model, it is desirable to have high cohesion and low coupling.

2. D. Botnets are used for a wide variety of malicious purposes, including scanning the network for vulnerable systems, conducting brute-force attacks against other systems, and sending out spam messages.

3. C. Code review takes place after code has been developed, which occurs after the design phase of the system's development life cycle (SDLC). Code review may use a combination of manual and automated techniques, or rely solely on one or the other. It should be a peer-driven process that includes developers who did not write the code. Developers should expect to complete the review of around 300 lines per hour, on average.

4. D. A social engineering attack may trick a user into revealing their password to the attacker. Other attacks that depend on guessing passwords, such as brute-force attacks, rainbow table attacks, and dictionary attacks, are unlikely to be successful in light of the organization's strong password policy.

5. C. One of the responsibilities of the release control process is ensuring that the process includes acceptance testing that confirms that any alterations to end-user work tasks are understood and functional prior to code release. The request control, change control, and configuration control processes do not include acceptance testing.

6. B. Cross-site request forgery (XSRF or CSRF) attacks exploit the trust that sites have in a user's browser by attempting to force the submission of authenticated requests to third-party sites. Session hijacking attacks attempt to steal previously authenticated sessions but do not force the browser to submit requests. SQL injection directly attacks a database through a web application. Cross-site scripting uses reflected input to trick a user's browser into executing untrusted code from a trusted site.

7. A. The SDLC consists of seven phases, in the following order: conceptual definition, functional requirements determination, control specifications development, design review, code review, system test review, and maintenance and change management.

8. D. The error message shown in the figure is the infamous "Blue Screen of Death" that occurs when a Windows system experiences a dangerous failure and enters a fail secure state. If the system had "failed open," it would have continued operation. The error described is a memory fault that is likely recoverable by rebooting the system. There is no indication that the system has run out of usable memory.

9. D. Software threat modeling is designed to reduce the number of security-related design and coding flaws as well as the severity of other flaws. The developer or evaluator of software has no control over the threat environment, because it is external to the organization.

10. C. In the diagram, Account is the name of the class. Owner and Balance are attributes of that class. AddFunds and RemoveFunds are methods of the class.

11. A. Primary storage is a technical term used to refer to the memory that is directly available to the CPU. Nonvolatile storage mechanisms, such as flash drives, DVDs, and hard drives, are classified as secondary storage.

12. A. Dynamic testing of software typically occurs in a black box environment where the tester does not have access to the source code. Static testing, white box testing, and code review approaches all require access to the source code of the application.

13. B. Inheritance occurs when a subclass (or child class) is able to use methods belonging to a superclass (or parent class). Polymorphism occurs when different subclasses may have different methods using the same interfaces that respond differently. Coupling is a description of the level of interaction between objects. Cohesion is the strength of the relationship between the purposes of methods within the same class.

14. C. Aggregate functions summarize large amounts of data and provide only summary information as a result. When carefully crafted, aggregate functions may unintentionally reveal sensitive information.

15. B. The best protection against buffer overflow attacks is server-side input validation. This technique limits user input to approved ranges of values that fit within allocated buffers. While firewalls and intrusion prevention systems may contain controls that limit buffer overflows, it would be more effective to perform filtering on the application server. Encryption cannot protect against buffer overflow attacks.

16. B. The log entries show the characteristic pattern of a port scan. The attacking system sends connection attempts to the target system against a series of commonly used ports.

17. C. Acme Widgets is clearly in the initial stage of the SW-CMM. This stage is characterized by the absence of formal process. The company may still produce working code, but they do so in a disorganized fashion.

18. B. The Repeatable stage is the second stage in the SW-CMM, following the Initial stage. It should be the next milestone goal for Acme Widgets. The Repeatable stage is characterized by basic life-cycle management processes.

19. A. The Defined stage of the SW-CMM is marked by the presence of basic life-cycle management processes and reuse of code. It includes the use of requirements management, software project planning, quality assurance, and configuration management practices.

20. D. The Managed stage is the fourth stage in the SW-CMM, following the Defined stage. It should be the next milestone goal for Beta Particles. The Managed stage is characterized by the use of quantitative software development measures.

21. C. Referential integrity ensures that records exist in a secondary table when they are referenced with a foreign key from another table. Foreign keys are the mechanism used to enforce referential integrity.

22. A. Macro viruses are most commonly found in office productivity documents, such as Microsoft Word documents that end in the .doc or .docx extension. They are not commonly found in executable files with the .com or .exe extensions.

23. C. The degree of a database table is the number of attributes in the table. Victor's table has six attributes: the employee's user ID, home telephone, office telephone, mobile telephone, office location, and job title.

24. C. The string shown in the logs is characteristic of a directory traversal attack where the attacker attempts to force the web application to navigate up the file hierarchy and retrieve a file that should not normally be provided to a web user, such as the password file. The series of "double dots" is indicative of a directory traversal attack because it is the character string used to reference the directory one level up in a hierarchy.

25. C. Design reviews should take place after the development of functional and control specifications but before the creation of code. The code review, unit testing, and functional testing all take place after the creation of code and, therefore, after the design review.

26. C. Regression testing is software testing that runs a set of known inputs against an application and then compares the results to those produced by an earlier version of the software. It is designed to capture unanticipated consequences of deploying new code versions prior to introducing them into a production environment.

27. D. Assurance, when it comes to software, is the level of confidence that software is free from vulnerabilities, either intentionally designed into the software or accidentally inserted at any time during its life cycle, and that the software functions in the intended manner. It is a term typically used in military and defense environments.

28. C. The change control process is responsible for providing an organized framework within which multiple developers can create and test a solution prior to rolling it out in a production environment. Request control provides a framework for user requests. Release control manages the deployment of code into production. Configuration control ensures that changes to software versions are made in accordance with the change and configuration management policies.

29. D. Aggregation is a security issue that arises when a collection of facts has a higher classification than the classification of any of those facts standing alone. An inference problem occurs when an attacker can pull together pieces of less sensitive information and use them to derive information of greater sensitivity. SQL injection is a web application exploit. Multilevel security is a system control that allows the simultaneous processing of information at different classification levels.

30. A. The two major classifications of covert channels are timing and storage. A covert timing channel conveys information by altering the performance of a system component or modifying a resource's timing in a predictable manner. A covert storage channel conveys information by writing data to a common storage area where another process can read it. There is no such thing as a covert firewall channel. Memory is a type of storage, so a memory-based covert channel would fit into the covert storage channel category.

31. A. Black box testing begins with no prior knowledge of the system implementation, simulating a user perspective. White box and gray box testing provide full and partial knowledge of the system, respectively, in advance of the test. Blue boxes are a phone hacking tool and are not used in software testing.

32. B. In this example, the two SQL commands are indeed bundled in a transaction, but it is not an error to issue an update command that does not match any rows. Therefore, the first command would "succeed" in updating zero rows and not generate an error or cause the transaction to rollback. The second command would then execute, reducing the balance of the second account by $250.

```
BEGIN TRANSACTION
UPDATE accounts
SET balance = balance + 250
WHERE account_number = 1001;

UPDATE accounts
SET balance = balance - 250
WHERE account_number = 2002;

END TRANSACTION
```

33. D. Worms have built-in propagation mechanisms that do not require user interaction, such as scanning for systems containing known vulnerabilities and then exploiting those vulnerabilities to gain access. Viruses and Trojan horses typically require user interaction to spread. Logic bombs do not spread from system to system but lie in wait until certain conditions are met, triggering the delivery of their payload.

34. C. A fail open configuration may be appropriate in this case. In this configuration, the firewall would continue to pass traffic without inspection while it is restarting. This would minimize downtime, and the traffic would still be protected by the other security controls described in the scenario. Failover devices and high availability clusters would indeed increase availability, but at potentially significant expense. Redundant disks would not help in this scenario because no disk failure is described.

35. D. An inference problem occurs when an attacker can pull together pieces of less sensitive information and use them to derive information of greater sensitivity. Aggregation is a security issue that arises when a collection of facts has a higher classification than the classification of any of those facts standing alone. SQL injection is a web application exploit. Multilevel security is a system control that allows the simultaneous processing of information at different classification levels.

36. B. Polymorphic viruses mutate each time they infect a system by making adjustments to their code that assists them in evading signature detection mechanisms. Encrypted viruses also mutate from infection to infection but do so by encrypting themselves with different keys on each device.

37. A. The message forum is clearly susceptible to a cross-site scripting (XSS) attack. The code that Linda discovered in the message is a definitive example of an attempt to conduct cross-site scripting, and the alert box that she received demonstrates that the vulnerability exists. The website may also be vulnerable to cross-site request forgery, SQL injection, improper authentication, and other attacks, but there is no evidence of this provided in the scenario.

38. A. The script that Linda discovered merely pops up a message on a user's screen and does not perform any more malicious action. This type of script, using an `alert()` call, is commonly used to probe websites for cross-site scripting vulnerabilities.

39. B. Web application firewalls (WAFs) sit in front of web applications and watch for potentially malicious web attacks, including cross-site scripting. They then block that traffic from reaching the web application. An intrusion detection system (IDS) may detect the attack but is unable to take action to prevent it. DLP and VPN solutions are unable to detect web application attacks.

40. C. Input validation verifies that user-supplied input does not violate security conditions and is the most effective defense against cross-site scripting attacks. Bounds checking is a form of input validation, but it is used to ensure that numeric input falls within an acceptable range and is not applicable against cross-site scripting attacks. Peer review and OS patching are both good security practices but are unlikely to be effective against a cross-site scripting attack.

41. C. Durability requires that once a transaction is committed to the database it must be preserved. Atomicity ensures that if any part of a database transaction fails, the entire transaction must be rolled back as if it never occurred. Consistency ensures that all transactions are consistent with the logical rules of the database, such as having a primary key. Isolation requires that transactions operate separately from each other.

42. D. JavaScript is an interpreted language that does not make use of a compiler to transform code into an executable state. Java, C, and C++ are all compiled languages.

43. B. Multipartite viruses use multiple propagation mechanisms to defeat system security controls but do not necessarily include techniques designed to hide the malware from antivirus software. Stealth viruses tamper with the operating system to hide their existence. Polymorphic viruses alter their code on each system they infect to defeat signature detection. Encrypted viruses use a similar technique, employing encryption to alter their appearance and avoid signature detection mechanisms.

44. C. User acceptance testing (UAT) is typically the last phase of the testing process. It verifies that the solution developed meets user requirements and validates it against use cases. Unit testing, integration testing, and system testing are all conducted earlier in the process leading up to UAT.

45. D. Functional requirements specify the inputs, behavior, and outputs of software. Derived requirements are requirements developed from other requirement definitions. Structural and behavioral requirements focus on the overall structure of a system and the behaviors it displays.

46. C. The Open Web Application Security Project (OWASP) is widely considered as the most authoritative source on web application security issues. They publish the OWASP Top Ten list that publicizes the most critical web application security issues.

47. B. When one object wishes to interact with another object, it does so by invoking one of the second object's methods, including required and, perhaps, optional arguments to that method.

48. D. This question is asking you to identify the blocking rule that should NOT be set on the firewall. Packets with public IP addresses will routinely be allowed to enter the network, so you should not create a rule to block them, making this the correct answer. Packets with internal source addresses should never originate from outside the network so they should be blocked from entering the network. Packets with external source addresses should never be found on the internal network, so they should be blocked from leaving the network. Finally, private IP addresses should never be used on the Internet, so packets containing private IP addresses should be blocked from leaving the network.

49. B. This is an example of a specific type of buffer overflow known as an off-by-one error. The first line of the code defines an array of 10 elements, which would be numbered 0 through 9. The second line of code tries to place a value in the 11th element of the array (remember, array counting begins at 0!), which would cause an overflow.

50. C. Lost updates occur when one transaction writes a value to the database that overwrites a value needed by transactions that have earlier precedence, causing those transactions to read an incorrect value. Dirty reads occur when one transaction reads a value from a database that was written by another transaction that did not commit. Incorrect summaries occur when one transaction is using an aggregate function to summarize data stored in a database while a second transaction is making modifications to the database, causing the summary to include incorrect information. SQL injection is a web application security flaw, not a database concurrency problem.

51. A. Transport Layer Security (TLS) provides the most effective defense against session hijacking because it encrypts all traffic between the client and server, preventing the attacker from stealing session credentials. Secure Sockets Layer (SSL) also encrypts traffic, but it is vulnerable to attacks against its encryption technology. Complex and expiring cookies are a good idea, but they are not sufficient protection against session hijacking.

52. C. When a system uses shadowed passwords, the hashed password value is stored in /etc/shadow instead of /etc/passwd. The /etc/passwd file would not contain the password in plaintext or hashed form. Instead, it would contain an x to indicate that the password hash is in the shadow file. The * character is normally used to disable interactive logins to an account.

53. B. Time of check to time of use (TOC/TOU) attacks target situations where there is a race condition, meaning that a dependence on the timing of actions allows impermissible actions to take place.

54. C. The single quotation mark in the input field is a telltale sign that this is a SQL injection attack. The quotation mark is used to escape outside of the SQL code's input field, and the text following is used to directly manipulate the SQL command sent from the web application to the database.

55. B. Client-side input validation is not an effective control against any type of attack because the attacker can easily bypass the validation by altering the code on the client. Escaping restricted characters prevents them from being passed to the database, as does parameterization. Limiting database permissions prevents dangerous code from executing.

56. B. PERT charts use nodes to represent milestones or deliverables and then show the estimated time to move between milestones. Gantt charts use a different format with a row for each task and lines showing the expected duration of the task. Work breakdown structures are an earlier deliverable that divides project work into achievable tasks. Wireframe diagrams are used in web design.

57. D. Regression testing is performed after developers make changes to an application. It reruns a number of test cases and compares the results to baseline results. Orthogonal array testing is a method for generating test cases based on statistical analysis. Pattern testing uses records of past software bugs to inform the analysis. Matrix testing develops a matrix of all possible inputs and outputs to inform the test plan.

58. B. Cross-site scripting (XSS) attacks may take advantage of the use of reflected input in a web application where input provided by one user is displayed to another user. Input validation is a control used to prevent XSS attacks. XSS does not require an unpatched server or any firewall rules beyond those permitting access to the web application.

59. A. In a white box test, the attacker has access to full implementation details of the system, including source code, prior to beginning the test. In gray box testing, the attacker has partial knowledge. In black box testing, the attacker has no knowledge of the system and tests it from a user perspective. Blue boxes are a phone hacking tool and are not used in software testing.

60. C. Heuristic-based anti-malware software has a higher likelihood of detecting a zero-day exploit than signature-based methods. Heuristic-based software does not require frequent signature updates because it does not rely upon monitoring systems for the presence of known malware. The trade-off with this approach is that it has a higher false positive rate than signature detection methods.

61. D. One possibility for the clean scan results is that the virus is using stealth techniques, such as intercepting read requests from the antivirus software and returning a correct-looking version of the infected file. The system may also be the victim of a zero-day attack, using a virus that is not yet included in the signature definition files provided by the antivirus vendor.

62. A. In URL encoding, the . character is replaced by %252E and the / character is replaced by %252F. You can see this in the log entry, where the expected pattern of ../../ is replaced by %252E%252E%252F%252E%252E%252F.

63. C. Attacks where the malicious user tricks the victim's web browser into executing a script through the use of a third-party site are known as cross-site scripting (XSS) attacks. This particular attack is a persistent XSS attack because it remains on the discussion forum until an administrator discovers and deletes it, giving it the ability to affect many users.

64. C. The Agile Manifesto includes 12 principles for software development. Three of those are listed as answer choices: maximizing the amount of work not done is essential, build projects around motivated individuals, and welcome changing requirements throughout the development process. Agile does not, however, consider clear documentation the primary measure of progress. Instead, working software is the primary measure of progress.

65. C. Unit testing works on individual system components, such as code modules. Regression testing is used to validate updates to code by comparing the output of the new version with previous versions. Samantha is developing new modules, so regression testing is not relevant. Integration and system testing require a broader scope than individual modules.

66. D. Expert systems have two components: a knowledge bank that contains the collected wisdom of human experts and an inference engine that allows the expert systems to draw conclusions about new situations based on the information contained within the knowledge bank.

67. D. A key-value store is an example of a NoSQL database that does not follow a relational or hierarchical model like traditional databases. A graph database is another example of a NoSQL database, but it uses nodes and edges to store data rather than keys and values.

68. C. A database failure in the middle of a transaction causes the rollback of the entire transaction. In this scenario, the database would not execute either command.

69. B. In the diagram, Account is the name of the class. Owner and Balance are attributes of that class. AddFunds and RemoveFunds are methods of the class.

70. B. Static testing performs code analysis in an offline fashion, without actually executing the code. Dynamic testing evaluates code in a runtime environment. Both static and dynamic testing may use automated tools, and both are important security testing techniques.

71. D. The chart shown in the figure is a Gantt chart, showing the proposed start and end dates for different activities. It is developed based on the work breakdown structure (WBS), which is developed based on functional requirements. Program Evaluation Review Technique (PERT) charts show the project schedule as a series of numbered nodes.

72. D. In a gray box test, the tester evaluates the software from a user perspective but has access to the source code as the test is conducted. White box tests also have access to the source code but perform testing from a developer's perspective. Black box tests work from a user's perspective but do not have access to source code. Blue boxes are a telephone hacking tool and not a software testing technique.

73. D. The Time of Check to Time of Use (TOC/TOU) attack exploits timing differences between when a system verifies authorization and software uses that authorization to perform an action. It is an example of a race condition attack. The other three attacks mentioned do not depend on precise timing.

74. A. In the diagram, Account is the name of the class. Owner and Balance are attributes of that class. AddFunds and RemoveFunds are methods of the class.

75. B. Incorrect summaries occur when one transaction is using an aggregate function to summarize data stored in a database while a second transaction is making modifications to the database, causing the summary to include incorrect information. Dirty reads occur when one transaction reads a value from a database that was written by another transaction that did not commit. Lost updates occur when one transaction writes a value to the database that overwrites a value needed by transactions that have earlier precedence, causing those transactions to read an incorrect value. SQL injection is a web application security flaw, not a database concurrency problem.

76. D. The fail closed approach prevents any activity from taking place during a system security failure and is the most conservative approach to failure management. Fail open takes the opposite philosophy, allowing all activity in the event of a security control failure. Fail clear and fail mitigation are not failure management approaches.

77. D. The illustration shows the spiral model of software development. In this approach, developers use multiple iterations of a waterfall-style software development process. This becomes a "loop" of iterations through similar processes. The waterfall approach does not iterate through the entire process repeatedly but rather only allows movement backward and forward one stage. The agile approach to software development focuses on iterative improvement and does not follow a rigorous SDLC model. Lean is a process improvement methodology and not a software development model.

78. B. Relational databases use the primary key to uniquely identify each of the rows in a table. The primary key is selected by the database designer from the set of candidate keys that are able to uniquely identify each row, but the RDBMS only uses the primary key for this purpose. Foreign keys are used to establish relationships between tables. Referential keys are not a type of database key.

79. A. The request process begins with a user-initiated request for a feature. Change and release control are initiated by developers seeking to implement changes. Design review is a phase of the change approval process initiated by developers when they have a completed design.

80. C. Polyinstantiation allows the storage of multiple different pieces of information in a database at different classification levels to prevent attackers from inferring anything about the absence of information. Input validation, server-side validation, and parameterization are all techniques used to prevent web application attacks and are not effective against inference attacks.

81. C. While Ursula may certainly use an object model, data dictionary, and primary key in her development effort, external developers cannot directly use them to access her code. An application programming interface (API) allows other developers to call Ursula's code from within their own without knowing the details of Ursula's implementation.

82. C. In the Establishing phase of the IDEAL model, the organization takes the general recommendations from the Diagnosing phase and develops a specific plan of action that achieves those changes.

83. D. Messages similar to the one shown in the figure are indicative of a ransomware attack. The attacker encrypts files on a user's hard drive and then demands a ransom, normally paid in Bitcoin, for the decryption key required to restore access to the original content. Encrypted viruses, on the other hand, use encryption to hide themselves from antivirus mechanisms and do not alter other contents on the system.

84. A. The bin2hex() function converts a string to a hexadecimal value that may then be passed to a database safely. The dechex() function performs a similar function but will not work for a string as it only functions on numeric values. The hex2bin() and hexdec() functions work in the reverse manner.

85. D. Neural networks attempt to use complex computational techniques to model the behavior of the human mind. Knowledge banks are a component of expert systems, which are designed to capture and reapply human knowledge. Decision support systems are designed to provide advice to those carrying out standard procedures and are often driven by expert systems.

86. B. In level 2, the Repeatable level of the SW-CMM, an organization introduces basic life-cycle management processes. Reuse of code in an organized fashion begins, and repeatable results are expected from similar projects. The key process areas for this level include Requirements Management, Software Project Planning, Software Project Tracking and Oversight, Software Subcontract Management, Software Quality Assurance, and Software Configuration Management.

87. C. The key to this question is that Lucas suspects the tampering took place before the employee departed. This is the signature of a logic bomb: malicious code that lies dormant until certain conditions are met. The other attack types listed here: privilege escalation, SQL injection, and remote code execution would more likely take place in real time.

88. A. The Agile approach to software development embraces four principles. It values individuals and interactions over processes and tools, working software over comprehensive documentation, customer collaboration over contract negotiation, and responding to change over following a plan.

89. C. API developers commonly use API keys to limit access to authorized users and applications. Encryption provides for confidentiality of information exchanged using an API but does not provide authentication. Input validation is an application security technique used to protect against malicious input. IP filters may be used to limit access to an API, but they are not commonly used because it is difficult to deploy an API with IP filters since the filters require constant modification and maintenance as endpoints change.

90. C. Signature detection is extremely effective against known strains of malware because it uses a very reliable pattern matching technique to identify known malware. Signature detection is, therefore, the most reliable way to detect known malware. This technique is not, however, effective against the zero-day malware typically used by advanced persistent threats (APTs) that does not exploit vulnerabilities identified in security bulletins. While malware authors once almost exclusively targeted Windows systems, malware now exists for all major platforms.

91. B. In the waterfall model, the software development process follows five sequential steps which are, in order: Requirements, Design, Coding, Testing, and Maintenance.

92. A. Atomicity ensures that database transactions either execute completely or not at all. Consistency ensures that all transactions must begin operating in an environment that is consistent with all of the database's rules. The isolation principle requires that transactions operate separately from each other. Durability ensures that database transactions, once committed, are permanent.

93. D. Input validation ensures that the data provided to a program as input matches the expected parameters. Limit checks are a special form of input validation that ensure the value remains within an expected range, but there was no range specified in this scenario. Fail open and fail secure are options when planning for possible system failures.

94. A. Cookies are used to maintain authenticated sessions, even when IP addresses change. Therefore, Mal can use the stolen cookies to conduct a session hijacking attack, taking over an authorized user's session with the website, potentially without the knowledge of the legitimate user.

95. D. Penetration tests of web-based systems may detect any possible web application security flaw, including cross-site request forgery (XSRF), cross-site scripting (XSS), and SQL injection vulnerabilities.

96. C. The DevOps approach to technology management seeks to integrate software development, operations, and quality assurance in a seamless approach that builds collaboration between the three disciplines.

97. B. nessus is a vulnerability testing tool designed for use by security professionals but also available to attackers. nmap may also assist attackers, but it only shows open ports and has limited capability to identify vulnerabilities. ipconfig displays network configuration information about a system, whereas traceroute identifies the network path between two systems.

98. D. Dirty reads occur when one transaction reads a value from a database that was written by another transaction that did not commit. Lost updates occur when one transaction writes a value to the database that overwrites a value needed by transactions that have earlier precedence, causing those transactions to read an incorrect value. Incorrect summaries occur when one transaction is using an aggregate function to summarize data stored in a database while a second transaction is making modifications to the database, causing the summary to include incorrect information. SQL injection is a web application security flaw, not a database concurrency problem.

99. B. A master boot record (MBR) virus redirects the boot process to load malware during the operating system loading process. File infector viruses infect one or more normal files stored on the system. Polymorphic viruses alter themselves to avoid detection. Service injection viruses compromise trusted components of the operating system.

100. C. Multipartite viruses use multiple propagation mechanisms to spread between systems. This improves their likelihood of successfully infecting a system because it provides alternative infection mechanisms that may be successful against systems that are not vulnerable to the primary infection mechanism.

Chapter 9: Practice Test 1

1. C. NIST SP 800-53 discusses security control baselines as a list of security controls. CIS releases security baselines, and a baseline is a useful part of a threat management strategy and may contain a list of acceptable configuration items.

2. B. A Content Distribution Network (CDN) is designed to provide reliable, low-latency, geographically distributed content distribution. In this scenario, a CDN is an ideal solution. A P2P CDN like BitTorrent isn't a typical choice for a commercial entity, whereas redundant servers or a hot site can provide high availability but won't provide the remaining requirements.

3. D. A forensic disk controller performs four functions. One of those, write blocking, intercepts write commands sent to the device and prevents them from modifying data on the device. The other three functions include returning data requested by a read operation, returning access-significant information from the device, and reporting errors from the device back to the forensic host. The controller should not prevent read commands from being sent to the device because those commands may return crucial information.

4. B. RAID 1, disk mirroring, requires two physical disks that will contain copies of the same data.

5. D. The TGS, or Ticket-Granting Service (which is usually on the same server as the KDC) receives a TGT from the client. It validates the TGT and the user's rights to access the service they are requesting to use. The TGS then issues a ticket and session keys to the client. The AS serves as the authentication server, which forwards the username to the KDC.

6. D. Asynchronous communications rely on a a built-in stop and start flag or bit. This makes asynchronous communications less efficient than synchronous communications, but better suited to some types of communication.

7. C. Wave pattern motion detectors transmit ultrasonic or microwave signals into the monitor area, watching for changes in the returned signals bouncing off objects.

8. C. Stateful packet inspection firewalls, also known as dynamic packet filtering firewalls, track the state of a conversation, and can allow a response from a remote system based on an internal system being allowed to start the communication. Static packet filtering and circuit level gateways only filter based on source, destination, and ports, whereas application-level gateway firewalls proxy traffic for specific applications.

9. B. A captive portal can require those who want to connect to and use Wi-Fi to provide an email address to connect. This allows Ben to provide easy-to-use wireless while meeting his business purposes. WPA2 PSK is the preshared key mode of WPA and won't provide information about users who are given a key. Sharing a password doesn't allow for data gathering either. Port security is designed to protect wired network ports based on MAC addresses.

10. B. Many modern wireless routers can provide multiple SSIDs. Ben can create a private, secure network for his business operations, but he will need to make sure that the customer and business networks are firewalled or otherwise logically separated from each other. Running WPA2 on the same SSID isn't possible without creating another wireless network and would cause confusion for customers (SSIDs aren't required to be unique). Running a network in Enterprise mode isn't used for open networks, and WEP is outdated and incredibly vulnerable.

11. D. Unencrypted open networks broadcast traffic in the clear. This means that unencrypted sessions to websites can be easily captured with a packet sniffer. Some tools like FireSheep have been specifically designed to capture sessions from popular websites. Fortunately, many now use TLS by default, but other sites still send user session information in the clear. Shared passwords are not the cause of the vulnerability, ARP spoofing isn't an issue with wireless networks, and a Trojan is designed to look like safe software, not to compromise a router.

12. D. The DES modes of operation are Electronic Codebook (ECB), Cipher Block Chaining (CBC), Cipher Feedback (CFB), Output Feedback (OFB), and Counter (CTR). The Advanced Encryption Standard (AES) is a separate encryption algorithm.

13. D. Clipping is an analysis technique that only reports alerts after they exceed a set threshold. It is a specific form of sampling, which is a more general term that describes any attempt to excerpt records for review. Thresholding is not a commonly used term. Administrators may choose to configure automatic or manual account lockout after failed login attempts but that is not described in the scenario.

14. B. RADIUS is a common AAA technology used to provide services for dial-up, wireless networks, network devices, and a range of other systems. OAuth is an authentication protocol used to allow applications to act on a user's behalf without sharing the password, and is used for many web applications. While both XTACACS and TACACS+ provide the functionality Sally is looking for, both are Cisco proprietary protocols.

15. C. In an inference attack, the attacker uses several pieces of generic nonsensitive information to determine a specific sensitive value.

16. A. The take rule allows a subject to take the rights belonging to another object. If Alice has take rights on Bob, she can give herself the same permissions that Bob already possesses.

17. B. Brute-force attacks try every possible password. In this attack, the password is changing by one letter at each attempt, which indicates that it is a brute-force attack. A dictionary attack would use dictionary words for the attack, whereas a man-in-the-middle or pass-the-hash attack would most likely not be visible in an authentication log except as a successful login.

18. B. Isolation requires that transactions operate separately from each other. Atomicity ensures that if any part of a database transaction fails, the entire transaction must be rolled back as if it never occurred. Consistency ensures that all transactions are consistent with the logical rules of the database, such as having a primary key. Durability requires that once a transaction is committed to the database it must be preserved.

19. B. Worms have built-in propagation mechanisms that do not require user interaction, such as scanning for systems containing known vulnerabilities and then exploiting those vulnerabilities to gain access. Viruses and Trojan horses typically require user interaction to spread. Logic bombs do not spread from system to system but lie in wait until certain conditions are met, triggering the delivery of their payload.

20. C. In a teardrop attack, the attacker fragments traffic in such a way that the system is unable to reassemble them. Modern systems are not vulnerable to this attack if they run current operating systems, but the concept of this attack illustrates the danger of relying upon users following protocol specifications instead of performing proper exception handling.

21. C. The TCP three-way handshake consists of initial contact via a SYN, or synchronize flagged packet, which receives a response with a SYN/ACK, or synchronize and acknowledge flagged packet, which is acknowledged by the original sender with an ACK, or acknowledge packet. RST is used in TCP to reset a connection, PSH is used to send data immediately, and FIN is used to end a connection.

22. B. MDM products do not have the capability of assuming control of a device not currently managed by the organization. This would be equivalent to hacking into a device owned by someone else and might constitute a crime.

23. A. Identity as a Service (IDaaS) provides an identity platform as a third-party service. This can provide benefits, including integration with cloud services and removing overhead for maintenance of traditional on-premise identity systems, but can also create risk due to third-party control of identity services and reliance on an offsite identity infrastructure.

24. A. Gina's actions harm the CISSP certification and information security community by undermining the integrity of the examination process. While Gina also is acting dishonestly, the harm to the profession is more of a direct violation of the code of ethics.

25. A. The annualized loss expectancy is the amount of damage that the organization expects to occur each year as the result of a given risk.

26. C. The whitelisting approach to application control allows users to install only those software packages specifically approved by administrators.. This would be an appropriate approach in a scenario where application installation needs to be tightly controlled.

27. A. This is a clear example of a denial-of-service attack—denying legitimate users authorized access to the system through the use of overwhelming traffic. It goes beyond a reconnaissance attack because the attacker is affecting the system, but it is not a compromise because the attacker did not attempt to gain access to the system. There is no reason to believe that a malicious insider was involved.

28. A. The Company ID is likely unique for each row in the table, making it the best choice for a primary key. There may be multiple companies that share the same name or ZIP code. Similarly, a single sales representative likely serves more than one company, making those fields unsuitable for use as a unique identifier.

29. C. Personally Identifiable Information (PII) includes data that can be used to distinguish or trace that person's identity, and also includes information like their medical, educational, financial, and employment information. PHI is personal health information, EDI is electronic data interchange, and proprietary data is used to maintain an organization's competitive advantage.

30. D. 129.53.44.124 is a valid public IP address and a legitimate destination for traffic leaving Bob's network. 12.8.195.15 is a public address on Bob's network and should not be a destination address on a packet leaving the network. 10.8.15.9 and 192.168.109.55 are both private IP addresses that should not be routed to the Internet.

31. D. Binary keyspaces contain a number of keys equal to 2 raised to the power of the number of bits. Two to the sixth power is 64, so a 6-bit keyspace contains 64 possible keys. The number of viable keys is usually smaller in most algorithms due to the presence of parity bits and other algorithmic overhead or security issues that restrict the use of some key values.

32. D. Research has shown that traditional methods of sanitizing files on SSDs were not reliable. SSDs remap data sectors as part of wear leveling, and erase commands are not consistently effective across multiple SSD brands. Zero fills can be performed on SSDs but may not be effective, much like erase commands. Degaussing doesn't work on SSDs because they are flash media, rather than magnetic media. SSDs don't have data remanence issues, but that doesn't create the need to destroy them.

33. A. Encrypting the files reduces the probability that the data will be successfully stolen, so it is an example of risk mitigation. Deleting the files would be risk avoidance. Purchasing insurance would be risk transference. Taking no action would be risk acceptance.

34. C. Sampling should be done randomly to avoid human bias. Choosing a timeframe may miss historic issues or only account for the current administrator's processes. Sampling is an effective process if it is done on a truly random sample of sufficient size to provide effective coverage of the userbase.

35. B. The European Data Protection Directive's seven primary tenets are:

Notice

Choice

Onward transfer

Security

Data integrity

Access

Enforcement

36. D. In a white box test, the attacker has access to full implementation details of the system, including source code, prior to beginning the test. In gray box testing, the attacker has partial knowledge. In black box testing, the attacker has no knowledge of the system and tests it from a user perspective. Blue boxes are a phone hacking tool and are not used in software testing.

37. C. The file clearly shows HTTP requests, as evidenced by the many GET commands. Therefore, this is an example of an application log from an HTTP server.

38. C. A blue box was used to generate the 2600 Hz tones that trunking systems required. White boxes included a dual-tone, multifrequency generator to control phone systems. Black boxes were designed to steal long-distance service by manipulating line voltages, and red boxes simulated the tones of coins being deposited into payphones.

39. B. Social engineering exploits humans to allow attacks to succeed. Since help desk employees are specifically tasked with being helpful, they may be targeted by attackers posing as legitimate employees. Trojans are a type of malware, whereas phishing is a targeted attack via electronic communication methods intended to capture passwords or other sensitive data. Whaling is a type of phishing aimed at high-profile or important targets.

40. C. Identity proofing that relies on a type of verification outside of the initial environment that required the verification is out-of-band identity proofing. This type of verification relies on the owner of the phone or phone number having control of it but removes the ability for attackers to use only Internet-based resources to compromise an account. Knowledge-based authentication relies on answers to preselected information, whereas dynamic knowledge–based authentication builds questions using facts or data about the user. Risk-based identity proofing uses risk-based metrics to determine whether identities should be permitted or denied access. It is used to limit fraud in financial transactions, such as credit card purchases. This is a valid form of proofing but does not necessarily use an out-of-band channel, such as SMS.

41. A. The modulo function is the remainder value left over after an integer division operation takes place.

42. C. A hybrid authentication service can provide authentication services in both the cloud and on-premise, ensuring that service outages due to interrupted links are minimized. An onsite service would continue to work during an Internet outage but would not allow the e-commerce website to authenticate. A cloud service would leave the corporate location offline. Outsourcing authentication does not indicate whether the solution is on or off-premise, and thus isn't a useful answer.

43. C. Federation links identity information between multiple organizations. Federating with a business partner can allow identification and authorization to occur between them, making integration much easier. Single sign-on would reduce the number of times a user has to log in but will not facilitate the sharing of identity information. Multifactor can help secure authentication, but again, doesn't help integrate with a third party. Finally, an Identity as a Service provider might provide federation but doesn't guarantee it.

44. B. Security Assertion Markup Language (SAML) is frequently used to integrate cloud services and provides the ability to make authentication and authorization assertions.

Active Directory integrations are possible but are less common for cloud service providers, and RADIUS is not typically used for integrations like this. Service Provisioning Markup Language (SPML) is used to provision users, resources, and services, not for authentication and authorization.

45. B. Rainbow tables use precomputed password hashes to conduct cracking attacks against password files. They may be frustrated by the use of salting, which adds a specified value to the password prior to hashing, making it much more difficult to perform precomputation. Password expiration policies, password complexity policies, and user education may all contribute to password security, but they are not direct defenses against the use of rainbow tables.

46. C. A honeypot is a decoy computer system used to bait intruders into attacking. A honeynet is a network of multiple honeypots that creates a more sophisticated environment for intruders to explore. A pseudoflaw is a false vulnerability in a system that may attract an attacker. A darknet is a segment of unused network address space that should have no network activity and, therefore, may be easily used to monitor for illicit activity.

47. C. The crossover error rate (CER) is the point where both the false acceptance rate and the false rejection rate cross. CER and ERR, or equal error rate, mean the same thing and are used interchangeably.

48. B. A Type 2 is something you have, like a smart card or hardware token. A Type 1 authentication factor is something you know. A Type 3 authentication factor is something you are, like a biometric identifier. There is no such thing as a Type 4 authentication factor.

49. C. Steganography is the art of using cryptographic techniques to embed secret messages within other content. Steganographic algorithms work by making invisible alterations to files, such as modifying the least significant bits of the many bits that make up image files. VPNs may be used to obscure secret communications, but they provide protection in transit and can't be used to embed information in an image. Watermarking does embed information in an image but with the intent of protecting intellectual property. A still image would not be used for a covert timing channel because it is a fixed file.

50. A. JavaScript is an interpreted language so the code is not compiled prior to execution, allowing Roger to inspect the contents of the code. C, C++, and Java are all compiled languages—a compiler produces an executable file that is not human-readable.

51. D. When a system is configured to use shadowed passwords, the /etc/passwd file contains only the character x in the place of a password. It would not contain any passwords, in either plaintext, encrypted, or hashed form.

52. D. Internet Control Message Protocol (ICMP) is used for normal pings, as well as Pings of Death. Ping of Death describes attacks that were used to overflow poorly implemented ICMP handlers; Smurf attacks, which spoof broadcast pings to create huge amounts of traffic on a network; and ping floods, which are a type of denial-of-service attack.

53. D. The due care principle states that an individual should react in a situation using the same level of care that would be expected from any reasonable person. It is a very broad

standard. The due diligence principle is a more specific component of due care that states an individual assigned a responsibility should exercise due care to complete it accurately and in a timely manner.

54. B. ISDN, cable modems, DSL, and T1 and T3 lines are all examples of broadband technology that can support multiple simultaneous signals. They are analog, not digital, and are not broadcast technologies.

55. C. Social engineering is the best answer, as it can be useful to penetration testers who are asked to assess whether staff members are applying security training and have absorbed the awareness messages the organization uses. Port and vulnerability scanning find technical issues that may be related to awareness or training issues but that are less likely to be directly related. Discovery can involve port scanning or other data-gathering efforts, but is also less likely to be directly related to training and awareness.

56. B. RAID level 5 is also known as disk striping with parity. It uses three or more disks, with one disk containing parity information used to restore data to another disk in the event of failure. When used with three disks, RAID 5 is able to withstand the loss of a single disk.

57. D. The Physical layer deals with the electrical impulses or optical pulses that are sent as bits to convey data.

58. A. In an IaaS server environment, the customer retains responsibility for most server security operations under the shared responsibility model. This includes managing OS security settings, maintaining host firewalls, and configuring server access control. The vendor would be responsible for all security mechanisms at the hypervisor layer and below.

59. B. Proactive monitoring, aka synthetic monitoring, uses recorded or generated traffic to test systems and software. Passive monitoring uses a network span, tap, or other device to capture traffic to be analyzed. Reactive and replay are not industry terms for types of monitoring.

60. D. Process isolation ensures that the operating system allocates a separate area of memory for each process, preventing processes from seeing each other's data. This is a requirement for multilevel security systems.

61. B. The use of an electcromagnetic coil inside the card indicates that this is a proximity card.

62. C. During a parallel test, the team actually activates the disaster recovery site for testing, but the primary site remains operational. During a full interruption test, the team takes down the primary site and confirms that the disaster recovery site is capable of handling regular operations. The full interruption test is the most thorough test but also the most disruptive. The checklist review is the least disruptive type of disaster recovery test. During a checklist review, team members each review the contents of their disaster recovery checklists on their own and suggest any necessary changes. During a tabletop exercise, team members come together and walk through a scenario without making any changes to information systems.

63. B. The Agile approach to software development embraces 12 core principles, found in the Agile Manifesto. One of these principles is that the best architecture, requirements, and designs emerge from self-organizing teams. Another is that teams should welcome changing requirements at any step in the process. A third is that simplicity is essential. The Agile approach emphasizes delivering software frequently, not infrequently.

64. B. Hand geometry scanners assess the physical dimensions of an individual's hand, but do not verify other unique factors about the individual, or even verify if they are alive. This means that hand geometry scanners should not be implemented as the sole authentication factor for secure environments. Hand geometry scanners do not have an abnormally high FRR, and do not stand out as a particular issue from an accessibility standpoint compared to other biometric systems.

65. A. The maximum tolerable downtime (MTD) is the amount of time that a business may be without a service before irreparable harm occurs. This measure is sometimes also called maximum tolerable outage (MTO).

66. D. Attacks that change a symlink between the time that rights are checked and the file is accessed, in order to access a file that the account does not have rights to, are time of check/time of use (TOC/TOU) attacks, a form of race condition. Unlinking removes names from a Linux filesystem, setuid allows a user to run an executable with the permissions of its owner, and tick/tock is not a type of attack or Linux command.

67. A. Smart cards are a Type II authentication factor, and include both a microprocessor and at least one certificate. Since they are something you have, they're not a Type I or III authentication factor. Tokens do not necessarily contain certificates.

68. C. Masquerading (or impersonation) attacks use stolen or falsified credentials to bypass authentication mechanisms. Spoofing attacks rely on falsifying an identity like an IP address or hostname without credentials. Replay attacks are a more specific type of masquerading attack that relies on captured network traffic to reestablish authorized connections. Modification attacks occur when captured packets are modified and replayed to a system to attempt to perform an action.

69. C. A T1 (DS1) line is rated at 1.544 Mbps. ISDN is often 64 or 128 Kbps, and T3 lines are 44.736 Mbps.

70. C. This scenario describes separation of duties—not allowing the same person to hold two roles that, when combined, are sensitive. While two-person control is a similar concept, it does not apply in this case because the scenario does not say that either action requires the concurrence of two users.

71. C. The parol evidence rule states that when an agreement between two parties is put into written form, it is assumed to be the entire agreement unless amended in writing. The best evidence rule says that a copy of a document is not admissible if the original document is available. Real evidence and testimonial evidence are evidence types, not rules of evidence.

72. A. Network Address Translation (NAT) translates an internal address to an external address. VLANs are used to logically divide networks, BGP is a routing protocol, and S/NAT is a made-up term.

73. A. SSAE-16 does not assert specific controls. Instead it reviews the use and application of controls in an audited organization. It is an attestation standard, used for external audits, and forms part of the underlying framework for SOC 1, 2, and 3 reports.

74. D. A constrained user interface restricts what users can see or do based on their privileges. This can result in grayed-out or missing menu items, or other interface changes. Activity-based controls are called context-dependent controls, whereas controls based on the content of an object are content-dependent controls. Preventing unauthorized users from logging in is a basic authentication function.

75. B. The recovery time objective (RTO) is the amount of time expected to return an IT service or component to operation after a failure. The maximum tolerable downtime (MTD) is the longest amount of time that an IT service or component may be unavailable without causing serious damage to the organization. The recovery point objective (RPO) identifies the maximum amount of data, measured in time, that may be lost during a recovery effort. Service-level agreements (SLAs) are written contracts that document service expectations.

76. C. Class variables exist only once and share their value across all instances of that object class. Instance variables have different values for each instance. Member variables are the combination of class and instance variables associated with a particular class. Global variables do not exist in an object-oriented programming language.

77. B. Class B fire extinguishers use carbon dioxide, halon, or soda acid as their suppression material and are useful against liquid-based fires. Water may not be used against liquid-based fires because it may cause the burning liquid to splash, and many burning liquids, such as oil, will float on water.

78. D. Notifications and procedures like the signs posted at the company Chris works for are examples of directive access controls. Detective controls are designed to operate after the fact. The doors and the locks on them are examples of physical controls. Preventive controls are designed to stop an event, and could also include the locks that are present on the doors.

79. D. The seven principles that the International Safe Harbor Provisions spell out for handling personal information are notice, choice, onward transfer, access, security, data integrity, and enforcement.

80. C. The DMCA provides safe harbor protection for the operators of Internet service providers who only handle information as a common carrier for transitory purposes.

81. B. According to NIST SP 800-18, a system owner should update the system security plan when the system they are responsible for undergoes a significant change. Classification, selection of custodians, and designing ways to protect data confidentiality might occur if new data was added, but should have already been done otherwise.

82. B. Provisioning that occurs through an established workflow, such as through an HR process, is workflow-based account provisioning. If Alex had set up accounts for his new hire on the systems he manages, he would have been using discretionary account provisioning. If the provisioning system allowed the new hire to sign up for an account on their own, they would have used self-service account provisioning, and if there was a central, software-driven process, rather than HR forms, it would have been automated account provisioning.

83. C. As Alex has changed roles, he retained access to systems that he no longer administers. The provisioning system has provided rights to workstations and the application servers he manages, but he should not have access to the databases he no longer administers. Privilege levels are not specified, so we can't determine if he has excessive rights. Logging may or may not be enabled, but it isn't possible to tell from the diagram or problem.

84. C. When a user's role changes, they should be provisioned based on their role and other access entitlements. De-provisioning and re-provisioning is time consuming and can lead to problems with changed IDs and how existing credentials work. Simply adding new rights leads to privilege creep, and matching another user's rights can lead to excessive privileges due to privilege creep for that other user.

85. B. EAL2 assurance applies when the system has been structurally tested. It is the second-to-lowest level of assurance under the Common Criteria.

86. C. Before granting any user access to information, Adam should verify that the user has an appropriate security clearance as well as a business need to know the information in question.

87. B. During the preservation phase, the organization ensures that information related to the matter at hand is protected against intentional or unintentional alteration or deletion. The identification phase locates relevant information but does not preserve it. The collection phase occurs after preservation and gathers responsive information. The processing phase performs a rough cut of the collected information for relevance.

88. D. Nessus, OpenVAS, the Open Vulnerability Assessment scanner and manager, and SAINT are all vulnerability scanning tools. All provide port scanning capabilities as well but are more than simple port scanning tools.

89. D. In the subject/object model, the object is the resource being requested by a subject. In this example, Harry would like access to the document, making the document the object of the request.

90. C. The process of removing a header (and possibly a footer) from the data received from a previous layer in the OSI model is known as de-encapsulation. Encapsulation occurs when the header and/or footer are added. Payloads are part of a virus or malware package that are delivered to a target, and packet unwrapping is a made-up term.

91. C. Metasploit is a tool used to exploit known vulnerabilities. Nikto is a web application and server vulnerability scanning tool, Ettercap is a man-in-the-middle attack tool, and THC Hydra is a password brute-force tool.

92. C. Service Provisioning Markup Language (SPML) uses Requesting Authorities to issue SPML requests to a Provisioning Service Point. Provisioning Service Targets are often user accounts, and are required to be allowed unique identification of the data in its implementation. SAML is used for security assertions, SAMPL is an algebraic modeling language, and XACML is an access control markup language used to describe and process access control policies in an XML format.

93. D. The use of a probability/impact matrix is the hallmark of a qualitative risk assessment It uses subjective measures of probability and impact, such as "high" and "low," in place of quantitative measures.

94. B. Mandatory access control systems can be hierarchical, where each domain is ordered and related to other domains above and below it; compartmentalized, where there is no relationship between each domain; or hybrid, where both hierarchy and compartments are used. There is no concept of bracketing in mandatory access control design.

95. C. RAID level 5 is also known as disk striping with parity. RAID 0 is called disk striping. RAID 1 is called disk mirroring. RAID 10 is known as a stripe of mirrors.

96. B. Category 5e and Category 6 UTP cable are both rated to 1000 Mbps. Cat 5 (not Cat 5e) is only rated to 100 Mbps, whereas Cat 7 is rated to 10 Gbps. There is no Cat 4e.

97. A. Developing a business impact assessment is an integral part of the business continuity planning effort. The selection of alternate facilities, activation of those facilities, and restoration of data from backup are all disaster recovery tasks.

98. D. Smurf attacks use a distributed attack approach to send ICMP echo replies at a targeted system from many different source addresses. The most effective way to block this attack would be to block inbound ICMP traffic. Blocking the source addresses is not feasible because the attacker would likely simply change the source addresses. Blocking destination addresses would likely disrupt normal activity. The Smurf attack does not use UDP, so blocking that traffic would have no effect.

99. C. Static packet filtering firewalls are known as first-generation firewalls and do not track connection state. Stateful inspection, application proxying, and next-generation firewalls all add connection state tracking capability.

100. A. TKIP is only used as a means to encrypt transmissions and is not used for data at rest. RSA, AES, and 3DES are all used on data at rest as well as data in transit.

101. C. Generational fuzzing is also known as intelligent fuzzing because it relies on the development of data models using an understanding of how the data is used by the program. Zzuf is a fuzzing program. Mutation simply modifies the inputs each time, and code based is not a description used for a type of fuzzing.

102. B. Latency is a delay in the delivery of packets from their source to their destination. Jitter is a variation in the latency for different packets. Packet loss is the disappearance of packets in transit that requires retransmission. Interference is electrical noise or other disruptions that corrupt the contents of packets.

103. B. Software tokens are flexible, with delivery options including mobile applications, SMS, and phone delivery. They have a relatively low administrative overhead, as users can typically self-manage. Biometrics require significant effort to register users and to deploy and maintain infrastructure, and require hardware at each authentication location. Both types of hardware tokens can require additional overhead for distribution and maintenance, and token failure can cause support challenges.

104. B. Web applications communicate with web browsers via an interface, making interface testing the best answer here. Regression testing might be used as part of the interface test, but is too specific to be the best answer. Similarly, the test might be a white box, or full knowledge test, but interface testing better describes this specific example. Fuzzing is less likely as part of a browser compatibility test, as it tests unexpected inputs, rather than functionality.

105. A. Role-based access control gives each user an array of permissions based on their position in the organization, such as the scheme shown here. Task-based access control is not a standard approach. Rule-based access controls use rules that apply to all subjects, which isn't something we see in the list. Discretionary access control gives object owners rights to choose how the objects they own are accessed, which is not what this list shows.

106. D. Fire suppression systems do not stop a fire from occurring but do reduce the damage that fires cause. This is an example of reducing risk by lowering the impact of an event.

107. D. Patents and trade secrets can both protect intellectual property in the form of a process. Patents require public disclosure and have expiration dates while trade secrets remain in force for as long as they remain secret. Therefore, trade secret protection most closely aligns with the company's goals.

108. D. The Security Content Automation Protocol (SCAP) is a suite of specifications used to handle vulnerability and security configuration information. The National Vulnerability Database provided by NIST uses SCAP. XACML is the eXtensible Access Control Markup Language, an OASIS standard used for access control decisions, and neither VSML nor SCML are industry terms.

109. B. The three components of the DevOps model are software development, operations, and quality assurance.

110. A. The Simple Security Property prevents an individual from reading information at a higher security level than his or her clearance allows. This is also known as the "no read up" rule. The Simple Integrity Property says that a user can't write data to a higher integrity level than their own. The *-Security Property says that users can't write data to a lower security level than their own. The Discretionary Security Property allows the use of a matrix to determine access permissions.

111. B. The work breakdown structure (WBS) is an important project management tool that divides the work done for a large project into smaller components. It is not a project plan because it does not describe timing or resources. Test analyses are used during later phases of the development effort to report test results. Functional requirements may be included in a work breakdown structure, but they are not the full WBS.

112. B. Network Access Control (NAC) systems can be used to authenticate users, and then validate their system's compliance with a security standard before they are allowed to connect to the network. Enforcing security profiles can help reduce zero-day attacks, making

NAC a useful solution. A firewall can't enforce system security policies, whereas an IDS can only monitor for attacks and alarm when they happen. Thus neither a firewall nor an IDS meets Kolin's needs. Finally, port security is a MAC address–based security feature that can only restrict which systems or devices can connect to a given port.

113. C. This scenario violates the least privilege principle because an application should never require full administrative rights to run. Gwen should update the service account to have only the privileges necessary to support the application.

114. B. Trace coverage is not a type of structural coverage. Common types of structural coverage include statement, branch or decision coverage, loop coverage, path coverage, and data flow coverage.

115. A. During the information gathering and discovery phase of a penetration test, testers will gather information about the target. Whois can provide information about an organization, including IP ranges, physical addresses, and staff contacts. Nessus would be useful during a vulnerability detection phase, and Metasploit would be useful during exploitation. zzuf is a fuzzing tool and is less likely to be used during a penetration test.

116. C. Test directories often include scripts that may have poor protections or may have other data that can be misused. There is not a default test directory that allows administrative access to PHP. Test directories are not commonly used to store sensitive data, nor is the existence of a test directory a common indicator of compromise.

117. A. Directory indexing may not initially seem like an issue during a penetration test, but simply knowing the name and location of files can provide an attacker with quite a bit of information about an organization, as well as a list of potentially accessible files. XDRF is not a type of attack, and indexing is not a denial-of-service attack vector. Directory indexing being turned on is typically either due to misconfiguration or design, or because the server was not properly configured at setup, rather than being a sign of attack.

118. B. Cross-site tracing (XST) leverages the HTTP TRACE or TRACK methods, and could be used to steal a user's cookies via cross-site scripting (XSS). The other options are not industry terms for web application or web server attacks or vulnerabilities.

119. D. The contents of RAM are volatile, meaning that they are only available while power is applied to the memory chips. EPROM, EEPROM, and flash memory are all nonvolatile, meaning that they retain their contents even when powered off.

120. C. Data loss prevention (DLP) systems specialize in the identification of sensitive information. In this case, Ursula would like to identify the presence of this information on endpoint devices, so she should choose an endpoint DLP control. Network-based DLP would not detect stored information unless the user transmits it over the network. Intrusion prevention systems (IPSs) are designed to detect and block attacks in progress, not necessarily the presence of sensitive information.

121. B. In the private cloud computing model, the cloud computing environment is dedicated to a single organization and does not follow the shared tenancy model. The environment may be built by the company in its own data center or built by a vendor at a co-location site.

122. D. Redundant Arrays of Inexpensive Disks (RAID) is designed to allow a system to continue operating without data loss in the event of a hard drive failure. Load balancing is designed to spread work across multiple servers. Intrusion prevention systems (IPSs) monitor systems and/or networks for potential attacks. Dual-power supplies protect against power supplies becoming a single point of failure.

123. D. Integrity ensures that unauthorized changes are not made to data while stored or in transit.

124. C. A star topology uses a central connection device. Ethernet networks may look like a star, but they are actually a logical bus topology that is sometimes deployed in a physical star.

125. C. Input validation ensures that the data provided to a program as input matches the expected parameters. Limit checks are a special form of input validation that ensure the value remains within an expected range, as is the case described in this scenario. Fail open and fail secure are options when planning for possible system failures. Buffer bounds are not a type of software control.

126. B. NIST SP 800-18 describes system owner responsibilities that include helping to develop system security plans, maintaining the plan, ensuring training, and identifying, implementing, and assessing security controls. A data owner is more likely to delegate these tasks to the system owner. Custodians may be asked to enforce those controls, whereas a user will be directly affected by them.

127. C. ESP's Transport mode encrypts IP packet data but leaves the packet header unencrypted. Tunnel mode encrypts the entire packet and adds a new header to support transmission through the tunnel.

128. B. In level 2, the Repeatable level of the SW-CMM, an organization introduces basic life-cycle management processes. Reuse of code in an organized fashion begins and repeatable results are expected from similar projects. The key process areas for this level include Requirements Management, Software Project Planning, Software Project Tracking and Oversight, Software Subcontract Management, Software Quality Assurance and Software Configuration Management. Software Quality Management is a process that occurs during level 4, the Managed stage of the SW-CMM.

129. A. Key risk indicators (KRIs) are often used to monitor risk for organizations that establish an ongoing risk management program. Using automated data gathering and tools that allow data to be digested and summarized can provide predictive information about how organizational risks are changing. KPIs are key performance indicators, which are used to assess how an organization is performing. Quantitative risk assessments are good for point-in-time views with detailed valuation and measurement-based risk assessments, whereas a penetration test would provide details of how well an organization's security controls are working.

130. D. The three-way handshake is SYN, SYN/ACK, ACK. System B should respond with "Synchronize and Acknowledge" to System A after it receives a SYN.

131. A. Systems that respond to ping will show the time to live for packets that reach them. Since TTL is decremented at each hop, this can help build a rough network topology map.

In addition, some firewalls respond differently to ping than a normal system, which means pinging a network can sometimes reveal the presence of firewalls that would otherwise be invisible. Hostnames are revealed by a DNS lookup, and ICMP types allowed through a firewall are not revealed by only performing a ping. ICMP can be used for router advertisements, but pinging won't show them!

132. C. Authorization defines what a subject can or can't do. Identification occurs when a subject claims an identity, accountability is provided by the logs and audit trail that track what occurs on a system, and authorization occurs when that identity is validated.

133. A. The commercial classification scheme discussed by (ISC)² includes four primary classification levels: confidential, private, sensitive, and public. Secret is a part of the military classification scheme.

134. B. All of these are objects. Although some of these items can be subjects, files, databases, and storage media can't be. Processes and programs aren't file stores, and of course none of these are users.

135. A. Testing for desired functionality is use case testing. Dynamic testing is used to determine how code handles variables that change over time. Misuse testing focuses on how code handles examples of misuse, and fuzzing feeds unexpected data as an input to see how the code responds.

136. C. When the author of a work is known, copyright protects that work for 70 years after the death of the author. Works created by a corporate author are protected for 95 years from publication or 120 years from creation, whichever expires first.

137. C. These are examples of private IP addresses. RFC1918 defines a set of private IP addresses for use in internal networks. These private addresses including 10.0.0.0-10.255.255.255, 172.16.0.0-172.31.255.255, and 192.168.0.0-196.168.255.255 should never be routable on the public Internet.

138. B. A cognitive password authenticates users based on a series of facts or answers to questions that they know. Preset questions for cognitive passwords typically rely on common information about a user like their mother's maiden name, or the name of their pet, and that information can frequently be found on the Internet. The best cognitive password systems let users make up their own questions.

139. D. A transformation procedure (TP) is the only process authorized to modify constrained data items (CDIs) within the Clark-Wilson model.

140. C. The blacklist approach to application control blocks certain prohibited packages but allows the installation of other software on systems. The whitelist approach uses the reverse philosophy and only allows approved software. Antivirus software would only detect the installation of malicious software after the fact. Heuristic detection is a variant of antivirus software.

141. C. Personal Health Information (PHI) is specifically defined by HIPAA to include information about an individual's medical bills. PCI could refer to the payment card industry's security standard but would only apply in relation to credit cards. PII is a broadly defined term for personally identifiable information, and personal billing data isn't a broadly used industry term.

142. D. Yagis, panel antennas, cantennas, and parabolic antennas are all types of directional antenna. Omnidirectional antennas radiate in all directions, whereas these types of antennas are not necessarily signal boosting. Finally, rubber duck antennas are a type of omnidirectional pole antenna.

143. C. Function, statement, branch, and condition are all types of code coverage metrics. Penetration testing methodologies use phases like planning, discovery, scanning, exploit, and reporting. Fuzzing techniques focus on ways to provide unexpected inputs, whereas synthetic transactions are generated test data provided to validate applications and performance.

144. B. Organizations should train at least two individuals on every business continuity plan task. This provides a backup in the event the primary responder is not available.

145. B. In this scenario, all of the files on the server will be backed up on Monday evening during the full backup. Tuesday's incremental backup will include all files changed since Monday's full backup: files 1, 2, and 5. Wednesday's incremental backup will then include all files modified since Tuesday's incremental backup: files 3 and 6.

File Modifications
Monday 8AM - File 1 created
Monday 10AM - File 2 created
Monday 11AM - File 3 created
Monday 4PM - File 1 modified
Monday 5PM - File 4 created
Tuesday 8AM - File 1 modified
Tuesday 9AM - File 2 modified
Tuesday 10AM - File 5 created
Wednesday 8AM - File 3 modified
Wednesday 9AM - File 6 created

146. A. Susan is performing passive monitoring, which uses a network tap or span port to capture traffic to analyze it without impacting the network or devices that it is used to monitor. Synthetic, or active, monitoring uses recorded or generated traffic to test for performance and other issues. Signature based technologies include IDS, IPS, and anti-malware systems.

147. A. While the differences between rights, permissions, and roles can be confusing, typically permissions include both the access and actions that you can take on an object. Rights usually refer to the ability to take action on an object, and don't include the access to it. Privileges combine rights and permissions, and roles describe sets of privileges based on job tasks or other organizational artifacts.

148. C. One of the core capabilities of Infrastructure as a Service is providing servers on a vendor-managed virtualization platform. Web-based payroll and email systems are examples of Software as a Service. An application platform managed by a vendor that runs customer code is an example of Platform as a Service.

149. D. The exposure factor is the percentage of the facility that risk managers expect will be damaged if a risk materializes. It is calculated by dividing the amount of damage by the asset value. In this case, that is $750,000 in damage divided by the $2 million facility value, or 37.5%.

150. C. The annualized rate of occurrence is the number of times each year that risk analysts expect a risk to happen. In this case, the analysts expect fires will occur once every 50 years, or 0.02 times per year.

151. A. The annualized loss expectancy is calculated by multiplying the single loss expectancy (SLE) by the annualized rate of occurrence (ARO). In this case, the SLE is $750,000 and the ARO is 0.02. Multiplying these numbers together gives you the ALE of $15,000.

152. A. Congestion Window Reduced (CWR) and ECN-Echo (ECE) are used to manage transmission over congested links, and are rarely seen in modern TCP networks.

153. B. The Tower of Hanoi; Grandfather, Father, Son; and First In, First Out backup rotation strategies are all used to rotate backup tapes and other media. Key rotation is a cryptographic concept not related to disaster recovery media.

154. A. An application programming interface (API) allows external users to directly call routines within Fran's code. They can embed API calls within scripts and other programs to automate interactions with Fran's company. A web scraper or call center might facilitate the same tasks, but they do not do so in a direct integration. Data dictionaries might provide useful information but they also do not allow direct integration.

155. A. A fault is a momentary loss of power. Blackouts are sustained complete losses of power. Sags and brownouts are not complete power disruptions but rather periods of low voltage conditions.

156. A. Lauren's team would benefit from a credential management system. Credential management systems offer features like password management, multifactor authentication to retrieve passwords, logging, audit, and password rotation capabilities. A strong password policy would only make maintenance of passwords for many systems a more difficult task if done manually. Single sign-on would help if all of the systems had the same sensitivity levels, but different credentials are normally required for higher sensitivity systems.

157. C. Windows systems will assign themselves an APIPA address between 169.254.0.1 and 169.254.255.254 if they cannot contact a DHCP server.

158. A. Enrollment, or registration, is the initial creation of a user account in the provisioning process. Clearance verification and background checks are sometimes part of the process that ensures that the identity of the person being enrolled matches who they claim to be. Initialization is not used to describe the provisioning process.

159. C. Repeated audit findings indicate a performance issue, making this a key performance indicator for Susan's organization. Audit findings may demonstrate risk, but are not guaranteed to do so. Safeguard metrics and audit tracking metrics are not common industry terms.

160. D. The business or mission owner's role is responsible for making sure systems provide value. When controls decrease the value that an organization gets, the business owner bears responsibility for championing the issue to those involved. There is not a business manager or information security analyst role in the list of NIST-defined data security roles. A data processor is defined but acts as a third-party data handler, and would not have to represent this issue in Olivia's organization.

161. A. The Electronic Communications Privacy Act (ECPA) makes it a crime to invade the electronic privacy of an individual. It prohibits the unauthorized monitoring of email and voicemail communications.

162. D. The kernel lies within the central ring, Ring 0. Ring 1 contains other operating system components. Ring 2 is used for drivers and protocols. User-level programs and applications run at Ring 3. Rings 0–2 run in privileged mode whereas Ring 3 runs in user mode.

163. B. The Common Vulnerability Scoring System (CVSS) uses measures such as attack vector, complexity, exploit maturity, and how much user interaction is required as well as measures suited to local concerns. CVE is the Common Vulnerabilities and Exposures dictionary, CNA is the CVE Numbering Authority, and NVD is the National Vulnerability Database.

164. C. An individual does not have a reasonable expectation of privacy when any communication takes place using employer-owned communications equipment or accounts.

165. D. During a tabletop exercise, team members come together and walk through a scenario without making any changes to information systems. The checklist review is the least disruptive type of disaster recovery test. During a checklist review, team members each review the contents of their disaster recovery checklists on their own and suggest any necessary changes. During a parallel test, the team actually activates the disaster recovery site for testing but the primary site remains operational. During a full interruption test, the team takes down the primary site and confirms that the disaster recovery site is capable of handling regular operations. The full interruption test is the most thorough test but also the most disruptive.

166. C. OpenID is a widely supported standard that allows a user to use a single account to log into multiple sites, and Google accounts are frequently used with OpenID.

167. D. Risk acceptance occurs when an organization determines that the costs involved in pursuing other risk management strategies are not justified and they choose not to pursue any action.

168. D. Fred should choose a fiber-optic cable. Copper cable types like 10Base2, 5, and 10BaseT, as well as 100Base-T and 1000BaseT, fall far short of the distance required, whereas fiber-optic cable can run for miles.

169. C. Decentralized access control makes sense because it allows local control over access. When network connectivity to a central control point is a problem, or if rules and regulations may vary significantly from location to location, centralized control can be less desirable than decentralized control despite its challenges with consistency. Since the problem does not describe specific control needs, mandatory access control and rule-based access controls could fit the need but aren't the best answer.

170. B. The U.S. government classifies data that could reasonably be expected to cause damage to national security if disclosed, and for which the damage can be identified or described, as Secret. The U.S. government does not use Classified in its formal four levels of classification. Top Secret data could cause exceptionally grave damage, whereas Confidential data could be expected to cause damage.

171. A. The purpose of a digital certificate is to provide the general public with an authenticated copy of the certificate subject's public key.

172. D. The last step of the certificate creation process is the digital signature. During this step, the certificate authority signs the certificate using its own private key.

173. C. When an individual receives a copy of a digital certificate, he or she verifies the authenticity of that certificate by using the CA's public key to validate the digital signature contained on the certificate.

174. A. Mike uses the public key that he extracted from Renee's digital certificate to encrypt the message that he would like to send to Renee.

175. C. Wireshark is a network monitoring tool that can capture and replay communications sent over a data network, including Voice over IP (VoIP) communications. Nmap, Nessus, and Nikto are all security tools that may identify security flaws in the network, but they do not directly undermine confidentiality because they do not have the ability to capture communications.

176. B. Studies consistently show that users are more likely to write down passwords if they have more accounts. Central control of a single account is also easier to shut off if something does go wrong. Simply decreasing the number of accounts required for a subject doesn't increase security by itself, and SSO does not guarantee individual system logging, although it should provide central logging of SSO activity. Since a SSO system was not specified, there is no way of determining whether a given SSO system provides better or worse encryption for authentication data.

177. D. Nonrepudiation is only possible with an asymmetric encryption algorithm. RSA is an asymmetric algorithm. AES, DES, and Blowfish are all symmetric encryption algorithms that do not provide nonrepudiation.

178. D. Modification of audit logs will prevent repudiation because the data cannot be trusted, and thus actions cannot be provably denied. The modification of the logs is also a direct example of tampering. It might initially be tempting to answer elevation of privileges and tampering, as the attacker made changes to files that should be protected, but this is an unknown without more information. Similarly, the attacker may have accessed the files, resulting in information disclosure in addition to tampering, but again, this is not specified in the question. Finally, this did not cause a denial of service, and thus that answer can be ignored.

179. C. Routing Information Protocol (RIP), Open Shortest Path First (OSPF), and Border Gateway Protocol (BGP) are all routing protocols and are associated with routers.

180. B. The Temporal Key Integrity Protocol (TKIP) was used with WPA on existing hardware to replace WEP. TKIP has been replaced by CCMP and 802.1x since 2012. PEAP and

EAP are both authentication protocols. Transport Layer Security (TLS) is used to secure web transactions and other network communications.

181. B. Each of the attributes linked to Ben's access provides information for an attribute-based information control system. Attribute-based information controls like those described in NIST SP 800-162 can take many details about the user, actions, and objects into consideration before allowing access to occur. A role-based access control would simply consider Ben's role, whereas both administrative and system discretionary access controls are not commonly used terms to describe access controls.

182. A. LOIC is an example of a distributed denial-of-service attack. It uses many systems to attack targets, combining their bandwidth and making it difficult to shut down the attack because of the number and variety of attackers. Ionization and Zombie horde attacks are both made-up answers. Teardrop attacks are an older type of attack that sends fragmented packets as a denial-of-service attack.

183. C. Certificates may only be added to a Certificate Revocation List by the certificate authority that created the digital certificate.

184. D. Remote journaling transfers transaction logs to a remote site on a more frequent basis than electronic vaulting, typically hourly. Transaction logging is not a recovery technique alone; it is a process for generating the logs used in remote journaling. In an electronic vaulting approach, automated technology moves database backups from the primary database server to a remote site on a scheduled basis, typically daily. Remote mirroring maintains a live database server at the backup site and mirrors all transactions at the primary site on the server at the backup site.

185. C. The Waiting state is used when a process is blocked waiting for an external event. The Running state is used when a process is executing on the CPU. The Ready state is used when a process is prepared to execute, but the CPU is not available. The Stopped state is used when a process terminates.

186. B. Operational investigations are performed by internal teams to troubleshoot performance or other technical issues. They are not intended to produce evidence for use in court and, therefore, do not have the rigid collection standards of criminal, civil, or regulatory investigations.

187. A. Non-disclosure agreements (NDAs) are designed to protect the confidentiality of an organization's data, including trade secrets during and after the person's employment. NDAs do not protect against deletion or availability issues, and non-compete agreements would be required to stop competition.

188. C. Adding a second factor can ensure that users who might be incorrectly accepted are not given access due to a higher than desired false acceptance rate (FAR) from accessing a system. The CER is the crossover between the false acceptance and false rejection rate (FRR), and is used as a way to measure the accuracy of biometric systems. Changing the sensitivity to lower the FRR may actually increase the FAR, and replacing a biometric system can be time consuming and expensive in terms of time and cost.

189. B. SOC 2 reports typically cover 6 months of operations. SOC 1 reports cover a point in time.

190. D. Over-the-shoulder reviews require the original developer to explain her code to a peer while walking through it. Email pass-around code reviews are done by sending code for review to peers. Pair programming requires two developers, only one of whom writes code while both collaborate. IDE forcing is not a type of code review; an IDE is an integrated development environment.

191. A. The Time of Check to Time of Use (TOC/TOU) attack exploits timing differences between when a system verifies authorization and software uses that authorization to perform an action. It is an example of a race condition attack. The other three attacks mentioned do not depend on precise timing.

192. B. Encapsulation is a process that adds a header and possibly a footer to data received at each layer before handoff to the next layer. TCP wrappers are a host-based network access control system, attribution is determining who or what performed an action or sent data, and data hiding is a term from object-oriented programming that is not relevant here.

193. C. Salting adds random text to the password before hashing in an attempt to defeat automated password cracking attacks that use precomputed values. MD5 and SHA-1 are both common hashing algorithms, so using them does not add any security. Double-hashing would only be a minor inconvenience for an attacker and would not be as effective as the use of salting.

194. A. Guidelines provide advice based on best practices developed throughout industry and organizations, but they are not compulsory. Compliance with guidelines is optional.

195. C. Usernames are an identification tool. They are not secret, so they are not suitable for use as a password.

196. C. Regression testing ensures proper functionality of an application or system after it has been changed. Unit testing focuses on testing each module of a program instead of against its previous functional state. White and black box testing both describe the amount of knowledge about a system or application, rather than a specific type or intent for testing.

197. C. Risk transference involves shifting the impact of a potential risk from the organization incurring the risk to another organization. Insurance is a common example of risk transference.

198. A. The four canons of the (ISC)² code of ethics are to protect society, the common good, necessary public trust and confidence, and the infrastructure; act honorably, honestly, justly, responsibly, and legally; provide diligent and competent service to principals; and advance and protect the profession.

199. C. A trust that allows one forest to access another's resources without the reverse being possible is an example of a one-way trust. Since Jim doesn't want the trust path to flow as the domain tree is formed, this trust has to be nontransitive.

200. B. Susan's team is performing static analysis, which analyzes nonrunning code. Dynamic analysis uses running code, whereas gray box assessments are a type of assessment done without full knowledge. Fuzzing feeds unexpected inputs to a program as part of dynamic analysis.

201. A. 201.19.7.45 is a public IP address. RFC 1918 addresses are in the ranges 10.0.0.0–0.255.255.255, 172.16.0.0–172.31.255.255, and 192.168.0.0–192.168.255.255. APIPA addresses are assigned between 169.254.0.0 to 169.254.255.254, and 127.0.0.1 is a loopback address (although technically the entire 127.x.x.x network is reserved for loopback).

202. A. Risks are the combination of a threat and a vulnerability. Threats are the external forces seeking to undermine security, such as the hacker in this case. Vulnerabilities are the internal weaknesses that might allow a threat to succeed. In this case the missing patch is the vulnerability. In this scenario, if the hacker attempts a SQL injection attack (threat) against the unpatched server (vulnerability), the result is website defacement.

203. C. The three categories of data destruction are clear (overwriting with nonsensitive data), purge (removing all data), and destroy (physical destruction of the media). Degaussing is an example of a purging technique.

204. A. Hot sites contain all of the hardware and data necessary to restore operations and may be activated very quickly.

205. B. Syslog uses UDP port 514. TCP-based implementations of syslog typically use port 6514. The other ports may look familiar because they are commonly used TCP ports: 443 is HTTPS, 515 is the LPD print service, and 445 is used for Windows SMB.

206. B. PSH is a TCP flag used to clear the buffer, resulting in immediately sending data, and URG is the TCP urgent flag. These flags are not present in UDP headers.

207. B. Fagan inspection is a highly formalized review and testing process that uses planning, overview, preparation, inspection, rework, and follow-up steps. Static inspection looks at code without running it, dynamic inspection uses live programs, and interface testing tests where code modules interact.

208. D. The system is set to overwrite the logs and will replace the oldest log entries with new log entries when the file reaches 20 MB. The system is not purging archived logs because it is not archiving logs. Since there can only be 20 MB of logs, this system will not have stored too much log data, and the question does not provide enough information to know if there will be an issue with not having the information needed.

209. B. Encapsulating Security Payload (ESP) provides the ability to encrypt and thus provides confidentiality, as well as limited authentication capabilities. It does not provide availability, nonrepudiation, or integrity validation.

210. A. Alejandro is in the first stage of the incident response process, detection. During this stage, the intrusion detection system provides the initial alert, and Alejandro performs preliminary triaging to determine if an intrusion is actually taking place and whether the scenario fits the criteria for activating further steps of the incident response process (which include response, mitigation, reporting, recovery, remediation, and lessons learned).

211. C. After detection of a security incident, the next step in the process is response, which should follow the organization's formal incident response procedure. The first step of this procedure is activating the appropriate teams, including the organization's computer security incident response team (CSIRT).

212. C. The root cause analysis examines the incident to determine what allowed it to happen and provides critical information for repairing systems so that the incident does not recur. This is a component of the remediation step of the incident response process because the root cause analysis output is necessary to fully remediate affected systems and processes.

213. D. When using symmetric cryptography, the sender encrypts a message using a shared secret key and the recipient then decrypts the message with that same key. Only asymmetric cryptography uses the concept of public and private key pairs.

214. A. Business logic errors are most likely to be missed by automated functional testing. If a complete coverage code test was conducted, runtime, input validation, and error handling issues are likely to have been discovered by automated testing. Any automated system is more likely to miss business logic errors, because humans are typically necessary to understand business logic issues.

215. A. During the Lessons Learned phase, analysts close out an incident by conducting a review of the entire incident response process. This may include making recommendations for improvements to the process that will streamline the efficiency and effectiveness of future incident response efforts.

216. B. The Digital Millennium Copyright Act (DMCA) prohibits attempts to circumvent copyright protection mechanisms placed on a protected work by the copyright holder.

217. B. Linda should choose a warm site. This approach balances cost and recovery time. Cold sites take a very long time to activate, measured in weeks or months. Hot sites activate immediately but are quite expensive. Mutual assistance agreements depend on the support of another organization.

218. B. Half-duplex communications allow only one side to send at a time. Full-duplex communications allow both parties to send simultaneously, whereas simplex communications describe one-way communications. A suplex would be a bad idea for most communications—it is a wrestling move!

219. D. Gray box testing is a blend of crystal (or white) box testing that provides full information about a target, and black box testing, which provides little or no knowledge about the target.

220. A. Test coverage is computed using the formula test coverage = number of use cases tested/total number of use cases. Code coverage is assessed by the other formulas, including function, conditional, and total code coverage.

221. C. TCP, UDP, and other transport layer protocols like SSL and TLS operate at the Transport layer.

222. C. Deterrence is the first functional goal of physical security mechanisms. If a physical security control presents a formidable challenge to a potential attacker, they may not attempt the attack in the first place.

223. A. In an automated recovery, the system can recover itself against one or more failure types. In a manual recovery approach, the system does not fail into a secure state but requires an administrator to manually restore operations. In an automated recovery without undue loss, the system can recover itself against one or more failure types and also preserve data against loss. In function recovery, the system can restore functional processes automatically.

224. A. Skip should use SCP—Secure Copy is a secure file transfer method. SSH is a secure command-line and login protocol, whereas HTTP is used for unencrypted web traffic. Telnet is an unencrypted command-line and login protocol.

225. C. The California Online Privacy Protection Act requires that commercial websites that collect personal information from users in California conspicuously post a privacy policy. The Act does not require compliance with the EU DPD, nor does it use the DPD concepts of notice or choice, and it does not require encryption of all personal data.

226. B. Callback disconnects a remote user after their initial connection, and then calls them back at a preauthorized number. CallerID can help with this but can be spoofed, making callback a better solution. CHAP is an authentication protocol, and PPP is a dial-up protocol. Neither will verify a phone number.

227. A. The reference monitor is a component of the Trusted Computing Base (TCB) that validates access to resources.

228. B. Iris scans have a longer useful life than many other types of biometric factors because they don't change throughout a person's lifespan (unless the eye itself is damaged). Iris scanners can be fooled in some cases by high-resolution images of an eye, and iris scanners are not significantly cheaper than other scanners.

229. B. Nondisclosure agreements (NDAs) prohibit employees from sharing sensitive information without authorization, even after their employment ends. They may also apply to business partners, contractors, customers and others. Service level agreements (SLAs) and operating level agreements (OLAs) specify the parameters of service that a vendor provides to a customer. Data loss prevention (DLP) technology prevents data loss but is a technical, rather than a policy control.

230. C. They need a key for every possible pair of users in the cryptosystem. The first key would allow communication between Matthew and Richard. The second key would allow communication between Richard and Christopher. The third key would allow communication between Christopher and Matthew.

231. A. The Gramm Leach Bliley Act is an example of civil law. The Computer Fraud and Abuse Act, Electronic Communications Privacy Act, and Identity Theft and Assumption Deterrence Act are all examples of criminal law.

232. C. The SMTP protocol does not guarantee confidentiality between servers, making TLS or SSL between the client and server only a partial measure. Encrypting the email content can provide confidentiality; digital signatures can provide nonrepudiation.

233. D. The single quotation mark in the input field is a telltale sign that this is a SQL injection attack. The quotation mark is used to escape outside of the SQL code's input field, and the text following is used to directly manipulate the SQL command sent from the web application to the database.

234. C. Record retention policies describe how long the organization should retain data and may also specify how and when destruction should occur. Classification policies describe how and why classification should occur and who is responsible, whereas availability and audit policies may be created for specific purposes.

235. A. The goal of the business continuity planning process is to ensure that your recovery time objectives are all less than your maximum tolerable downtimes.

236. C. The Remediation phase of incident handling focuses on conducting a root cause analysis to identify the factors contributing to an incident and implementing new security controls, as needed.

237. A. The S/MIME secure email format uses the P7S format for encrypted email messages. If the recipient does not have a mail reader that supports S/MIME, the message will appear with an attachment named `smime.p7s`.

238. A. Aggregation is a security issue that arises when a collection of facts has a higher classification than the classification of any of those facts standing alone. An inference problem occurs when an attacker can pull together pieces of less sensitive information from multiple sources and use them to derive information of greater sensitivity. In this case, only a single source was used. SQL injection is a web application exploit. Multilevel security is a system control that allows the simultaneous processing of information at different classification levels.

239. B. Polyinstantiation allows the storage of multiple different pieces of information in a database at different classification levels to prevent attackers from conducting aggregation or inference attacks. Kim could store incorrect location information in the database at lower classification levels to prevent the aggregation attack in this scenario. Input validation, server-side validation, and parameterization are all techniques used to prevent web application attacks and are not effective against inference attacks.

240. B. The tail number is a database field because it is stored in the database. It is also a primary key because the question states that the database uniquely identifies aircraft using this field. Any primary key is, by definition, also a candidate key. There is no information provided that the tail number is a foreign key used to reference a different database table.

241. B. Foreign keys are used to create relationships between tables in a database. The database enforces referential integrity by ensuring that the foreign key used in a table has a corresponding record with that value as the primary key in the referenced table.

242. B. The waterfall model uses an approach that develops software sequentially, spending quite a bit of time up front on the development and documentation of requirements and design. The spiral and agile models focus on iterative development and are appropriate when requirements are not well understood or iterative development is preferred. DevOps is an approach to integrating development and operations activities and is not an SDLC model.

243. A. The data owner is a senior manager who bears ultimate responsibility for data protection tasks. The data owner typically delegates this responsibility to one or more data custodians.

244. C. A unique salt should be created for each user using a secure generation method and stored in that user's record. Since attacks against hashes rely on building tables to compare the hashes against, unique salts for each user make building tables for an entire database essentially impossible—the work to recover a single user account may be feasible, but large scale recovery requires complete regeneration of the table each time. A single salt allows rainbow tables to be generated if the salt is stolen or can be guessed based on frequently used passwords. Creating a unique salt each time a user logs in does not allow a match against a known salted hashed password.

245. D. NIST SP800-53 describes three processes:

- Examination, which is reviewing or analyzing assessment objects like specifications, mechanisms, or activities

- Interviews, which are conducted with individuals or groups of individuals

- Testing, which involves evaluating activities or mechanisms for expected behavior when used or exercised

Knowing the details of a given NIST document in depth can be challenging. To address a question like this, first eliminate responses that do not make sense; here, a mechanism cannot be interviewed, and test and assess both mean the same thing. This leaves only one correct answer.

246. B. Anomaly-based intrusion detection systems may identify a zero-day vulnerability because it deviates from normal patterns of activity. Signature-based detection methods would not be effective because there are no signatures for zero-day vulnerabilities. Strong patch management would not be helpful because, by definition, zero-day vulnerabilities do not have patches available. Full-disk encryption would not detect an attack because it is not a detective control.

247. B. Credential management systems provide features designed to make using and storing credentials in a secure and controllable way. AAA systems are authorization, authentication, and accounting systems. Two-factor authentication and Kerberos are examples of protocols.

248. A. The emergency response guidelines should include the immediate steps an organization should follow in response to an emergency situation. These include immediate response procedures, a list of individuals who should be notified of the emergency, and secondary response procedures for first responders. They do not include long-term actions such as activating business continuity protocols, ordering equipment, or activating disaster recovery sites.

249. D. A mantrap uses two sets of doors, only one of which can open at a time. A mantrap is a type of preventive access control, although its implementation is a physical control.

250. B. When following the separation-of-duties principle, organizations divide critical tasks into discrete components and ensure that no one individual has the ability to perform both actions. This prevents a single rogue individual from performing that task in an unauthorized manner and is also known as two-person control.

Chapter 10: Practice Test 2

1. D. The recovery point objective (RPO) identifies the maximum amount of data, measured in time, that may be lost during a recovery effort. The recovery time objective (RTO) is the amount of time expected to return an IT service or component to operation after a failure. The maximum tolerable downtime (MTD) is the longest amount of time that an IT service or component may be unavailable without causing serious damage to the organization. Service-level agreements (SLAs) are written contracts that document service expectations.

2. D. Fred should choose a router. Routers are designed to control traffic on a network while connecting to other similar networks. If the networks were very different, a bridge can help connect them. Gateways are used to connect to networks that use other protocols by transforming traffic to the appropriate protocol or format as it passes through them. Switches are often used to create broadcast domains and to connect endpoint systems or other devices.

3. B. Crystal box penetration testing, which is also sometimes called white box penetration testing, provides the tester with information about networks, systems, and configurations, allowing highly effective testing. It doesn't simulate an actual attack like black and gray box testing can, and thus does not have the same realism, and it can lead to attacks succeeding that would fail in a zero- or limited-knowledge attack.

4. D. The discovery phase includes activities like gathering IP addresses, network ranges, and hostnames, as well as gathering information about employees, locations, systems, and of course, the services those systems provide. Banner information is typically gathered as part of discovery to provide information about what version and type of service is being provided.

5. B. A class B network holds 2^16 systems, and its default network mask is 255.255.0.0.

6. D. Device fingerprinting via a web portal can require user authentication and can gather data like operating systems, versions, software information, and many other factors that can uniquely identify systems. Using an automated fingerprinting system is preferable to handling manual registration, and pairing user authentication with data gathering provides more detail than a port scan. MAC addresses can be spoofed, and systems may have more than one depending on how many network interfaces they have, which can make unique identification challenging.

7. B. The data owner is normally responsible for classifying information at an appropriate level. This role is typically filled by a senior manager or director, who then delegates operational responsibility to a data custodian.

8. A. The ping flood attack sends echo requests at a targeted system. These pings use inbound ICMP echo request packets, causing the system to respond with an outbound ICMP echo reply.

9. C. While all of the listed controls would improve authentication security, most simply strengthen the use of knowledge-based authentication. The best way to improve the authentication process would be to add a factor not based on knowledge through the use of multifactor authentication. This may include the use of biometric controls or token-based authentication.

10. C. Software-defined networking (SDN) is a converged protocol that allows virtualization concepts and practices to be applied to networks. MPLS handles a wide range of protocols like ATM, DSL, and others, but isn't intended to provide the centralization capabilities that SDN does. Content Distribution Network (CDN) is not a converged protocol, and FCoE is Fiber Channel over Ethernet, a converged protocol for storage.

11. C. The best way to ensure that data on DVDs is fully gone is to destroy them, and pulverizing DVDs is an appropriate means of destruction. DVDs are write-only media, meaning that secure erase and zero wipes won't work. Degaussing only works on magnetic media and cannot guarantee that there will be zero data remnance.

12. D. The five stages of the SW-CMM are, in order, Initial, Repeatable, Defined, Managed, and Optimizing. In the Optimizing stage, a process of continuous improvement occurs.

13. A. All packets leaving Angie's network should have a source address from her public IP address block. Packets with a destination address from Angie's network should not be leaving the network. Packets with source addresses from other networks are likely spoofed and should be blocked by egress filters. Packets with private IP addresses as sources or destinations should never be routed onto the Internet.

14. D. Security best practices dictate the use of shadowed password files that move the password hashes from the widely accessible /etc/passwd file to the more restricted /etc/shadow file.

15. A. While developers may feel like they have a business need to be able to move code into production, the principle of separation of duties dictates that they should not have the ability to both write code and place it on a production server. The deployment of code is often performed by change management staff.

16. A. Applying a digital signature to a message allows the sender to achieve the goal of nonrepudiation. This allows the recipient of a message to prove to a third party that the message came from the purported sender. Symmetric encryption does not support nonrepudiation. Firewalls and IDS are network security tools that are not used to provide nonrepudiation.

17. A. System A should send an ACK to end the three-way handshake. The TCP three-way handshake is SYN, SYN/ACK, ACK.

18. B. TACACS+ is the most modern version of TACACS, the Terminal Access Controller Access-Control System. It is a Cisco proprietary protocol with added features beyond what RADIUS provides, meaning it is commonly used on Cisco networks. XTACACS is an earlier version, Kerberos is a network authentication protocol rather than a remote user authentication protocol, and RADIUS+ is a made-up term.

19. C. Call managers and VoIP phones can be thought of as servers or appliances and embedded or network devices. That means that the most likely threats that they will face are denial-of-service (DoS) attacks and attacks against the host operating system. Malware and Trojans are less likely to be effective against a server or embedded system that doesn't browse the Internet or exchange data files; buffer overflows are usually aimed at specific applications or services.

20. C. The blacklist approach to application control blocks certain prohibited packages but allows the installation of other software on systems. The whitelist approach uses the reverse philosophy and only allows approved software. Antivirus software would only detect the installation of malicious software after the fact. Heuristic detection is a variant of antivirus software.

21. B. The exposure factor is the percentage of the facility that risk managers expect will be damaged if a risk materializes. It is calculated by dividing the amount of damage by the asset value. In this case, that is $20 million in damage divided by the $100 million facility value, or 20%.

22. B. The annualized rate of occurrence is the number of times each year that risk analysts expect a risk to happen in any given year. In this case, the analysts expect floods once every 200 years, or 0.005 times per year.

23. B. The annualized loss expectancy is calculated by multiplying the single loss expectancy (SLE) by the annualized rate of occurrence (ARO). In this case, the SLE is $20 million and the ARO is 0.005. Multiplying these numbers together gives you the ALE of $100,000.

24. B. The most frequent target of account management reviews are highly privileged accounts, as they create the greatest risk. Random samples are the second most likely choice. Accounts that have existed for a longer period of time are more likely to have a problem due to privilege creep than recently created accounts, but neither of these choices is likely unless there is a specific organizational reason to choose them.

25. A. In an Infrastructure as a Service (IaaS) cloud computing model, the customer retains responsibility for managing operating system security while the vendor manages security at the hypervisor level and below.

26. A. Type 1 errors occur when a valid subject is not authenticated. Type 2 errors occur when an invalid subject is incorrectly authenticated. Type 3 and Type 4 errors are not associated with biometric authentication.

27. B. The Company ID is a field used to identify the corresponding record in another table. This makes it a foreign key. Each customer may place more than one order, making Company ID unsuitable for use as a primary or candidate key in this table. Referential keys are not a type of database key.

28. B. Application programming interfaces (APIs), user interfaces (UIs), and physical interfaces are all tested during the software testing process. Network interfaces are not typically tested, and programmatic interfaces is another term for APIs.

29. D. The hearsay rule says that a witness cannot testify about what someone else told them, except under very specific exceptions. The courts have applied the hearsay rule to include the concept that attorneys may not introduce logs into evidence unless they are authenticated by the system administrator. The best evidence rule states that copies of documents may not be submitted into evidence if the originals are available. The parol evidence rule states that if two parties enter into a written agreement, that written document is assumed to contain all of the terms of the agreement. Testimonial evidence is a type of evidence, not a rule of evidence.

30. B. While key risk indicators can provide useful information for organizational planning and a deeper understanding of how organizations view risk, KRIs are not a great way to handle a real-time security response. Monitoring and detection systems like IPS, SIEM, and other tools are better suited to handling actual attacks.

31. B. Worms have built-in propagation mechanisms that do not require user interaction, such as scanning for systems containing known vulnerabilities and then exploiting those vulnerabilities to gain access. Viruses and Trojan horses typically require user interaction to spread. Logic bombs do not spread from system to system but lie in wait until certain conditions are met, triggering the delivery of their payload.

32. A. In this scenario, the vendor is providing object-based storage, a core infrastructure service. Therefore, this is an example of Infrastructure as a Service (IaaS).

33. C. In the community cloud computing model, two or more organizations pool their resources to create a cloud environment that they then share.

34. A. The Agile approach to software development states that working software is the primary measure of progress, that simplicity is essential, and that business people and developers must work together daily. It also states that the most efficient method of conveying information is face-to-face, not electronic.

35. C. Encryption, access controls, and firewalls would not be effective in this example because the accountants have legitimate access to the data. Integrity verification software would protect against this attack by identifying unexpected changes in protected data.

36. C. Class C fire extinguishers use carbon dioxide or halon suppressants and are useful against electrical fires. Water-based extinguishers should never be used against electrical fires due to the risk of electrocution.

37. A. Frame Relay supports multiple private virtual circuits (PVCs), unlike X.25. It is a packet switching technology that provides a Committed Information Rate, which is a minimum bandwidth guarantee provided by the service provider to customers. Finally, Frame Relay requires a DTE/DCE at each connection point, with the DTE providing access to the Frame Relay network, and a provider supplied DCE which transmits the data over the network.

38. B. SOC 2 reports are released under NDA to select partners or customers, and can provide detail on the controls and any issues they may have. A SOC 1 report would only provide financial control information, and a SOC 3 report provides less information since it is publicly available.

39. C. A SOC 2, Type 2 report includes information about a data center's security, availability, processing integrity, confidentiality, and privacy, and includes an auditor's opinion on

the operational effectiveness of the controls. SOC 3 does not have types, and an SOC 2 Type 1 only requires the organization's own attestation.

40. B. SAS 70 was superseded in 2010 by the SSAE 16 standard with three SOC levels for reporting. SAS 70 included Type 2 reports, covered data centers, and used 6-month testing periods for Type 2 reports.

41. C. Both a logical bus and a logical ring can be implemented as a physical star. Ethernet is commonly deployed as a physical star but placing a switch as the center of a star, but Ethernet still operates as a bus. Similarly, Token Ring deployments using multistation access unit (MAU) were deployed as physical stars, but operated as rings.

42. C. Bell-LaPadula uses security labels on objects and clearances for subjects, and is therefore a MAC model. It does not use discretionary, rule-based, role-based, or attribute-based access control.

43. D. The Family Educational Rights and Privacy Act (FERPA) protects the privacy of students in any educational institution that accepts any form of federal funding.

44. D. The Health Insurance Portability and Accountability Act (HIPAA) mandates the protection of Protected Health Information (PHI). The SAFE Act deals with mortgages, the Graham Leach Bliley Act (GLBA) covers financial institutions, and FERPA deals with student data.

45. C. Windows system logs include reboots, shutdowns, and service state changes. Application logs record events generated by programs, security logs track events like logins and uses of rights, and setup logs track application setup.

46. D. Implementations of syslog vary, but most provide a setting for severity level, allowing configuration of a value that determines what messages are sent. Typical severity levels include debug, informational, notice, warning, error, critical, alert, and emergency. The facility code is also supported by syslog, but is associated with which services are being logged. Security level and log priority are not typical syslog settings.

47. B. In RAID 1, also known as disk mirroring, systems contain two physical disks. Each disk contains copies of the same data, and either one may be used in the event the other disk fails.

48. B. An application-level gateway firewall uses proxies for each service it filters. Each proxy is designed to analyze traffic for its specific traffic type, allowing it to better understand valid traffic and to prevent attacks. Static packet filters and circuit-level gateways simply look at the source, destination, and ports in use, whereas a stateful packet inspection firewall can track the status of communication and allow or deny traffic based on that understanding.

49. C. Interviews, surveys, and audits are all useful for assessing awareness. Code quality is best judged by code review, service vulnerabilities are tested using vulnerability scanners and related tools, and the attack surface of an organization requires both technical and administrative review.

50. B. The Digital Millennium Copyright Act extends common carrier protection to Internet service providers who are not liable for the "transitory activities" of their customers.

51. C. Tokens are hardware devices (something you have) that generate a one-time password based on time or an algorithm. They are typically combined with another factor like a password to authenticate users. CAC and PIV cards are US government–issued smart cards.

52. B. A non-disclosure agreement (NDA) is a legal agreement between two parties that specifies what data they will not disclose. NDAs are common in industries that have sensitive or trade secret information they do not want employees to take to new jobs. Encryption would only help in transit or at rest, and Fred will likely have access to the data in unencrypted form as part of his job. An AUP is an acceptable use policy, and a stop-loss order is used on the stock market.

53. A. Multitasking handles multiple processes on a single processor by switching between them using the operating system. Multiprocessing uses multiple processors to perform multiple processes simultaneously. Multiprogramming requires modifications to the underlying applications. Multithreading runs multiple threads within a single process.

54. C. Binary keyspaces contain a number of keys equal to 2 raised to the power of the number of bits. Two to the eighth power is 256, so an 8-bit keyspace contains 256 possible keys.

55. C. Scoping is the process of reviewing and selecting security controls based on the system that they will be applied to. Tailoring is the process of matching a list of security controls to the mission of an organization. Baselines are used as a base set of security controls, often from a third-party organization that creates them. Standardization isn't a relevant term here.

56. D. During the preservation phase, the organization ensures that information related to the matter at hand is protected against intentional or unintentional alteration or deletion. The identification phase locates relevant information but does not preserve it. The collection phase occurs after preservation and gathers responsive information. The processing phase performs a rough cut of the collected information for relevance.

57. D. Systems and media should be labeled with the highest level of sensitivity that they store or handle. In this case, based on the US government classification scheme, the highest classification level in use on the system is Secret. Mixed classification provides no useful information about the level, whereas Top Secret and Confidential are too high and too low, respectively.

58. C. She has placed compensation controls in place. Compensation controls are used when controls like the locks in this example are not sufficient. While the alarm is a physical control, the signs she posted are not. Similarly, the alarms are not administrative controls. None of these controls help to recover from an issue and are thus not recovery controls.

59. A. Rainbow tables rely on being able to use databases of precomputed hashes to quickly search for matches to known hashes acquired by an attacker. Making passwords longer can greatly increase the size of the rainbow table required to find the matching hash, and adding a salt to the password will make it nearly impossible for the attacker to generate a table that will match unless they can acquire the salt value. MD5 and SHA1 are both poor choices for password hashing compared to modern password hashes, which are designed to make hashing easy and recovery difficult. Rainbow tables are often used against lists of hashes acquired by attacks rather than over-the-wire attacks, so over-the-wire encryption is not particularly useful here. Shadow passwords simply make the traditionally world-readable list of password hashes on Unix and Linux systems available in a location readable only by root. This doesn't prevent a rainbow table attack once the hashes are obtained.

60. C. External auditors can provide an unbiased and impartial view of an organization's controls to third parties. Internal auditors are useful when reporting to senior management of the organization but are typically not asked to report to third parties. Penetration tests test technical controls but are not as well suited to testing many administrative controls. The employees who build and maintain controls are more likely to bring a bias to the testing of those controls and should not be asked to report on them to third parties.

61. A. Using encryption reduces risk by lowering the likelihood that an eavesdropper will be able to gain access to sensitive information.

62. B. Provisioning includes the creation, maintenance, and removal of user objects from applications, systems, and directories. Registration occurs when users are enrolled in a biometric system; population and authenticator loading are not common industry terms.

63. A. In the subject/object model of access control, the user or process making the request for a resource is the subject of that request. In this example, Ricky is requesting access to the VPN (the object of the request) and is, therefore, the subject.

64. C. The formula for determining the number of encryption keys required by a symmetric algorithm is $((n*(n-1))/2)$. With six users, you will need $((6*5)/2)$, or 15 keys.

65. B. Patents have the shortest duration of the techniques listed: 20 years. Copyrights last for 70 years beyond the death of the author. Trademarks are renewable indefinitely and trade secrets are protected as long as they remain secret.

66. C. In a risk acceptance strategy, the organization chooses to take no action other than documenting the risk. Purchasing insurance would be an example of risk transference. Relocating the data center would be risk avoidance. Reengineering the facility is an example of a risk mitigation strategy.

67. C. Uninterruptible power supplies (UPSs) provide immediate, battery-driven power for a short period of time to cover momentary losses of power. Generators are capable of providing backup power for a sustained period of time in the event of a power loss, but they take time to activate. RAID and redundant servers are high-availability controls but do not cover power loss scenarios.

68. C. Password histories retain a list of previous passwords (or, preferably, a list of salted hashed for previous passwords) to ensure that users don't reuse their previous passwords. Longer minimum age can help prevent users from changing their passwords, then changing them back, but won't prevent a determined user from eventually getting their old password back. Length requirements and complexity requirements tend to drive users to reuse passwords if they're not paired with tools like single-sign on, password storage systems, or other tools that decrease the difficulty of password management.

69. B. The Single Loss Expectancy (SLE) is the amount of damage that a risk is expected to cause each time that it occurs.

70. B. Sanitization includes steps like removing the hard drive and other local storage from PCs before they are sold as surplus. Degaussing uses magnetic fields to wipe media; purging is an intense form of clearing used to ensure that data is removed and unrecoverable from media; and removing does not necessarily imply destruction of the drive.

71. D. During the Reporting phase, incident responders assess their obligations under laws and regulations to report the incident to government agencies and other regulators.

72. B. Service Provisioning Markup Language (SPML) is an OASIS developed markup language designed to provide service, user, and resource provisioning between organizations. Security Assertion Markup Language (SAML) is used to exchange user authentication and authorization data. Extensible Access Control Markup Language (XACML) is used to describe access controls. Service-oriented architecture (SOA) is not a markup language.

73. B. While full device encryption doesn't guarantee that data cannot be accessed, it provides Michelle's best option for preventing data from being lost with a stolen device when paired with a passcode. Mandatory passcodes and application management can help prevent application based attacks and unwanted access to devices, but won't keep the data secure if the device is lost. Remote wipe and GPS location is useful if the thief allows the device to connect to a cellular or wifi network. Unfortunately, many modern thieves immediately take steps to ensure that the device will not be trackable or allowed to connect to a network before they capture data or wipe the device for re-sale.

74. D. SMTP servers that don't authenticate users before relaying their messages are known as open relays. Open relays that are Internet exposed are typically quickly exploited to send email for spammers.

75. D. Sending logs to a secure log server, sometimes called a bastion host, is the most effective way to ensure that logs survive a breach. Encrypting local logs won't stop an attacker from deleting them, and requiring administrative access won't stop attackers who have breached a machine and acquired escalated privileges. Log rotation archives logs based on time or file size, and can also purge logs after a threshold is hit. Rotation won't prevent an attacker from purging logs.

76. C. A Security Information and Event Management tool (SIEM) is designed to provide automated analysis and monitoring of logs and security events. A SIEM that receives access to logs can help detect and alert on events like logs being purged or other breach indicators. An IDS can help detect intrusions, but IDSs are not typically designed to handle central logs. A central logging server can receive and store logs, but won't help with analysis without taking additional actions. Syslog is simply a log format.

77. B. Requiring authentication can help provide accountability by ensuring that any action taken can be tracked back to a specific user. Storing logs centrally ensures that users can't erase the evidence of actions that they have taken. Log review can be useful when identifying issues, but digital signatures are not a typical part of a logging environment. Logging the use of administrative credentials helps for those users but won't cover all users, and encrypting the logs doesn't help with accountability. Authorization helps, but being able to specifically identify users through authentication is more important.

78. B. Port Address Translation (PAT) is used to allow a network to use any IP address set inside without causing a conflict with the public Internet. PAT is often confused with Network Address Translation (NAT), which maps one internal address to one external address. IPSec is a security protocol suite, Software Defined Networking (SDN) is a method of defining networks programmatically, and IPX is a non-IP network protocol.

79. C. Each of the precautions listed helps to prevent social engineering by helping prevent exploitation of trust. Avoiding voice-only communications is particularly important, since establishing identity over the phone is difficult. The other listed attacks would not be prevented by these techniques.

80. C. L2TP is the only one of the four common VPN protocols that can natively support non-IP protocols. PPTP, L2F, and IPSec are all IP-only protocols.

81. D. Remnant data is data that is left after attempts have been made to remove or erase it. Bitrot is a term used to describe aging media that decays over time. MBR is the master boot record, a boot sector found on hard drives and other media. Leftover data is not an industry term.

82. C. During a parallel test, the team activates the disaster recovery site for testing but the primary site remains operational. A simulation test involves a roleplay of a prepared scenario overseen by a moderator. Responses are assessed to help improve the organization's response process. The checklist review is the least disruptive type of disaster recovery test. During a checklist review, team members each review the contents of their disaster recovery checklists on their own and suggest any necessary changes. During a tabletop exercise, team members come together and walk through a scenario without making any changes to information systems.

83. C. Discretionary access control gives owners the right to decide who has access to the objects they own. Role-based access control uses administrators to make that decision for roles or groups of people with a role, task-based access control uses lists of tasks for each user, and rule-based access control applies a set of rules to all subjects.

84. C. Trusted paths that secure network traffic from capture and link encryption are both ways to help prevent man-in-the-middle attacks. Brute-force and dictionary attacks can both be prevented using back-off algorithms that slow down repeated attacks. Log analysis tools can also create dynamic firewall rules, or an IPS can block attacks like these in real time. Spoofed login screens can be difficult to prevent, although user awareness training can help.

85. D. The four canons of the (ISC)² code of ethics are to protect society, the common good, necessary public trust and confidence, and the infrastructure; act honorably, honestly, justly, responsibly, and legally; provide diligent and competent service to principals; and advance and protect the profession.

86. A. The emergency response guidelines should include the immediate steps an organization should follow in response to an emergency situation. These include immediate response procedures, a list of individuals who should be notified of the emergency, and secondary response procedures for first responders. They do not include long-term actions such as activating business continuity protocols, ordering equipment, or activating DR sites.

87. C. Security Assertion Markup Language (SAML) is the best choice for providing authentication and authorization information, particularly for browser-based SSO. HTML is primarily used for web pages, SPML is used to exchange user information for SSO, and XACML is used for access control policy markup.

88. D. Individuals with specific business continuity roles should receive training on at least an annual basis.

89. B. Triple DES functions by using either two or three encryption keys. When used with only one key, 3DES produces weakly encrypted ciphertext that is the insecure equivalent of DES.

90. B. RFC 1918 addresses are in the range 10.0.0.0–10.255.255.255, 172.16.0.0–172.31.255.255, and 192.168.0.0–192.168.255.255. APIPA addresses are assigned between 169.254.0.01 and 169.254.255.254, and 127.0.0.1 is a loopback address (although technically the entire 127.x.x.x network is reserved for loopback). Public IP addresses are the rest of the addresses in the space.

91. C. Since Lauren wants to monitor her production server she should use passive monitoring by employing a network tap, span port, or other means of copying actual traffic to a monitoring system that can identify performance and other problems. This will avoid introducing potentially problematic traffic on purpose while capturing actual traffic problems. Active monitoring relies on synthetic or previously recorded traffic, and both replay and real time are not common industry terms used to describe types of monitoring.

92. B. For web applications, input validation should always be performed on the web application server. By the time the input reaches the database, it is already part of a SQL command that is properly formatted and input validation would be far more difficult, if it is even possible. Input validation controls should never reside in the client's browser, as is the case with JavaScript, because the user may remove or tamper with the validation code.

93. A. RSA is an asymmetric encryption algorithm that requires only two keys for each user. IDEA, 3DES, and Skipjack are all symmetric encryption algorithms and would require a key for every unique pair of users in the system.

94. D. The image clearly shows a black magnetic stripe running across the card, making this an example of a magnetic stripe card.

95. D. The log entries contained in this example show the allow/deny status for inbound and outbound TCP and UDP sessions. This is, therefore, an example of a firewall log.

96. D. Zero-day vulnerabilities remain in the dangerous zero-day category until the release of a patch that corrects the vulnerability. At that time, it becomes the responsibility of IT professionals to protect their systems by applying the patch. Implementation of other security controls, such as encryption or firewalls, does not change the nature of the zero-day vulnerability.

97. A. All of the techniques listed are hardening methods, but only patching the leaky roof is an example of physical infrastructure hardening.

98. C. Using a virtual machine to monitor a virtual span port allows the same type of visibility that it would in a physical network if implemented properly. Installing Wireshark would allow monitoring on each system but doesn't scale well. A physical appliance would require all traffic to be sent out of the VM environment, losing many of the benefits of the design. Finally, netcat is a network tool used to send or receive data, but it isn't a tool that allows packet capture of traffic between systems.

99. C. The sender of a message encrypts the message using the public key of the message recipient.

100. D. The recipient of a message uses his or her own private key to decrypt messages that were encrypted with the recipient's public key. This ensures that nobody other than the intended recipient can decrypt the message.

101. D. Digital signatures enforce nonrepudiation. They prevent an individual from denying that he or she was the actual originator of the message.

102. B. An individual creates a digital signature by encrypting the message digest with his or her own private key.

103. D. The comparison of a factor to validate an identity is known as authorization. Identification would occur when Jim presented his user ID. Tokenization is a process that converts a sensitive data element to a nonsensitive representation of that element. Hashing transforms a string of characters into a fixed-length value or key that represents the original string.

104. B. Decentralized access control empowers people closer to the resources to control access but does not provide consistent control. It does not provide redundancy, since it merely moves control points, the cost of access control depends on its implementation and methods, and granularity can be achieved in both centralized and decentralized models.

105. C. A mantrap, which is composed of a pair of doors with an access mechanism that allows only one door to open at a time, is an example of a preventive access control because it can stop unwanted access by keeping intruders from accessing a facility due to an opened door or following legitimate staff in. It can serve as a deterrent by discouraging intruders who would be trapped in it without proper access, and of course, doors with locks are an example of a physical control. A compensating control attempts to make up for problems with an existing control or to add additional controls to improve a primary control.

106. C. Sally needs to provide nonrepudiation, the ability to provably associate a given email with a sender. Digital signatures can provide nonrepudiation and are her best option. IMAP is a mail protocol, encryption can provide confidentiality, and DKIM is a tool for identifying domains that send email.

107. D. In most situations, employers may not access medical information due to healthcare privacy laws. Reference checks, criminal records checks, and credit history reports are all typically found during pre-employment background checks.

108. C. In a land attack, the attacker sends a packet that has identical source and destination IP addresses in an attempt to crash systems that are not able to handle this out-of-specification traffic.

109. A. An SSAE-16 Type I report covers controls and design of controls at the time of the report. A Type II report adds a historical element, covering controls over time. SAS-70 is outdated and should not be used.

110. A. When a data stream is converted into a segment (TCP) or a datagram (UDP) it transitions from the Session layer to the Transport layer. This change from a message sent to an encoded segment allows it to then traverse the network layer.

111. C. The user has successfully explained a valid need to know the data—completing the report requested by the CFO requires this access. However, the user has not yet demonstrated that he or she has appropriate clearance to access the information. A note from the CFO would meet this requirement.

112. B. Kathleen's needs point to a directory service, and the Lightweight Directory Access Protocol (LDAP) would meet her needs. LDAP is an open, industry standard and vendor-neutral protocol for directory services. Kerberos and RADIUS are both authentication protocols, and Active Directory is a Microsoft product and is not vendor neutral, although it does support a number of open standards.

113. A. Application firewalls add Layer 7 functionality to other firewall solutions. This includes the ability to inspect application-layer details such as analyzing HTTP, DNS, FTP, and other application protocols.

114. C. The create rule allows a subject to create new objects and also creates an edge from the subject to that object, granting rights on the new object.

115. A. Metasploit provides an extensible framework, allowing penetration testers to create their own exploits in addition to those that are built into the tool. Unfortunately, penetration testing can only cover the point in time when it is conducted. When conducting a penetration test, the potential to cause a denial of service due to a fragile service always exists, but it can test process and policy through social engineering and operational testing that validates how those processes and policies work.

116. D. EAL7 is the highest level of assurance under the Common Criteria. It applies when a system has been formally verified, designed, and tested.

117. C. X.509 defines standards for public key certificates like those used with many smart cards. X.500 is a series of standards defining directory services. The Service Provisioning Markup Language (SPML) and the Security Assertion Markup Language (SAML) aren't standards that Alex should expect to see when using a smart card to authenticate.

118. C. The Children's Online Privacy Protection Act (COPPA) regulates websites that cater to children or knowingly collect information from children under the age of 13.

119. A. The Health Insurance Portability and Accountability Act (HIPAA) applies to healthcare information and is unlikely to apply in this situation. The Federal Information Security Management Act (FISMA) and Government Information Security Reform Act regulate the activities of all government agencies. The Homeland Security Act (HSA) created the US Department of Homeland Security, and more importantly for this question included the Cyber Security Enhancement Act of 2002 and the Critical Infrastructure

Information Act of 2002. The Computer Fraud and Abuse Act (CFAA) provides specific protections for systems operated by government agencies.

120. C. Turnstiles are unidirectional gates that prevent more than a single person from entering a facility at a time.

121. C. Access control systems rely on identification and authentication to provide accountability. Effective authorization systems are desirable, but not required, since logs can provide information about who accessed what resources, even if access to those resources are not managed well. Of course, poor authorization management can create many other problems.

122. B. EAP was originally intended to be used on physically isolated network channels and did not include encryption. Fortunately, it was designed to be extensible, and PEAP can provide TLS encryption. EAP isn't limited to PEAP as an option as EAP-TLS also exists, providing an EAP TLS implementation, and the same extensibility allows a multitude of other authentication methods.

123. C. The 192.168.0.0-192.168.255.255 address range is one of the ranges defined by RFC 1918 as private, non-routable IP ranges. Scott's ISP (and any other organization with a properly configured router) will not route traffic from these addresses over the public Internet.

124. B. She should use a KPI (Key Performance Indicator). KPIs are used to measure success, typically in relation to an organization's long-term goals. Metrics are measures, and although a KPI can be a metric, metrics are not all KPIs. SLAs are service-level agreements, and metrics can help determine whether they are being met. Objectives and key results (OKRs) are used to connect employee performance to results using subjective measures for objectives and quantitative measures for key results.

125. A. A well-designed set of VLANs based on functional groupings will logically separate segments of the network, making it difficult to have data exposure issues between VLANs. Changing the subnet mask will only modify the broadcast domain and will not fix issues with packet sniffing. Gateways would be appropriate if network protocols were different on different segments. Port security is designed to limit which systems can connect to a given port.

126. C. Captive portals are designed to show a page that can require actions like accepting an agreement or recording an email address before connecting clients to the Internet. NAC is designed to verify whether clients meet a security profile, which doesn't match the needs of most coffee shops. A wireless gateway is a tool to access a cellular or other network, rather than a way to interact with users before they connect, and 802.11 is the family of IEEE wireless standards.

127. A. Active monitoring is also known as synthetic monitoring and relies on prerecorded or generated traffic to test systems for performance and other issues. Passive monitoring uses span ports, network taps, or similar technologies to capture actual traffic for analysis. Reactive monitoring is not a commonly used industry term.

128. B. TCP headers can be 20 to 60 bytes long depending on options that are set.

129. A. Cellular networks have the same issues that any public network does. Encryption requirements should match those that the organization selects for other public networks like hotels, conference Wi-Fi, and similar scenarios. Encrypting all data is difficult, and adds overhead, so it should not be the default answer unless the company specifically requires it. WAP is a dated wireless application protocol and is not in broad use; requiring it would be difficult. WAP does provide TLS, which would help when in use.

130. D. Fred's best option is to use an encrypted, trusted VPN service to tunnel all of his data usage. Trusted Wi-Fi networks are unlikely to exist at a hacker conference, normal usage is dangerous due to the proliferation of technology that allows fake towers to be set up, and discontinuing all usage won't support Fred's business needs.

131. B. Remote wipe tools are a useful solution, but they only work if the phone can access either a cellular or Wi-Fi network. Remote wipe solutions are designed to wipe data from the phone regardless of whether it is in use or has a passcode. Providers unlock phones for use on other cellular networks rather than for wiping or other feature support.

132. C. The goal of business continuity planning exercises is to reduce the amount of time required to restore operations. This is done by minimizing the recovery time objective (RTO).

133. D. NIST Special Publication 800-53 describes depth and coverage. These terms describe depth, specifying the level of detail. Coverage measures breadth by using multiple assessment types and ensuring that each line of code is covered. If you encounter a question like this and are not familiar with the details of a standard like NIST 800-53, or may not remember them, focus on the meanings of each word and the details of the question. We can easily rule out affirmation, which isn't a measure. Suitability is a possibility, but depth fits better than suitability or coverage.

134. C. A structured walk-through uses only role-playing to test a disaster recovery plan. It does not involve the use of any technical controls. Simulation tests, parallel tests, and full interruption tests actually use some or all of the disaster recovery controls.

135. C. Interference is electrical noise or other disruptions that corrupt the contents of packets. Latency is a delay in the delivery of packets from their source to their destination. Jitter is a variation in the latency for different packets. Packet loss is the disappearance of packets in transit that requires retransmission.

136. A. Fagan inspections follow a rigorous, highly structured process to perform code review, using a planning, overview, preparation, inspection, rework, and follow-up cycle. Fuzzing feeds unexpected input to programs, while over-the-shoulder code review is simply a review by having another developer meet with them to review code using a walk-through. Pair programming uses a pair of developers, one of whom writes code while both talk through the coding and development process.

137. B. While removing the <SCRIPT> tag from user input, it is not sufficient, as a user may easily evade this filter by encoding the tag with an XSS filter evasion technique. Frank was correct to perform validation on the server rather than at the client, but he should use validation that limits user input to allowed values, rather than filtering out one potentially malicious tag.

138. C. Fortran is a functional programming language. Java, C++, and C# are all object-oriented languages, meaning that they use the object model and approach programming as describing the interactions between objects.

139. C. HIPAA requires that anyone working with personal health information on behalf of a HIPAA covered entity be subject to the terms of a business associates agreement (BAA).

140. A. During a full interruption test, the team takes down the primary site and confirms that the disaster recovery site is capable of handling regular operations. The full interruption test is the most thorough test but also the most disruptive. During a parallel test, the team actually activates the disaster recovery site for testing but the primary site remains operational. The checklist review is the least disruptive type of disaster recovery test. During a checklist review, team members each review the contents of their disaster recovery checklists on their own and suggest any necessary changes. During a tabletop exercise, team members come together and walk through a scenario without making any changes to information systems.

141. D. Ed's best option is to install an IPv6 to IPv4 gateway that can translate traffic between the networks. A bridge would be appropriate for different types of networks, whereas a router would make sense if the networks were similar. A modern switch might be able to carry both types of traffic but wouldn't be much help translating between the two protocols.

142. C. The Rijndael block cipher was selected as the winner and is the cryptographic algorithm underlying the Advanced Encryption Standard (AES).

143. C. The International Safe Harbor Privacy Principles listed here are part of the Safe Harbor provisions intended to address the European Union's Data Privacy Directive. The DPD provides seven slightly different key principles to ensure data security and privacy. The Children's Online Privacy Act (COPA), the NY SAFE Act is not an information security or privacy law, and the Federal Information Security Modernization Act (FISMA) is a key part of the US federal government's security posture.

144. B. The EU Data Protection Directive does not require that organizations provide individuals with employee lists.

145. B. Tammy should choose a warm site. This type of facility meets her requirements for a good balance between cost and recovery time. It is less expensive than a hot site but facilitates faster recovery than a cold site. A red site is not a type of disaster recovery facility.

146. B. When data reaches the Transport layer, it is sent as segments (TCP) or datagrams (UDP). Above the Transport layer, data becomes a data stream, while below the Transport layer they are converted to packets at the Network layer, frames at the Data Link layer, and bits at the Physical layer.

147. D. The Advanced Encryption Standard supports encryption with 128-bit keys, 192-bit keys, and 256-bit keys.

148. D. An application programming interface (API) allows developers to create a direct method for other users to interact with their systems through an abstraction that does not require knowledge of the implementation details. Access to object models, source code, and data dictionaries also indirectly facilitate interaction but do so in a manner that provides other developers with implementation details.

149. D. The PGP email system, invented by Phil Zimmerman, uses the "web of trust" approach to secure email. The commercial version uses RSA for key exchange, IDEA for encryption/decryption, and MD5 for message digest production. The freeware version uses Diffie-Hellman key exchange, the Carlisle Adams/Stafford Tavares (CAST) encryption/decryption, and SHA hashing.

150. B. The permissions granted on files in Linux designate what authorized users can do with those files—read, write, or execute. In the image shown, all users can read, write, and execute `index.html`, whereas the owner can read, write, and execute `example.txt`, the group cannot, and everyone can write and execute it.

151. C. Detective access controls operate after the fact and are intended to detect or discover unwanted access or activity. Preventive access controls are designed to prevent the activity from occurring, whereas corrective controls return an environment to its original status after an issue occurs. Directive access controls limit or direct the actions of subjects to ensure compliance with policies.

152. C. A honeypot is a decoy computer system used to bait intruders into attacking. A honeynet is a network of multiple honeypots that creates a more sophisticated environment for intruders to explore. A pseudo flaw is a false vulnerability in a system that may attract an attacker. A darknet is a segment of unused network address space that should have no network activity and, therefore, may be easily used to monitor for illicit activity.

153. C. The CER is the point where FAR and FRR cross over, and it is a standard assessment used to compare the accuracy of biometric devices.

154. A. At point B, the false acceptance rate (FAR) is quite high, whereas the false rejection rate (FRR) is relatively low. This may be acceptable in some circumstances, but in organizations where a false acceptance can cause a major problem, it is likely that they should instead choose a point to the right of point A.

155. B. CER is a standard used to assess biometric devices. If the CER for this device does not fit the needs of the organization, Ben should assess other biometric systems to find one with a lower CER. Sensitivity is already accounted for in CER charts, and moving the CER isn't something Ben can do. FRR is not a setting in software, so Ben can't use that as an option either.

156. B. Personally Identifiable Information (PII) can be used to distinguish a person's identity. Personal Health Information (PHI) includes data like medical history, lab results, insurance information, and other details about a patient. Personal Protected Data is a made-up term, and PID is an acronym for process ID, the number associated with a running program or process.

157. D. The figure shows the waterfall model, developed by Winston Royce. The key characteristic of this model is a series of sequential steps that include a feedback loop that allows the process to return one step prior to the current step when necessary.

158. B. Encapsulation creates both the benefits and potential issues with multilayer protocols. Bridging can use various protocols but does not rely on encapsulation. Hashing and storage protocols typically do not rely on encapsulation as a core part of their functionality.

159. B. The five COBIT principles are meeting stakeholder needs, covering the enterprise end-to-end, applying a single integrated framework, enabling a holistic approach, and separating governance from management.

160. A. The onward transfer principle requires that organizations only exchange personal information with other organizations bound by the EU Data Protection Directive's privacy principles. The United Kingdom, Italy, and Germany, as EU member states, are all bound by those principles. The United States does not have a comprehensive privacy law codifying those principles, so the onward transfer requirement applies.

161. C. The Domain Name System (DNS) provides human-friendly domain names that resolve to IP addresses, making it possible to easily remember websites and hostnames. ARP is used to resolve IP addresses into MAC addresses, whereas TCP is used to control the network traffic that travels between systems.

162. B. Ben is assessing a specification. Specifications are document-based artifacts like policies or designs. Activities are actions that support an information system that involves people. Mechanisms are the hardware-, software-, or firmware-based controls or systems in an information system, and an individual is one or more people applying specifications, mechanisms, or activities.

163. C. When done properly, a sanitization process fully ensures that data is not remnant on the system before it is reused. Clearing and erasing can both be failure prone, and of course destruction wouldn't leave a machine or device to reuse.

164. C. In a gray box test, the tester evaluates the software from a user perspective but has access to the source code as the test is conducted. White box tests also have access to the source code but perform testing from a developer's perspective. Black box tests work from a user's perspective but do not have access to source code. Blue boxes are a telephone hacking tool and not a software testing technique.

165. D. The DevOps approach to technology management seeks to integrate software development, operations, and quality assurance in a cohesive effort. It specifically attempts to eliminate the issue of "throwing problems over the fence" by building collaborative relationships between members of the IT team.

166. B. A Security Information and Event Management (SIEM) tool is designed to centralize logs from many locations in many formats, and to ensure that logs are read and analyzed despite differences between different systems and devices. The Simple Network Management Protocol (SNMP) is used for some log messaging but is not a solution that solves all of these problems. Most non-Windows devices, including network devices among others, are not designed to use the Windows event log format, although using NTP for time synchronization is a good idea. Finally, local logging is useful, but setting clocks individually will result in drift over time and won't solve the issue with many log sources.

167. C. Mike should use overwriting to protect this device. While degaussing is a valid secure data removal technique, it would not be effective in this case, since degaussing only works on magnetic media. Physical destruction would prevent the reuse of the device. Reformatting is not a valid secure data removal technique.

168. A. The single quotation mark in the input field is a telltale sign that this is a SQL injection attack. The quotation mark is used to escape outside the SQL code's input field and the text that follows is used to directly manipulate the SQL command sent from the web application to the database.

169. D. Procedures are formal, mandatory documents that provide detailed, step-by-step actions required from individuals performing a task.

170. D. Durability requires that once a transaction is committed to the database it must be preserved. Atomicity ensures that if any part of a database transaction fails, the entire transaction must be rolled back as if it never occurred. Consistency ensures that all transactions are consistent with the logical rules of the database, such as having a primary key. Isolation requires that transactions operate separately from each other.

171. D. Watermarking alters a digital object to embed information about the source, either in a visible or hidden form. Digital signatures may identify the source of a document but they are easily removed. Hashing would not provide any indication of the document source, since anyone could compute a hash value. Document staining is not a security control.

172. C. Data centers should be located in the core of a building. Locating it on lower floors makes it susceptible to flooding and physical break-ins. Locating it on the top floor makes it vulnerable to wind and roof damage.

173. A. The due care principle states that an individual should react in a situation using the same level of care that would be expected from any reasonable person. It is a very broad standard. The due diligence principle is a more specific component of due care that states an individual assigned a responsibility should exercise due care to complete it accurately and in a timely manner.

174. B. Criminal investigations have high stakes with severe punishment for the offender that may include incarceration. Therefore, they use the strictest standard of evidence of all investigations: beyond a reasonable doubt. Civil investigations use a preponderance of the evidence standard. Regulatory investigations may use whatever standard is appropriate for the venue where the evidence will be heard. This may include the beyond-a-reasonable-doubt standard, but it is not always used in regulatory investigations. Operational investigations do not use a standard of evidence.

175. D. Differential backups do not alter the archive bit on a file, whereas incremental and full backups reset the archive bit to 0 after the backup completes. Partial backups are not a backup type.

176. B. Warm sites contain the hardware necessary to restore operations but do not have a current copy of data.

177. C. A power spike is a momentary period of high voltage. A surge is a prolonged period of high voltage. Sags and brownouts are periods of low voltage.

178. A. Subjects are active entities that can access a passive object to retrieve information from or about an object. Subjects can also make changes to objects when they are properly authorized. Users are often subjects, but not all subjects are users.

179. A. OSPF is a link state protocol. Link state protocols maintain a topographical map of all connected networks and preferentially select the shortest path to remote networks for traffic. A distance vector protocol would map the direction and distance in hops to a remote network, whereas shortest path first and link mapping are not types of routing protocols.

180. A. Machine languages are examples of first-generation programming languages. Second-generation languages include assembly languages. Third-generation languages include compiled languages. Fourth- and fifth-generation languages go beyond standard compiled languages to include natural languages and declarative approaches to programming.

181. A. Tara first must achieve a system baseline. She does this by applying the most recent full backup to the new system. This is Sunday's full backup. Once Tara establishes this baseline, she may then proceed to apply differential backups to bring the system back to a more recent state.

182. B. To restore the system to as current a state as possible, Tara must first apply Sunday's full backup. She may then apply the most recent differential backup, from Wednesday at noon. Differential backups include all files that have changed since the most recent full backup, so the contents of Wednesday's backup contain all of the data that would be contained in Monday and Tuesday's backups, making the Monday and Tuesday backups irrelevant for this scenario.

183. A. In this scenario, the differential backup was made at noon and the server failed at 3 p.m. Therefore, any data modified or created between noon and 3 p.m. will not be contained on any backup and will be irretrievably lost.

184. D. By switching from differential to incremental backups, Tara's weekday backups will only contain the information changed since the previous day. Therefore, she must apply all of the available incremental backups. She would begin by restoring the Sunday full backup and then apply the Monday, Tuesday, and Wednesday incremental backups.

185. D. Each incremental backup contains only the information changed since the most recent full or incremental backup. If we assume that the same amount of information changes every day, each of the incremental backups would be roughly the same size.

186. A. Information that is modifiable between a client and a server also means that it is accessible, pointing to both tampering and information disclosure. Spoofing in STRIDE is aimed at credentials and authentication, and there is no mention of this in the question. Repudiation would require that proving who performed an action was important, and elevation of privilege would come into play if privilege levels were involved.

187. B. Record retention ensures that data is kept and maintained as long as it is needed, and that it is purged when it is no longer necessary. Data remanence occurs when data is left behind after an attempt is made to remove it, whereas data redaction is not a technical term used to describe this effort. Finally, audit logging may be part of the records retained but doesn't describe the life cycle of data.

188. D. The Authentication Header provides authentication, integrity, and nonrepudiation for IPSec connections. The Encapsulating Security Payload provides encryption and thus provides confidentiality. It can also provide limited authentication. L2TP is an independent VPN protocol, and Encryption Security Header is a made-up term.

189. B. The attack described in the scenario is a classic example of TCP scanning, a network reconnaissance technique that may precede other attacks. There is no evidence that the attack disrupted system availability, which would characterize a denial-of-service attack, that it was waged by a malicious insider, or that the attack resulted in the compromise of a system.

190. C. Attackers may use algorithmic complexity as a tool to exploit a TOC/TOU race condition. By varying the workload on the CPU, attackers may exploit the amount of time required to process requests and use that variance to effectively schedule the exploit's execution. File locking, exception handling, and concurrency controls are all methods used to defend against TOC/TOU attacks.

191. D. The kernel lies within the central ring, Ring 0. Ring 1 contains other operating system components. Ring 2 is used for drivers and protocols. User-level programs and applications run at Ring 3. Rings 0-2 run in privileged mode, whereas Ring 3 runs in user mode.

192. A. RAID level 0 is also known as disk striping. RAID 1 is called disk mirroring. RAID 5 is called disk striping with parity. RAID 10 is known as a stripe of mirrors.

193. A. This is an example of a time of check/time of use, or TOC/TOU attack. It exploits the difference between the times when a system checks for permission to perform an action and when the action is actually performed. Permissions creep would occur if the account had gained additional rights over time as the other's role or job changed. Impersonation occurs when an attacker pretends to be a valid user, and link swap is not a type of attack.

194. B. RAID 0, or disk striping, requires at least two disks to implement. It improves performance of the storage system but does not provide fault tolerance.

195. B. Fred's company needs to protect integrity, which can be accomplished by digitally signing messages. Any change will cause the signature to be invalid. Encrypting isn't necessary because the company does not want to protect confidentiality. TLS can provide in-transit protection but won't protect integrity of the messages, and of course a hash used without a way to verify that the hash wasn't changed won't ensure integrity either.

196. A. An attribute-based access control (ABAC) system will allow Susan to specify details about subjects, objects, and access, allowing granular control. Although a rule-based access control system (RBAC) might allow this, the attribute-based access control system can be more specific and thus is more flexible. Discretionary access control (DAC) would allow object owners to make decisions, and mandatory access controls (MACs) would use classifications; neither of these capabilities was described in the requirements.

197. C. Synchronous communications use a timing or clock mechanism to control the data stream. This can permit very fast communication.

198. B. The maximum allowed length of a Cat 6 cable is 100 meters, or 328 feet. Long distances are typically handled by a fiber run or by using network devices like switches or repeaters.

199. B. One of the main functions of a forensic drive controller is preventing any command sent to a device from modifying data stored on the device. For this reason, forensic drive controllers are also often referred to as write blockers.

200. A. Setting the Secure cookie will only allow cookies to be sent via HTTPS TLS or SSL sessions, preventing man-in-the-middle attacks that target cookies. The rest of the settings are problematic: Cookies are vulnerable to DNS spoofing. Domain cookies should usually have the narrowest possible scope, which is actually accomplished by not setting the Domain cookie. This allows only the originating server to access the cookie. Cookies without the Expires or Max-age attributes are ephemeral and will only be kept for the session, making them less vulnerable than stored cookies. Normally, the HTTPOnly attribute is a good idea, but it prevents scripting rather than requiring unencrypted HTTP sessions.

201. D. Data remanence describes data that is still on media after an attempt has been made to remove it. Failed clearing and data pooling are not technical terms, and data permanence describes how long data lasts.

202. B. Mandatory access control (MAC) applies labels to subjects and objects and allows subjects to access objects when their labels match. Discretionary access control (DAC) is controlled by the owner of objects, rule-based access control applies rules throughout a system, and role-based access control bases rights on roles, which are often handled as groups of users.

203. B. Identity as a Service (IDaaS) provides capabilities such as account provisioning, management, authentication, authorization, reporting, and monitoring. PaaS is Platform as a Service, IaaS is Infrastructure as a Service, and SaaS is Software as a Service.

204. C. Eavesdropping, denial-of-service attacks, and caller ID spoofing are all common VoIP attacks. Blackboxing is a made-up answer, although various types of colored boxes were associated with phone phreaking.

205. D. This broad access may indirectly violate all of the listed security principles, but it is most directly a violation of least privilege because it grants users privileges that they do not need for their job functions.

206. C. The Secure File Transfer Protocol (SFTP) is specifically designed for encrypted file transfer. SSH is used for secure command-line access, whereas TCP is one of the bundles of Internet protocols commonly used to transmit data across a network. IPSec could be used to create a tunnel to transfer the data but is not specifically designed for file transfer.

207. B. TACACS+ uses TCP, and encrypts the entire session, unlike RADIUS, which only encrypts the password and operates via UDP.

208. C. The client sends its existing valid TGT to the KDC and requests access to the resource.

209. A. The KDC must verify that the TGT is valid and whether the user has the right privileges to access the service it is requesting access to. If it does, it generates a service ticket and sends it to the client (step B).

210. C. When a client connects to a service server (SS), it sends the following two messages:

- The client-to-server ticket, encrypted using service's secret key
- A new authenticator, including the client ID and timestamp which is encrypted using the Client/Server session key.

211. B. The service ticket in Kerberos authentication provides proof that a subject is authorized to access an object. Ticket granting services are provided by the TGS. Proof that a subject has authenticated and can request tickets to other objects, uses ticket granting tickets, and authentication host is a made-up term.

212. C. A series of questions that the user has previously provided the answer to or which the user knows the answers to like the questions listed is known as a cognitive password. A passphrase consists of a phrase or series of words, whereas multifactor authentication consists of two or more authenticators, like a password and a biometric factor or a one-time token-based code.

213. B. CDMA, GSM, and IDEN are all 2G technologies. EDGE, DECT, and UTMS are all examples of 3G technologies, whereas 4G technologies include WiMax, LTE, and IEE 802.20 mobile broadband.

214. A. Dry pipe, deluge, and preaction systems all use pipes that remain empty until the system detects signs of a fire. Closed-head systems use pipes filled with water that may damage equipment if there is damage to a pipe.

215. A. Protected Health Information (PHI) is defined by HIPAA to include health information used by healthcare providers, like medical treatment, history, and billing. Personally Identifiable Information is information that can be used to identify an individual, which may be included in the PHI but isn't specifically this type of data. Protected Health Insurance and Individual Protected Data are both made-up terms.

216. B. Manual testing uses human understanding of business logic to assess program flow and responses. Mutation or generational fuzzing will help determine how the program responds to expected inputs but does not test the business logic. Interface testing ensures that data exchange between modules works properly but does not focus on the logic of the program or application.

217. A. A Type 1 authentication factor is something you know. A Type 2 is something you have, like a smart card or hardware token. A Type 3 authentication factor is something you are, like a biometric identifier. There is no such thing as a Type 4 authentication factor.

218. B. System owners have to ensure that the systems they are responsible for are properly labeled based on the highest level of data that their system processes, and they have to ensure that appropriate security controls are in place on those systems. System owners also share responsibility for data protection with data owners. Administrators grant appropriate access, whereas data owners own the classification process.

219. A. Jack is performing misuse case analysis, a process that tests code based on how it would perform if it was misused instead of used properly. Use case testing tests valid use cases, whereas static code analysis involves reviewing the code itself for flaws rather than testing the live software. Hacker use case testing isn't an industry term for a type of testing.

220. D. Vendors complete security targets (STs) to describe the controls that exist within their product. During the review process, reviewers compare those STs to the entity's Protection Profile (PP) to determine whether the product meets the required security controls.

221. C. Both TCP and UDP port numbers are a 16-digit binary number, which means there can be 2^{16} ports, or 65,536 ports, numbered from 0 to 65,535.

222. A. MITRE's Common Vulnerabilities and Exploits (CVE) dictionary and NIST's National Vulnerability Database (NVD) both provide information about vulnerabilities.

223. D. The military classification scheme contains three major levels. They are, in descending order of sensitivity: Top Secret, Secret, and Confidential. Unclassified is a default, and not a classification, whereas Sensitive But Unclassified (SBU) has been replaced with Controlled Unclassified Information (CUI).

224. D. In an automated recovery, the system can recover itself against one or more failure types. In an automated recovery without undue loss, the system can recover itself against one or more failure types and also preserve data against loss. In function recovery, the system can restore functional processes automatically. In a manual recovery approach, the system does not fail into a secure state but requires an administrator to manually restore operations.

225. A. Antenna placement, antenna design, and power level control are the three important factors in determining where a signal can be accessed and how usable it is. A captive portal can be used to control user logins, and antenna design is part of antenna types. The FCC does provide maximum broadcast power guidelines but does not require a minimum power level.

226. C. Physically destroying the drive is the best way to ensure that there is no remnant data on the drive. SSDs are flash media, which means that you can't degauss them, whereas both random pattern writes and the built-in erase commands have been shown to be problematic due to the wear leveling built into SSDs as well as differences in how they handle erase commands.

227. A. Confidentiality ensures that data cannot be read by unauthorized individuals while stored or in transit.

228. B. The recovery time objective (RTO) is the amount of time that a business believes it will take to restore a function in the event of a disruption.

229. D. The United States Code (USC) contains the text of all federal criminal and civil laws passed by the legislative branch and signed by the President (or where the President's veto was overruled by Congress).

230. B. A post-admission philosophy allows or denies access based on user activity after connection. Since this doesn't check the status of a machine before it connects, it can't prevent the exploit of the system immediately after connection. This doesn't preclude out-of-band or in-band monitoring, but it does mean that a strictly post-admission policy won't handle system checks before the systems are admitted to the network.

231. B. The principle of implicit denial states that any action that is not explicitly allowed is denied. This is an important concept for firewall rules and other access control systems. Implementing least privilege ensures that subjects have only the rights they need to accomplish their job. While explicit deny and final rule fall-through may sound like important access control concepts, neither is.

232. B. Risks are the combination of a threat and a vulnerability. Threats are the external forces seeking to undermine security, such as the hacker in this case. Vulnerabilities are the internal weaknesses that might allow a threat to succeed. In this case, web defacement is the risk. In this scenario, if the hacker attempts a SQL injection attack (threat) against the unpatched server (vulnerability), the result is website defacement (risk).

233. A. The kernel of an operating system is the collection of components that work together to implement a secure, reliable operating system. The kernel contains both the Trusted Computing Base (TCB) and the reference monitor.

234. A. Val can use statistical sampling techniques to choose a set of records for review that are representative of the entire day's data. Clipping chooses only records that exceed a set threshold so it is not a representative sample. Choosing records based on the time they are recorded may not produce a representative sample because it may capture events that occur at the same time each day and miss many events that simply don't occur during the chosen time period.

235. D. Fiber-optic cable is more expensive and can be much harder to install than stranded copper cable or coaxial cable, but it isn't susceptible to electromagnetic interference (EMI). That makes it a great solution for Jen's problem, especially if she is deploying EMI-hardened systems to go with her EMI-resistant network cables.

236. D. The request control process provides an organized framework within which users can request modifications, managers can conduct cost/benefit analyses, and developers can prioritize tasks.

237. B. Change control provides an organized framework within which multiple developers can create and test solutions prior to rolling them out into a production environment.

238. C. Release control ensures that any code inserted as a programming aid during the change process is removed before releasing the new software to production. It also includes acceptance testing to ensure that any alterations to end-user work tasks are understood and functional.

239. A. Configuration control ensures that changes to software versions are made in accordance with the change control and configuration management process. Updates can be made only from authorized distributions in accordance with those policies.

240. B. Ben is reusing his salt. When the same salt is used for each hash, all users with the same password will have the same hash, and the attack can either attempt to steal the salt or may attempt to guess the salt by targeting the most frequent hash occurrences based on commonly used passwords. Short salts are an issue, but the salts used here are 32 bytes (256 bits) long. There is no salting algorithm used or mentioned here; salt is an added value for a hash, and plaintext salting is a made-up term.

241. B. Risk transference involves actions that shift risk from one party to another. Purchasing insurance is an example of risk transference because it moves risk from the insured to the insurance company.

242. C. The Online Certificate Status Protocol (OCSP) eliminates the latency inherent in the use of certificate revocation lists by providing a means for real-time certificate verification.

243. D. Static code analysis uses techniques like control flow graphs, lexical analysis, and data flow analysis to assess code without running it. Dynamic code analysis runs code on a real or virtual processor and uses actual inputs for testing. Fuzzing provides unexpected or invalid input to test how programs handle input outside of the norm. Manual analysis is performed by reading code line by line to identify bugs or other issues.

244. B. TCP's use of a handshake process to establish communications makes it a connection-oriented protocol. TCP does not monitor for dropped connections. nor does the fact that it works via network connections make it connection-oriented.

245. A. The LDAP bind operation authenticates and specifies the LDAP protocol version. Auth, StartLDAP, and AuthDN operations do not exist in the LDAP protocol.

246. C. The two most important elements of a qualitative risk assessment are determining the probability and impact of each risk upon the organization. Likelihood is another word for probability. Cost should be taken into account but is only one element of impact, which also includes reputational damage, operational disruption, and other ill effects.

247. B. When a message reaches the Data Link layer, it is called a frame. Data streams exist at the application, presentation, and session layers, whereas segments and datagrams exist at the transport layer (for TCP and UDP, respectively).

248. A. If the (ISC)² peer review board finds that a certified individual has violated the (ISC)² code of ethics, the board may revoke their certification. The board is not able to terminate an individual's employment or assess financial penalties.

249. D. SDLC approaches include steps to provide operational training for support staff as well as end-user training. The SDLC may use one of many development models, including the waterfall and spiral models. The SDLC does not mandate the use of an iterative or sequential approach; it allows for either approach.

250. A. The Bell-LaPadula model includes the Simple Security Property, which prevents an individual from reading information that is classified at a level higher than the individual's security clearance.

Index

Comprehensive Online Learning Environment

Register on Sybex.com to gain access to the online interactive test bank to help you study for your CISSP certification—included with your purchase of this book! All of the practice tests in this book are included in the online test bank so you can practice in a timed and graded setting.

Go to www.wiley.com/go/sybextestprep to register and gain access to this study tool.

Do you need more? If you have not already read Sybex's CISSP (ISC)[2] Certified Information Systems Security Professional Official Study Guide, 7th Edition by James M. Stewart, Mike Chapple, and Darril Gibson (ISBN: 978-1-119-04271-6) and are not seeing passing grades on these practice tests, this book is an excellent resource to master any CISSP topics causing problems. This book maps every official exam objective to the corresponding chapter in the book to help track exam prep objective by objective, challenging review questions in each chapter to prepare for exam day, and online test prep materials with flashcards and additional practice tests.

30% off on-demand IT video training from ITProTV

ITProTV and Sybex have partnered to provide 30% off a Premium annual or monthly membership. ITProTV provides a unique, custom learning environment for IT professionals and students alike, looking to validate their skills through vendor certifications. On-demand courses provide over 1,000 hours of video training with new courses being added every month, while labs and practice exams provide additional hands-on experience. For more information on this offer and to start your membership today, visit http://itpro.tv/sybex30/.